ACROSS OUR WIDE MISSOURI

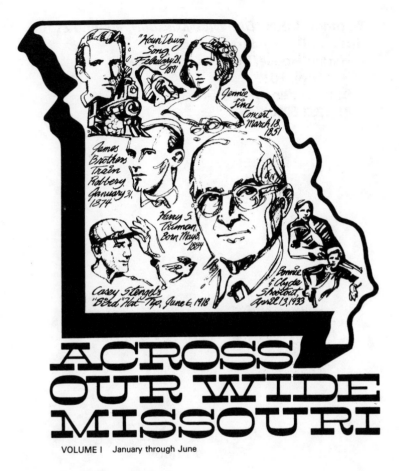

Labels within illustration:
"Houn' Dawg" Song, February 21, 1891
Jennie Lind Concert March 18, 1851
James Brothers Train Robbery January 31, 1874
Harry S. Truman, Born May 8, 1884
Casey Stengel's "Bird Hat" Trip, June 6, 1918
Bonnie & Clyde Shootout, April 13, 1933

ACROSS OUR WIDE MISSOURI

VOLUME I   January through June

By Bob Priddy

INDEPENDENCE PRESS
P.O. Box HH
Independence, MO 64055

To order *Across Our Wide Missouri,* volume 2 (July
through December) contact:
  Herald House/Independence Press
  P.O. Box HH
  Independence, MO 64055
  816/252-5010

To my children,
to whom history is a bore.
Perhaps someday
they will understand
that I am their past
and they are my future.

FOREWORD

Clyde Lear was my assistant at KLIK radio in Jefferson City when I was news director. One day he looked across the desk at me and said, "Priddy, you ought to make this into a book."

It is now ten years later. Clyde Lear is now my boss at the Missouri Network.

And this is that book.

For more than a decade the folks in Jefferson City knew this as "Missouri in Retrospect," the daily radio program I originated on February 8, 1971, as part of the state's sesquicentennial. The program began with a more important goal, however, than simply observing the state's 150th birthday. The program was intended to emphasize history for its own sake—to convince people that history goes beyond presidents, wars, and generals, memorized dates, and remote events. I wanted people to understand that history is not something dull to be stored between hard covers and left on a shelf to gather dust, but is instead human, dynamic, and virile.

Although many people still find history worthless, many others find it exciting and human, an opportunity to understand that what we are today is based on what we were yesterday, and tomorrow's Missourians and the issues they face will spring from what we are and what we do today.

A study of history shows no generation has a monopoly on grace, dignity, narrowness, greatness, or folly. Understanding the human nature which creates these ingredients of history leads not to the acceptance of the continued negative but, one hopes, to a striving for the positive.

History is the blood and sweat, tears and smiles of real people—our ancestors socially, politically, and geographically. Whatever they were, we are. Whatever possibilities for greatness or failure they had within them exist within us. Realizing that and understanding those things about the people who shaped our past, we should be better able to shape our present and future.

That is the value of history and, I hope, the value of the series of programs which have led to this book.

Just as history is not an isolated event or individual, this book is not the creation of a single person. It is derived from the lives and activities of the figures described here, and from the work of other writers who have described them. A few come quickly to mind.

Floyd Shoemaker, the head of the State Historical Society of Missouri for so many years, created a format similar to the one used in these programs in a series of newspaper articles and two books almost a half-century ago. I have expanded on his format and have filled in some of the blank dates he left.

Lew Larkin, a predecessor of mine in the press corps covering state government, also wrote historical vignettes often tied to specific dates. His articles, published in the *Kansas City Star,* later appeared in two books.

The format, then, is only mildly original. The research which went into these articles came from sources readily available at the Missouri State Library, the Thomas Jefferson Library in Jefferson City, and the State Historical Society in Columbia. I stumbled onto a few stories, but most of what many have heard and what you will read here is drawn from more than 300 available references, not the result of hours of sifting through piles of dusty documents. I say this only to emphasize to those who have term papers to write that the material is readily available if they will but look. (I have had many students write or call asking if they could have a copy of a particular program. I always refuse, but I usually give them the references I used to prepare the script so they can do the work themselves.)

I am grateful to the staff and ownership of radio stations KLIK and KJFF-FM in Jefferson City and their managers Stan Grieve and Chuck Larson, for their continuing support and encouragement of this effort. The program began, grew, and matured while I was news director there. The continuing support, interest, and response of those stations and their large listening audience early led to thoughts of publishing this material in book form. I am deeply grateful for their enthusiastic interest and encouragement.

Margaret Baldwin might not want to be mentioned. But I forbid her to remove from this section my thanks to her. She has been the editor of this book. She has convinced me I have forgotten almost everything Miss Rachael Richardson tried to teach me about writing back in Sullivan, Illinois. This book could not be in your hands without her interest and work.

Missouri Life magazine has published some of these items and some expanded versions of them. I appreciate their support.

Since 1975 the Missouri Network has been broadcasting these programs as "Across Our Wide Missouri" on more than fifty radio stations. I greatly appreciate the opportunities the Missouri Net has given me to develop this work and the encouragement Clyde and so many others have given.

For about five years, one-minute versions of this program have been syndicated by Northeast Missouri State University in Kirksville as public affairs programs for more than two-dozen stations. I hope it has generated interest in history, in Northeast Missouri State University, and, of course, in this book.

No married author can produce something like this without a massive amount of tolerance from his family. My wife would have preferred I not spend a vacation locked in a trailer on a farm near Rolla typing. My children suffered through long hours of a clacking typewriter that competed with the volume of their favorite television programs. To all of the others, thank you. To my family, this warning: there is another volume to go.

Bob Priddy
Jefferson City, Missouri
January, 1982.

James
Brothers
Train
Robbery
January 31,
1874

JANUARY

JANUARY 1
THE COMMUNIST UTOPIA IN A MISSOURI VILLAGE

Communism has been part of Missouri life and history for more than a century. Not the great "red menace" from Russia or China, or elsewhere behind the iron curtain—this was the communism of the utopian society. The movement was quite popular in the 19th century and Missouri was as much involved as any state in the Union. In fact, it was more involved than most.

One of the leaders of the Missouri movement was Etienne Cabet, a famous writer, diplomat, and exile from France. He had studied law and medicine, and gained favor during the reign of King Louis Phillipe after the 1830 revolution. Cabet was appointed Procurer General for Corsica by the King. But Cabet was recalled when his activities took an anti-establishment turn. He served in the Chamber of Deputies, but got into trouble three years later through his articles in a workingman's paper, *Le Populaire.* The articles were branded traitorous by the government and he was exiled for five years to England. When he returned he published a book, a romantic novel which made him famous. The main ingredient of that book was a communistic utopia.

But unlike other dreamers and philosophers, Cabet did more than just dream. He and about 70 of his followers came to this country to set up a colony in the Red River valley of Texas. They called themselves "Icarians." But the group learned the land agent who had promised them one million acres had swindled them.

They moved to Nauvoo, Illinois, having heard that Joseph Smith's Mormons had recently been driven from the town. Cabet's Icarians numbered 281 when they arrived in Nauvoo. But the colony was not to survive long in that town. When Cabet demanded virtual dictatorial powers, the colony split. Cabet turned out to be part of the minority and left Nauvoo with those who supported him.

He went to St. Louis because of its French heritage and its business potential. But before Cabet could see his colony firmly established on the western bank of the Mississippi, he died. It was November 8, 1856. Cabet was 68.

But his town went ahead.

In May of 1858, the Icarians purchased an estate called Cheltenham, about six miles west of St. Louis, close enough for residents to work in the city. It had a large stone house and six other structures to house the group of colonists. Cheltenham became noted worldwide as the only genuine Icarian community. Everyone shared ownership and community responsibility. The colony had a community center, printing offices, school and theatre, and workshops.

But the community ran into difficulty in 1859.

One group wanted to establish a democracy within the community. The other, larger group wanted to keep things as Cabet would have wanted them. The rest of the community refused to accept that idea and pulled out. The withdrawal killed Cheltenham as an organized settlement. Cheltenham fell behind in its mortgage payments as aid from France was cut off when the colony's troubles became known back home.

It was an interesting experiment in community organization. Men were supposed to work until they were 65. Women would retire at the age of 50. A day's labor was seven hours in the summer and five in the winter. Women worked four-hour days. Everyone got up at the same time each morning when the community alarm bell was rung. They all ate at a common table. Religion was a matter of personal preference. But philosophically and politically, common bonds held them together. They were recognized by the Paris bureau as the only Icarian colony in America.

Etienne Cabet was a dreamer who brought his flock to Missouri. He didn't live to see his colony established and flourish but he was also spared the sad experience of seeing his ideal community fail. It suffered the same troubles conventional society endures: a crisis over who should govern and how the government should be run.

Etienne Cabet, the dreamer of a Missouri utopia, was born on January 1, 1788.

****

JANUARY 2
THE MISSOURIAN CALLED "TEX."

The promoter took the young boxer aside and told him, "You get in there and fight him the best you can. But if he hits you hard and you think he's going to kill you, just go down and stay down."

But the young boxer knocked his opponent down seven times in the first round. He defeated his opponent in three. A Missourian named "Tex" arranged this historic fight which would mark the beginning of a golden age for boxing.

It was July 4, 1919. The fight matched heavyweight champion Jess Willard, six feet seven inches tall and 245 pounds, against a youngster half a foot shorter named William Harrison Dempsey. Dempsey destroyed Willard in three rounds on a sweltering day in Toledo, Ohio. The great boxing writer, Nat Fleischer, said the fight was "the beginning of the lush period of ring spectacles."

The man who promoted it was George Lewis Rickard. Born in a cabin in Clay County, Missouri, Rickard was described by Fleischer as one of the "golden people of sports in the golden decade" of the 1920s.

Rickard was the son of a millwright in Clay County in the 1870s. But they pulled up stakes not long after some Pinkerton men blew up a neighbor's cabin looking for members of the neighbor's family—Frank and Jesse James. The Rickards moved to Texas where young George eventually realized a dream of becoming a cowboy. He married and settled down. But in 1895 his wife died and George decided to leave Texas.

Gold had been discovered in Alaska. So George, or "Tex" as he was called by then, headed north. He prospected, speculated, and ran gambling establishments in the Yukon. It was a boom and bust time. Rickard was part of it at both ends. Once he celebrated the opening of a new saloon in Rampart by staging a boxing match. From that time on, Rickard was a boxing promoter.

When Rickard was approached by Jack Dempsey's manager, Jack Kearns, with a proposition that Dempsey should fight Willard, Rickard honestly feared Willard would kill the man from Manassa, Colorado. But when Dempsey won, Rickard knew his greatest gold strike was in the boxing ring promoting the young fighter, not in Alaska.

In 1921 Rickard promoted a match between Dempsey, who was viewed as something of a villain because of his non-involvement in the recent war, with a French war hero, Georges Carpentier. The fight took place at Boyle's Thirty Acres, New Jersey. Wooden bleachers were built to hold more than 90,000 people. Rickard watched people pour into the stadium and said, "If it takes all sorts to make up the world, the world must be here already.... I never seed anything like it."

The occasion was historic. A preliminary fight was the first boxing match ever broadcast in America and the main event was the first title fight broadcast. Dempsey kayoed the Frenchman in the fourth round. But the fight is most memorable because it was the first time gate receipts for a boxing match totalled more than one million dollars. In fact, the receipts reached almost $1.8 million.

The skill of Dempsey, his manager Kearns, and the ability of Rickard to promote them made sports history. Two years later Rickard lined up another foreigner for Dempsey to fight — Luis Firpo. It lasted two historic rounds and was another million-dollar gate. Then came the really big ones. Dempsey signed to fight a young man named Gene Tunney. Tunney won and the gate was over a million dollars again. Before the rematch Dempsey met Jack Sharkey in another Rickard-arranged fight. It too was a million-dollar gate.

One year and four days after their first meeting, Dempsey and Tunney fought their famous long-court fight at Soldier's Field in Chicago. More than 100,000 people watched. It was Tex Rickard's last great promotion. Gate receipts were an astounding $2,659,000, an unheard-of amount for a sporting event in 1927. Rickard knew a third match would produce a million more than that. But Dempsey didn't want it. He sent a telegram reading, "Count me out, Tex."

Early in 1929 Rickard was in Miami to arrange a fight matching Young Stribling and Jack Sharkey. But his appendix burst and he died four days after his fifty-eighth birthday.

Tex Rickard, the greatest fight promoter of all time, the man who made boxing into big business, was born in Missouri on January 2, 1871.

****

JANUARY 3
MISSOURI PREACHER, MOUNTAIN MAN

As a Baptist minister, he hoped to convert the Osage Indians of Missouri. But instead he found himself converted, becoming more Indian than white man. He had a mule he called "Ol' Flopear," a horse he named "Santyfee," and a Hawken rifle he called "Fetchum," because it always fetched home the game. Kit Carson is said to have remarked that you never walked in front of him during starving times. His name was William Sherley Williams, but he was called "Ol Bill."

His family moved to the St. Louis area a decade before the Louisiana Purchase. Their first child, John William, is claimed by descendants to have been the first white child born in St. Louis. John would later settle in Maries County. But the quiet, narrow life was not for his younger brother, Bill Williams.

Young Bill got involved in the religious revival sweeping the country in the 1800s. He became an itinerant Baptist preacher, visiting small villages and scattered cabins. Williams was a powerful hellfire and brimstone preacher. But he gave up circuit riding suddenly. Some say he quit right in the middle of a sermon when he couldn't keep from looking at a pretty girl. Others say he went into the woods and prayed for God to release him from his duty. God apparently did.

Bill Williams had grown up with the Indians in the St. Louis area. He respected them and they came to respect him. He tried to convert them but wound up, as his family once put it, two-thirds Indian. He married an Osage girl in 1813 and they had two children.

In 1825, when the government started a survey of the Santa Fe Trail, Williams was hired as an interpreter. He was a key figure in negotiating important treaties guaranteeing safe passage along the trail. The turning point in his life came when the party reached Taos, New Mexico. He lived there for twenty years. The Utes adopted him and he took an Indian wife, his first wife having died.

He became more of a loner, although Old Bill—they called him that by now—liked to sit around the campfire and spin tales of his exploits. He gambled extensively, sometimes losing a thousand dollars a game at cards, and consumed large quantities of "Taos Lightning."

William's biographer, Alpheus H. Taylor, says that within seven years after his arrival at Taos, Williams had "no peer as a hunter, trapper, marksman and horseman, or in his intimate knowledge of the several Indian tribes in the mountains of the region." A contemporary described him as an inch over six feet tall with red hair flecked with grey as the years went by, "with a hard, weather beaten face, marked deeply with small pox...all muscle and sinew, and the most indefatigable hunter and trapper in the world." Old Bill was so proud of his marksmanship that he'd bet a hundred dollars on a shot, although Albert Pike says, "He always shot with a double wobble for he never could hold his gun still." He wore dirty, greasy buckskins, a long beard and shoulder-length hair. He had the alertness of a mountain man, felt like he would strangle if he stayed under a roof at night, and thought a bed was the work of the devil. He spoke in a high voice with a peculiar speech pattern that resulted from the use of so many dialects. On returning to Missouri, he so frightened his granddaughter that she hid under a bed and wouldn't come out. Williams said that after his death, he'd come back as a buck elk.

After the fur trapping frontier declined, he played a role as pathfinder. Twice Fremont chose him as a guide. The last time, 1848, Fremont ignored Williams' advice and tried to scale the Sangre de Cristo Mountains in the dead of winter. Only 21 of the 32 members of the party survived. Williams was accused by Fremont of being a cannibal, a charge which was never substantiated. Later, on a trip back to the mountains to recover baggage left behind, Williams was killed by the Utes, seeking revenge for an earlier army raid.

Two years after his death, a river and a mountain in Arizona were named for him. And today, Old Bill Williams is regarded as one of the greatest of that most independent breed of men this country has ever known—the mountain man. He was a man whom Pike says "had no glory except in the woods." He was Old Bill Williams, the Missouri preacher turned mountain man, who was born on January 3, 1787.

****

JANUARY 4
THE WICKED CITY OF ROSES

A woman once wrote that the town was "a beautiful place but it is very wicked. There is no chance to hear the gospel preached without going ten miles over a wretched road to a chapel. The main way the men spend their Sundays is in drinking and gambling, horse racing and chicken fighting."

It isn't surprising, really, that such a town was established by a man who used to pay Indians for American scalps, and it was named for a Frenchman who deserted his country's military to first settle the area.

The town is Cape Girardeau.

Sometime about 1720 a French marine ensign left his post on the eastern side of the Mississippi River and set up a canoe landing at a place on the west bank called Cape Rock. His name was Jean

Girardot. Over the years, the spelling of the town was based on how his name sounded, not how it was spelled.

Many years later, a Canadian came to this territory, a man whose scalp-buying activities in Ohio had been broken up by George Rogers Clark in 1782. Pierre Louis Lorimier couldn't read, but he could write his name. He brought with him many of his wife's people, Shawnee and Delaware Indians, and settled near Ste. Genevieve. A few years later the Spanish who controlled this territory gave him authority to set up a trading post further south. The Osage Indians had been troubling Spanish settlers and it was hoped Lorimier and his Indian friends would act as buffers between the Osages and those settlers.

Lorimier settled in the area and founded a town which he wanted to call "Lorimont." But the town was actually named for that little-known ensign, Girardot.

Lorimier became a Spanish citizen and was strongly loyal. During the American Revolution he hated Americans enough to pay Indians in gold for their scalps. Once he and his Indian allies made a raid into Kentucky and captured Daniel Boone, who later escaped.

As years passed, however, Lorimier's attitude softened and American immigrants began to flow into the area. Lorimier was willing to arrange land grants for them. Many of those grants were based on the 30,000 arpents, or 38,400 acres of land the Spanish had given him. By the beginning of the 19th century, Cape Girardeau was the most populous district west of the Mississippi. But it was a sad day for Louis Lorimier when the Louisiana Territory came under American ownership. The last Governor-General of Spanish Missouri stopped at Cape Girardeau on his way back to New Orleans. Lorimier wept openly and presented him with the Spanish flag which he had loyally flown over his settlement.

Lorimier died in 1812. His large funeral was attended by representatives from 20 Indian tribes he had befriended. His city stagnated for several years as the Spanish land grants were contested in the courts. They were finally confirmed a decade and a half after Lorimier's death. Even today, real estate in Cape Girardeau is based on his original grants. The first courthouse was built in 1854 on land Lorimier had donated years before. In 1873 the town gained a college which is now Southeast Missouri State University.

Long ago, someone discovered beautiful roses could be grown in Cape Girardeau. Today, with no apologies whatever to Pasadena,

California, Cape Girardeau calls itself "The City of Roses." In fact, there once was a ten-mile-long rose garden along the highway between Cape Girardeau and Jackson. It's gone now, destroyed by the new road. But the city has a large municipal rose garden that is popular with tourists.

Cape Girardeau traces its history as a community back to when Pierre Louis Lorimier was given trading privileges in the area by the Spanish government on January 4, 1796.

****

JANUARY 5
FOUR GOVERNORS IN TEN MONTHS

Sterling Price's term as Governor was running out. He was to be succeeded by Trusten Polk, victor in one of Missouri's most hotly-contested elections. The change in power began a frantic scramble at the top of Missouri government. In ten months four men would be Governor and in four years destiny would weave their lives together.

It began in 1857 as the four-year reign of Sterling Price came to an end. Trusten Polk won a three-way race over Robert C. Ewing and former Senator Thomas Hart Benton. Benton had finished a distant third although he was still a powerful influence in Missouri politics. One observer said, "Few elections anywhere have been more exciting than the national, state, and Congressional elections of 1856 in Missouri." It was the time of the border troubles with Kansas. The Civil War was nearing. The state was growing rapidly.

Trusten Polk told the joint legislative session in his inaugural speech:

"It will be a never-failing source of gratification to me, if I shall be able to contribute in any degree, towards inspiring a more sacred reverence for the Constitution...under which the several peoples of all the States are united as one people—a stronger attachment to that Union thus established and the free institutions of which is at once the conservator and guaranty—and a fraternal regard for each of our sister states and for the people of every section of our widely extended country...."

But just over a month later, a joint session of the legislature named Polk to succeed Henry S. Geyer as U.S. Senator from Missouri and

Trusten Polk would go down in history as serving the shortest term of any Governor in Missouri history.

Next in line was Hancock Lee Jackson, the Lieutenant Governor. In those days, the sole duty of the Lieutenant Governor was to act as Governor until a new one could be chosen in a special election. Less than two months after Polk resigned as Governor, Hancock Jackson called for the special election. It was held in August. In October, Robert M. Stewart was sworn in, the fourth man to serve as Governor of Missouri in ten months.

Hancock Jackson later served as a District Marshall in Missouri and went to Oregon in 1865. He died there eleven years later.

Robert Stewart won the governorship with a narrow victory over James Rollins, a figure prominent in the establishment of the University of Missouri. Stewart was remembered as one of our more eccentric chief executives. He was a bachelor. He drank a great deal and was known for his "toots."

He dressed well but sloppily. He kicked an inmate out of the state penitentiary once, claiming the inmate wasn't good enough to be kept there.

During his term, Robert Stewart saw the war clouds deepen. And so, in the final days of his term, in 1861, he told the legislature, "As matters are at present, Missouri will stand to her lot, and hold to the Union so long as it is worth an effort to preserve it...."

Shortly after Stewart's speech, his successor called for Missouri to cast her lot with the Southern states. The new Governor was Claiborne Fox Jackson, a cousin to Hancock Lee Jackson, the man who called the election which put Stewart in the Governorship.

Under Claiborne Jackson, the decision to stay in the Union or leave it would be made by a special convention presided over by a former Governor: Sterling Price. When that special convention decided to stay in the Union, Governor Jackson set up a militia to repel any invaders. Former Governor Price, the first of the four Governors of 1851, was named commander of that unit.

Sterling Price's successor as Governor, Trusten Polk—who wanted to increase reverence in the constitution—was expelled from the United States Senate. Charge—disloyalty. He became a Confederate officer, was taken prisoner, and eventually fled to Mexico after the war.

Robert Stewart continued in Missouri as a strong supporter of the Union and helped build an important railroad despite the war.

But all of that was far down the road the day that first inauguration of that historic year was held—when Trusten Polk took the oath of office on January 5th, 1857.

****

JANUARY 6
A NEW, RADICAL CONSTITUTION

In 1865, 45 years had passed since the first Constitution of Missouri had been written. Times had changed. The state was no longer a mass of frontier settlements. It was still involved in the Civil War. There were open political wounds needing strong action. The time had come for a new constitution. One was developed, only to produce controversy, conflict and the greatest housecleaning of political officeholders in Missouri history.

Some call it the Drake Constitution because of the role played by Charles Daniel Drake in drafting it. It will be remembered as a document of harsh revenge which overshadows some of its more positive aspects. It went into effect even though voters in the state did not approve it. More than 800 sheriffs, judges and other officials were thrown out of office under the constitution. Two members of the Missouri Supreme Court were escorted out by the state militia.

The Constitution of 1865 was the product of the Radical Republican movement which materialized in the closing years of the Civil War. The Radicals believed the state had not acted strongly enough punishing disloyal citizens and freeing slaves. The party posted a strong victory in the election of 1864. A constitutional convention was called by the legislature which asked that amendments be drafted freeing slaves and restricting voting privileges to loyal citizens.

The convention assembled at the Mercantile Library Hall in St. Louis. The delegates elected St. Louis lawyer Charles Daniel Drake their leader. Duane Meyer describes him as "an intense, intelligent, dogmatic, aggressive man who had held a variety of political views in Missouri." Once Drake defended slavery as just. Then he advocated gradual emancipation. By 1865 he had adopted the radical stance demanding immediate freedom for slaves. Those who were either against him or favored a milder approach were branded by him as "traitors." Five days after the convention started, delegates voted

60-4 in favor of immediate emancipation of slaves. This was almost eleven months before the 13th amendment to the federal constitution formalized national freedom for slaves.

Missouri thus became the first slave state to totally renounce slavery.

That was one of three major accomplishments. The other two were not as positive. One of the others was the so-called "ousting ordinance" which declared all judges, circuit attorneys, sheriffs, and county recorders to be removed from office. Radical Republicans then were named to fill those vacancies. This came about because the delegates at the convention feared the state supreme court would declare the emancipation amendment unconstitutional. To keep that from happening, Radicals were put on the high court.

The second questionable accomplishment was the "ironclad oath." It required all voters, jurors, officeholders, officers and directors of corporations, trustees, attorneys, teachers, and preachers to swear they had never been in armed hostility against the federal government or had ever aided those who had been hostile to the United States.

The new constitution passed by less than 2,000 votes. Citizens in the state itself voted it down by 965 votes. But Missouri soldiers stationed outside the state were allowed to vote too and they passed it 43,670 to 41,808.

It went into effect July 4, 1865, but almost immediately started to crumble.

A Catholic priest, Father John Cummings, refused to take the oath. He was arrested and fined. He refused to pay. He was jailed. He appealed to the U.S. Supreme Court. In 1867 the court ruled the oath for professional activity was unconstitutional.

Two members of the Missouri Supreme Court, William V. N. Bay and John D. S. Dryden, refused to relinquish their jobs under the "ouster ordinance." Governor Fletcher ordered militiamen to force them from their courtrooms and seize their records.

These controversial issues overshadow other, more routine, parts of the document. It was twice as long as the 45-year-old constitution it replaced. Taxes, although high, enabled the state to support schools and colleges. A state insurance department and board of statistics were created under this constitution. Missouri started paying off its railroad and war debts.

Voters later repealed the loyalty oath and within a decade the

Drake Constitution, a document of revenge and little else, was dead. A new one, drafted in 1875, lasted 70 years.

The constitution of 1865 had a short and stormy life. Like many other parts of Reconstruction, the vengeful feelings gave way to time and reason. But the Drake Constitution stands as the mark of what the Radical political mind, supported by a vengeful citizenry, can accomplish. The Drake Constitution was drawn up by the Radical Republican convention which began its deliberations on January 6, 1865.

****

JANUARY 7
METHODISM AND THE CITADEL OF WICKEDNESS

Getting a church started in the frontier territory of Missouri in the early 1800s was a task which called for inventiveness, initiative, and action. When Jesse Walker wanted to build a Methodist church in St. Louis he had little money to purchase the material for the building or the furnishings to go in it. But his small congregation was given a valuable gift—logs. Unfortunately they were in a rather unfinished state. As a matter of fact they were still trees. And they were growing on the other side of the river, in Illinois. Jesse Walker and his group of Methodists went across the river, chopped down those trees, ferried them across the river, and sawed them into lumber. The church they built measured 25 by 30 feet. By now the Episcopalians were interested in the effort too. They had just lost their pastor and it looked as if it might be a while before their next one came. So they gave Walker's church the pulpit and the pews it needed. Thus the Reverend Jesse Walker built Missouri's first Methodist church. He built it in a town many Methodists feared—St. Louis.

Methodists thought the Protestant movement would never be established in St. Louis. The town was predominantly French-Catholic and the non-Catholic population contained a large element of so-called "godless adventurers" who came to the town because it was wide open. Methodist historian Frank Tucker says the opinion on the part of most Methodists was that "for Methodists to assault such a citadel of wickedness was folly."

Jesse Walker was born on the 9th of June, 1766, to a Baptist family, but he joined the Methodist Church at the age of ten. He had only twenty days of formal schooling but was studious enough to learn much on his own. He was admitted to the Western Annual Methodist Conference on a trial basis in 1804. He was 38 years old.

Just two years after that, Walker was appointed to the Hartford circuit in Kentucky, and later that year circuit director William Mc-Kendree chose him as his companion to explore the Illinois country. Walker impressed McKendree and that fall was appointed to a circuit in Illinois. He bought a farm near Belleville, Illinois, and made it his home base.

In 1805, John Clark, believed to have been the first Methodist minister to arrive in this area, set up the first Methodist class at a camp meeting at Coldwater Creek, a village in the wilds of St. Louis County. Another one was organized in 1806 but they both apparently dissolved soon afterwards.

It was up to Jesse Walker to establish the first permanent Methodist organization there. It numbered 20 members in 1807, but at a camp meeting that summer he converted about 40 more people. For the next 15 years or so he was part of the circuit around St. Louis. He had no formal congregations or churches. He met with Methodist groups from time to time and conducted camp meetings. In 1821 he was appointed "Missionary to Missouri," at the annual conference. The conference sent him to St. Louis to establish a church and build a house of worship. Walker rented a small log house with two rooms. He lived in one room and made the other a chapel and schoolroom. Then he rented a nearby building in which he conducted services. The membership grew until it became apparent the congregation needed its own building and that's when the logs in Illinois were donated. In 1822 the Methodists held their annual conference in St. Louis, a city many had feared just a decade or two earlier. Walker reported a congregation of 95 white and 32 black members. About two years later the blacks had their own church.

Reverend Walker did not become rich in his ministry or even well off. He helped pay the way with income from the sale of meal and flour produced on his Illinois farm. His peak salary in any one of his 32 years on the frontier was probably no more than $50.

It was largely due to the efforts of Jesse Walker that the Methodist church was established in Missouri. It was he who put together the first lasting Methodist group, converted the first size-able number of Missourians to Methodism and built St. Louis's first Methodist church which had its origins the day Jesse Walker organized the first permanent Methodist group in Missouri on this date, January 7, 1821.

****

JANUARY 8
THE WRITER OF THE UNWRITTEN EPIC

He went west as a young boy to live with his grandparents in a sod house on the Upper Solomon River, near Stockton, in Western Kansas. He was eight years old when he moved to Kansas City and first saw the Missouri River. It was at flood stage. The big river would be a part of his life for the next 84 years. He would come to call it "The River of an Unwritten Epic."

His name was John G. Neihardt.

Neihardt called the Missouri River, "My brother—the eternal Fighting Man." In 1908, after a long trip down the Missouri from Fort Benton, Montana, Neihardt wrote of the ghosts who haunt the river: "I am more thrilled by the history of the Lewis and Clark expedition than by the tale of Jason. John Colter, wandering three years in the wilderness and discovering Yellowstone Park, is infinitely more heroic to me than Theseus. These moderns made no Gods of the ele-ments—they merely conquered them! The ancients idealized the material. These moderns materialized the ideal."

The book he wrote based on that journey, *The River and I,* tells of a Missouri River now gone, altered by straighter channels and flood-controlling dams. It was left to John Neihardt to write the epic poetry which would give ancient heroic stature to the men of the Missouri River. In fact, after his 30 years work he would be described as "An American Homer," and his books would be listed among the 3,000 greatest books published in the 3,000 years between Homer and Hemingway.

John Neihardt was a man born just five years after Custer and his men were wiped out at the Little Big Horn, nine years before Wounded Knee. He would always take pride in knowing many of those who were at both places as well as places before and in between. Neihardt was born in a two-room cabin where the curtains were made of newspaper and the rug was an old wagon cover stained with the juice of green walnuts. In 1891 the family moved to Nebraska. In 1898 he graduated from Nebraska Normal College at the age of 16.

John Neihardt first began dealing with Indians when he became secretary to a trader working with the Omahas. He relished his contacts with the "old long hairs," the Indians who lived as they did in the old days—or as close to it as they could—forever refusing to be strictly reservation Indians.

In 1921 Neihardt left Nebraska and moved to Branson, Missouri. But Nebraska would always claim him, even as Missouri does. He would later become Nebraska's Poet Laureate. By then he was writing his "Cycle of the West," the five lengthy poems or "songs" which told the story of the westward movement from the first group of Ashley-Henry men going upriver on the Missouri to the virtual closing of the frontier and the crushing of the Plains Indians at Wounded Knee.

For a dozen years he was the literary editor for the *Post-Dispatch* in St. Louis. Then in 1930 he met a man who would give him his most famous work—an old Sioux Indian holy man named Black Elk who seemed to know Neihardt was coming. "There is much to teach you," the old Indian told the author. "What I know was given to me for men and it is true and it is beautiful. Soon I shall be under the grass and it will be lost. You were sent to save it, and you must come back so that I can teach you."

Neihardt did go back and, with an interpreter, he translated Black Elk's story. It is a book which provides the reader not only with a fascinating story, but also with the spirit of the man telling it and the people who lived it.

In 1948, John Neihardt became a lecturer in English at the University of Missouri. He sold the farm at Branson and bought one near Columbia which he called "Skyrim." For the next 20 years he lectured, using his "Cycle" as the main text, teaching not so much about himself and the way he wrote as he taught about the people of whom he wrote—Jed Smith, Hugh Glass, Crazy Horse, Sitting Bull and dozens of others great and foolish came to life in his classroom. History, through the voice of the poet, became flesh-and-blood people.

At age 67 he wrote, "I can see now that I grew up on the farther slope of a veritable 'watershed of history', the summit of which is already crossed, and in a land where the old world lingered longest. It is gone, and, with it, all but two or three of the old-timers, white and brown, whom I have known. My mind and most of my heart are with the young....But something of my heart stays yonder, for in the years of my singing about a time and a country that I loved, I note, without regret, that I have become an old-timer myself."

John Neihardt died on November 3, 1973. He had just seen the publication of the first volume of his autobiography, which covered the first twenty years of his life. He was editing the second volume, which was published a few years later.

John G. Neihardt, one of the greatest authors in world history, was born on this date, the 8th of January, in 1881.

****

JANUARY 9
THE HERITAGE OF THE COLUMNS

Even as the fire reached its height that night, plans were being made to keep operations going as close to normal as possible. The next day there would be meetings throughout the town. The community would rally around, and although the main administration building was gone, the University of Missouri would go on.

Or would it? The fire which destroyed a building built up the hopes of critics of the University and would almost bring about a dismantling of the state school in Columbia.

Faulty wiring has always been listed as the reason the administration building burned that night in 1892. The only water supply to fight the fire was in a cistern in the building's basement. It was soon drained. Efforts to save things from the building were hampered by exploding ammunition, part of the supply for the cadet corps.

By midnight the building was gutted.

The next morning, University President Richard H. Jesse met with students and citizens at a mass meeting. From that meeting came an overwhelming amount of cooperation. Churches, halls, and public buildings were put at the disposal of the University and classes went on.

Governor David Francis sent a telegram urging the student body to stay together. He was warmly greeted a few days later when he went to Columbia to address the group. He pledged to call a special

27

legislative session to deal with the disaster and provide for a new building. A month after the fire, University officials had approved a plan for rebuilding the campus and had set aside money to start. Further funding would have to come from the legislature.

But while progress was being made in Columbia, the fate of the University hung in the balance in the legislative halls in Jefferson City. The destruction of the main building on the University campus badly weakened the University's existence. As long as the school was a going and growing operation with sizeable buildings, it was foolish to consider moving it or fragmenting it. But now its main building was gone. Its student body was meeting in opera houses, churches, and other buildings and might not hold together. Now was the time to move the University if it was ever going to be moved.

The situation also provided a chance for disgruntled farmers and farm groups to voice their criticisms of the University for its alleged lack of development of the College of Agriculture. Many felt the Agriculture College would never progress as long as it was part of the University.

In addition to that was the long-standing hostility toward Boone County, the home county of the University. The original founding of the University had been marred by controversy and bitter competition. The choice of Boone County was not completely popular in the 1830s and it was still not popular 60 years later.

Governor Francis always assumed the school would be rebuilt in Columbia. But the House voted not to appropriate any money at all until a site for the University had been agreed upon. That was on the third day of the special session. On the fifth day a committee was named to consider relocating the University. Cities were invited to submit bids for the institution. On top of that, the House passed a resolution stating the College of Agriculture should be moved somewhere else.

On March 10, a committee report recommended leaving the Agriculture College in Columbia, but made provisions for putting other departments elsewhere. It was a confusing and chaotic time in the Missouri legislature. On March 15, the House balloted on the bids of several towns wanting the University. Four towns were serious contenders: Columbia, Independence, Clinton, and Sedalia. The contest quickly became a match between Sedalia and Columbia. On the third ballot, Sedalia had 69 votes. Columbia had 67.

It took 71 votes to pass a motion.

Although only two votes short of getting the University, Sedalia faction leaders gave up. They decided they could get no more votes. Independence had the only other votes cast. But Sedalia supporters apparently felt the 67 votes for Columbia would never switch. Experienced floor leaders finally gained control of the situation, further dampening Sedalia's hopes. Then there was the realization that the Governor would probably veto the bill if it went through with Sedalia included.

In the meantime, citizens of Columbia had put up almost $53,000 for a new building and promised adequate fire protection.

The House finally approved a bill saying the building would be rebuilt in Columbia. The Senate promptly passed it and the Governor signed it.

The University stayed in Columbia by a bare margin and the last great threat to its existence had been turned back.

Six columns stand on the Columbia campus of the University of Missouri today. They stand on Francis Quadrangle, an area named for the Governor who stood by the University in its great hour of challenge. Those six columns are the symbol of the University. They are more than remnants of an old building. They are reminders of a time when, for lack of only two votes, the University might have been dismantled and scattered about the state.

It all started with the fire which destroyed old Academic Hall on this date, January 9, in 1892.

****

JANUARY 10
JOHNSON, POLK, AND 46 DAYS

For two years Missouri had only one U.S. Senator. He was Henry S. Geyer who served while the legislature was unable to select a companion. But that's not the most unusual occurrence. A few years later Missouri went 46 days with *no* Senators in Washington because Congress had accused them of disloyalty and kicked them out.

Their names were Waldo Porter Johnson and Trusten Polk.

Waldo Porter Johnson became a United States Senator on the 15th ballot of voting in the legislature. Back in those days the legislature picked our Senators, not the public. Johnson became a

Senator four years after his colleague, Trusten Polk, had resigned as Governor to become a member of the U.S. Senate. Both men favored slavery. A resolution passed by the Missouri legislature in 1861 which stated that freeing slaves would be "impracticable, inexpedient, impolitic, unwise, and unjust," was acceptable to them.

Early that year, delegations were sent to Washington seeking ways to sidestep the looming Civil War. One of the five delegates to that so-called "peace conference" was Waldo Porter Johnson. Johnson was not an avowed secessionist. He thought slavery was acceptable but he believed the Union should stay together if at all possible. The special session of Congress ended that August. The United States was plummeting into a conflict between the states. Johnson went to visit friends and relatives in Virginia, the state in which he'd been born. He came back to Missouri that fall. By then the lines had been drawn. He had a choice to make. He chose the Confederacy.

Congress and the federal government, of course, were interested in crushing the rebellion before it got off to a good start. Both Polk and Johnson knew they couldn't go back to Washington. It would do them no good to plead the Southern cause.

December 2, 1861. The roll is called in the Senate of the United States.

There is no one to answer when "Missouri" is called.

No one was there the next day. Or the next. Or the day after that.

A week went by and the Senators from Missouri were still absent.

Finally, eight days after the session convened, the first resolution declaring Missouri's Senate seats vacant was prepared. Senator Solomon Foote of Vermont introduced it. The resolution called on the Senate to expel Senator Johnson, the junior Senator. The matter was referred to the Judiciary Committee.

Another eight days passed and still neither man was present.

Now another resolution was created. This one sought the expulsion of Senator Polk from Missouri. It had the backing of the influential Massachusetts Senator, Charles Sumner.

The resolutions contained similar charges. They said the Senators had voluntarily absented themselves from the chamber. Furthermore, they had supported the rebellion with speeches on behalf of the secessionist movement. They had entered Confederate territory and service. Because of this behavior they were considered in open rebellion against the federal government and no longer deserved to sit in the national assembly. An additional charge against Polk was that he had given money to finance Confederate newspapers in his home state.

Shortly after the first of the year, commitee chairman Lyman Trumbull of Illinois presented the committee's recommendations to the floor. The vote: For expulsion of Polk, 36-0; and for expulsion of Johnson, 35-0.

Back in Missouri, it had been obvious the expulsions were coming. Lieutenant Governor Willard Hall acting in the absence of Governor Hamilton Gamble named Andrew County State Representative Robert Wilson to replace Waldo Porter Johnson. He named John Brooks Henderson to take the place of Polk. Henderson would go on to achieve particular distinction. Some credit him with authoring the 13th amendment. He was one of five Republicans who voted against the impeachment of Andrew Johnson seven years later, putting his own political career in jeopardy.

Wilson served for about a year. His successor was Benjamin Gratz Brown who would become a Governor of Missouri a decade later.

What happened to the two displaced Senators?

Polk rose to become a Confederate Colonel and a judge in the military courts of the Department of the Mississippi.

Johnson became a Lieutenant Colonel and was wounded twice at Pea Ridge. Later he was a member of the Confederate Senate. Afterwards, the man expelled from the U.S. Senate for disloyalty became the President of Missouri's 1875 Constitution Convention.

Missouri had gone from December 2, 1861, until January 17, 1862, with no Senators, 46 days when the entire nation was falling apart, plunging deeper into the bloody War Between the States. It happened because two men could not accept the actions of the U.S. Senate and placed their personal principles above service to their state.

Because they took that stand, Missouri's two Senators were both expelled on this date, the 10th of January, 1862.

****

JANUARY 11
THE STATE SEAL

The Governor was most disturbed by the lack of an official State Seal. He told the legislature "considerable inconvenience daily arises from the want of a seal of state." About two years after the drafting of a constitution was authorized and seven months after statehood had been formally granted, Missouri finally had a State Seal.

The man who designed it is largely forgotten today, although he was a distinguished figure of his time.

Robert William Wells is the man who created the State Seal. He was in his late 20s when he designed it and during the next forty years he would play an important role in the development of our state.

Robert Wells came from Virginia. Some believe he went to school with Hamilton Gamble, the man who would later be our Civil War Governor. Wells moved to St. Louis, as a surveyor, during Missouri's territorial days. By 1820 he had taken up the practice of law in St. Charles, destined to be the first Capital City of our state. The early legislatures show him as a member representing St. Charles County. On several occasions he served as acting Speaker of the House.

Wells became Missouri's Attorney General in 1826, the third person to hold that job. Five years later he challenged the prominent fur-trading entrepreneur and St. Louis businessman William H. Ashley for a seat in Congress, a seat which had fallen vacant because of the death of Spencer Pettis in a duel. But Ashley beat him by about 700 votes.

In later years, Robert Wells was the President of the 1845 State Constitutional Convention, a curator for the University of Missouri, and a United States District Attorney. He died in 1864.

Through the years there have been disagreements about the meanings of some of the symbols on the seal he designed. Some have attacked the use of the bears on the seal, noting that bears are vicious and deadly.

More than 25 years after he designed the seal, Wells wrote a letter in which he explained the symbolism.

The creation of a State Seal relies on heraldry and in heraldry only the good properties of animals are emphasized. For instance, wrote Robert Wells in 1847, "the United States, in adopting the eagle, is not supposed to indicate that the U.S. are like a bird of prey or will prey upon and devour other nations." Therefore Wells chose the White or Grizzly Bear because of its "vast power, great courage and prodigious hardihood; emblematical of the great resources of the state, of the courage and hardihood of its citizens."

32

A line surrounds the Seal of the United States. Wells said it symbolizes "that the whole make one government, yet are separate and distinct governments for certain purposes."

The crest over the arms of the state is a gold helmet with six bars. It "indicates that the state, although sovereign as to some matters is not sovereign as to all; the helmet being that of a prince but not that of a king." The helmet represents military enterprise also.

The Seal shows one star rising to a field of 23 other stars. Wells wrote that "The large star ascending from a cloud into a constellation of 23 smaller stars indicates the rise of Missouri into the . . . union of 23 states and the difficulty attending to it . . . the Missouri Compromise."

The bears are standing on a banner on which is written in Latin the state motto: *Salus Populi Suprema Lex Esto.* Translated, that means "Let the welfare of the people be the supreme law," which Wells says is the foundation of state government.

The State Seal carries the date 1820. That wasn't the year Missouri was admitted to the union. That was the year the state was allowed to draft a constitution.

The original seal design had no date on it. But Henry Geyer, later a U.S. Senator, suggested it should carry the year 1820 and it was incorporated into the design.

The original State Seal no longer exists. When the Capitol burned in Jefferson City in 1837, the original design by Wells was lost. The State Seal we have today shows some refinements. The bears look a little more realistic and they face each other. The first seal had the bears looking out at the viewer.

The present State Seal has an interesting history as well. It was in Confederate hands for a while. It was taken south by Governor Jackson and not returned to the state until some time after the Civil War, when former Lieutenant Governor Thomas Reynolds brought it back. Reynolds became the Confederate Governor when Jackson died.

Missouri's State Seal finally became a part of our state and ended a Governor's inconvenience a year and a half after statehood when Governor McNair approved the bill creating it on this date, January 11, 1822.

****

JANUARY 12
ROSATI AND THE ROME OF AMERICA

Much of the early history of what is now Missouri is dominated by the Catholic Church. This is logical since some of the earliest explorers up the Mississippi River were Catholic priests. The first settlers were French Catholics. As we recount in other stories, the Roman Catholic Church in St. Louis was considered so strong that some Protestant sects were almost afraid to try establishing their faith there. The first mass was said in St. Louis in the year of its founding, 1764. A church was built at a location which has since been the site of a Catholic Church for the more than two centuries. Despite the strong Catholic heritage, only one man is known for making St. Louis into the "Rome of America."

His name is Joseph Rosati.

Father Joseph Rosati arrived in St. Louis in 1817. He was 28 years old and he had an immediate complaint. Rosati found the facilities in which he was to preach and live atrocious.

"The rectory," he wrote, "looks more like a barn and the church is small, poor and falling into ruins." That was 1817. But within six years he would transform the entire religious life in St. Louis, and leave a landmark still used today.

Joseph Rosati was born in Naples, Italy, in 1789. He became a novitiate in the Lazarist Order of Rome and was 26 when he came to America. He went to seminary at Bardstown, Kentucky. There he learned English and did some teaching. Rosati served under Bishop DuBourg when he arrived in St. Louis. DuBourg, among other things, is remembered as a leader in early Missouri Catholic education, establishing what later became St. Louis University, and bringing nuns to run a private school for the poor.

Rosati worked in Perry County for a time. He served there as the head of St. Mary's Seminary and as pastor of the village church. While there, he directed construction of the seminary, drawing up the plans and supervising the building.

In 1820, when Father DeAndreis died, Rosati became the head of the Lazarist community in America. Just six years later Bishop DuBourg resigned and Rosati became his successor.

What an area he had under his jurisdiction! For some time his diocese extended from New Orleans to Canada and from the Mississippi River to the Rocky Mountains. Later, when that territory was divided into two parts, Rosati became the first official Bishop of the St. Louis Catholic Diocese.

By the time Rosati had been Bishop for five years, St. Louis was becoming a jumping-off point of the missionaries to the west. Five missionaries arrived from France in 1831. Several were sent westward, two of them to achieve great fame on the frontier. One was Father Pierre Jean DeSmet, who gained considerable stature among the Indian tribes. The Indians called him "Chief Black Robe." The other missionary was Father Benedict Roux. In 1833 he founded the first Catholic parish in what is now Kansas City.

Perhaps the most evident achievement of Rosati is the St. Louis cathedral. Still standing, it is now a historical as well as a religious shrine. He started it in 1831. It was completed in 1834.

By now Rosati's work had attracted worldwide attention within the Catholic Church. But no one watched his success with more interest than a former Italian schoolmate who had become Pope Gregory XVI. He granted Rosati's cathedral an indulgence usually reserved only for pilgrims visiting the seven Roman basilicas. The Pope ruled that indulgence could be gained by visiting the three altars of St. Louis. No other church or cathedral in America is so honored. That is why some call St. Louis "the Rome of America."

In 1840 Bishop Rosati sailed for Rome and was commissioned to improve relations between the Vatican and Haiti. He succeeded in that work, but became ill on a trip to Haiti and died in Rome in September of 1843 at the age of 54.

Bishop Joseph Rosati, the first Bishop of St. Louis, the man who made the Gateway City the "Rome of America," was born on this date, January 12, 1789.

****

JANUARY 13
THE POTATO CHIP LADY'S SON

He was making state history that crisp winter day as he stood in Jefferson City, his right hand upraised. For the second time he was taking the oath of office as Missouri's Governor. It had been a long time since his mother had gone to work to raise money so she could buy a potato chip machine to give the family an income. Her son had repeatedly ignored the advice of those who thought he was too young and moving too fast to become the first Missouri Governor to serve two consecutive four-year terms.

Warren Hearnes had learned as a growing boy in Southeast Missouri that success comes through hard work and often despite great odds. His father ran into business trouble in the 1930 depression. The hardware store went bankrupt and his mother became an important financial contributor to the Hearnes family. When the general store failed, Mrs. Hearnes went to work selling cakes and pies until she had raised enough to buy a potato chip machine. Then she drove a panel truck around distributing chips, peanuts, candy, cupcakes, and snacks to grocery stores, saloons, and other outlets.

Warren Hearnes wanted a military career early in his life. He enlisted in the National Guard when he was 16. But it didn't work out. He was under age. The National Guard found out and young Warren quickly became a civilian again.

He turned his interest toward the United States Military Academy at West Point. He was accepted, completed the rigorous course of study, and graduated in 1946, the year after the war ended. Upon graduation he was stationed in Puerto Rico. Two years later he married a preacher's daughter after only three dates. They settled down in Puerto Rico where he was still stationed. The first of their three daughters was born there.

Only two days after he retired from the military in 1949 he became a candidate for the Missouri House of Representatives from Mississippi County. Some people thought he was too young. But they were wrong. He won and became the youngest member of the legislature ever to serve from Mississippi County.

Hearnes wasted little time moving into a leadership position. He was twice elected Majority Floor Leader in the House. But he had his sights set on bigger things. In 1960 he became a candidate for Secretary of State. His main competition in the Democratic primary was James C. Kirkpatrick, who would later hold the job when Hearnes moved on. After one term as Secretary of State, Hearnes ran for Governor. Throughout his gubernatorial campaign, Hearnes hammered at the "establishment," the group of politicians and financial figures connected in one way or another with the Central Trust Bank in Jefferson City. He was an underdog. But his strong campaign and efficient organization put him on the Capitol steps as the Governor-elect on January 11, 1965.

In his first term the legislature passed 42 of his 45 proposals, one of them an amendment allowing him to succeed himself as Governor.

The second time he stood as Governor-elect on those Capitol steps, he called for the state to sacrifice to improve. "To do and be better," he said that day, "is a goal few achieve. To do it we are required to make sacrifices. Sacrifice in the sense of the giving of a part of those material things which we enjoy in abundance."

But his second term was a disappointment in many ways. Hearnes suffered his first big political loss in a fight with former supporter Earl Blackwell over a tax increase. Sixty percent of his proposals were passed by the legislature. Not bad, but it wasn't 42 out of 45.

He talked of returning to private life after his term ended. But after a couple of years as a lawyer in Charleston and St. Louis, he became restless. In 1976 he ran for the U.S. Senate. He lost twice, once in the August primary and then in November as the replacement candidate for the August winner, Jerry Litton. Litton and his family were killed in an airplane crash the night of the primary election. Hearnes lost in the general election to John Danforth.

But even that didn't keep him down. Warren and Betty Hearnes were not comfortable on the outside looking in. In 1978, Warren Hearnes ran for state auditor. But a political novice, James Antonio, a Republican, beat a man once considered politically unbeatable.

In 1979, a special election was called to fill a vacancy in the legislature created by the resignation of the incumbent representative from the district which included Charleston. Betty Hearnes won, becoming the first woman in Missouri history to become a member of the legislature after having been First Lady.

That same year, Warren Hearnes missed out on an appointment as circuit judge, an action which prompted him to refer to then-Governor Joseph Teasdale as a "buffoon" because of Teasdale's choice of Lloyd Briggs. In 1980, after the Missouri Supreme Court had ordered Briggs off the bench for impropriety, Hearnes and Teasdale patched up their differences and Hearnes became a Circuit Judge by appointment. However, the former Governor could not even retain his judgeship. Voters refused to elect him to a full term. Warren Hearnes said afterward he doubted that he would ever again seek public office.

It was a long way from that history making day when Warren E. Hearnes became the first Missourian to be sworn in for a second straight four-year term as Governor on this date, January 13, 1969.

****

JANUARY 14
FREEDOM OF RELIGION: A POLITICAL RIGHT?

Missouri once had a law saying religious liberty is not an inborn right, as the Bill of Rights states, but is a right granted by governments to people wishing to practice a belief. Even more astonishing in America, the Missouri Supreme Court upheld that position! The law is as frightening today as it was in the 1860s. The challenge to it was led by a modest, gentlemanly young priest who was indicted by a Pike County Grand Jury for preaching illegally.

Radicals had gained control of state government at the close of the Civil War and drawn up a constitution containing what was called the "ironclad oath." It was designed to keep former southern loyalists out of political office. All professional men were required to take that oath before they could practice their professions.

Ministers, for example, couldn't preach, marry people, or teach unless they took the oath. But many of them felt their loyalty was to God before it was to the state and decided to ignore it. The Catholic Church began an opposition movement.

The day after the deadline for signing the oath, Father John Cummings gave a quiet, ordinary sermon. He didn't advocate any radical theology or government overthrow. But a week later he was indicted. He pleaded guilty to the charge of preaching illegally. Acting as his own attorney, he told the court his constitutional rights were being violated and his church was being persecuted. He was fined $500.

Cummings refused to pay that fine and he was thrown into jail. He refused to be released on bail and appealed to the Supreme Court of Missouri.

In October of 1865, the case went to the Missouri Supreme Court. Representing the priest was former Postmaster General Montgomery Blair. Blair and others argued on behalf of Cummings that the oath violated the fundamental right of all men to practice their religion in freedom, the right on which our country was founded.

Those who favored the oath argued that a church is only an association of individuals sharing a common view and practice, and claiming authority for such activities is divine. But since each member of those associations is a citizen of Missouri and must therefore follow state laws, the state has the authority to regulate the activities of those individuals and associations.

The ruling was unanimous. It was against Father Cummings.

The ruling said the state had the right to act in the field of municipal regulation for the public good. Eventually, eighty-five more preachers were indicted. But enforcement difficulties grew. An effort was made in the legislature to remove the oath, but it failed. One lawmaker, Thomas J. Babcock of Miller County, said, "No class of people between Heaven and Earth or outside Heaven and Hell deserve the curse of God more than disloyal ministers."

The Cummings case went all the way to the United States Supreme Court. The arguments were the same there as before the Missouri Court. The waiting began for the decision, and the wait was a long one. By the summer of 1866 Governor Fletcher had decided the oath should be repealed because it couldn't be enforced. Finally the Supreme Court handed down its decision early in 1867. Today it is hard to believe the issue could have gone so far. But no less astonishing is the fact that the nation's highest court struck down the oath on a vote of only 5-4.

The court did not rule on the religious issue. It ruled on the constitutionality of the oath. It said the requirement to sign the oath constituted punishment without judicial trial. Those charged under the law were presumed guilty until proven innocent—the reverse of proper legal procedure—and those required to take the oath were being punished for past events, not protected for the future.

Most of the cases against clergymen were soon dismissed. It was impossible to enforce the law and arrest all the violators anyway. It is estimated only about one percent of the 1,500 ministers of all faiths in Missouri at the time took the hated oath.

Cummings versus the State of Missouri stands today as a major stroke for freedom. It is ironic that it occurred because many Missourians were threatened with the loss of basic rights after the nation had fought a tragic war to make men free.

The Cummings Case, a landmark for freedom, was decided by the United States Supreme Court on this date, the 14th of January, in 1867.

****

JANUARY 15
MARION COLLEGE: DREAMS KILLED BY SPECULATION

A Presbyterian minister named David Nelson moved to Missouri in 1830 with a dream for a college. He settled in the Palmyra area and set aside about eleven acres for his unique school. He called it Marion College, an institution which led to some wild wheeling and dealing in its time. It fostered rampant speculation in the area and when it died, many dreams died with it.

The first building for Marion College was a log cabin. The school's first president was David Nelson. There were two other men listed as co-founders, William Muldrow and Doctor David Clark. Their small one-cabin school became the first chartered college in Missouri, and the second educational institution in the state to give degrees.

Although the founders figured it would take little money to get it going, they found it impossible to raise even that small amount. So they settled on a manual labor plan to sustain the school—a plan other colleges use even today.

Originally they wanted to buy 5,000 acres which they felt could support a college of 420 students and a dozen faculty. The college would have three departments: a theological department, a literary school, and a preparatory school. The college farm would be divided into 300-acre tracts to support the literary school. The department head would have supervision over the land and see that 30 students would work three hours a day each. It was thought that land could produce 3,000 dollars a year, a third of which would go to the professor-overseer, the rest going to finance student needs. The theological department would have 500 acres and 50 students per professor. They were to raise hay, a crop the backers throught would produce $12,000 to $15,000 profit a year.

The Presbyterian Church had internal problems which kept the school from gaining the support from that quarter. The state had a seminary fund and the legislature was interested in manual labor schools. But the founders overlooked that. Instead they put up personal holdings as collateral and borrowed $20,000 in New York. They bought the 5,000 acres. Soon another $19,000 came in from the east not to pay off the debt, but to put up buildings and fences.

A number of learned men back east decided to invest in Marion College and they also went there to teach. One was the Reverend

Ezra Stiles Elzy, a pastor for 20 years at an important Philadelphia Presbyterian Church. He is said to have sunk $60,000 to $100,000 in Marion and Shelby County real estate.

David Nelson was anti-slavery and that wasn't popular. In the middle of the 1830s he resigned as school President and had to leave Missouri. His school continued, however. The first annual catalogue lists 85 students. The records show the greatest number of students attending the school was 91 in the 1837-38 school year.

Speculators sold $150,000 worth of lots in Marion City to eastern investors and another $35,000 worth of lots in New Philadelphia. The number of acres sold by the Palmyra land office increased by five times from 1834 to 1835 and doubled in the next year. A railroad company was planned.

Then disaster hit.

In 1837 the United States suffered a depression known as the Panic of '37. Missouri, for various reasons, didn't feel the impact as much as many areas back East. But much of the funding for Marion College came from the East. The panic weakened school finances and the finances of those supporting it. The entire web of speculation began to collapse.

By 1841 the student body was only half what it had been five years earlier. The college was weakening. In 1842 it was refinanced, but that didn't help. It died later that year. The great dreams of a major college, a major metropolis, several communities and a railroad died with Marion College.

In 1842 the Grand Lodge of Missouri bought the college buildings for $9,500 and made them into a school and orphan asylum. In 1848 it was relocated in Lexington to become the first Masonic College in the world. But in 1858 the doors closed for good.

Marion College, the first institution of higher learning chartered by the state of Missouri, was a school based on self-supporting labor and killed by self-serving speculation. It was incorporated on this date, January 15, 1831.

****

JANUARY 16
MISSOURI'S LOATHSOME STONE PURGATORY

Wilson Eidson walked through the gate that day and heard it clang shut behind him. He was in prison to serve two years and 45 days for a Greene County grand larceny conviction.

Eidson had plenty of room because he was the first inmate to enter the Missouri State Penitentiary that day in 1836. Thus began a long and generally unflattering history for the penitentiary, sometimes called the worst in the nation.

The groundwork for the institution was laid three years before Eidson became the first inmate. Early in 1833 the legislature called for two commissioners to plan and let a contract for construction of a "jail and penitentiary house" in Jefferson City. The legislature allowed $25,000 for the work with the institution to be located on a hill set aside by a law passed in 1821. The place was supposed to be ready in the fall of 1834. But the contractor failed to complete it by then and the legislature authorized another contractor to complete the job. In 1836 the penitentiary opened with a warden to run it and a three-member board of prison inspectors to oversee it.

At first the prison was only a few small buildings on four acres of land surrounded by a wooden stockade. Eight months after Eidson arrived there were 13 more inmates. By 1838 the prison population reached 46. The original population limit was 40. It already was overcrowded, headed toward becoming the "loathsome stone purgatory" it would be called 127 years later.

Only three years after it first opened, the prison was made self-supporting under a law leasing the institution to contractors who would employ the inmates in profitable labor. There would be no warden under that system. It would be up the contractors to feed and clothe the inmates. In 1843 the prison was leased for $50,000. All but $5,000 of that went into the state treasury.

The system didn't work out. When the state resumed control of the prison in 1854 the place was in pitiful condition. The buildings were run down. The contractors, using free labor, had done little to sustain the prisoners. Living conditions were atrocious. Bedding was filthy. The cells were little more than kennels. The terrible conditions continued for years. In 1860 the warden told the legislature the institution was "little better than a school for rogues," a comment which would be echoed for more than a century. Sometimes there were riots because of inmate anger over brutal treatment and poor food. The contract system was later reestablished and lasted until 1913 when a bill was passed gradually abolishing it.

Thirteen years later, in 1926, the National Society of Penal Institutions ranked Missouri's prison one of the three worst in the United States. The place was overcrowded, filthy, undisciplined and poorly administered. The inmate crowd was eased in the 1930s with the opening of the Algoa Intermediate Reformatory east of Jefferson City. Some renovation money was approved by the legislature. But conditions remained terrible. In 1933 the State Board of Penal Commissioners was created with the reorganized corrections system placed under it. Things still didn't improve. Just three years later the prison was packed with 4,800 inmates.

After World War II, in 1946, the state Department of Corrections was organized. Nine years after that, the Division of Penal Institutions was disbanded. Six divisions were set up within the Department of Corrections. Further modernization came after a disastrous riot in 1954 took many lives and destroyed several buildings. The shake-up within the administration, however, didn't bring about much modernization.

In the 1960s internal warfare began behind the big walls and strong steps were finally taken. The situation forced a response. Seven convicts had been killed and 205 others injured. Governor John Dalton ordered an investigation. When the report was made public, the warden committed suicide. The Director of Corrections resigned not long afterwards. In 1966 Fred Wilkinson, a top figure for years in the federal prison system, took over at the top of Missouri's corrections department.

He wasted little time making improvements. Prisoners were given utensils other than a spoon to eat with. They got mattresses and pillows instead of bug-infested straw pallets. Wilkinson ordered the opening of 17 acres of the 45-acre facility for inmate use. The guard force and personnel services were improved. Old buildings were renovated.

More than a decade earlier one newspaper reporter had written that the Missouri Penitentiary was "conceived in the traditions of Bedlam, The Black Hole of Calcutta and Devils Island." When Fred Wilkinson resigned in 1972, he said Missouri's correction system could stand equal to any in the nation.

But it is clear that progress comes only through great effort, often in lengthy and loud battles — not inside the walls, but outside them in various political arenas. Missouri's corrections system today is better than it has ever been, but there is still room for improvement. It began its long and undistinguished life with the passage of a bill establishing a state prison on this date, January 16, 1833.

****

JANUARY 17
THOMAS A. DOOLEY, M.D.

As a young man he once listed his prime interests as "pretty girls, snappy roadsters, and bourbon on the rocks."

Later he wrote to his family in St. Louis, "I am a doctor. This is the root of me — I am a doctor. Everything else, everyone, is second to that. First, I am a doctor....Everything else is second. Home life, social life, writing life, living life, loving life, family, friends, romance, fame, fortune, all these are secondary because I am a doctor."

He wore a St. Christopher medal around his neck, engraved with the words of Robert Frost:

"The woods are lovely, dark and deep.
But I have promises to keep
And miles to go before I sleep."

He traveled those miles and wanted to go more, but an insidious disease cut short his meteoric career one day after his 34th birthday.

He was a singular man who believed in people.

His name was Doctor Thomas A. Dooley.

Dr. Dooley could have been a spoiled playboy in the lucrative medical profession, but he learned to care about people among the refugees in Haiphong in 1954. He lost 60 pounds there and was on the last plane to leave that city as the Communists poured in. He would later say, "What we did in dying Haiphong was far less important than what we learned there. We had seen simple tender loving care...change a people's fear and hatred into friendship and understanding....I knew the promises I had to keep. I knew the keeping of them would take me many miles back to Southeast Asia to the very edge of tomorrow, where the future might be made or lost."

Thomas Dooley was born in St. Louis. He loved horses, showed an early talent for medicine, and was extremely religious. His brother

Earle was killed in World War II, in Europe. Tom carried with him for years a letter Earle had written in case of his death. "Never again must you allow human stupidity to look idly aside while this scourge is permitted to fester and spring out on such a scale....We can never get rid of war entirely, but it must be limited," it said.

Tom Dooley attended Notre Dame, graduated from the St. Louis University School of Medicine, then went into the Navy where he met his destiny at Haiphong. It was in Haiphong that he gained the experience for his first book, *Deliver Us From Evil.* Money from that book helped form MEDICO, a privately-financed, non-secular medical mission in Laos in 1958.

In February of 1959 he fell down an embankment and later complained of chest pains. Doctors removed a tumor from his chest and told him it was malignant. Tom Dooley had incurable cancer. Later he would say, "The cancer went no deeper than my flesh. There was no cancer in my spirit."

In the last year of his life he went back to Asia three times and published the third of his three books. He established a new hospital, had an audience with the Pope, concentrated on medical work at various hospitals, and made many speeches and personal appearances.

A contemporary, Doctor Alex Zlatanos, said a month before Dooley's death, "I saw his overwhelming sadness, and knew that his real agony came not primarily from his physical condition but from an awareness that it would never permit him to do all the things he had to do."

The day after his 34th birthday, he died.

He once told a school group in Harrisburg, Illinois, "You must never think that what I do or anyone like me does, is because I am an extraordinary man. I am not. I am an ordinary man. America was founded on the idea that the ordinary man can accomplish extraordinary things."

Tom Dooley was one of the symbols of the idealism of the early 1960s. Efforts were made to erect a statue to his honor in his hometown. Two decades after his death, however, there is still no statue. A new generation of Americans have not heard of Tom Dooley, and many of his generation have forgotten.

Thomas Dooley, doctor and humanitarian, was born in Missouri on this date, the 17th of January, 1927.

****

JANUARY 18
CHARLES PHILLIP JOHNSON, OUTLAW'S LAWYER

Standing at the grave of the executed killer he had represented in court in 1897, Charles Phillip Johnson felt moved to speak. He hadn't planned to and his words formed no eulogy for the man being buried that day. But his impromptu speech at graveside is considered by some to be a classic on justice, especially when conditions of the day were considered.

He had been a lawyer for 40 years by then and was known as a man unafraid to speak his mind. Johnson was an Illinois native who at 19, had already been a newspaper editor for two years before he took up the study of law. Just four years later he became city attorney in St. Louis.

Johnson was one of the disciples of Frank Blair, a prominent pro-Union political leader of the time. Johnson helped organize Missouri troops for the northern cause during the Civil War. When the Republicans split, he went with the radicals, favoring prompt and vigorous measures for coercion of the South and immediate emancipation. He turned down a nomination to Congress and became a state legislator. Johnson tried to gain support for his proposal that loyal slaveowners be paid for their slaves. But he failed. He came out in favor of immediate emancipation without compensation. He drafted the bill calling for the constitutional convention of 1865 in which a new state charter was drawn up. But he found that constitution too harsh and opposed it.

In 1872 Johnson ran for Lieutenant Governor and won. Silas Woodson was elected Governor. As the presiding officer in the Senate, Johnson led a widely-discussed reform fight. The legislature had unthinkingly given St. Louis the power to regulate prostitution. St. Louis passed a so-called "social evil" law, saying prostitution was wrong *unless* licensed by the city. Johnson led the fight for repeal of the law and won.

After his term, he returned to private law practice. Another touchy subject came up: the prevalance of public gambling and the rise of gamblers as the ruling element in St. Louis politics. Johnson was elected to the legislature again on this issue and pushed through a bill making gambling a felony.

That done, he returned to his private law practice.

46

In the 1880s the James gang was breaking up. St. Joseph newspaperman John Edwards started arranging legal assistance for Frank James and obtained Johnson's services as one of the defense attorneys. Some thought the agreement to defend Frank James was a move by Johnson to become a candidate for Governor. The fact that he did it without a fee further encouraged critics to say he was trying to gain favor with the political friends of the James family. There is a touch of irony in the situation. Johnson, a strong Union supporter during the war, defended a man who had ridden with some of the worst of the Confederate guerillas in those years.

Johnson successfully defended Frank James.

But there is more irony to the James family situation. About this time, Frank Triplett wrote a book about Jesse, now dead, allegedly dictated by Jesse's widow, Zee, and the outlaw's mother. But Zee repudiated that statement after receiving $500 royalties. Zee then declared the book a fraud and filed suit for more money. Johnson represented the women and won for them another $492.

In 1897 Johnson found himself standing next to the grave of Doctor Arthur Duestrow at Union. Duestrow had been executed for killing his wife and children. Johnson thought Duestrow insane and at the gravesite that day called Duestrow a victim of "judicial murder." He said punishment should be left to God, who inflicted insanity upon the man in the first place.

"It is claimed," he said, "that this is a triumph of law and a just punishment of the victim. I say here that it is a disgrace to the humanity of the age...a triumph of ignorance and prejudice. It is illustrative of a retrogression to the cruel savagery of the past ages."

Johnson was part of the law faculty at Washington University for many years. He and his brothers were law partners, J. D. Johnson handling the civil cases, while Charles took care of the criminal proceedings. He was 84 when he died in 1920.

Charles P. Johnson, a moving force in legislative halls and courtrooms of our state, was born on this date, January 18, 1836.

****

JANUARY 19
THOMAS LAWSON PRICE: A VICTIM OF HIS TIMES

In 1864 the Missouri Democratic Party was all but dead. The Civil War and the Radical movement had badly crippled the conservative, traditionally-southern Democratic political organization. With absolutely no hope of winning, the party nominated a former Lieutenant Governor. Sure enough he lost—by more than 40,000 votes. The party would be in trouble for several years. But it might have staved off its own death by accepting defeat rather than quitting entirely.

Thomas Lawson Price was the man thrown into the political breach. Price was the first Mayor of Jefferson City. He first came to Missouri in 1831, from Virginia. He decided to settle in St. Louis but that city was ravaged by cholera so he moved west to Jefferson City. There, Price opened a mercantile business which he ran shrewdly. He invested the profits in land and became wealthy.

In 1838 Price opened the first stage line from St. Louis to Jefferson City. It wasn't the first of its kind in Missouri. The first one had been set up back in 1819. He got out of the business in 1849, eventually he founded a bank and organized a building and loan agency. When railroads came along, Thomas Lawson Price was one of the first major financial supporters. He became involved in state government and took his railroad interests with him to their benefit. He supported funding for the Iron Mountain Railroad which ran south out of St. Louis, and the Hannibal-St. Joseph Railroad. He was a major contractor of the Pacific Railroad, which later became the Missouri Pacific.

In 1838 and '39 he ran for State Treasurer but lost. It was his first political venture. In 1839 Jefferson City incorporated and Price became its first Mayor. Six years later he tried for the U.S. Senate and lost again. Four years later he ran for public office again, and this time he won, becoming Lieutenant Governor under Austin King.

Price served a term in the legislature in 1860 and in 1862 became a Congressman, filling the vacancy created by the expulsion of the delegate from what was then the Fifth District. The next November he tried for a full term but was beaten by Joseph McClurg, who later would become Governor.

Price was a robust man, a couple of inches over six feet in height. But his health began to fail in the 1860s. He died at his home in

Jefferson City in July of 1870. He was 61.

Price's home was a landmark in the city. For many years it was customary for the new Governor and First Lady to be received at their first formal reception in that house. The land on which it stood figured in a lawsuit which challenged the existence of Jefferson City as the Capital City of Missouri.

The house has been gone for years. In its place is the Missouri Supreme Court building, an ironic yet appropriate situation since the Missouri Supreme Court handled that important case. Thomas Lawson Price was a man whose political star rose at the wrong times, a Benton man in the days of anti-Benton feeling, a Democrat when Democrats couldn't vote, a man who was a candidate for Governor when he knew he couldn't win but ran to save his party and then didn't live to see that party recover.

Thomas Lawson Price was born on this date, the 19th of January in 1809.

****

JANUARY 20
THE HOUSE

It's quite a house, with three stories and a basement. It cost almost $75,000 to build. In the first one hundred years after it was occupied it cost more than ten times that amount to operate it, repair it, and renovate it. Great people and scoundrels alike have lived in it, been entertained in it, or just visited it. It has been the scene of grand celebrations and great tragedy.

Lodgings for Missouri's Governors in the first half century of statehood had not been universally popular among the chief executives and their families. Several Governors had complained that their quarters weren't adequate. Two rooms in the first Capitol in Jefferson City were set aside for Governor's quarters. That was fine for John Miller, a bachelor and the first to live there. But when Daniel Dunklin took over, he needed room for his family and a mansion was started.

It would be thirty years later, though, before a decent home was provided. Governor McClurg once referred to his residence as "antiquated, dilapidated, and uncomfortable, unsuited to the reasonable requirements of the public."

His successor, Benjamin Gratz Brown, pushed for a new residence altogether. He lived in the house then used as the mansion, but his wife stayed at their St. Louis home except for formal occasions. That in itself was somewhat unusual since his wife had grown up in Jefferson City, living just a few blocks from where her husband maintained his quarters as Governor. Early in January of 1871, Cole County Representative John Wielandy introduced a bill calling for $50,000 to be spent on a new house for the Governor. It was passed. Work started quickly, with penitentiary inmates and citizen volunteers. Governor Brown had stone columns quarried from an Iron County quarry he owned. The columns turned out to be nine inches too short. But adjustments were made and the columns still stand today on the front porch of the mansion. The front doors are hand-carved walnut and weigh about a ton each. Nine fireplaces were built inside. A sweeping staircase led to the second floor.

The Browns moved in about a year after the bill had been introduced providing for the mansion. Just three days later, their first guest arrived—the Russian Grand Duke, Alexis, who was touring the country hunting buffalo and, some say, trying to forget an unfortunate love affair back home.

The Brown children gave the mansion a lived-in look almost immediately. Jerri Giffen, in her book about the mansion and the First Ladies who have lived there, tells the story of 10-year-old Gratz Brown practicing sawing one day on the legs of several dining room chairs. His parents didn't learn about it until some guests were unceremoniously dumped onto the floor when they sat down. The Browns lived in the mansion about a year before the Governor's term ended.

The first mansion wedding took place in the next administration when a relative of Governor Silas Woodson's was married. A few weeks later the first baby was born in the mansion to another Woodson relative. Carrie Crittenden, daughter of Governor and Mrs. Thomas Crittenden, was the first child to die in the mansion. She was nine when she died, just five days before Christmas. The funeral was held in the big house, amidst the holiday decorations.

It was common practice for bachelor Governor John Marmaduke to hold an annual Christmas party for relatives and the children of Jefferson City. But he died in 1887, on the night the third party was scheduled. He was the first Governor to die in that house. On New

Year's day, 1903, Mary Dockery died, the first Governor's wife to die in the mansion.

A fire broke out in a chimney during the Folk administration. The Governor was seen, clad in his nightshirt, throwing fire dust at the flames until firemen arrived.

During World War I, the yard of the mansion was plowed up and became Mrs. Gardner's victory garden.

National headlines were made at the mansion in the 1950s when Governor Blair refused to move in. He complained the place was infested with rats, the toilets were old-fashioned, the woodwork was worm-eaten and it needed an elevator. His complaints were reminiscent of those of Governor McClurg years before. Renovation was started once more. But it was several months before the Blairs moved in. They had another house in Jefferson City and there was no pressure to leave it for a mansion of less impressive living conditions.

Restoration continued with the Hearnes administration on a scope not previously seen. When the first Bond administration took over, further restoration and renovation efforts were made and a special trust organization was established to oversee continued restoration and maintenance of the old house.

Renovation and restoration will probably go on as long as the building is used, a special house which began its long, colorful and often expensive history when Governor B. Gratz Brown and his family moved in on this date, January 20, 1872.

****

JANUARY 21
A BRAVE MAN'S WIDOW

It was a day to celebrate in Columbia in 1837. There were banners and ceremonies. Men were marching off to war. There were good-byes and high-spoken words. Missourians were to go off for a glorious fight. They were to meet the murderous savage and succeed where others had failed. That's what they thought; what they hoped. But there were many in the crowd that day who would become widows.

One was Ann Hawkins Gentry. Her husband Richard was a founder of Columbia, a member of the legislature, a man prominent in the life of early Missouri. They were married twenty-seven years.

Ann Hawkins was nineteen years old when she married Richard Gentry. Their first child was born during the War of 1812 while Richard was serving with General William Henry Harrison on Lake Erie. It was bitterly cold in that area. Richard and the other volunteers from Kentucky were ill-prepared for the weather. So Ann gathered all the wool she could find, carded it, spun the yarn, and wove the cloth to make a suit of heavy clothes for her husband.

She rode sidesaddle on a Kentucky thoroughbred, carrying the youngest of their four children, from Madison County, Kentucky, to St. Louis in 1818—373 miles. In years to come she and Richard would have nine more children for a total of thirteen. They settled in St. Louis County but stayed for only a short time. They soon moved further west, upriver, to old Franklin, across the river from Boonville.

In 1820 her husband and some other men founded a new community called Smithton, the forerunner of Columbia. The Gentrys set up housekeeping in Smithton in a double cabin which also became the new village's first tavern. Her husband, an ambitious man and an adventurous one, was often away from home, leaving her to care for and raise the ever-increasing family. She was left behind while he served as State Senator, while he was a Marshall on an expedition to Santa Fe and while he fought as a Major General in the Black Hawk War. He was Columbia's first Mayor during one stretch when he was at home. In all of these absences, some lasting for months on end, it was Ann Hawkins Gentry who kept the house together.

In 1831, the Gentry Tavern, later known as the Columbia Hotel, was relocated in an L-shaped two-story brick building where the present Boone County Courthouse now stands. Her husband, Columbia's second postmaster, ran the post office from one corner of their hotel.

In October 1837 Richard Gentry left his wife and family behind for the last time to seek further adventure fighting the Seminoles in the Florida Everglades. He was a Colonel, leading his men on a mission which came about largely because Senator Benton had chided the President about lack of military success against those Indians. Benton had boasted that Missourians could turn things around. Students of the Columbia Female Academy, which Gentry had helped found, made a silk banner for the troops to carry. On it were sewn the words "Gird, Gird for the Conflict, Our Banner Wave High. For our country we live, for our country we die." Richard was wounded several times in one of the swamp battles and died. The banner was returned to Mrs. Gentry and still exists. It is state property now and for many years was on display at Jefferson Barracks near St. Louis.

Ann Gentry was left a widow with a large family.

Senator Thomas Hart Benton came to her aid. He secured for her the appointment of postmaster at Columbia. It was a historic appointment in a time when women's place was definitely limited. In fact, she became only the second woman in the nation to receive an official appointment of that type from the federal government. Ann Gentry served in the position for 27 years, from 1838 to 1865. She was in her mid-70s when she retired. She died just short of her 79th birthday in January of 1870.

Her family went on to lives of distinction for generations. The name Gentry is still a familiar one in Columbia. In many ways she was typical of the hardy pioneer woman who settled Missouri and elsewhere on the frontier. You can study your history books for hours on end and you will seldom, if ever, find a better example of a woman's courage and loyalty than you will find in the story of Ann Hawkins Gentry who was born on this date, the 21st of January, 1791.

****

JANUARY 22
MISSOURI'S SWAMP FOX

Sizeable numbers of Union soldiers either spent much of their time searching the swamps of southern Missouri for an elusive Confederate leader or fearing he would come out to make an attack. He seldom appeared and when he did he rarely used more than a fragment of his forces. Actually he didn't have very many men, but he was a master at keeping federal forces busy thinking he did. He was known as the Swamp Fox of Missouri's Civil War.

Meriwether Jeff Thompson first attracted the attention of Union leaders in the city of St. Joseph. The federal government planned to make it plain that Missouri was a state of northern allegiance after war had been declared. A federal flag was run up the pole of the St. Joseph post office. But the Mayor of the town scaled that pole and cut it down. The crowd watching below tore it to shreds.

That mayor, Meriwether Jeff Thompson, wrote later in his journal, "I had cut down the flag that I once loved. I had as yet drawn no blood from its defenders, but I was determined to strike it down wherever I found it and to cast my lot with my southern brethren, who were building a new nation."

Once when Governor Jackson was having problems at the start of the war, Thompson strode into his office and told him, "I wish to tell you the two qualities of a soldier. One he must have, but he needs both. One of them is common sense and the other is courage, and by God! You have neither!"

He clerked at a store in Liberty for a while, then in the 1850s he became a civic leader in St. Joseph. Biographer Jay Monaghan says Thompson was, at one time, president of the gas works; president of two railroads, secretary of a third, and general agent for a fourth; a Colonel of the militia; and head of the Catholic Benefit Society. As Mayor, he formally dispatched the first Pony Express rider bound west. He was at the throttle when the first Hannibal and St. Joseph Railroad locomotive pulled into town.

With the coming of the Civil War, Thompson was named Commander of the First Military District of Missouri. He quickly established his reputation as the "Swamp Fox" by leading his men through those swampy areas along the border, escaping from federal forces and reappearing without warning. He demanded discipline, but had trouble obtaining it. He once hanged four men for horse stealing and had a firing squad kill a deserter.

Thompson and his men raided the bank of Charleston in 1861, taking $56,000. He captured New Madrid with only 20 men and held it several days before the small size of his force became known. Then he melted back into the swamps.

Halfway through the war, his men elected a kleptomaniac swamp preacher to replace Thompson as Commander. Thompson tried to recruit another force. But he was captured and held captive until 1864. After he was exchanged, he came back to Missouri to fight again. During a skirmish about ten miles from Jefferson City, Brigadier General David Shanks was killed. Thompson succeeded him, and gained the rank of Brigadier which had been denied him earlier.

While detached from Jo Shelby's force, he captured Sedalia, held it briefly and then went on to the Battle of Westport, called by many "The Gettysburg of the West." He and Shelby had to cut their way through the encircling Union forces and then fought the rearguard action on the long flight southward.

It was the last great Confederate surge in Missouri.

The next April Thompson found it impossible to believe Lee had surrendered. But he finally wrote President Johnson asking to take the amnesty oath. He said, "Apologies for the past or promises for the future would be an evidence of want of confidence in my own integrity. I have simply done what I conceived to be my duty and am actuated by the same incentive now in making this application for your pardon."

He took part in Louisiana politics for the next decade. He did not return to Missouri until he was seriously ill with tuberculosis. He died in September of 1876. The St. Joseph *Weekly Herald* described him as "a fair type of the southerner physically, the northerner mentally and the westerner in his manner and broad progressive ideas, one of the bravest men our country ever produced."

General Meriwether Jeff Thompson, the Swamp Fox of Missouri's Civil War, was born on this date, January 22, 1826.

****

JANUARY 23
THE FARM VOTE AND THE CONGRESSMAN

George Christopher was a farmer. He believed in the centuries-old idea that virtue is found close to the soil. When the time came in the mid 1900s to build his political fortunes, he constructed them in the farming areas of outstate Missouri.

Christopher surprised many by winning when he did and the way he did, winning when the farm vote justified his faith in rural Missouri. He knew what he was talking about when he spoke of the farm vote, unlike many politicians who speak of that voting bloc in abstract terms. For 25 years he was a tenant farmer in the Butler area. Tenant farmers aren't generally known for becoming wealthy, but George Christopher managed to put enough aside so that he was able to buy a farm near the small community of Amoret. He spent the rest of his life farming 975 acres in Bates County.

Christopher was born in December, 1888. His limited education was in Butler. He didn't attend high school. But he later graduated from a business college in Sedalia. His interest in politics was late-blooming.

He was almost 60 when he took his first run at the United States Congress. He posted a narrow primary victory, polling just over 10,000 votes with a victory margin of just over 2,000 votes. The Republican primary winner, meanwhile, had rolled up almost 21,500 votes, some 18,000 more than his nearest challenger. But two months later, Christopher upset the applecart and beat his opponent. He rolled up more than 63,000 votes to become a member of the 81st Congress. It was a slim victory though, only 3,400 votes. Narrow victories would continue to mark his career as an elected official.

After his first term, Christopher left the Congress to become Assistant Director of the United States Department of Agriculture's conservation program. Conservative in farming practices, he believed that time, sweet clover, and alfalfa were the best techniques for renewing and saving land.

He was 65 when he decided to try again for Congress in 1954. Christopher rolled over his primary opponents, then crushed his Republican opposition in the November election by more than 40,000 votes. It was not a typical Christopher election.

In his first term he had served on only one committee, a fairly insignificant one—the House Administrative and Printing Committee. But his return to Washington put him on two more important ones: Interior and Insular Affairs, and the Committee on Veterans Affairs.

Congressmen must run every two years. In 1956, George Christopher tried again. In that election he compiled his highest vote total ever, 98,000 votes. His victory margin was about 68,000. But his biggest challenge came two years later. In 1958 he faced a tough battle against a Jackson County coalition backing former Independence Mayor Robert Weatherford, Jr., for the Democratic nomination. In this election, however, Weatherford had the support of a man named Harry Truman. Jackson County Democrats had decided to try to send a more urban-oriented representative to Congress. But Christopher once again banked on a strong farm vote.

He lost badly in Jackson County, almost two to one. Weatherford piled up 15,125 votes while Christopher had about 7,200. But Barton County went with Christopher 424-81. He outpolled Weatherford in Bates County 2,500 to 200; beat him in Cass County 1,500 to 400. Henry County went to Christopher, 2,800 to 600. He carried Johnson County, 1,062 to 232 for Weatherford. Lafayette County was his 1,380 to 503 and Vernon County went his way 2,858 to 824. In the final tally Weatherford had 18,057. Christopher had 19,862. His loyal supporters in rural Missouri did not let him down. He beat Weatherford in outstate Missouri almost four to one.

That November he ran up a 32,000 vote victory to go back to Congress for a fourth term. He had just a few months to savor those victories, though. His wife had died in 1952 and his daughter was married to the doorkeeper in the U.S. House of Representatives. Just after the 86th Congress began its session, George Christopher died of a heart attack at his daughter's home. He was 70. Three months after his death, a special election named William Randall of Independence, to take his place.

George Christopher was a Congressman and farmer who believed in the strength of the rural vote and saw that belief justified. He died on this date, the 23rd of January, in 1959.

****

JANUARY 24
THE LIFE OF THE LIBERAL REVOLT

Liberal Republicans had had enough of the Radicals and the corrupt Grant administration. Led by Senator Carl Schurz, they walked out of the state Republican convention, nominated their own candidate, and made him the winner of the Governor's office. When B. Gratz Brown won, it shook the Radical movement throughout Reconstruction America. The next step would be one of the more bizarre episodes in American political history.

Senator Schurz, Governor Brown, and St. Louis newspaper publisher Joseph Pulitzer set the national Republican party convention of 1872 as their next target after their state victory of 1870. They won at the state level although the Grant people had suspended the federally-appointed officeholders in Missouri, levied a five percent tax on government salaries to finance the Radical cause, and exerted other pressures to hinder their efforts. But it became obvious before April of 1872 that these events in Missouri weren't going to intimidate the regular Republican party. Disenchantment with Grant was growing.

The Liberals met in Cincinnati with some leaders hoping for a groundswell of anti-Grantism, a coalition with the Democrats, and the emergence of a reformist candidate who could win. Although

Schurz didn't trust the Democrats, he was willing to accept their help as long as the Republicans had the candidates and the platforms. The Democrats were still reeling from their Civil War setbacks, and they realized the Liberals offered the only chance they had in 1872 of making a rapid recovery.

Governor Brown had visions of a Presidential nomination. But Schurz thought he had been rewarded well enough with the office of Governor. Besides, thought Schurz, Brown didn't have the necessary national appeal. Schurz didn't make his stand public though because he didn't want to split the Missouri delegation. He favored Charles Francis Adams and so did many others. But the field was still wide open. Brown was staying back in Missouri while all of this was happening.

A day before the balloting, Missouri delegation chairman William Grosvener told his 30 delegates Brown didn't have a chance, but could probably get the vice-presidential nomination. Somebody telegraphed this to Brown who promptly climbed on a train with his cousin Frank Blair, and arrived in Cincinnati that night bent on revenge.

All night Brown worked to foil the plans of his former ally Schurz by making a deal with backers of New York newspaperman Horace Greeley. On the first ballot, Adams had 205 votes, but Greeley had a surprising 147 and Brown 95. Brown then gained the floor and dramatically threw his support to Greeley. Joseph Pulitzer thought Schurz could have stopped the surge then and there with a simple command. But he didn't and the tide turned. Greeley took the lead on the second ballot, and on the sixth won the nomination. Brown was named his running mate.

Schurz also suffered reverses in the formulation of the platform. He wound up at a friend's house, heavily disappointed, pounding out Chopin's Funeral March on the piano. He was so sure his newspaper in St. Louis would be hurt by the Cincinnati travesty that he sold it to Pulitzer, giving the soon-to-be-famous editor his first newspaper ownership.

As for Greeley—his was a sad case. His mind was slipping. He seldom buttoned his vest straight. His cravat was always stained with food. His wife died a week before the election, further adding to his mental collapse. Despite this, he and Brown carried six states including Missouri by 32,000 votes. They received 2.8 million votes nationally. But they were crushed in the overall tally. By then many knew Horace Greeley was insane. He died in a mental hospital about three weeks after the election.

The Liberal Republican movement had a short life in Missouri as well as nationally. It was born at the state level as the first national break with Grantism. It died pathetically on the national level when it tried to put an insane man in the White House. But it was an open signal that the Radical days were numbered and that the Grant administration government-by-crony would come under greater scrutiny.

It all started with the Liberal Republican convention which met in Jefferson City on this date, the 24th of January, in 1870.

****

JANUARY 25
THE SCULPTRESS, THE SENATOR, AND THE IMPEACHMENT SCANDAL

The bearded man and the small girl walked into the sculptor's studio one day in the 1850's so she could see the famous Clark Mills at work. She was fascinated. Mills gave her a bucket of potter's clay and told her to go into the next room and make something. She was back in an hour, with the clay model of the head of an Indian.

It was the first of many works which would lead her to become one of the nation's most famous sculptresses. But life was more than a bucket of clay for Vinnie Ream.

She was born in an Indian village in Madison, Wisconsin, where her father was a U.S. Government engineer and surveyor, charting the public lands of that state. In 1854, when she was seven, her father was transferred to Fort Leavenworth, Kansas, where he served as chief clerk to land surveyor John Calhoun. During this time the family made friends with two men who would play important roles in Vinnie's life. One was James Rollins, the other was Edmund Gibson Ross.

The family moved to Columbia three years later. Vinnie and her sister studied at Christian College—now Columbia College. The home in which she lived later became Williams Hall on the college campus. It is the oldest junior college building in permanent use west of the Mississippi. History records that Vinnie was an outstanding student in literature and art.

When the family moved to Washington at the start of the Civil War, Clark Mills—the sculptor—was persuaded to make Vinnie his pupil. For two years she studied with him and eventually received commissions for her work. Prominent politicians called upon her. But her dream was to do a bust of Abraham Lincoln. She turned to Congressman James Rollins along with Illinois Senator Orville Browning. They made a personal appeal to the President and Lincoln agreed to let Vinnie sculpt him. For five months just before his death, Lincoln set aside time each day for sitting with Vinnie Ream.

Later she would recall that Lincoln seemed to find a kind of companionship with her although they seldom talked. It was shortly after his son, Willie, had died. Lincoln often wept. Vinnie thought it was because she reminded him of his dead son. Sometimes, she noted, he would stand at the window gazing at the section of the yard where Willie had played.

Vinnie Ream carved the sadness and compassion of Abraham Lincoln into that bust. It turned out to be the last likeness from life ever made of Abraham Lincoln. She was putting the finishing touches on it when he was killed.

When Lincoln was assassinated, Congress provided for a statue of him but held a 20-person competition for the right to sculpt it. Vinnie Ream won the contract, the first contract of its kind ever granted to a woman in this country. The bust of Lincoln, life-size, is now a much-admired part of the statuary in the national Capitol. To work on that bust, she set up a studio in the basement of the Capitol. Her studio quickly became a gathering place of many of the leading conservatives in Congress during the administration of Lincoln's successor, Andrew Johnson.

Her old friend Edmund Ross came to visit her one day. He was now a Senator from Kansas and he was looking for a room to rent. She had one. He moved in. Neither foresaw the political struggle ahead that would deeply involve both of them.

By now agitation had reached the boiling point in Congress on the issue of Andrew Johnson's removal. The Radicals knew they had to have Ross's vote. But Ross kept quiet. So the conflict descended on Vinnie Ream. She was hounded by politicians demanding she deliver the vote of Ross. She sometimes went home at night in a state of nervous exhaustion because of the growing pressure. Threats drove her to the verge of hysteria. The day of the vote came, May 16, 1867. History records Edmund Ross cast the crucial "no" vote which saved the Johnson administration. Through it all, Vinnie Ream had withstood the hounding, badgering, and threatening of those who demanded she influence Ross to go with the impeachment vote.

Frustrated by their failure, some of the congressional conspirators turned on the little sculptress and ordered her out before the Lincoln statue was finished. She immediately appealed to one of the impeachment ringleaders, Thaddeus Stevens. His chivalrous nature surfaced. He was appalled at the expulsion of the lady from her studio and without consulting his associates, he moved that her studio be restored and rammed his resolution through the Senate.

Vinnie Ream would go on to create many other great works of sculpture including one of Thaddeus Stevens. She was 67 when she died in Washington in 1914. At her death, her greatest work was still the one she created of a brooding President, the sorrow of his child's death and the Union's division on his shoulders and in the lines of his face.

Vinnie Ream's statue of Abraham Lincoln, her greatest triumph, finished despite the turmoil of the Johnson impeachment, was unveiled on this date, January 25, 1871.

****

JANUARY 26
"TUTT," FATHER OF THE ANGLICAN CHURCH IN THE WEST

The three Concord stagecoaches, each pulled by six-horse teams, plunged across the prairies. It was 1867, a dangerous time. Indians were about. Cavalrymen served as outriders, half a mile on either side of the coaches. The coaches careened through the dust and across the rocks for four days, stopping only for quick meals. A dozen people were crammed into each coach, sitting on the mail bags. Other passengers rode on top. Each man had to carry a rifle, even the new Episcopal Bishop who was one of those passengers. It took a month to travel through the Indian territories between Omaha and Salt Lake City. Bishop Daniel Sylvester Tuttle, just turned 30, would launch his church's future course in the home city of Mormonism.

One of the first things he did when he arrived in Salt Lake City was contact Brigham Young. He told Young who he was and what he intended to do. His attitude toward the Mormon Church was one of friendship and respect. But he was there to establish the Episcopal Church.

He came from New York, where he had been baptized into the Episcopal Church at the age of 16. He was a Rector in Morris, New York, when he was elected Bishop of Montana. His parish at Morris had been about ten miles square. As Bishop of Montana, he also had jurisdiction over Utah and Idaho, an area of 300- to 350,000 square miles. On Saturdays, in Morris, he would go into a grove near his rector and practice his sermon on the birds and animals. The next morning, he was able to give his sermon from memory.

Tuttle was only 29 when he was elected Bishop of Montana. But he had to wait until he passed his 30th birthday in 1867 before he could go west. The territory was yet to see the worst of the Indian wars. The nearest railroad was still a thousand miles away. Of the 155,000 people scattered about, 100,000 were Mormons. No Episcopal clergyman had ever been to Montana. But in his first twelve days in Salt Lake City, Tuttle confirmed eleven persons as members of the Episcopal Church. That winter he went to the mining camp of Virginia City, Montana, and the next year moved his family to Helena where he paid sixty dollars a month in gold to rent a house.

In 1868 Bishop Tuttle was called to Missouri, but he refused to come. He had barely started work in Montana. Eighteen years later the call went out again and that time he accepted. He left behind two parishes, 13 organized missions, a dozen clergy, and about 1,000 communicants in an area unseen by an Episcopal clergyman until he arrived. For almost four decades he would be important to the religious life of Missouri. So rapid was the growth of the church in this state during his term that in 1891 the Episcopal Diocese was split into an eastern and western division. The Eastern Division retained the "Missouri" title.

For 25 years Tuttle worked without an assistant. In 1903 he became the Presiding Bishop of the church in the United States. He served in that post until his death 20 years after his election. Historian Floyd Shoemaker notes that when Tuttle first took charge in Missouri, there were 58 Episcopal clergymen and about 6,600 communicants. When he died in April of 1923 at the age of 86, there were 74 churches and about 10,000 communicants in eastern Missouri alone.

At the time of his death, Tuttle was the oldest Anglican Bishop in point of service in the world. Among the institutions he left behind are St. Mark's Hospital, and a school for girls—Rowland Hall—in Montana. Both facilities were in use a century after he founded them. His sculptured figure stands in Christ Church Cathedral in St. Louis, and a Bishop Tuttle Memorial Building was funded in the late 1920s in St. Louis.

Bishop Daniel Sylvester Tuttle, who went west stuffed into a fear-filled stagecoach, established the Episcopal Church in the far west, and later expanded it in Missouri, was born on this date, January 26, 1837.

****

JANUARY 27
A MAN BOND AND HIS WORDS

The scene was the State Law Library in Jefferson City. A young man was studying one of the many reference books when an older man walked up to him.

The elder man asked the younger what he was doing.

"Trying to learn a little law," replied the younger man.

"Well," said the older man sarcastically, "if that is true, you certainly should not be looking among some of the recent reports of the Supreme Court of Missouri."

The younger man was North Todd Gentry, later Missouri's Attorney General. The crusty older lawyer was an outspoken man and an outstanding jurist. In fact, he was a member of the court he had just maligned.

Henry Whitelaw Bond was his name. Bond was born near Brownsville, Tennessee, and was educated there in private schools and by private tutors during his primary years. He was sent to St. Louis when he was 16 to attend another private school, and after that went on to study for a year at Harvard. He didn't graduate however. He returned to Tennessee to study law in the office of Tennessee Supreme Court judge Thomas Freeman. When Bond reached the age of 21 he applied for, and was granted, admission to the Tennessee bar.

He practiced law in Brownsville for nine years before coming back to Missouri. He was 31 before formally beginning a practice of law in this state, but he quickly established himself as an able attorney. In 1885 he was elected to the Missouri General Assembly where he served as chairman of the Committee on Banks and Corporations. His election to the legislature ended a six-year partnership with Judge J. J. Lindsley which had brought their firm into wide prominence and paved the way to his eventual election to the St. Louis Court of Appeals in 1892. Bond served almost nine years of his 12-year term before resigning in 1901 to enter a law partnership with his son.

In 1911 he was elected a member of the Supreme Court Commission. The next year he was named to a ten-year term as a Judge. He had differences with his associates on the high bench about opinions written by the Commissioners although he had been one himself. Sometimes he was quite sarcastic about those opinions, prompting the remarks to Gentry we discussed earlier. He advocated changes in the date of the Fall court term, wanting it to be shifted from October to September. That finally came about several years after his death.

Bond believed in the highest ethics of the legal profession. He wrote part of a book published in the early 1900s about the history of the Missouri courts and those who practiced in them. He wrote, "Courts constitute one of the three primary and coordinate divisions of political power. It is so ordained by the people—the source of all government—in the exercise of their natural right to appoint agencies for making, expounding and executing such laws as are designed to promote the good of all. . . . American judges derive all their power and authority from the limitations of the law, and acknowledge no higher source."

He served a long and distinguished career on the state's highest court. He was still a member of it, in his 70s, when he died in 1919.

Incidentally, that young lawyer studying in the law library that day, North Todd Gentry, became a Supreme Court Judge in 1928.

Henry Whitelaw Bond was a remarkable man who in only 14 years rose from total stranger in St. Louis to the second highest position in the state's judicial circles, then moved to Missouri's highest court. Henry Whitelaw Bond was born on this date, January 27th, 1848.

****

JANUARY 28
MR. STOCKTON, MRS. CULVER, AND THE COLLEGE ON THE HILL

Teaching religion in the schools was a problem long before the United States Supreme Court outlawed prayer in the public schools. Citizens have argued for years the merits of restricting religious instruction to the home or church or whether it should be allowed in the schools too. This question apparently was one of the main reasons a college was established by the Disciples of Christ in Missouri.

A former school president, B. H. Smith, wrote in the 1870s that an aversion to teaching the gospel in public schools appeared early in the nation's history. Part of the problem, he said, was that those in charge of the schools yielded to the pressure of "an anti-religious element which, though weak at the time, promised rapid growth." It was with this situation facing them that a group of clergymen met in 1851 to set up a college. They sincerely believed that all knowledge and morals were based on teachings from God.

The driving force behind that early organization was the Reverend David Patterson Henderson, a minister of the Disciples of Christ, or as it is more commonly known, the Christian Church. A special committee visited the town of Canton. The members saw the view from a hill overlooking the town, a view which took in the dramatic curve of the Mississippi River, and the states of Iowa and Illinois. They decided that would be the place for their new college. The town contributed $50,000 to put up a building, and one of its citizens, Chauncey Durkee, gave 34 acres of land.

B. H. Smith said the school wasn't designed to advocate any particular faith, but to expand the student's general knowledge of God. Henderson traveled throughout the state looking for financial support for the new school and is said to have raised more than a million dollars.

A charter was granted by the legislature, a charter which made Christian University unique in its time. It demanded the school be coeducational, a point Henderson extensively supported. The school thus became the first coeducational institution of higher learning west of the Mississippi, and one of the earliest ones in the nation.

The new building was ready in the fall of 1856.

The University was fortunate to attract James Shannon as its first formal President. Shannon was the second president of the

University of Missouri. But he left that job after criticism of his work as a minister while head of the state University.

The endowment gathered strength in the five years or so before the Civil War. But when war came, the financial support given by railroads in the south vanished. An estimated $1,000,000 of the endowment just disappeared. The main building was turned into a barracks during the conflict. But in 1865 the school resumed, and was revived under B. H. Smith's leadership. By 1867, the student body numbered 200.

Disaster struck in 1903 with a fire which destroyed the old main building as well as most of the papers and records of Christian University's earliest days. The school president then was Carl Johann, who launched a vigorous effort to put up a new building, later named for Henderson.

It was through his efforts and appeals, as well as those of the next president, J. H. Wood, that two St. Louis residents made sizeable bequests to the school for dormitories and a gymnasium. Their names were Mary Culver and Robert Stockton. In 1917 the trustees and the legislature agreed to rename Christian University Culver-Stockton College.

Culver-Stockton, by the time it reached the century mark, had become a campus of 111 acres. The student body continued to show a slow but strong growth.

Carl Johann served as school president until 1914 and became President Emeritus, a position he held for another 16 years. A library-educational center on the Culver-Stockton camplus carries his name.

Through the years the college maintained the principle it set forth in its earliest days of not forcing denominational beliefs onto the students, but as one catalog put it, "to develop committed moral and spiritual leaders who are responsible in witnessing to their faith through service to the brotherhood of man."

Culver-Stockton College, the former Christian University, in Canton, was incorporated as the first coeducational institution of higher education west of the Mississippi on this date, the 28th of January, in 1853.

****

JANUARY 29
THE MECHANICAL DOCTOR

The next time you break a bone, dislocate a joint, swallow something that stops halfway down, or eat something which reaches your stomach and threatens to do you in, the work of a mechanically-minded Missouri surgeon and medical teacher might either save your life or ease your pain. The mechanic/medicine man was Doctor John Thompson Hodgen, and we are still benefiting from his work although he's been dead since 1882.

John Hodgen was born just down the road from the birthplace of Abraham Lincoln, in Hodgensville, Kentucky, 17 years after Lincoln's birth. Lincoln by then had gone from the area, but Hodgen did follow in Lincoln's footsteps. He, like Lincoln, moved from Kentucky to Illinois. There, Hodgen received some of his education in Pittsfield. Later he attended Bethany College in Virginia. He came to Missouri for his medical education, graduating from the University of Missouri medical department in 1848.

At that time, the medical department was in St. Louis and was overseen by an eccentric doctor named Joseph Nash McDowell who believed, for example, that bodies are best preserved if they are suspended in caves, not buried. Fortunately, little of his eccentricity rubbed off on Hodgen. Early in the Civil War, McDowell's southern sympathies got him in trouble with Union officials. St. Louis was a strongly pro-Union town. The federals appropriated McDowell's hospital, eventually turning the structure into a military hospital and later into a military prison.

Hodgen saw this coming and fought against it. He wasn't disloyal to the Union. But he was loyal to his profession. In time he became a Surgeon General of the Western Sanitary Commission, a special group set up to provide proper medical treatment for wounded soldiers. Later he became the Surgeon General for the entire state of Missouri. During part of that time, and until the year he died, Hodgen was the consulting surgeon at the City Hospital in St. Louis.

He was a member of the St. Louis Board of Health until 1871, and President of it for two years. He constantly pushed for more sanitary living conditions in the city.

This was a golden age for medical discoveries. Medicine was becoming more modernized in those years and in the years to follow as new vaccines were discovered. New equipment was being devised.

New experiments were being performed. Doctor Hodgen was a leader in his field. Today, however, he is largely forgotten.

The fracture of a thigh is still a painful problem today, one which leads to a long convalescence and much discomfort. But John Thompson Hodgen helped make things a little better. It still takes a while to recover from such an injury, but it was Hodgen who invented a wire splint for fractured thighs. He perfected the suspension cord and pulley arrangement allowing the flexion, extension and rotation of leg fractures. He invented the forceps-dilator instrument for the removal of foreign bodies from the air passages, which ended the need for a trachaeotomy in many instances. He invented a wire suspension splint for arm injuries. He also invented a double-action syringe and the stomach pump.

Hodgen became so well known because of his mechanical work that he was named the President of the American Medical Association the year before he died. He already had been the head of the state medical society and was a charter member of the American Surgical Association. He was only 56 years old when he died. Today many of his inventions are still in use, although they have been modernized and improved. Doctor John Thompson Hodgen, a distinguished Missouri physician, surgeon and inventor, was born on this date, January 29, 1826.

****

JANUARY 30
CHIEF BLACKROBE

In May, 1873, a St. Louis priest, old and infirm, dedicated a new riverboat named for him. It was fitting the boat should be named for the priest who often had been carried upriver by its captain and who had referred to the Missouri as "my river."

Ten days later the old priest was dead.

His name was Pierre Jean DeSmet, a Flemish Jesuit priest. He and several other Jesuits came to Missouri in 1823 to establish an Indian school in St. Louis. Although he was a faculty member there for years, he was also a roving missionary and it is in that role that he is best remembered.

In the 1840s the Jesuits responded to efforts by the Flathead Indians to establish a mission in the Bitterroot Valley of the Rocky

Mountains, 1,500 miles west of St. Louis. DeSmet headed west and in July of 1840 celebrated the first Catholic mass in Wyoming history near the site of what is now Daniel, Wyoming. He and his party stayed throughout the summer, then returned to St. Louis. On the way the met a tribe of Sioux Indians. A fur trader with DeSmet's party introduced the priest as Chief Blackrobe of the Frenchmen. The Indians were intrigued by the title and immediately started asking about the robe and the large crucifix DeSmet carried. In making his explanations, DeSmet gained the tribe's respect. Albert Antrei wrote for the Montana Historical Society, "The Sioux knew who Chief Blackrobe of the Frenchmen was, and that he demanded neither land, women, horses nor pelts. It was understood that he sold neither whiskey nor guns, but was a man of peace...a great rarity among the white man!"

In 1841 he established St. Mary's Mission near what is now Stevensville, Montana. It would become his favorite mission, and one to which he often returned.

DeSmet preached against polygamy, something the Indians were surprised to learn was a sin. And they couldn't understand his priestly celibacy. The Flatheads finally decided DeSmet's religion must be very hard and, because of that, must have many truths.

He dreamed of a chain of Jesuit missions from the Rockies to the Pacific and as far north as the far borders of Alberta and British Columbia. He spent three years laying the groundwork for this vast religious empire. Later, speaking of those years crossing and recrossing the Rockies, he wrote, "I have been several years a wanderer in the desert. I was three years without receiving a letter from any quarter. I was two years in the mountains without tasting bread, salt, coffee, tea or sugar. I was for years without a bed, without a roof. I have been six months without a shirt on my back, and passed whole days and nights without a morsel of anything to eat, not even a drop of water to quench my parching thirst. I thank God for it, and most gladly would exchange my present situation for the like again."

DeSmet's "present situation" was in the 1840s and 1850s when he was confined to the St. Louis area. The St. Louis Diocese restricted his activities, fearing his fame might hurt his humility and mindful that his efforts to raise money for his missions might be infringing on violations of vows of poverty. DeSmet sat in St. Louis and worried about the white man's push west, knowing what might happen if the gold he knew was in the Black Hills was found.

The Indian Department called on him to persuade the Indians to sign an 1851 treaty at Fort Laramie calling for peace on the Oregon Trail. In 1858 he helped settle the Yakima War in the Oregon Country. But DeSmet was a sick and tired old man when he went west in 1868 to find Sitting Bull and persuade him to sign a peace treaty. He succeeded at a time of extreme unrest for the Sioux were angry over violations of a treaty signed a few years earlier involving settlements along the Bozeman Trail. Later that year the Sioux would wipe out an eighty-man detachment in the Fetterman Massacre near Fort Kearney, Wyoming. DeSmet succeeded in getting Sitting Bull to sign the treaty at a time when the Sioux leader had promised to kill any white man on sight.

It was his last contribution to the frontier. His career was over. Now all he could do for the next five years in St. Louis was sit, study, and write his journals until death in 1873. He was 72.

Chief Blackrobe, Father Pierre Jean DeSmet, a man whose travels in the west and ten times to Europe and back seeking support for his work totalled an estimated 265,000 miles, perhaps the most unusual and certainly one of the greatest of all missionaries in the American West, was born on this date, January 30, 1801.

****

JANUARY 31
THE MOST DARING TRAIN ROBBERY ON RECORD

The red flag fluttering in the middle of the railroad tracks that day was a signal for the 5:40 to stop for a passenger or a message at Gads Hill, a flag stop on the Iron Mountain Railroad about 100 miles south of St. Louis. It was late afternoon when the train stopped at the station. The conductor and engineer climbed down to see what was needed. They found themselves staring into the gaping barrels of pistols.

Missouri's first train robbery had just begun.

It was the James gang.

There are those who think the James boys originated train robbery in America. But that's not true and this wasn't the first train robbery in American history. It wasn't even the first train robbery by the

James boys. But it was the first in Missouri and it created an international stir.

The first train robbery for the James bunch was a crude one. In July of 1873, the gang jerked a rail lose in front of a Rock Island train as it was rounding a blind curve east of Council Bluffs, Iowa. Only the locomotive went off the tracks but the engineer was killed and the fireman and several passengers were hurt. The bandits got between $200 and $700 from the express safe and passengers, depending on the source of the information. They missed a large gold shipment by 12 hours.

Six months later, five men walked into the station at Gads Hill, Missouri, and took the station agent and most of the male population of the town captive. It was an astounding event. Train robbery was unknown in Missouri at the time. The passengers were even more astonished by the antics of the robbers. The gang suspected one of the passengers was a Pinkerton man. He was ordered to strip, apparently in the belief that he bore some kind of mark of identity since he carried no card from the famous detective agency. The hands of the passengers were examined for callouses. The robbers said they didn't want to rob working men or ladies, just gentlemen "in plug hats." The take from the passengers, mail bags, and express safe has been estimated as high as $22,000 and as low as $2,000.

When the robbery was over the leader ordered the engineer to go on to Little Rock. Just before fleeing into the woods, one of the gang left a sheet of paper with the engineer. It was a press release, prepared before the robbery. But it set out details of exactly what happened, leaving a blank so the amount of money taken could be filled in later! The release even had a headline: "The Most Daring Train Robbery on Record."

The train went on to Piedmont, seven miles down the track where telegraph messages were sent out and posses were formed. But it was useless. The robbers apparently retreated westward. There are stories of them stopping at farms for meals and always acting like gentlemen.

Governor Silas Woodson didn't think so, however. He put up a $2,000 reward for the bodies of each one of them. The Pinkertons immediately sent men to Missouri to track down the robbers. One agent, 26-year old John W. Whicher, planned to disguise himself as a farm hand, gain employment at the home of Jesse's mother, then

71

capture the outlaws at the first opportunity. A few days later, Whicher's body was found, shot through the head, on a road near Independence.

A few days after that the Younger brothers killed two other Pinkertons in a fight that left one of the Youngers dead as well.

European newspapers began to print accounts of Missouri's lawlessness. Senator Carl Schurz noted one paper printed an account of the Gads Hill robbery as "a racy anecdote to show what can be done in this commonwealth with impunity."

The Iowa robbery, the Gads Hill holdup, and the Pinkerton killings focused national attention on Missouri during 1874. It made lawlessness a political issue. It would be several years before the James gang was finally run into the ground, literally and figuratively. It took a much bigger reward, fears for their own safety among the gang members, a botched bank job in Minnesota and, finally, the shooting of Jesse by one of the gang members to bring about the gang's downfall.

All of that was a long way down the track from the fluttering red flag that day at Gads Hill. Missouri's first train robbery began the afternoon a startled station agent at Gads Hill looked up to see five visitors stroll into his depot with guns drawn and orders to stop a train on this date, January 31, 1874.

"Houn' Dawg" Song, February 21, 1891

FEBRUARY

FEBRUARY 1

THE WHEELS OF JOSEPH MURPHY

First came the explorers, the hunters and trappers. They would be followed by the missionaries, then the farmers and businessmen. The explorers, hunters and trappers would return with stories that made other men dream. But dreams are only frustration on the hoof unless the mechanical means are available to make them come true. Joseph Murphy put wheels under those dreams.

Lewis and Clark were just starting back to civilization when Joseph Murphy was born in Ireland. When he died in St. Louis, Henry Ford was making automobiles.

He came to America as a child because his family thought he would have a better chance here than in Ireland where Catholics were oppressed. When he arrived in Creve Coeur, Missouri, he was barely a teenager, his formal schooling ended. The farm which relatives were supposedly going to set up had failed and the landlord had foreclosed on the mortgage. So young Joseph Murphy went to work as a four-dollar-a-month farmhand. Later he moved to St. Louis to live with his aunt and her husband. He was apprenticed to a wagon maker named Daniel Custer. His experience with Custer was the turning point of his life. Murphy learned the trade so well that he became one of the foremost wagon makers of the American West. He learned to judge the quality of lumber, sight unseen, just by feeling the grain.

He was twenty when he went into business for himself.

Joseph Murphy, described by biographer Emily O'Neill Bott as "tall and serious minded, reticent, gentle and peace-loving, although shrewd and hard-headed as a businessman," began to build his business slowly. Government officials in Santa Fe provided Murphy with his first big order. The Spanish Governor of Santa Fe had decided to impose a tax of $500 on each wagonload of goods entering the province from the United States, regardless of value or quantity. Murphy immediately started building wagons which could hold four to five times the capacity of earlier wagons. These wagons were gigantic. The wheels were seven feet high with eight-inch rims. The tongue was fifty feet long and four oxen pulled it. A man could easily stand up inside.

The Army turned to Murphy when the Mexican War broke out, to make repairs on old wagons and build new ones. He built wagons to last, of durable wood, using techniques to keep the wood from splitting. He didn't drill holes. He made holes with red hot iron rods, exactly one size smaller than the bolts.

A Murphy wagon paved the way to Oregon. In 1830, Bill Sublette paid Murphy $200 for a new wagon. Less than a month later he took it to the Wind River area of Wyoming. It was the first wheeled passenger/cargo vehicle to go to the Continental Divide, the first of hundreds of Murphy wagons to travel the Oregon Trail. The St. Louis *Globe-Democrat,* writing of Murphy's death in 1901, said that Murphy made all of the wagons which left St. Louis in 1849 bound for California. It was not uncommon for entire wagon trains to be composed of Murphy wagons.

When the rush west ended, Murphy began to build all-purpose wagons, many of which were dismantled and shipped west by steamboats to be assembled in Westport, Omaha, or Fort Benton—the first wagons built in the far west.

He had quarters built upstairs over his shop for his bachelor employes. This was more than a fringe benefit. It was an effort to keep his rivals from stealing his help!

Joseph Murphy outlived three wives and many of his twelve children. He attended night school in St. Louis, and although his formal education had ended at age 12, he went on to become a learned man and a millionaire. He became a naturalized citizen in 1853. His sons continued the wagon building business after he retired. But the railroads gradually killed off the need for those wagons and the company closed its doors in 1894. Murphy was 95 years old when he died in 1901.

The ruts made by wheels of the wagons for the Santa Fe businessman, the California gold seeker, and the Oregon dreamer can still be seen in many parts of the west, carved for decades to come in the land by the 200,000 wagons built in St. Louis by a man named Murphy. He came to this country to find opportunity, found it, and in doing so provided the means for thousands of Americans to find theirs. Joseph Murphy was born on this date, February 1, 1806.

****

FEBRUARY 2
THE BANK OF THE STATE OF MISSOURI

It was a long time in Missouri before you could write a check on your favorite bank. There were few banks and those that did exist were all too often quite shaky.

The first Bank of St. Louis was chartered in 1813, but did little business for three years. By then the Bank of Missouri was in business. The charter for the latter bank was granted in 1817. Its first president was Auguste Chouteau, prominent St. Louis businessman. Future Governor Lilburn Boggs was the first cashier. The bank was located in the basement of Chouteau's home. It was created over the strenuous objections of the organizers of the first St. Louis bank. They had fallen on hard times because their bank, anxious to encourage commercial expansion in the West, had overextended itself in issuing worthless money.

The Bank of St. Louis was also hampered by internal problems which got worse as its financial condition deteriorated. Once, in 1818, a group of stockholders held an impromptu stockholder's meeting outside the front door of the bank and demanded the keys from bank officials. The bank officials refused and the protestors immediately ordered them out of the building, padlocked the door and announced the bank wouldn't reopen until stockholders had been assured it would operate on a more solid footing. The Bank of St. Louis closed for good in 1819.

By then the state bank—the Bank of Missouri—was in operation. It became the westernmost depository for federal funds, giving it some solidity. But the Panic of 1819 weakened it and it finally closed in 1821. By now the public had had enough of Missouri banks. It would be sixteen years before the state chartered another financial operation.

In 1837 the former cashier, Lilburn Boggs, was now Governor and pushing for a new state bank. In the sixteen years since the failure of those earlier banks, Missouri had been served by a few private banking institutions, mostly branches of banks located elsewhere. St. Louis had a branch of the Bank of the United States, but it closed when President Jackson refused to allow the parent bank to be rechartered.

The first bill to go before the legislature in 1837 called for creation of the "Union Bank of Missouri." The legislature fought over the philosophies involved in setting up a state bank for some time before finally passing a bill much like Boggs had recommended. It called for a bank in St. Louis with a branch in Fayette. This bank could issue no notes for less than ten dollars. Six of the twelve directors and the bank president would be chosen by the legislature. There would be some private ownership of bank stock, but the state kept 50%. The facility would be the state's fiscal agent but could not be required to make loans to the state. State money deposited in the facility for more than one year would draw six percent interest. The bank was capitalized in 1837 with John Brady Smith as its first president. Smith was a prominent St. Louis man with a spotless reputation. The chief cashier was Henry Shurlds who is given even more credit for keeping the bank solvent for thirty years.

William H. Thompson, writing a turn-of-the-century history of St. Louis banking, said the notes from the Bank of the State of Missouri were as good as gold and maybe better. He says they were "in the mountains, among the trappers and hunters and at military posts among officers and soldiers, esteemed better than gold."

In 1837 the bank started issuing its own currency. But two years later it suffered a sizeable loss when $120,000 in foreign coin was determined to be missing from its vaults. The money was never recovered, but the bank survived.

The Panic of 1857 forced many private banks to close. The state bank shut its doors for two days and suspended specie payment, but survived that one too.

In 1866 the state passed a law getting itself out of the banking business, selling the state stock in the facility to a syndicate headed by James B. Eads, later to gain fame as a bridge builder. The price was about 1.2 million dollars. The bank became known as the National Bank of the State of Missouri. Its attitude changed. It started speculating. It was weakened by the Panic of 1873 and in June of 1877 directors admitted it was insolvent. The bank took ten years to pay, with interest, all proven claims. Final cause of the death of the bank was listed as excessive loans to officers and directors, fraudulent management, and depreciation of securities.

The first and only Bank of the State of Missouri lasted forty years, fifty if you count the decade it took to pay off its debts. But it was a steadying influence during the important growing years of the American West. For a while it was the only American financial institution west of the Mississippi. The Bank of the State of Missouri was chartered when Governor Boggs signed the enabling legislation on this date, February 2, 1837.

****

FEBRUARY 3
THE BANDIT QUEEN

Judge John Shirley was a man of wealth and social standing in Carthage when the Civil War began. He had two sons and a daughter and was pro-Southern in sympathy. His eldest son, Preston, not in the war, would die later in a Texas tavern shooting. His second son, Ed, became a member of Quantrill's guerrillas and was killed in a skirmish near Sarcoxie in 1863. It was his daughter who made the greatest mark of the family. Her name was Myra Belle. We know her as Belle Starr.

The Shirleys left Carthage, where the judge owned most of the city block on the north side of the square and ran a hotel called "The Shirley House." They settled in Texas where sometime in 1866 Myra Belle had an affair which left her with an illegitimate daughter. She named the child Pearl Younger and claimed the father was the Missouri outlaw Cole Younger. Myra Belle always claimed, however, that she and Younger were married although Younger steadfastly denied it.

After Cole Younger, Myra Shirley became acquainted with Jim Reed, a young man who had ridden with Quantrill and the James gang. He was a Missourian who had grown up near Rich Hill and might have known the Shirley family earlier. But the judge didn't want him around and locked his daughter in the second floor room of their Texas farmhouse. Reed rounded up some 20 men and rescued the girl. They lived together for several years and had a son.

In one of their flights from justice, Reed became allied with a Cherokee Indian family in Oklahoma named Starr. In 1874 a bounty hunter killed Reed, making Myra Belle what one might call a widow.

Six years later she moved in with Sam Starr, settling at a place she called Younger's Bend near Eufala, Oklahoma. There she adopted the name Starr. She and Sam became the head of a successful horse and cattle rustling operation and moonshine-running business. The only time the two were convicted of anything, though, was when Judge Isaac Parker sentenced them to a term in the Michigan prison for stealing a horse. They both got off on good behavior after nine months.

Back at Younger's Bend, Belle started taking in boarders. One was John Middleton who lived with her for about six months while Sam was hiding out. Middleton's record included burning the courthouse in Scott County, Arkansas, killing a sheriff in Texas, and stealing horses. It is believed he was killed by Sam Starr.

Sam Starr is also suspected of killing Belle's next lover, a guy known as Blue Duck, in 1886. Five months later, however, Sam Starr himself was dead, killed in a family feud.

Meanwhile, Belle had been having words with a neighbor and their disagreement had become quite heated. On her 43rd birthday her riderless horse trotted into the yard at Younger's Bend. Another neighbor, Milo Hoyt, found her lying in the road a few miles away, terribly wounded. She was shot in the back with a shotgun and died within a few minutes, never naming her assailant.

She was buried with Cherokee Indian rites in the front yard of her home, her hand grasping a fine revolver said to have been given her by Cole Younger years before. The neighbor with whom she'd been feuding was tried and acquitted of her murder.

Myra Belle Shirley is said to have been the first white woman in Oklahoma. She also is called "The Bandit Queen of the West." Belle Starr, born in 1846, shot to death on her 43rd birthday on this date, the 3rd of February, in 1889.

****

FEBRUARY 4
PRUDHOMME'S TOWN

The old man, Gabriel Prudhomme, had died. His estate couldn't be settled amiably among the heirs, so the land went up for sale. It was advertised as "admirably calculated for a ferry across the Missouri River, also one of the best steamboat landings on the river, also an excellent situation for a warehouse or townsite."

Fourteen men got together and bought Prudhomme's 256 acres for about $4,200. Some suggested calling the settlement Kawsmouth, since it was near the mouth of the Kaw River. But eventually the town came to be known as Kansas, the other name for the Kaw. Much later it gained the name by which we know it today: Kansas

City. At the time the community was named, the territory or state of Kansas didn't exist.

The first known white man to live in the area for any length of time is believed to have been Daniel Morgan Boone, son of the famous Kentucky-Missouri frontiersman. He established residence near Westport where he trapped along the Blue River in the late 1780s and 90s. In 1815 two Frenchmen, Louis Grand Louis and Jacques Fournaise, lived in the vicinity for a while. But it wasn't until 1821 that the settlement really began to take hold.

In that year, Francois Chouteau, a member of the family that helped organize St. Louis, was authorized to establish a trading post for furs nearer the source of supply. His fur post was in what is now Kansas City's northeast industrial district. The post was later moved to the present side of Troost Avenue to protect it from high water. But that didn't work. The historic flood of 1844, the worst in recorded Missouri River history, wiped it out.

It was a Baptist missionary's son, John C. McCoy, who saw the location as a possibility for something other than a fur trading post. He built a store to tap the westward trade and his area became known to residents of Westport and Independence as "Westport Landing." In 1835 he filed a plat of Westport and by 1845 his community had replaced Independence as the eastern end of the Santa Fe trail. The town was also rounding up most of the business of the Colorado and Oregon fur trade.

When Prudhomme died, McCoy and thirteen others organized a special company and bought his estate, then immediately laid out a new townsite. Fifteen acres were laid off in lots and sold at public auction in 1839. The going price was between $32 and $200 per lot. It took seven years to clear up some of the legal difficulties, but in that year, 127 lots were laid out and sold for about $8,100.

By now the town was flourishing. In 1850 nearly 700 people lived there. A decade later the population was 4,000. In 1850 the Jackson County court gave the town the right to govern itself and three years later the legislature allowed the town a city charter. The community called "Kansas" became the "City of Kansas." At the time the municipal treasury showed a balance of $7.22. It collected less than $5,000 worth of taxes in the first year of its corporate existence. But by 1859 the city had raised enough to spend $30,000 on street improvements alone and had an assessed valuation of about $3,000,000.

By 1870 the town reached 30,000 population and in another decade that figure doubled. It became a major railroad and cattle center in those brawling frontier years around the Civil War. It was a primary target for the Confederates in 1864. One of the biggest battles in the western theater was fought at Westport.

The original town charter underwent a number of amendments in the 35 years just before the 20th century. In 1889 an entirely new charter was adopted. And it was only then that the town became known officially as "Kansas City," although it had been called that for many years.

The twentieth century saw a modern city on the edge of the plains. The nation's first major shopping center tailored to the motoring public was built in Kansas City. Urban renewal has been a constant effort in the town. Severe floods hit the city but the people just shoveled out the mud and kept on going.

Kansas City is a town of major proportions now. It is a dynamic and growing city, proud of its heritage as a frontier community. To call Kansas City a cowtown is no insult today and never has been. It is a recognition of its past. To call it a major metropolis on the plains is to recognize its present and its future. The town of Kansas, the forerunner to Kansas City, a town created on the banks of the Missouri River as a French trading post, was first incorporated by the Jackson County Court on this date, the 4th of February, 1850.

****

FEBRUARY 5
FIRE AND LIGHTNING

It was a Sunday night, 1911, in Jefferson City. Local residents were preparing for the evening church services. In the Governor's Mansion the first lady, Mrs. Hadley, was writing letters.

Then there was a brilliant flash of lightning!

A shattering clap of thunder.

Mrs. Hadley thought the mansion might have been hit. But it wasn't. The lightning hit the Capitol a block away and in a few hours only the walls remained.

In February, 1837, the state legislature approved bills providing money for erection of a new Capitol, one which would be fireproof. But that November, before any work could be done on the new building, the old Capitol burned. Sixty-three years later the legislature was pushing for another new Capitol. The one built in 1840 had been modified in 1880, but it looked terrible. The Capitol's central portion was 71 years old. The original 192-by-85-foot structure was built of stone quarried from a nearby bluff along the Pacific Railroad line. The limestone for the columns came from Callaway County, just across the river. The original building was a graceful structure with a low dome, facing east and west, a 90-degree difference from today's building. By the 1880s the building needed expansion. So two additions were tacked on in T-fashion at each end of the building. That made it 300 feet long and 112 feet deep. An awkward 185-foot dome was built on top. The entire work was finished in 1888 at a cost of $220,000. James E. Ford, who wrote a history of Jefferson City in the 1930s, complained of the modifications, saying the building "was defiled by changing its outlines from its beautiful simplicity to a monstrosity of neither beauty or character. Fortunately this travesty of architecture was later destroyed by fire."

A few minutes after the lightning hit, citizens strolling along Main Street saw flames flickering from the dome. The alarm was sounded. Firemen rushed to the scene. They dashed to the second floor and smashed through a door where steps led to the roof. But they couldn't stop the flames. The fire spread rapidly. About 8:00 p.m. fire fighters from the prison arrived, fifteen convicts and their equipment. At 8:30 p.m., the dome collapsed over the north side of the building and set fire to the roof of the House of Representatives. The dense smoke chased out those who had entered the building to rescue valuable paintings and papers. The fire department from Lincoln Institute arrived along with departments from city wards. Altogether, fifteen hoses poured water on the blaze. Then the big water main broke, and there was no longer any hope of saving the building.

Men continued to dash in and out of the burning building, rescuing books and papers. The Sedalia fire department arrived by train a little after 11:00 p.m. making the sixty-four mile trip in seventy-five minutes. But with no water, the Sedalia firemen could only stand with the rest of the people and watch.

Nobody could reach the valued paintings in the Senate chamber, paintings 12 to 15 feet tall originally done by the great Missouri artist George Caleb Bingham. They burned. By morning Missouri's Capitol was a smoldering, steaming mass of debris surrounded by giant stone walls. Government went on in churches, the Supreme Court building, and wherever office space was available.

Only two days after the fire, bills were introduced in both houses for a $3½ million bond issue for a new building. The new structure would have six times the floor space of the one that burned. It would face north and south instead of east and west. It would be built slightly south of the old building's location. The new building would have three acres of sub-basement alone. This time the voters said yes by 100,000 votes in an August election.

Ground was broken in May of 1914. The cornerstone was laid on June 24, 1915. The new building was completed in record time, by the fall of 1917. A decoration commission went to work. Dedication came in the fall of 1924, ending a long process which began with a brilliant flash of lightning, a roar of thunder, and a tragic fire one Sunday evening, on this date, February 5, 1911.

****

FEBRUARY 6
MISSOURI'S SECOND NEWSPAPER

It is 1814 and then, as now, a newspaper printed something which aroused the ire of some of the citizens. Of course, in those days, editors had a habit of being considerably more pointed in their comments than they are today. In this instance, the editor had certainly been candid. For several years Joseph Charless had been the only newspaper editor in Missouri. His paper, the *Missouri Gazette,* was the only newspaper. Charless was outspoken on such things as military discipline and Indian suppression. He also favored abolition of slavery and this triggered a visit to his office by a group of people who disagreed with him. Harsh words were exchanged but apparently no fisticuffs resulted. Charless told them to get out of his office. The group left, seething, and decided the only way they could counter Charless was to start their own paper. But first they needed an editor.

An advertisement was placed in the *Kentucky Reporter,* published in Lexington, Kentucky. It said the people of St. Louis were dissatisfied with their present newspaper editor and would like to have one of "correct republican principle." He wouldn't have to be outstanding. They'd take someone of "moderate abilities."

Charless wrote that only five or six persons opposed him, one of them being an ambitious politician he called in print "the little lawyer and would be Lord Mayor." He was talking about Thomas Hart Benton, already a leader in pre-statehood days. Charless referred to the people advertising for an editor in Kentucky as the "military junto." In March of 1815 the newspaper ad had its desired results. Joshua Norvell went to St. Louis to establish what was called the *Western Journal.* The thousand dollars the so-called "junto" had raised apparently helped lure him from Tennessee.

But Norvell failed.

In September of 1816 he moved to Arkansas. The newspaper, founded to wipe out the only other St. Louis newspaper, was dead. But only for a short time. The paper was revived as the *Emigrant and General Advertiser.* The first edition came out in May of 1817. A Cincinnati lawyer named Sergeant Hall was its publisher. It didn't last long either. In August of 1818, Isaac Henry and Evarist Maury took it over. They renamed the sheet the *Enquirer.*

None of this made any difference to Charless. He continued to refer to the editors as the "hireling press" operating under the Benton clique. Benton, in fact, was the editor for a while. He used the paper to put his name and platform before the public.

Isaac Henry, meanwhile, had promised to "print a clear and decent paper, devoted to the general services, and holding itself above the filth of private scandal and personal abuse," something of a rarity in those early newspapers.

When Isaac Henry died in 1821, the paper was sold to two other men. They continued to support Benton and Missouri's first Congressman, John Scott. The *Enquirer* was one of several papers in the state to print the new state constitution in its entirety.

Owners, editors and publishers came and went. A rival newspaper noted in 1827, "...then came Patrick H. Ford and Company, then Ford and Orr, afterwards Ford and Stine, then Green and Ford, Duff Green then became sole editor; to him succeeded Foreman and Keemle; then W. W. Foreman solus, then Foreman and Birch; soon afterwards S. W. Foreman again; and now it is said, James H. Birch..."

Charles Keemle, the publisher of the *Missouri Advocate,* finally merged his paper with the *Enquirer.* By then the paper had had five names in 11 years. Sometime around 1829 the paper became known as the St. Louis *Beacon.* It tried to be semi-weekly again late in 1829, but gave that up in March of 1830. Missouri's second newspaper finally staggered to its grave in 1832.

Such were the perils of trying to run a newspaper on the frontier. The *Western Journal* lasted longer than many. Born as the *Western Journal* in 1815, the second newspaper in Missouri blinked out in 1832 as the St. Louis *Beacon*. Its story, with all its editors and names, began when the editor of the state's first newspaper told some critics to get out of his office on this date, February 6, in 1814.

****

FEBRUARY 7
THE LADY OF THE LITTLE HOUSE

For years she told stories of her childhood to her daughter. When her daughter grew up to become a prominent author, she encouraged her mother time and again to write down those recollections. The mother's resistance finally weakened and she wrote eight books about her life, the life of her husband, and her family. Today those books are a treasured part of children's literature and Laura Ingalls Wilder is one of Missouri's most famous authors.

There is a real problem in telling the story of Laura Ingalls Wilder's life. There is no way to improve on the way she told it. So let us begin with her own words: "Once upon a time, sixty years ago, a little girl lived in the Big Woods of Wisconsin, in a little gray house made of logs.

"The great, dark trees of the Big Woods stood all around the house, and beyond them were other trees and beyond them were more trees. As far as a man could go to the north in a day, or a week, or a whole month, there was nothing but woods. There were no houses. There were no roads. There were no people."

The family numbered five: Ma and Pa, Laura, her older sister Mary, and baby Carrie. She was five years old when the first story begins and had never been to town, had never seen a store, and had never seen two houses standing together.

Her father wanted to go west. It was the early 1870s. They left the little house in the big woods and went to the Indian Territory, what is now Oklahoma. They forded streams, one of which rose suddenly and nearly killed them. Their cabin was almost destroyed by a chimney fire, then by a prairie fire. They came down with malaria and might have died if neighbors hadn't found them. Indians sometimes came around.

But the federal government didn't want settlers in the area, so the Ingalls family packed up and went to Minnesota to settle at Plum Creek. Since they were about two miles from town instead of the forty as they had been in Oklahoma, Laura went to school for the first time. She was eight years old.

The family survived a grasshopper plague which destroyed the wheat crop. Pa had to leave to find work and the family endured loneliness and blizzards. If you want to feel the fury of a winter storm, you'll find no better description than in the books of Laura Ingalls Wilder. The family grew with the addition of Grace, another baby, and was touched with sadness when scarlet fever left the oldest daughter, Mary, blind.

Laura was growing up. She became a certified teacher. She met Almanzo Wilder who saved her family and others by making a daring run during a Dakota winter to get wheat for the starving townsfolk.

In 1893 the depression got the best of them in Dakota. Laura and Almanzo packed up and headed south to Missouri. They travelled for fifty-five days before arriving at Mansfield in the Ozarks.

The Wilders lived at a place called Rocky Ridge Farm and it was there that Laura finally wrote the stories we have come to love. They both lived long and rewarding lives. Laura died in 1957 at the age of 90, although through her books she'll never be older than 20. Almanzo died in 1949 at the age of 92.

The *Little House* books of Laura Ingalls Wilder might be children's stories. But they are certainly not beneath the enjoyment of adults. Why? Maybe the reason is in the last paragraphs of her first book.

"Laura lay awake a little while, listening to Pa's fiddle softly playing and to the lonely sound of the wind in the Big Woods. She looked at Pa sitting on the bench by the hearth, the firelight gleaming on his brown hair and beard. . . . She looked at Ma, gently rocking and knitting.

"She thought to herself, 'This is now.'"

At the end of *Little House in the Big Woods,* Laura says, "She was glad that the cozy house, and Pa and Ma and the firelight and the music were now. They could not be forgotten, she thought, because now is now. It can never be a long time ago."

The past "can never be a long time ago" in the books of Laura Ingalls Wilder, born on this date, the 7th of February, in 1867.

FEBRUARY 8
"OLD SARCASM," COOPER COUNTY'S FIRST LAWYER

Cooper County's first lawyer was called "Old Sarcasm" by friend and foe alike because of his sharp wit, his keen legal mind, and his outspokenness. He came from an area which produced governors and judges. When he was angry he was a firebrand. His indignation was expressed in the sharpest terms. But he was so respected that when he died at the age of 59 the Missouri Supreme Court passed a resolution to wear mourning for thirty days.

The stories of Peyton Hayden, the sarcastic wit, the practical joker, the benefactor of young lawyers, are found in various references. Less available are specific indications of his capabilities as an attorney, but his name is often listed as representing clients before the Supreme Court of Missouri. That in itself is testimony to the regard in which he was held.

Hayden practiced law in Cooper County with other men who would later make their marks on the state—men like Hamilton Gamble, our Civil War Governor, and Abiel Leonard, George Tompkins and John F. Ryland, all of whom became members of the state supreme court.

Hayden came west to Missouri in 1817, staying in Cape Girardeau for a year. Then he taught school for a year at Franklin. One of his pupils at Franklin later ran away to go farther west—Kit Carson. Hayden had taken up the study of law at the age of 15, while he was in Kentucky. In Missouri, Hayden rode the circuit that took in Cooper, Howard, Boone, and Saline counties.

John F. Phillips, who knew Hayden well, wrote in a history of the bar in Missouri: "In his tongue was the sting of the asp. He was known as 'old sarcasm.' In invective he was a terror. He wore his hair in a long queue like a Chinaman. In speaking he had the habit of flipping with his forefinger his queue into the form of a periphery. Whenever he began to flip it violently it was an unmistakable warning signal that opposing counsel, witness or litigant, was about to get 'a skinning.' And when he turned loose the artillery of his raillery or invective the courtroom became lurid and woe to him who caught its fire!"

Phillips recalled the time Hayden defended a man of low reputation who had been accused of slandering another man. Hayden produced "character" witnesses on behalf of his client. To the court's astonishment, all of them said his client was a liar of the highest degree. They stated that nothing Hayden's client uttered could be believed. Hayden then argued before the jury that testimony showed his client such a proven liar no man's character could be affected by his client's remarks because everybody knew he wasn't telling the truth! Furthermore, the plaintiff, the man who claimed to have been slandered, was a low, greedy and selfish man who only wanted to take some of the poor liar's hard-earned money. The jury awarded the plaintiff only nominal damages. But when Hayden went to collect his fee, his client threatened to whip him for the way he conducted the defense!

For all his legal prowess, Hayden was not a literary giant. When asked once what he thought of Lord Byron's work "Childe Harold," he told his questioner, "Egad, sir, I did not know Byron had a child, Harold."

He sometimes showed little respect for the highest court in Missouri. Once he spent his time before the Supreme Court arguing a case on its weak points, almost totally ignoring the important ones. When asked why, he told Judge George Tompkins, "because I find in my long practice in this court that the weak points win fully as often as the strong ones!"

Peyton Hayden probably wouldn't do well in the courts today. Courts have become more sophisticated and less fun. But it is people like Peyton Hayden who make history interesting. Peyton Hayden was a good lawyer. But first he was an individual, a human being. He died in 1855 at his home in Boonville. Peyton Hayden, Cooper County's first attorney, was born on this date, February 8, in 1796.

****

FEBRUARY 9
THE TRAGEDY OF THOMAS REYNOLDS

The note was addressed to Colonel William G. Minor. It was from one of the most popular men in the state. But the note charged that its writer had been slandered and abused by his enemies. The writer complained that his best efforts had not been appreciated. Those things, and failing health, are considered reasons why a shot rang out in the Governor's office one day in 1844. When a passerby went to see what had happened, he found the Governor of Missouri had committed suicide.

Thomas Reynolds had achieved political renown in Illinois before coming to Missouri in the late 1820s. He was born in Kentucky and had gone to Springfield, Illinois, a decade before Abraham Lincoln. There he became clerk for the Illinois House of Representatives. Later he was Attorney General of the state, then Speaker of the House. In 1822 he was named Chief Justice of the Illinois Supreme Court, a position he held until January of 1825.

Reynolds moved to Fayette, Missouri. Three or four years after he arrived he became the Howard County representative. Not long afterwards he was named Speaker of the House in Missouri. Governor Lilburn Boggs nominated him for the judgeship of the Second Judicial Circuit of Missouri in 1837. Just three years later the Democratic State Convention, meeting in Jefferson City, nominated him for Governor.

He won.

Thomas Reynolds, a lawyer, a Democrat, a Methodist, a slave owner and editor of a newspaper in Fayette, spoke in his inaugural address in November of 1840 about the obligation of public servants to their constituency, of general education, of good roads, the need to maintain a strong and stable currency, corporations and their privileges, of the condition of the Bank of Missouri, slavery, formation of new counties, and the need to protect the ballot.

Reynolds was a man of vision. He pushed for improvements in the state educational system. He sought a limited number of internal improvements, limiting them because he didn't want the state to carry a large public debt. He also believed each state had the right to settle the question of slavery within its own limits.

Two years after he was sworn in, he addressed the legislature again, speaking of the danger slaveholding Missourians faced from outsiders trying to lure their slaves to "free" states. Reynolds told lawmakers, "I would respectfully urge the propriety and necessity of placing this question, by suitable enactments, beyond all doubt, and providing such penalties as will put an end to the increasing evil. The penitentiary for life seems punishment scarcely too severe for perpetrators of such atrocious offenses."

The issue which really intrigued Reynolds, however, was imprisonment for debt. He believed it was wrong and he wanted to do away with it. In the 1842 legislative session's address, he deplored the situation created by a U.S. Supreme Court ruling which allowed Congress to create a federal bankruptcy law. "It is presumed that the baneful effects of the bankrupt act will, at no distant period, include its repeal," he said, "but it is unwise and unjust that during its continuance, debtors should be forced into the federal courts, at an enormous expense, to find relief from imprisonment, which must be their condition while the bankrupt act remains in force, unless the laws authorizing imprisonment for debt are repealed." On January 17th, Thomas Reynolds signed the act ending imprisonment for debt in Missouri. The act has been included in every state consitution since. That fall, Reynolds issued the first proclamation for an official state observance of Thanksgiving.

In the summer of 1843, items began to appear in the Jefferson City newspaper hinting Governor Reynolds' health was not good.

Then early the next year, just after breakfast one day, Governor Reynolds sent for a rifle and asked it be brought to his office. He wrote to his friend, Colonel Minor, "In every situation in which I have been placed, I have labored to discharge my duty faithfully to the public, but this has not protected me for the last twelve months from the slanders and abuse of my enemies, which has rendered my life a burden to me. I pray God to forgive them, and teach them more charity. Farewell." He put the muzzle of the rifle to his forehead and pulled the trigger. He was survived by a wife and one son.

In years to come, Reynolds County would be named for him. Contemporaries say he had given up too soon, that his possibilities at the time were greater than those of any man in the state. But our seventh Governor, Thomas Reynolds, cut short those possibilities when he killed himself in his office on this date, February 9, 1844.

****

FEBRUARY 10
AN UNCOMMON MAN WITH A COMMON NAME

Like so many of Missouri's early leaders, John Jones was born in a foreign country. He came from Wales in the late 1700s, an Oxford graduate, a doctor, and a lawyer. He was the first English-speaking lawyer and first Attorney General of what was then the Indiana territory. He helped draft Indiana's first state constitution. He had been part of George Rogers Clark's force which took Vincennes in 1786. He stayed there and gained prominence in the then Northwest Territory. In 1789 Jones moved to the Illinois country and in 1809 he became the first practicing lawyer in Illinois Territory.

Jones was 41 when he came to Missouri.

He settled at Ste. Genevieve. One of his business partners later became known as the man who started the American colonization of Texas—Moses Austin. He and Austin ran a lead mine in Southeast Missouri and it became the richest mine in America. Jones and Austin donated the land on which the city of Potosi now stands. In 1814, Jones was elected to the second General Assembly of Missouri Territory. He became President of that Council, a position he held for two years. In 1815 his signature was one of those on a petition calling for statehood for Missouri.

John Rice Jones was Washington County's delegate to the state constitutional convention in 1820 where he and 40 others drafted the first state charter. Some of its provisions are still in existence. One of the most prominent, limiting the Governor to one four-year term, wasn't repealed until 1965. Floyd Shoemaker, the state's foremost historian, wrote that Jones was certainly the most learned member of that convention and the "greatest lawyer west of Ohio if not west of the Allegheny Mountains."

Jones's European education and his continuing thirst for knowledge made him proficient in mathematics and classical studies. He could speak six languages: French, Greek, Spanish, English, Latin and Welsh. His law practice was widespread, covering the state of Ohio, the territories of Indiana, Illinois, Kentucky and Upper Louisiana, which became Missouri. He was almost our first Senator, but he lost to another constitutional convention delegate, David Barton.

But Jones's usefulness to the state was far from over. In November of 1820 Governor McNair appointed Jones to Missouri's first Supreme Court. He was known during his time on the high court as the author of minority opinions. In just over three years as a Supreme Court Judge, and out of 140 opinions the court rendered during that time, Jones wrote a dissenting opinion 28 times.

He died in St. Louis, February 1, 1824.

Interestingly enough the influence of John Rice Jones extended far beyond his lifetime. His family ranks as one of the more influential in Missouri history. His oldest son, Rice Jones, was an Indiana lawyer and member of the Indiana House of Representatives. He participated in the successful fight to separate Illinois from Indiana before he was murdered. Another son, also named John Rice Jones, was prominent in the settlement of Texas. After helping the state win its independence, he became the first Postmaster General in the Republic. Among other things, he was the executor of the estate of William Barret Travis, commander of the Alamo garrison. Two other sons, Augustus and Myers Fisher Jones, were also influential in the early days of Texas history. Another son, George Wallace Jones, shaped the history of four states. He held office in Missouri, served in the Blackhawk War, was a delegate to Congress from Michigan Territory and a Congressman from Wisconsin Territory. In 1848 he was one of the first two U.S. Senators from Iowa.

Jones's daughter, Harriet, married John Scott, Missouri's third territorial delegate to Congress. Another daughter, Elizabeth, married Andrew Scott, later a federal judge in Arkansas.

Few families carrying the common name of Jones have had such an uncommon impact on America. John Rice Jones, a man who shaped the destiny of Missouri and America, was born on this date, the 10th of February in 1759.

****

FEBRUARY 11
THE TRIUMPH AND TRAGEDY OF ALEXANDER DOCKERY

By the time his term as Governor had ended, Alexander Monroe Dockery could say that all state debts except for long-term school bonds had been paid off and that Missouri had the lowest tax rate in the nation. Not only that, but he had helped the federal government streamline itself for more economic operation and had helped improve the mail service halfway across the country. He achieved great success but also experienced great sorrow—more of both than most men.

Dockery was a young doctor when he filled his first elective office. He was 26 when he became President of the Chillicothe Board of Education. Just a year later he was a member of the University of

Missouri Board of Curators and seven years after that became a city councilman in Gallatin. At 36 he became Mayor of that city. Alexander Dockery was a loyal Democratic party worker, heading the Tenth Congressional Committee for four years. The district was redrawn during the Crittenden administration and seven of the ten counties were Democratic. That is when Alexander Dockery saw the chance to realize his potential. He went to Congress for the first of eight terms.

Dockery was born near Gallatin, educated at public schools there and an academy near Macon. The academy was closed during the Civil War and Dockery took up the study of medicine at Keytesville. By the end of the Civil War, he had graduated from the St. Louis Medical College. He practiced medicine in Linneus for a couple of years, moved to Chillicothe for a few more, and finally returned to Gallatin.

In 1869 he married a banker's daughter, Mary Bird. Mary and Alexander Dockery would have eight children. But none would live longer than seven years. Six died in infancy. One son lived only to the age of three and a daughter died when she was seven years old. Mrs. Dockery had a heart condition which curtailed many of her activities, but while her husband was in Congress, she devotedly read every newspaper from the home district to help him keep up on what people were thinking at home.

Dockery became known in Congress for his revisions of the government accounting system. The Treasury Department adopted the "Dockery Accounting System" with good results. He proposed the substitution of salaries for fees in certain federal court offices and saved the federal government $2.5 million a year. He also played an important role in getting laws passed requiring special delivery of some letters, and for extending the free delivery of mails to small cities. He was important in securing the second fast-mail service in America, from New York to Kansas City, by way of St. Louis.

Dockery was elected Governor in 1900 and sworn in in January of 1901. Those were momentous years for the state. Although Dockery had been thrifty in Congress, he wasn't above opening the purse strings during his gubernatorial term. Taking advantage of the prosperity of the times, he raised school appropriations. He established juvenile courts, created a board of arbitration and mediation to settle labor disputes, and organized a staff of factory inspectors to examine the manufacturing establishments of the state and report infractions of the law. The beer inspection law was revised. A law was passed giving preference to Missouri stone in erecting public buildings. Franchises and public utilities were taxed for the first time. The first school district consolidation bill was passed. New election laws were enacted.

But sadness came again. Mrs. Dockery fell ill during the Christmas season of 1902. Although growing worse, she insisted preparations continue in the mansion for the New Year's Day reception and military ball. Guests were already arriving in Jefferson City for that event when Mrs. Dockery died on January 1, 1903. The Governor had his executive clerk, Al Morrow, and his wife move into the mansion with him to conduct the social affairs, and, one suspects, to keep him company in the big house.

After his term Dockery returned to Gallatin, still a loyal Democratic party member. He was a treasurer for the Democratic State Committee for two years. In 1913 he was named an Assistant Postmaster General and served eight years. He died in 1926, nearly 82 years old.

Alexander Monroe Dockery, a Governor and Congressman with success enough for any man and sadness enough for many, was born on this date, the 11th of February, 1845.

****

FEBRUARY 12
THE G.I. GENERAL

He wanted to go to college, but he couldn't afford it. After high school he went to work for the Wabash Railroad in Moberly. One night the young man was talking with John Crewson, superintendent of the Sunday School at the Moberly Christian Church. Crewson, knowing how much the young man wanted a college education, suggested he go to a college that paid the students—West Point. Although almost too discouraged to try for an appointment the young man did and succeeded. Many years he would be known as "The G.I. General," Omar Bradley.

Bradley had thought of being a soldier earlier and the talk with Crewson rekindled that interest. Bradley wrote directly to Congressman W. W. Rucker asking for an appointment to the U.S. Military Academy. But Rucker wrote back saying the principal appointment had already been filled. The only chance was as an alternate.

Bradley had to pass exams to qualify. After being out of school for a year, he feared his study habits were weak. He couldn't give up his job with the railroad to study during the daytime, since he'd just been promoted to the boiler shop and given a raise to seventeen cents an hour. He was concerned about wasting money traveling to St. Louis for what he feared would be a hopeless trip. Family friends encouraged him to get a pass from the railroad, which he did. He made the trip, took the test and three weeks later he received a letter. The principal appointee had flunked. Omar Bradley was ordered to West Point, to report by August 1, 1911.

After graduation, Bradley had a number of "going-nowhere" stations. He was in charge of a guard company at the Butte, Montana, copper pits while many of his colleagues were fighting in Europe. But he worked to improve and by 1929 he had graduated from the Command and General Staff School and was a faculty member at Fort Benning's infantry school. It was there he learned the basics of command from General George Marshall, then a Lieutenant Colonel.

Marshall became Brigadier General in 1936 and Bradley was soon afterward promoted to Assistant Secretary of the General Staff. In 1943, Marshall told him it was time Omar Bradley took a major part in World War II. He was sent to command a unit in Africa. For the first time in his 32 years as a soldier, Bradley was going to war.

That fall, Eisenhower issued orders for Bradley to go to England to command the army gearing up for the invasion of France. By then Bradley had cut his teeth on a large operation against the Germans in Tunisia and a large-scale amphibious assault in Sicily. His importance to the Allied war effort continued to increase until by the end of the war he commanded the Twelfth Army Group of four armies and 1.3 million combat troops. The kid who almost gave up on going to West Point ended World War II commanding the largest body of American soldiers ever to serve under a single field commander.

In 1945, the Senate confirmed Bradley as a four-star general. He was known as the G.I. General. He never adopted the individual style of uniform favored by some of his contemporaries such as Eisenhower and Patton. He often wore the fatigues of the combat trooper. He seldom raised his voice.

Bradley became General of the Army in 1950 and received his fifth star. He reorganized the Veterans Administration, was Army Chief of

Staff in 1948 and 1949, and was Chairman of the Joint Chiefs of Staff from 1949 to 1953.

Five-star Generals never retire although the army lets them follow their own pursuits. Even as he moved into his ninth decade, Bradley said he would serve again: "I don't think anyone can ever say 'I've done enough.'" He wrote, "In the rear areas, war may sometimes assume the mask of adventure. On the front it seldom lapses far from what General Sherman declared it to be."

Bradley died April 8, 1981, at the age of 88.

Omar Bradley, the G.I. General, a man who rose from a discouraged railroad employe in Moberly to command the greatest army in world history, was born in Clark, Missouri, on this date, the 12th of February, 1893.

****

FEBRUARY 13
AMERICA'S FIRST SECRETARY OF AGRICULTURE

It is sometimes hard to believe that early in our country's history, when we were still a largely agrarian society, there was opposition to establishing a federal cabinet office just for agriculture. It finally happened 20 years after the Civil War. The first Secretary of Agriculture was a St. Louis farm newspaper publisher called "Governor" by his friends although he never held that job, and who shares the title of "Father of the Agriculture Experiment Station."

Several days after Grover Cleveland's inauguration, Missouri Senator George Graham Vest went to the White House, angered because no Missourians had been named to high federal positions or ambassadorships. He spoke heatedly to Cleveland and mentioned in his tirade the position of Commissioner of Agriculture. That rang a bell with Cleveland who looked down at his desk and saw there the nomination of George W. Glick of Kansas. The President thought about it. Then he made up a new nomination form with the name of Norman J. Colman of Missouri inserted.

Norman Colman was a farmer and lawyer from St. Louis, a newspaperman known nationwide. His nomination as Commissioner of Agriculture prompted one person to write to the St. Louis *Republican,* "Well, at least we, the people, have the office well-filled—no padding needed.... No appointment made at Washington for the last 25 years has so reached the masses or been so truly a representative one as the appointment of Governor Colman of Missouri."

Norman Colman came from New York where he was born in May, 1827, to a farm family. He would stay up late at night after farming and schoolwork were finished to read books borrowed from neighbors, or read the "Albany Cultivator," a farm newspaper that came in the mail. Colman became a schoolteacher when he was 16. He taught in the winters to make money for his schooling in the summer. He moved to Kentucky where he studied law and received a degree. He practiced for a while with M. C. Kerr in Indiana. Kerr would later be Speaker of the House in Washington. But law wasn't Colman's big interest. He resigned as a District Attorney in Indiana and came to Missouri, buying a farm near St. Louis. Three years later Colman bought out a magazine called *Valley Farmer,* and in 1865 he started a new publication, *Colman's Rural World.* It soon became the leading farm paper in the Mississippi Valley.

Colman was a strong Democrat, a member of the St. Louis Board of Aldermen, a member of the Missouri Legislature and victorious in 1874 in a race for Lieutenant Governor, which is where he got his nickname "Governor."

Colman was President of the State Board of Agriculture from 1865 until his death 46 years later. It was that board which organized the State Fair in Sedalia. He maintained a model farm in St. Louis. He believed a teacher of or spokesman for agriculture must have a practical as well as a theoretical knowledge about it. He raised about one hundred fine standard bred horses.

Under President Cleveland, as Commissioner of Agriculture, Colman pushed to make the position part of the cabinet, citing the growing complexity of agriculture. Opposition came from, among others, Attorney General Augustus Garland, who said the only question Colman could discuss at the cabinet meetings was "whether it is best to plant potatoes in the dark of the moon...." But the President disagreed and when Congressman Hatch's bill making the post part of the cabinet reached his desk, he signed it. Although he had only three weeks left in his administration, Cleveland named Norman Colman the first Secretary of Agriculture.

At the end of his term, Colman came back to Missouri to his farm and his newspaper. He believed in fresh air, good eating habits, sunshine and exercise. "Most of us dig our graves with our teeth," he once said. He liked Turkish baths, and on his 84th birthday he noted,

"I have taken a Turkish bath at least once a week for 50 years, and while I was in Washington mingling with some of the politicians there, from 1885 to 1889, I always took three a week."

Norman J. Colman, a Missouri lawyer who found farming and newspaper editing to be his field, became the nation's first Secretary of Agriculture on this date, the 13th of February, in 1889.

****

FEBRUARY 14
CUMP

Although he was born a Presbyterian he had never been baptized. The family he was living with was Catholic. They thought he should be properly blessed, and asked a priest to do so. But when the priest learned the young man had been named "Tecumseh," in honor of the great Indian chief, the priest decided he could not baptize anyone unless he had a Christian name. And so it became *William* Tecumseh Sherman. His family and close friends called him "Cump," short for Tecumseh.

Sherman was still a youngster when his father died. The family had to be broken up, the children sent to other homes for proper raising. It was Sherman's good fortune to live with the family of Thomas Ewing, prominent lawyer, member of Congress, and this country's first Secretary of the Interior. Sherman went to West Point at the age of 16 and graduated sixth in his class. He might have graduated third, but he constantly piled up demerits.

He served the army in the Seminole War, but after that ended it was a long time before he saw combat again. He visited St. Louis for the first time in 1843, while on leave. Sherman liked it so much he wanted to make St. Louis his permanent home. In 1850 he was stationed at Jefferson Barracks in St. Louis and was there promoted to Captain. Two years later he was transferred to New Orleans. But when he had a chance to set up a California branch of the famous St. Louis banking house of Lucas, Turner, and Company, he resigned from the army and took that job. Unfortunately the bank went out of business. Sherman repaid many depositors out of his own pocket.

He had a chance to become Assistant Secretary of War under Lincoln; however, he thought Lincoln's plea for 75,000 volunteers to put down the rebellion was worthless. He believed volunteers would never make good soldiers. Sherman refused an appointment as Brigadier General in charge of St. Louis volunteers.

Finally in May of 1861 he offered his services to the Union Army. Sherman was in the crowd at Camp Jackson when disorder broke out and several people died. This, he felt, supported his contention that untested volunteers couldn't be trusted. Sherman became a Colonel in 1861, but the next year was difficult for him and he resigned as head of the Department of the Cumberland. He was near a mental collapse. Some newspapers reported Cump Sherman had gone insane. He came back to Missouri where General Halleck took him in tow. Sherman toured the state, with authority to take command of divisions at Sedalia, Syracuse, and Tipton if he wished. He also was given a three week vacation.

When Sherman returned, Halleck made him commander of Benton Barracks where training was under way for 12,000 recruits. Refreshed, he plunged into the job and in a month had four infantry and two cavalry regiments ready to fight. Sherman regained his confidence and with Halleck he created the idea of a massive offensive to clear the Confederates out of the Mississippi River area. It put Sherman into the limelight along with another St. Louisan named Ulysses Grant. Later, Sherman would make his lasting mark on the history of American warfare with his famous march to the sea.

After the Civil War, with a nation divided into military divisions and districts, Sherman was given command of the Military Division of the Missouri, and established his headquarters in St. Louis. There he resisted with all his power attempts to involve him in the political conflict in Washington, often refusing either to run for President or accept a job of Secretary of War under President Johnson. His interest turned more and more toward Indians. He worried about the fate of the Indian, although he was known as their enemy.

Sherman became the commander of the entire U.S. Army and served as interim Secretary of War during the Grant administration. His biographer, James Merrill, says Sherman yearned to leave his Washington job and return to Missouri. But his loyalty to Grant stood in the way.

When Sherman's son Tom graduated from Yale, the younger Sherman returned to St. Louis to watch over family business affairs. The elder Sherman had often dreamed of leaving Washington, retiring to St. Louis, and letting Tom run the business interests. But Tom became a priest, smashing his father's dreams. It was years before the split between father and son healed. Sherman did eventually return to St. Louis and set up his headquarters in the mid 1870s.

A decade later when Sherman was pushed again to run for President he wrote that he would not "commit the folly of giving up the peace and quietude of the remainder of my life for such an empty honor."

The Shermans later settled in New York. When his wife died, she was taken to St. Louis for burial. He died at the age of 71. His body was returned to Missouri and buried in St. Louis next to his wife.

Tecumseh Sherman died on this date, February 14, 1891.

****

FEBRUARY 15
THE SECOND OLDEST COMMUNITY IN MISSOURI

It had been more than three decades since French settlers moved to the area. Others had followed, setting up camps and mines. Now two men stood on a hill overlooking the Mississippi River. One turned to the other and said he thought this place, too, would be a good place for a trading post or town.

The trading post came first. Then the town was built around it. Today that town is the second oldest permanent settlement in Missouri.

A short time after deciding on the location for the new town, one of the men—his name was Liguest—told the commander of a fort in Illinois, "I have found a situation where I am going to form a settlement which might become hereafter one of the finest cities in America." Almost immediately upon organization of that trading post, settlers began to come in. Many of them were people who didn't want to be part of England when France gave up its lands east of the Mississippi. But those people learned later that even then they weren't on French soil.

The story of Missouri's second oldest permanent settlement actually begins in 1763 when Pierre Laclede Liguest started up the Mississippi River from New Orleans with trade goods for the Indians. Arriving at Ste. Genevieve in November, his trading party found no place to store those goods. So they went on to a French military post six miles farther upstream on the Illinois side. They were given permission to spend the winter there. At Fort Chartres they found French settlers ready to leave for New Orleans. They had heard rumors that France had given her lands east of the Mississippi to the English.

The next month, Laclede, as he was more commonly called, set out with one of his companions, young Auguste Chouteau, for a short exploratory trip west of the Mississippi. They found a place they thought suitable for their trading post and notched trees to mark the spot. Laclede turned to the younger man and outlined why it would be a good place for a settlement.

Then Laclede and Chouteau went back to Fort Chartres. Laclede easily presuaded the disappointed inhabitants at the Fort to move to the site of his new trading post and form a regular settlement. He sent Chouteau with about 30 men and boys back across the river ordering them "to have the place cleared, build a large shed to protect the provisions and tools, and some cabins to shelter the men."

In the meantime, however, France had ceded its lands west of the Mississippi to Spain. None of the settlers knew about this though. Laclede laid out the streets and developed a system of property ownership. Many of his land grants were verbal and since the land was now Spanish he really had no authority to do anything about property ownership to begin with. Again, he didn't know that. The Spanish later sustained those first grants anyway.

The village was known for some time as "Laclede's Village." But in time it acquired its formal name which honors a French King who led the crusades and who since had been canonized by the Catholic Church.

Pierre Laclede Liguest would live only long enough to see a rough pioneer settlement, nowhere near "one of the finest cities in America" he dreamed it would be. He died in 1778 on his way back to New Orleans. He was buried on shore somewhere near the junction of the Mississippi and the Arkansas rivers. The mantle of leadership passed to young Chouteau who continued to guide the town's expansion and promote friendly relations with the Indians. The town would not be immune to Indian attacks, but would survive them as it would survive floods, tornadoes, epidemics, wars and financial panics. Growth over the years would be slow but steady. Historian Logan Reavis notes that by 1790, a merchant in the town was "a man who, in the corner of his cabin had a large chest which contained a few pounds of powder and shot, a few knives and hatchets, a little red paint, two or three rifles, some hunting shirts of buckskin, a few tin cups and iron pots and perhaps a little tea, coffee, sugar and spice. There was no post office, no ferry over the river and no newspaper."

Today evidence of the two men who founded the town survives in the names of streets, buildings, utility companies, historical markers and many other ways. The hill they stood on is now the site of a domed building which is a national monument. The riverfront of their town is dominated by a 600-foot gleaming stainless steel arch, a tribute in part to Laclede and Chouteau, who founded the city of St. Louis, the second oldest permanent settlement in Missouri, on this date, February 15, 1764.

****

FEBRUARY 16
THE HANNIBAL-ST. JOE

It was just a small group of businessmen from the Hannibal area meeting in the office that day in 1846. One of them was John M. Clemens whose son Samuel would be more remembered than he. One of the others was State Senator Robert Stewart, later to be Governor. The small group was excitedly discussing a large business proposition. Stewart vowed he would push the legislature into giving the go-ahead for the project. He did and the next year the legislature granted incorporation for a railroad which deserves an important place in our history—the Hannibal and St. Joseph.

In 1846 the St. Joseph *Gazette* had run an editorial calling for a railroad connecting St. Joseph with the Mississippi to the east. The editorial suggested Hannibal, St. Louis, or even Quincy, Illinois, as likely places for an eastern connection. Later that year Stewart traveled the proposed route of the tracks to make a preliminary survey. He found no geographical problems. But railroads take money to build and the only money available was in the east where railroads had taken hold. Eastern investors were reluctant to sink money into a venture through sparsely settled territory. But in September of 1850, Congress passed a bill allowing more than $2,000,000 worth of public lands to be given to the state of Illinois to build what became the Illinois Central Railroad.

Missouri promoters immediately put pressure on Congress for a similar deal. It took two years. But when it came, the legislature gave more than 600,000 acres to the Hannibal and St. Joe. By then the state had loaned the railroad $1 ½ million, an amount it would match in 1855.

The state and federal action cleared the way for eastern investors. A corporation headed by John and Robert Forbes was set up in 1854 in Boston to finance the railroad. Construction had started in March of 1853 but progress was slow and the future was uncertain because of shaky finances. It wasn't until the fall of 1856 that the first twenty-five miles of track west of Hannibal was operating.

On February 13, 1859, the last spike was driven near Chillicothe. The next day the first through passenger train made a trip and nine days after that, regular passenger service was set up on an eleven-hour schedule. That fall the railroad opened its first land office and sold 14,000 acres in four months. In the first nine and one-half months of operation the railroad made about $380,000.

In April of 1860 the Hannibal and St. Joe carried the first mail across Missouri for the Pony Express trip to Sacramento. The record set in that wild trip across the state—192 miles in about four hours—lasted for 50 years.

In July the first mail car in American history went into business on the Hannibal and St. Joe. But by now the Civil War was hurting the railroad. Operating costs, high enough anyway, were increasing because of damage to the railroad by guerrillas under orders from Confederate officers. One of the big financial backers of the line, Erastus Corning, wrote to Secretary of War Simon Cameron in 1861 pleading for federal protection for the railroad because, he pointed out, it helped maintain communcations with the territories of Kansas, Nebraska and Utah and other outlying military areas. Federal help came in time.

By 1863, though, bonds had fallen to 25 percent of their value and the stock was worthless. Strong financial realignment kept the railroad alive and allowed it to stay out of receivership. It became the only one of Missouri's railroads which did not default on its bonds. All others forfeited their payments and became property of the state.

The Boston investors were also working to set up other lines in Illinois and Iowa. They arranged a joint lease with the young Chicago, Burlington and Quincy; the Wabash; and the Hannibal and St. Joseph to build a bridge at Quincy. It was completed and profits jumped.

But by the mid-1870s the financial picture was shaky again. The Burlington finally bought the Hannibal and St. Joe stock. Now it is only a small part of the sprawling Burlington Northern system. But it is a historic part. The Hannibal and St. Joseph Railroad was incorporated on this date, February 16, 1847.

****

FEBRUARY 17
THE DOCTOR, THE MIRRORS, THERMOMETERS, AND PRACTICAL JOKES

Good doctors were rare on the frontier. Rarer still was one who went beyond simply treating disease in the traditional way. Missouri has had a number of physicians who made history. Many have been recognized for inventions or for their scientific explorations in their field. One of those recognized for his experiments as well as his treatments was Dr. Antoine Francois Saugrain. In two decades he became widely known as an intellectual and scientific leader in eastern Missouri.

Saugrain not only was a highly skilled doctor, but he had interests in mineralogy, chemistry and physics. It is said he built furnaces, chemical laboratories, and electrical batteries wherever he went.

In 1800 he went to St. Louis. The city was still in Spanish hands, not yet having passed into French ownership. Saugrain became the post physician for the Spanish Governor. When Spain gave up its territory in this part of the United States, the Spanish Governor left St. Louis. Many people went with him, French and Spanish alike. But Saugrain liked the town and stayed.

In 1804, when Lewis and Clark started assembling a force of men and equipment in the St. Louis area to make their great trip to the Pacific Northwest, they went to Saugrain for medical supplies. They carried with them thermometers, medicines and other scientific tools supplied by the doctor.

He made the thermometers for them out of his wife's best mirror, brought all the way to the wilds of St. Louis from France with great care to keep it from breaking. Saugrain scraped the mercury from the back of the mirror, melted down the glass, and enclosed the mercury inside. He determined where the mercury would stand at the temperature of blood, and at freezing, then marked off degrees on the tubes as best he could. He must have made several thermometers out of the mirror. The journals of the expedition tell of the last thermometer breaking during a crossing of the Rocky Mountains.

The expedition needed a reliable way to make fire, too. Saugrain provided Lewis and Clark with matches 20 years before the friction match came into general use. He put some sulphur on the end of a sliver of wood, then tipped it with phosphorous. A Lewis and Clark biographer, John Bakeless, says that 50 years later old Indians recalled the amazing speed with which Lewis and Clark made fire.

In years to come Saugrain and Clark became good friends. Clark enjoyed Saugrain's experiments. The doctor fiddled with electricity to the delight and consternation of visiting Indians. They were told to open a door only to get a shock out of it because the doctor had electrified the knob. Sometimes the doctor dropped a coin in the water and told the Indians they could have it. But when they reached for it, Doctor Saugrain turned on the current. Indians from time to time were seen running from the Clark home in St. Louis with painful memories of the doctor and his "big medicine."

One of the most feared diseases in those days was smallpox which could wipe out an entire village in a couple of days. Saugrain is thought to have been the first Missouri doctor to use vaccine for the prevention of that dread disease. He made it available for all, regardless of their economic situation. The State Historical Society of Missouri has on record one of the doctor's advertisements from this state's first newspaper offering vaccine to all persons of indigent circumstances, paupers, and Indians. It also offers the vaccine to doctors and other intelligent persons residing outside the doctor's usual territory.

Saugrain died in 1820 at the age of 57.

Dr. Antoine Francois Saugrain, a pioneering Missouri doctor and scientist, was born on this date, the 17th of February, 1763.

****

FEBRUARY 18
CONVENTION OF NINETY-NINE

What might have happened if Missouri had seceded from the Union?

The consequences could have been immediate and tragic.

Our economy could have been destroyed, since most of the markets for the things we grew or manufactured were in the north. Eastern capital developed and maintained our mines and railroads. Some economic historians think the slave holdings would have disappeared entirely or quickly deteriorated because many of those slaves would have fled to free states around us. Missouri might have become, like Virginia, a major battleground of the war. Of course, the state did suffer during the war. But a group of ninety-nine men, taking extraordinary action, blocked its destruction.

Governor Claiborne Jackson's hopes of taking Missouri out of the Union began to suffer a series of disastrous political setbacks. A House committee recommended calling a convention of citizens to determine Missouri's relations with the Union. The act set no restrictions on the powers of that convention as it was originally drawn. The convention could have voted secession and Missouri would have been out of the Union. But the act was amended to say no action of the convention would be final unless ratified by the voters of the state. This in itself was a major defeat for the group headed by Jackson and former Governor, Sterling Price.

The need to call the convention was so urgent there was little time for campaigning. There were no party labels. Men were voted on because of their avowed sentiments. Jackson and Price were shocked when not a single secessionist was elected. It was a crushing defeat for Jackson, who had miscalculated the feelings of the people.

It was a distinguished group. W. L. Webb writes that fifty-two of the ninety-nine were unconditional Unionists. The rest would accept secession only under the most severe circumstances. Ninety-five of the ninety-nine were southern-oriented or had a southern heritage. Eighty-five of them were slave-owners. There were forty-five lawyers, twenty-six farmers, and eleven merchants. Seven judges were in the group and so were three doctors. Average age: 45.

When the group held its first meeting in Jefferson City, it elected former Governor Sterling Price its chairman. A resolution calling for all members to take a loyalty oath was strongly debated, then passed 65-30.

Members of the Convention decided not to stay in Jefferson City. Some historians think the members wanted to escape the partisan pressures they faced there. But a more logical reason for the shift of convention work to St. Louis might have been the lack of hotel rooms in the Capital City.

The convention reconvened in March. A few days later its Committee on Federal Relations, chaired by Hamilton Gamble of St. Louis, came in with a report containing a series of resolutions. The resolution saying there was no adequate cause to secede was adopted 89-1. A resolution saying the people wanted the Union preserved was approved 90-0. Afterwards, Price told fellow convention member Thomas Shackelford of Glasgow, "I believe war is inevitable. I am a military man. I can't fight against the South; so I must go with the border states. I was, as you know, against secession, but in favor of revolution. This will be a revolution, the greatest in the world." Price never met with the convention again.

State Senator George Graham Vest, not a member of the convention, but a member of the House committee which brought out the resolution calling for the convention to assemble, disliked what was happening. He called the delegates "political cheats, jugglers and charlatans who foisted themselves upon the people by ditties and music and striped flags." But the resolutions had sealed off any hope of Missouri leaving the Union. By May, Jackson and Price had fled the state. Robert Wilson became the new convention President, when the convention was reassembled in July for nine days. The convention declared all legislative seats vacant, partly because of disloyalty, and vacated all high state offices. The Convention of ninety-nine, in effect, seized power with those recommendations. Hamilton Gamble was named Provisional Governor. The convention set November as the time for a new election to pick state officials and a new legislature.

In October, Gamble called the convention back into session to delay the elections until August of 1862 because of civil disorder. The convention abolished many state offices and cut the salaries of state officials by 20% in an economy move. It arranged for the issuance of a million dollars worth of bonds and another million dollars worth of defense warrants to be used for money. Tougher loyalty oaths were enacted. But in June, 1862 the convention re-convened and called off the elections again. Still more oaths were instituted to guarantee a loyal electorate when a new legislature finally was picked in November, 1862.

The convention met once more, in June, 1863. It came forth with a plan to free the slaves in Missouri as of July 4, 1870, although those slaves over 40 years old could stay with their masters as indentured servants for the rest of their lives if they chose. Missouri thus

107

became the first slave state to take steps to free its slaves. The Emancipation Proclamation signed a few months earlier by President Lincoln did not affect Missouri. It applied only to the southern states and they, of course, did not recognize it. The convention adjourned for the last time on July 1, 1863.

The convention, although it operated without restrictions as far as running Missouri's government was concerned, kept Missouri in the Union. It changed constitutional laws without regard to constitutional procedure. But Missouri could have fared much worse in the Civil War than it did. One reason it did not was because the citizens, as we hope citizens always will, recognized if not the greatest good, at least the least evil, and elected those ninety-nine members on this date, the 18th of February, in 1861.

****

FEBRUARY 19
FRANK BLAIR

It is the Republican Convention of 1860. William Seward has carried two ballots, but not by enough to win a nomination. A Missouri delegation will help turn the tide on the third ballot. In that delegation are three men with the last name of Blair, a father and two sons. One of the sons is regarded by many as a man who saved Missouri for the Union through his bold political and military action. He was Francis Preston Blair, Jr. He went by the nickname "Frank."

Frank Blair came from Kentucky. He studied law in North Carolina and Kentucky and practiced law in St. Louis for a while. But when General Phil Kearney took possession of New Mexico, he named Blair that territory's first Attorney General. When Blair returned to St. Louis, he jumped into the political arena almost immediately. A free-soiler, he established a newspaper to voice his views. Blair didn't believe the federal government should dictate to the states on the question of slavery, although he believed slavery was outdated and wrong.

In 1857 a momentous meeting took place which altered Blair's life. He was visiting lawyer John Herndon in Springfield, Illinois, when he met Herndon's law partner, a gangling, homely man named Abraham Lincoln. By then Blair was a first-term Congressman. He would serve three terms as a Congressman and later one term as

U.S. Senator. He had pulled out of the Democratic party earlier that year because of its pro-slavery leanings. Lincoln felt even then that Missouri was a key to maintaining the Union. In Blair, he saw a strong ally, an alliance which never slackened.

The favored candidate in the convention of 1860 was William Seward. The three Blairs and Edward Bates constituted the power bloc of the Missouri delegation. Bates was the favorite son candidate from Missouri. The southern politicians who backed Seward believed this would hurt Lincoln. Seward led for two ballots, but couldn't get the necessary majority. On the third ballot, the Missouri bloc went for Lincoln and the tide was turned.

Missouri didn't vote for Lincoln, though, in the Presidential election. This angered the Blairs and Bates. But Lincoln appointed Montgomery Blair his Postmaster General, and Bates was named his Attorney General, the first cabinet members from west of the Mississippi. It is said Frank Blair could have had any position he wanted, but he cautioned Lincoln against loading the cabinet with too many men from a state which hadn't supported the President at the polls.

When war came, Frank Blair resigned from Congress. He was the leader of one of the factions prompting the Convention of 1861. He had organized anti-slavery German groups in St. Louis into Wide-Awake Clubs for political purposes in the 1860 elections and, as he saw the conflict approaching, he began to reorganize them into Home Guard units. When Governor Jackson refused the President's request for troops after the capture of Fort Sumter, Blair offered his unit and the President accepted. He and General Nathaniel Lyon thwarted hopes by Governor Jackson that the state could take the St. Louis Arsenal and contain federal troops in St. Louis. They did it by taking the arsenal themselves, forcing the retirement of General Harney, who commanded the region. Some historians say that this one move might have saved Missouri more than any other single military move in the war. Certainly it damaged, at the very beginning, the Governor's hopes for a pro-southern state and started the ball rolling which would force Jackson to leave Missouri.

A year later, when the Confederate troops were carrying the battle, Blair raised seven regiments of troops from Missouri. He led the troops at the siege of Vicksburg and had command of a unit in Sherman's army during the march to the sea in 1864.

A few days after war ended, Blair's friend Lincoln was murdered. His plans for a benevolent reconstruction died with him. The Blairs favored readmitting the southern states. Frank took a strong stand against registry laws, test oaths and punishment of the South. When the Republican party became infiltrated with carpetbaggers, Blair left it.

Blair was appointed to the Senate in 1870 when Charles Drake resigned. Blair claimed he was entitled to the job since he had helped his party rebuild after the war. He served three years, much of the time as a member of the Committee on Outrages, touring the South, blasting the radical movement and urging Democrats to unite and assert themselves.

Frank Blair was a man whose influence was felt on national politics in trying times, a man who was one of the most important figures in keeping Missouri in the Union. Francis Preston Blair, Jr., was born the year Missouri entered the Union, on this date, February 19th, in 1821.

****

FEBRUARY 20
BOTANIST, PUBLISHER, GERMAN SCOUT

If you want to check the weather records for the Missouri-Mississippi River Valley, you can do so as far back as 1836. That was when a St. Louis doctor and scientist started keeping those records. He was a remarkable man, forced to leave Europe's schools because of what were called "democratic tendencies." He was a member of thirty-five scientific societies at home and abroad, and an organizer of the first Academy of Science west of the Allegheny Mountains.

On January 1, 1836, Dr. George Engelmann set up a thermometer, barometer, and hydrometer in St. Louis, and started keeping history's first regular weather statistics for the Missouri Valley region. It was a habit he continued for 47 years, three times a day. In fact, his devotion to keeping accurate records of the weather eventually killed him. His journals over those decades are the only reliable source of weather information we have for the Mississippi Valley for that time period.

Engelmann started his medical studies at the University of Heidelberg, but had to transfer to the University of Berlin where he graduated in 1831. His graduation paper on plant monstrosities was widely circulated in Europe and gave an early indication of his constant love of botany. He came to America at the age of 23 and lived for a while in Illinois before moving to Missouri. Engelmann came to this state representating people in Germany who had been hearing glowing reports of the area. He was sent to see if things really were that good. With a guide, Engelmann conducted scientific studies of the St. Louis region, southern Illinois, southern Missouri and Arkansas. His reports on the resources of the Mississippi Valley were important enough to encourage continued German migration. After that he settled in St. Louis, practiced medicine, helped publish the first German newspaper in that city, the *Anzeiger,* and helped build the first German high school.

Highly-trained doctors were still rare, and Engelmann became one of the busiest in St. Louis. He aroused bitter criticism from some colleagues, however, when he became the first in the region to use obstetrical forceps. Engelmann also pioneered in the use of quinine to treat malaria.

His interest in botany eventually drew him away from his practice of medicine more and more. He would work all day as a doctor. At night, sometimes after nine o'clock, he would study botany. He became an international authority on cactus and gymnosperms—pines and other cone-bearing plants. In 1840 he met another nationally-prominent botanist, Dr. Asa Gray, at Harvard. His relationship with Gray and another famous plant scientist, Thomas Nuttall, brought him continued success and gave the world a trio of great scientific minds in the field of botany. Nuttall and Gray recommended to all their explorer friends they go to St. Louis to compare and adjust their instruments with Engelmann's, or have him build proper instruments for their expeditions.

The State Historical Society of Missouri states that Engelmann examined and classified most of the botanical specimens collected on government expeditions. Many others were forwarded to Gray for his work. Gray helped finance more expeditions by selling the specimens back east. A plant from the Rocky Mountains could bring ten dollars; one from Texas was worth eight—vast sums in those days.

Engelmann's enthusiasm for Missouri was always great. Once he wrote Gray that St. Louis is "the center of North America, if not the world, and of civilization! The great focus of the West and Southwest...We burn one-third of our steamboats, destroy one-tenth of the wealth of our citizens in one night, kill one-tenth by cholera—try

111

our hand at burning again—all only to show how much we can stand without succumbing."

The general public probably isn't familiar with Engelmann's research. But he did leave behind a large and lasting monument well-known to those in the St. Louis area. It was George Engelmann, the great botanist, who materialized the dreams of Henry Shaw into the massive botanical gardens known today as Shaw's Gardens.

In 1884, on a snowy day in February, Dr. Engelmann tried to clear a path through the snow to his weather instruments. He caught cold and died two days past his 75th birthday on February 4th.

Doctor George Engelmann, doctor, scientist, botanist, came to Missouri on this date, February 20, 1833.

****

FEBRUARY 21
HOUN' DAWG

Many years ago, about 1911, an old man from Taney County claimed this famous song originated in the Forsyth area before the Civil War, based on problems encountered by one Zeke Parrish. Parrish, the story goes, once got into trouble for fighting with a boy who had kicked his dog. The incident was soon set to music. The song became part of a Presidential campaign, believe it or not, and later was associated with a distinguished military group.

You have probably heard the chorus:

> Every time I go to town,
> the boys start kickin' my dog around.
> Makes no difference if he is a hound,
> they gotta quit kickin' my dog around.

The verses run something like this, in the original version, as near as Susan Marsh and Charles Vannest were able to trace it down:

> Wunst me 'n' Lem Briggs 'n' ol' Bill Brown
>   Tuk a load of cawn to town
> An ol' Jim Dawg, the ornry cuss,
>   He jus' nachelly follored us.
>
> As we driv' past Sam Johnson's store
>   Passel o' yawps kem out the door;
> When Jim he stops to smel a box,
>   They shied at him a bunch of rocks.

112

They tied a tin can to his tail
  An' run him a past the county jail,
'N' that plum nachelly made me sore—
  'N' Lem he cussed 'n' Bill he swore.

Me 'n' Lem Briggs 'n' ol' Bill Brown
  We lost no time in jumpin' down
An' we wiped them ducks up on the ground
  Fer kickin' my old dawg aroun'.

Folks say a dog kain't hold no grudge
  But wunst when I got too much to budge
Them town ducks tried to do me up,
  But they didn't count on ol' Jim pup.

Jim seed his duty thar and then,
  An' he lit into them gentlemen,
An' he shore mussed up the courthouse square
  With rags 'n' meat 'n' hide 'n' hair.

The origin of this great piece of poetry is obscure. Aaron Weatherman of Taney County claimed the boys around Forsyth sang it until the Civil War broke out and then, he said, "there wasn't time to sing anymore." But some long-time residents of the area dispute that, saying they'd never heard the song until many years later. One writer, Mark Sullivan, claimed that Daniel Boone and his associates sang it when they came to Missouri, but offered no proof of his findings. A woman in Springfield claimed to have published it about 1910 and in October of 1911 a Hound Dog Society was formed in Mountain Grove, with each member required to sing the "hound dog" song.

The song was strongly identified with Missouri. In 1912 Congressman Champ Clark of Louisiana, Missouri, was a prime candidate for the Democratic presidential nomination and the Hound Dog song became his theme song. Champ Clark lost the nomination. The song, however, survived. By then, in fact, it was closely tied to a Missouri military unit. The Second Missouri Infantry, a National Guard unit formed in 1891, was one of many units called up for the Spanish-American War which never saw battlefield action before the war ended. The Second Infantry was stationed at Camp Clark and is said to have played the song constantly. The unit was dubbed "the Hound Dawg" regiment. The tune they played apparently came from an old fiddle song called "Big Sweet Taters in the Sandy Land."

When American troops were sent to Mexico under Pershing to find Pancho Villa, the Second Missouri was mobilized. The commanding officer at the time, Colonel W. A. Raupp, thought the Hound Dog song would be an interesting regimental air. Lew Larkin notes that during a parade in Laredo, Texas, a Missouri hound dog actually marched in review with the unit for the first time. The Second Missouri served seven months on the border and the hound stayed with it. The dog later became the symbol, not only of the Second, but of other Southwest Missouri regiments.

The spelling changed with the re-designation of the regiment. They were called *Houn' Dawgs* in World War I. The Second Missouri went to France to become part of the famed 35th Division as the 130th, 129th and 128th machine gun battalions and the 110th trench mortar battery. The unit was back in World War II as Southwest Missourians enlisted to re-form the *Houn' Dawgs.* The unit became part of the 203rd coast artillery and anti-aircraft regiment.

The Hound Dog, or Houn' Dawg, if you will, was the symbol on patches, uniform insignia and designs on regimental vehicles. And so the lowly houn' dawg, immortalized in song because somebody kicked him around, became the symbol of a group that wasn't about to let anybody kick them around.

Whether the story really did start with Zeke Parrish in Taney County or whether it was created in Springfield in 1910, the Hound Dog song lives on, as a humorous folk song, and as the symbol of a famous group of Missouri fighting men, the Second Missouri Division, formed on this date, February 21, in 1891.

****

FEBRUARY 22
SOLDIER IN GREASEPAINT

She had just barely started singing her first number that night in Boston in 1943 when the audience of 3,500 soldiers and other servicemen rose to give her a standing ovation. Her mere appearance on that stage was all it took. She weighed only 85 pounds and was lugging around a 35-pound cast. The audience couldn't tell it, but the entire production had been designed to get her on and off the stage without revealing she could neither walk, stand, nor use her right arm properly. She should have been dead. But luck helped her live. Courage would make her life an inspiration. Her name was Jane Froman.

Actually, it was Ellen Jane Froman. She was born in St. Louis and was in a convent school from the age of five through twelve. She made her singing debut at the age of eight at a church party. Her mother, Anna Froman Hetzler, was an instructor in the music conservatory at Christian College in Columbia and Jane enrolled there. But music was not her main interest at the time. She graduated from Christian College in 1926 and went to the University of Missouri to study journalism.

Jane Froman first saw her name in lights in 1927 when she had the lead in the annual journalism school review, called "Bag Daddies." A scout saw her and offered her a contract to appear Christmas week at the Grand Central Theatre in St. Louis. They called her the "Blues-Singing Coed from Missouri University," and gave her a dressing room with a child dancer who later gained fame, as would Jane, in World War II. Jane's dressing room partner was Betty Grable. From there it was on to Cincinnati to study music.

One night she went to a party in Cincinnati and wound up at the piano entertaining other guests. She sang the "St. Louis Blues," and had just started her next number when Powell Crosley offered her a job on his radio station, one of the best in the country—WLW. She did as many as twenty-two shows a week for Crosley and began to attract national attention.

Crosley contacted NBC. Would they be interested in her? They were. But the day after Paul Whiteman wired her to rush to Chicago for an audition, Jane came down with tonsilitis. The tonsils were removed. The doctor said she couldn't sing for a year. But she thought otherwise and went to Chicago. As she left the train, she slipped on some ice, fell and broke her ankle. She persuaded the taxi driver to half-carry her to the studios where she sang, signed the contract, fainted, and spent the next month in the hospital. But after six months with NBC Jane Froman had her own show.

Nightclub appearances continued to build her popularity. She sang five times for President Roosevelt, who liked to hear her sing "It Ain't Necessarily So." By 1940 Jane was in a Broadway play, "Keep Off the Grass," with Jimmy Durante and Ray Bolger. A year later she appeared in "Laugh Clown Laugh," with Ed Wynn.

In 1941 the Japanese attacked Pearl Harbor and within months Jane Froman became the first entertainer to agree to go overseas with USO troupes. She had performed earlier for the servicemen, appearing at what might have been the first of the camp shows, at Camp Meade and Fort Belvoir. Early in 1943, Jane Froman and a troupe of performers were in a plane headed for Europe. The plane crashed into the Tegus River near Lisbon. Jane should have been killed, but she and another performer, Tamara Swan, changed seats. Tamara Swan died in the crash. Surrounded by darkness and icy cold water, in shock and great pain, Jane Froman groped toward a voice she heard swearing continuously and loudly. For the next 45 minutes she and co-pilot John Burn carried on a casual conversation until they were picked up.

Jane was badly hurt with a compound fracture of the right leg just above the ankle. Her left leg was nearly severed below the knee; her ribs were broken and she had multiple fractures of the right arm. She would undergo 25 operations to keep from losing her leg. Bone grafts, therapy, and surgery brought hospital bills of $350,000.

Doctors told her work would be the best therapy. Jane went back on stage. She wore long skirts and dresses with long sleeves to hide the scars, braces and bandages. She devised an electric piano to which she chained herself so she and the piano would move together. Nightclubs paid well and she needed the money to pay her bills. Congress finally appropriated $200,000 to pay some of them. She was named to the Philco Radio Hall of Fame in 1944, known as the "Soldier in Grease Paint."

By the end of the war she had recovered enough to go back to Europe, entertaining the troops left behind. She was there for 3½ months until a dislocated bone put her back in the hospital for surgery. She almost died, from shock after surgery. By that time she had divorced her first husband and married John Burn, the copilot of the plane that crashed in Lisbon.

These were the early days of television, and Jane Froman was hostess or guest on several shows. In 1952 she was given her own show, *Jane Froman's USA Canteen*. Her version of "You'll Never Walk Alone" was the first song to become a nationwide hit because of its play on television. In 1952 Susan Hayward starred in a biographical movie about Jane Froman. Jane sang while Susan Hayward mouthed the words on film.

Jane Froman retired from her stage career in 1961. In 1962 she married Columbia newspaperman Rowland Smith and moved to Columbia. She painted, did needlework and worked with civic and theatre groups. She died in April, 1980. She was 72.

Jane Froman stands as a woman who showed that talent and courage often must go hand-in-hand, a woman whose determination brought her back to stardom after a terrible airplane crash on this date, the 22nd of February, in 1943.

****

FEBRUARY 23
THE COLLEGE OF COLLEGE MOUND

The members of the Cumberland Presbytery knew they wanted to found a college when they met at Huntsville on March 8, 1852. They wanted it to be a special school, but not just for Presbyterians and not just for future Presbyterian ministers. The discussion went on at length before it was agreed the school would be co-educational. It would be a unique school despite a brief life. And from its ashes would come another distinguished school still with us.

McGee College came first, then the town of College Mound, in southern Macon county. The town was named for the college and the Indian burial mounds in the area. Professor J. W. Blewett opened McGee College in 1852, operating it under the sponsorship of the Cumberland Presbytery. The college was to be free of "offending sectarianism," and Blewett was to make sure no one was turned away on religious grounds. Cumberland Presbytery historian Milton L. Baughn has written that "the most immediate and paramount purpose of Cumberland Presbyterians in their educational work was to provide literary and theological training for prospective ministers. Denominational interest was broader than the need for an educated ministry; an educated laity was needed as well."

McGee College was part of a national trend in which the religious denominations led the way in higher education, secular and otherwise. Baughn cites figures showing 152 of the 182 "permanent" colleges established in the United States before the Civil War were founded by religious denominations.

One could study to become a minister of any denomination at McGee. The only charge for ministerial students was for the English or classical courses at two dollars per session. Students preparing for Cumberland Presbyterian ministry were furnished, at no charge, rooms and coal stoves.

The Reverend J. B. Mitchell succeeded Blewett in 1853 and expanded the curriculum until it included modern and medieval history, literature, mathematics, physics, political and moral philosophy, rhetoric, Latin, Greek and various other courses in religion and theology. The quality of education offered seems consistent with the statement of the 1855 Presbyterian General Assembly which said, "Education is pre-eminently the handmaid of religion. No church can accomplish the ends of its creation without the correlative influence of education."

The first graduate of McGee College received his degree in 1857. The next year there were eight graduates. Enrollment reached 216 by the 1859-60 school year, 70 students more than at the State University in Columbia. In 1859 the main building which housed the library and science laboratory burned down. Classes were held in temporary quarters until a new $43,000 building was opened.

The Civil War forced the school to close not long after that. It reopened in 1866 and quickly regained its popularity. By the 1869-70 school year it was one faculty member and 22 students larger than the University of Missouri. The next year was its best when it counted a dozen faculty members and 280 students. But the school was in financial trouble. Debts continued to pile up. The school lacked an endowment to fall back on and in 1874, McGee College had to close.

Later that year delegates representing the various synods of the Cumberland Presbytery met in Sarcoxie to plan a new college, one with a proper endowment and a stronger financial footing. Two cities put in bids. Sedalia offered land and money, but Marshall, with a pledge of $138,000 worth of land, endowment and building funds, won the contest. One of those pushing hardest for Marshall was Erasmus Darwin Pearson, one of the trustees of McGee College. He noted that the famous Arrow Rock doctor, John Sappington, had established an educational trust fund to help Saline County students go to college. Pearson argued that the fund would almost guarantee students from the area. But it took 15 years to build the solid finances needed before the new college could be opened.

On September 17, 1889, the new school opened in Marshall with 92 students. By the end of its first year the school which became

Missouri Valley College had 153 students. In 1892 that number had reached 270.

"The God of Nature is the author of Revelation," the Presbyterian General Assembly said in 1855. "Education is the talisman which unfolds the treasures, the mysteries and the beauties of one, and of the other: of Revelation no less than of...Nature." Through the years education has remained that "talisman." Today, a fine Missouri college traces its lineage back to an earlier institution which sought to unfold those treasures, mysteries, and beauties. McGee College, incorporated on this date, February 23rd, in 1853.

****

FEBRUARY 24
THE BORDER WAR

The Missouri Compromise, which let this state into the Union in 1821 as a possible slave state and let Maine into the Union as a free state, would cause trouble for decades. It would be forty years before a compromise was no longer possible and there would be civil war. It has been said Missourians would go a long way to get into a fight. In the 1850s we didn't have to go very far at all—just to Kansas.

It began with the Kansas-Nebraska act which some saw as a welcome chance to give Missouri a slave-holding western neighbor. Senator Stephen A. Douglas of Illinois had proposed the bill in 1854 calling for the establishment of two new territories west of Missouri and Iowa. He suggested those two states decide for themselves whether they would allow slaves. The assumption was that Nebraska, which would receive an influx of emigrants from Iowa, would stay free. Kansas, because of its nearness to slave-holding Missouri, would go to the pro-slavery forces and keep the precarious political balance between the free and slave states. But it didn't work out that way, despite the best efforts of many Missourians.

Missouri's slave owners intended to push slavery westward, but they were blocked by the sudden anti-slavery movement which developed in Kansas as Northern abolitionists poured men and money into the state in an effort to hold it as a free state. In 1855 the first territorial legislature election was held in Kansas and Missourians flocked across the border to cast pro-slavery votes. At that time

Kansas had about 2,900 legal voters. But more than 6,300 votes were cast, many of them by Missourians. A newspaper of the day told how the Missourians came into the polling places armed with rifles, revolvers and Bowie knives. They didn't use them, however. Nobody wanted to force the issue with such determined voters. That fall, Kansas had a pro-slavery legislature and a pro-slavery congressional delegate. The Governor was anti-slavery, but the pro-slavery legislature kicked him out.

The next year anti-slavery forces began to grow and formed their own government. Things began to change. The pro-slavery forces continued to try to intimidate Kansans. Missourians, of course, played a great role in that intimidation attempt. These men earned the nickname "border ruffians," as they tried to stop the emigration of northern abolitionists into the state.

Once they stopped a riverboat at Lexington, Missouri, and removed rifles intended for anti-slavery forces. In December of 1855, a group of Missourians attacked the United States Arsenal at Liberty, Missouri, and removed its arms and ammunition. The incident caused less trouble than it might have caused. The federal army demanded the weapons be returned and they were. In 1855 and '56 the border war flared to full intensity. A large band of Missourians raided Lawrence, attacking the hotel, the printing offices and several private homes. John Brown, who would later become a martyr for the abolitionist cause, was determined to gain revenge. He led a raid across the border and hacked five men to death with an axe. When the Westport Sharpshooters were assembled to capture Brown, he captured them. But Missourians got their revenge when they set the match to Brown's headquarters, burning the entire town of Osawatomie, Kansas.

The raid led by John Brown, a year before his abortive attempt at Harpers Ferry, Virginia, prompted the Missouri government to try to end things. The legislature passed a law in 1859 appropriating $30,000 to establish a military force to protect the western border of Missouri. The force had as its aim not only keeping marauding Jayhawkers out, but keeping Missouri's border ruffians in. A year later an outbreak of border trouble prompted another callup of the militia. But it would take the Civil War to bring the border war to its bitter and violent climax.

The Missouri-Kansas Border War settled nothing. Many people were forced to leave their homes on both sides of the border. It provided a chance for a few people to gain some authority politically and materially. It was an indication of things to come when guerrillas would go on rampages in Missouri and Kansas during the Civil War.

But the end of the first stage of the Missouri-Kansas Border War began when the legislature passed a bill setting up that border-guarding military operation on this date, February 24, 1859.

****

FEBRUARY 25
THE CHURCH OF GEORG WALL

As a student of the Missionary Society in Basel, Switzerland, he had intended to go to Southern Russia to preach. But Czar Nicholas abolished the church's missions and decreed that the only churches to be allowed were Greek Catholic churches. So when the call went out from the American west for a young man to come to this country and minister to the large number of German emigrants who were flowing into Middle America, Georg Wendelin Wall answered. He and Joseph Reiger came to this country in 1836 on the basis of a request from church officials in Hartford, Connecticut. Wall's first church, when he arrived in St. Louis, was the German Protestant Evangelical Church of the Holy Ghost, a small congregation meeting in a building loaned by the Methodist and Presbyterian churches.

Wall soon started a campaign to raise money for the group's own church building, one that would be forty-two by sixty feet and cost $8,000 to build. There was opposition to the building from other Germans, but in 1840 the first German Protestant Church in St. Louis was constructed, four years after Wall had arrived. About 500 persons attended the communion service on the first Sunday in the new church.

By then there were three other graduates of the Basel Academy in St. Louis: Reiger, Johan Jacob Riess, and Johannes Gerber. They noted that the steadily increasing German population was fragmenting into a series of small German churches. Wall and his companions were distressed at the growing sectarianism they saw and felt the need for unity.

St. Louis had a population of 16,419 in 1840. By 1850 the population was almost 78,000. Of that number more than 22,000 were Germans. Many of the German settlers were independent, refusing to call themselves either Lutheran or Reformed. A migration of Saxon Lutherans about this time took dead aim at the suggestions for a unified church. They told Wall they considered it a "sin to serve a united church, since, according to their opinion, the Reformed are the children of Satan."

The brethren invited their fellow German Evangelical clergymen to a meeting in October of 1840 at the Gravois settlement, where Louis Edward Nollau was serving. Six men came to the conference. On the second day of their meeting, October 15, 1840, they laid the foundation for a United Church, the German Evangelical Church of the West. It later became known as the German Evangelical Synod of America. That night Well went back to St. Louis, the only Evangelical clergyman in the entire city. He was strengthened now by an organization, small though it might be, to deal with an area his countrymen in the East referred to as the "German Cemetery."

But the new organization was attacked by many as a "priestly conspiracy," and those in it were subjected to some fierce verbal abuse by their critics. Wall finally resigned as pastor of the German Protestant Evangelical Church of the Holy Ghost and founded his own church in St. Louis County in 1843. It was to become a bulwark of the new association. In 1850 the organization was strong enough to set up a seminary for teachers and preachers of the German Evangelical Church at Marthasville, in Warren County.

Wall went to Germany in 1852 to attend the Fifth Evangelical Church Diet at Bremen and seek support for the seminary. He received two thousand books. He also got into trouble with the King when he asked to solicit an offering from German churches. The German Counsel at St. Louis had reported the seminary was a disreputable, backwoods school run by men of questionable character. But Wall continued his efforts in Germany, built confidence in the institution, and eventually gained support for it.

The church continued to grow. It had a missionary society among its own members and received a graduate of the Basel Mission House to start a mission among the Indians. The Reverend Wall would live to see the church he founded become the German Evangelical Synod of the West. A decade after his death in 1867, it became the German Evangelical Synod of North America. In later years the term "German" would be dropped and the church would merge with the Reformed Church of the United States, creating the Evangelical and Reformed Church. In 1957, ninety years after Wall's death, the Evangelical and Reformed Church merged with the Congregational Christian Church and became the United Church of Christ.

It takes some unscrambling, but somewhere back through the mergers and name changes and the addition and subtraction of words is the German Evangelical Church of the West, founded in Missouri by a German emigrant who came to minister to other German emigrants, Georg Wendelin Wall, born on February 25th, in 1811.

****

FEBRUARY 26
THE SHOEMAKER GOVERNOR

In the space of one year, shortly after Missouri became a state, it had three different Governors.

Missouri's second Governor, Frederick Bates, caught pleurisy in the summer of 1825 and died in August. The state constitution provided that the Lieutenant Governor would step into the vacated office. But our Lieutenant Governor, Benjamin Reeves, had resigned a few months earlier to become a commissioner to survey the new federal road from Fort Osage to Santa Fe. Next in line was President pro tem, Abraham J. Williams, the presiding officer of the state Senate.

Williams' career as Governor turned out to be less distinguished than his careers leading to the office and the years afterward. Williams was born in what is now West Virginia. He had a birth defect, one leg was missing. He came to Missouri sometime between 1816 and 1820 and lived in old Franklin, opposite Boonville, for a short time. He moved to Boone County not long afterwards and established a tobacco warehouse at Nashville, in the southern part of the county, near the Missouri River. Later when he went to Columbia, he expanded his operations, put up the first storehouse in that city, became a manufacturer-dealer in tobacco products, sold dry goods and, tradition says, made boots and shoes.

When the county was organized that same year, Williams became its first state Senator. During his second term, Governor Bates died and Williams became the third Governor of Missouri. No regular legislative session was held during his short term of office. He did appoint a Supreme Court Judge and under constitutional requirement called an election for December of 1825 to pick a successor to Bates.

He set that election date reluctantly, telling the legislature, "Knowing the embarrassed condition of the treasury, at the first view of the subject, I felt much disposed to postpone the election until the next biennial election for senators and representatives." But, Williams said, "another consideration of more equal importance to the government induced an entire abandonment of that position. The state would have been left without any person vested with the powers of government, as my term as senator will expire on the first Monday in August next, and the present Speaker of the House of Representatives will be out of office on the same day."

Williams went back to the Senate where he had been Chairman of the Committee on Accounts and of the Committee on Education. He was a member of the committee recommending plans for a new capitol building. In those days the legislature was still meeting in St. Charles and the new building would be the first Capitol in Jefferson City.

A few years later Williams tried for re-election but lost to Richard Gentry, one of Columbia's founders. In 1832 he tried for U.S. Senator, finishing a distant second to Thomas Hart Benton, who by then already was a political institution in the state. Williams died seven years later at his home in Columbia and is buried there.

Tradition tells us Abraham Williams, Missouri's third Governor, was tall and slender and used a crutch because of his missing leg. He was not a good public speaker, although he was respected for his thinking, as witnessed by his memberships on important Senate committees and his membership on the committee to plan a new Capitol. His elevation to President pro tem of the state Senate is another tribute to his effectiveness in the legislature.

Williams was not highly educated. Few men were in those times. But he was educated enough to run a successful business and amass something of a fortune. Williams was President of the Boone County Agricultural Society which in 1835 held the first county fair west of the Mississippi. He never married.

When you look up the records of Missouri Governors, you will probably notice that Williams is not pictured anywhere. As far as we know, no one ever photographed or painted a portrait of Missouri's third Governor. Abraham J. Williams, our one-legged, bachelor, shoemaker Governor, was born on this date, February 26, 1781.

****

FEBRUARY 27
ROADS OF WOOD

As we drive down our fine highways today, it is difficult to understand the thinking of some of our forefathers in the 1840s and '50s who were saying that gravel and paved roads were inadequate. Some thought the best thing you could build roads of was wood. The idea wasn't bad. But the execution was impossible. The rough wooden roads were called "corduroy roads" for obvious reasons. It was a noble experiment in Missouri which failed miserably. But the wooden roads were the first major attempt at highway improvements in this state.

The idea of building wooden roads was logical one hundred and twenty years ago. After all, Missouri had a lot of trees and people built everything from them—fences, homes, stores, offices, bridges, sidewalks. So why not roads? Plank roads were thought to be cheaper and better adapted to the timber areas than gravel and macadamized roads. Certainly they would be an improvement over the roads of the day which weren't much more than dirt trails. If a man traveled on a plank road in wet weather, he wouldn't get stuck in the mud. So on paper the roads made of wooden planks seemed practical. But we have none today.

The legislature adopted a plank roads law allowing the formation of corporations to build and operate the roads. The roads were to start at the Mississippi and Missouri Rivers and work inland, opening up inner Missouri to settlement. The only one of the roads which didn't have that concept was one from Versailles, in Central Missouri, to the Pacific Railroad, then working its way along the Missouri River toward Jefferson City. The idea of the plank roads was greeted with enthusiasm throughout the state. Forty-nine corporations filed to build those roads. The most ambitious one was designed to connect Glasgow and St. Charles, a distance of 150 miles. It was never built. The shortest road was planned to be only one and three-quarters miles long. The law required the roads to be at least 50 feet wide with the wooden part to be eight to 12 feet wide. The rest would be dirt, gravel, macadam or some other substance. Seventeen roads were actually built but most went out of business in 20 years. The freezing and thawing of winter played havoc with the wood roads. Some simply sank into the mud. Others warped and rotted. Many just wore out when the wood didn't hold up under heavy traffic.

Perhaps the longest and most famous was the Ste. Genevieve, Iron Mountain and Pilot Knob Plank Road. It was 42 miles long and connected Ste. Genevieve and Iron Mountain by way of Farmington when it was completed in 1853. It had five toll gates. Only one of the roads was not a toll road. Tolls could be collected when a road was one-third finished. Most of the tolls were based on the means of transportation and the mileage to be traveled. Pedestrians, suckling cows and suckling horses, for example, could travel free. It was illegal to avoid a toll gate. A tollkeeper could detain a traveler until the toll was paid, although there was a penalty if the tollkeeper held the traveler longer than necessary.

But operating costs for the roads quickly outdistanced revenue. The Glasgow and Huntsville Road, which went by way of Roanoke, lasted eight years before the directors declared the situation hopeless. The cost of producing enough wooden planks was monumental. The Glasgow *Times* reported in 1852, when the road was started, that the contractor brought in three steam sawmills and employed one hundred men chopping, sawing and grading. The Hannibal, Ralls County and Paris Plank Road Company faced a lawsuit from its contractor who said it cost $2,300 a mile to build. But the road wasn't up to specs so the court ruled against the contractor.

The Cape Girardeau Plank Road Company was authorized to build a road from Cape Girardeau to Dallas, now Marble Hill, by way of Jackson, and on to Mine LaMotte. But the heavy traffic of the Civil War ruined the road. The old Providence Plank Road connecting Columbia with the Boone County river community of Providence opened in July of 1855 with a big ceremony but failed just two years later. The road cost $30,000 to build but was sold later for $8,700. The new owners cut their tolls in half, but couldn't save it. Finally the road was sold and the owners gave up their right to it in March of 1866. By the time the Providence Plank Road went under, the legislature had approved the gravel roads, some say at the request of the bankrupt corduroy road operators.

Today some of the old plank road routes are covered by modern highways. Part of 54 between Louisiana and Bowling Green covers an old plank road. So does part of 61 from Cape Girardeau to Marble Hill and parts of Highways 5 and 20 between Glasgow and Huntsville. Even Highway 40 followed the path of a plank road between St. Louis and St. Charles years after the planks failed.

Now only weeds grow where most of Missouri's first paved highways were laid. Occasionally you hear of a Boy Scout troop taking a hike along the route of the old roads. But today we travel on the successors to those old wooden roads, our state's first major highway improvements, authorized by the legislature on this date, February 27, 1851.

****

FEBRUARY 28
THE BATTLE OF SACRAMENTO PASS

In 1847 a small army of Missourians struggled toward the city of Chihuahua, Mexico, through deserts of blowing sand. There was little water. The horses died. The men suffered. They were Doniphan's First Missouri Volunteers who filled the pages of history with their battles and played a major role in the Mexican War.

When the Mexican War broke out, Governor Edwards called for Missouri volunteers to help other American forces take Santa Fe. About 1,200 Missourians volunteered and marched with General Stephen Kearney. They captured Santa Fe without firing a shot. The Missourians then elected Colonel Alexander Doniphan their commander.

It was a remarkable group of men from Missouri. They had gathered at Fort Leavenworth where Kearney tried to whip them into an organized fighting unit in three weeks, then they rode and marched south. There was no supply line. For months at a time they operated with no word from their government. They had to rely on the last orders they had been given weeks before. Most of them ran out of money buying food along the way. They didn't receive a single cent in pay during their service.

But they could fight. The Mexicans, big on flashy uniforms and showy tactics, thought the Missourians were a rag-tag army. A young observer wrote of them later, after seeing them in New Orleans, "The greatest attraction in the city at present is Colonel Doniphan and his regiment of Missouri Volunteers, who are called 'Lions' here, but in my opinion they look more like Rocky Mountain Bears than any sort of 'Lions' that I have ever seen. Col. Doniphan looks like a 'host' himself. He is six feet four inches high—weighs about two hundred and forty to sixty pounds—raw boned—has fingers about nine inches long—feet in proportion—his hair is sort of sandy red and sticks out something like Porcupine quills and his men say that he is not afraid of the Devil or the God that made him. His men, a great many of them, look more like giants than men, being from six feet to six feet four inches and a half in height. If you can imagine a man about six feet two to four and a half inches high, well proportioned, with a deer skin (hair on) hunting shirt and pantaloons, the seams fringed with the same material cut into strings and a bear skin stretched over his face with nothing but eyeholes cut in it, you can see a large proportion of Doniphan's regiment."

These, then, were the men who moved toward Chihuahua. Fifteen miles from that city the Mexicans planned to stop them. Sacramento Pass stood in the way, guarded by 4,000 Mexican troops. The Mexicans were confident they could easily defeat the Missourians, who were now weary of battle and the 235 miles of hard marching across the desert. In the city of Chihuahua, citizens were making handcuffs and leg-irons for the Missouri soldiers. Mexicans at Sacramento are said to have had a thousand lengths of rope with which to lead the captured Missourians back to Chihuahua.

Doniphan told his men they faced only two possibilities: victory, or another Alamo. He formed his units into four columns 30 paces apart. Two artillery battalions were placed at the front, and the Missourians began to march toward the entrenched Mexicans. The gap between the two armies narrowed from three miles to a mile and a half before Doniphan, with a sudden gesture, ordered the troops to make a flanking attack which seized the Mexican position on nearby high ground.

That was the cue for the artillery duel to begin. Doniphan ordered his men to stay scattered so they could warn each other of approaching cannon fire. Sometimes they simply jumped over the rolling Mexican cannonballs!

Then came a charge by 1,200 Mexicans. The Missourians waited until the Mexicans came close enough and then cut the charging troops to ribbons with accurate fire. They followed that up with a surprise charge of their own. Eight hundred Missourians rushed 4,000 Mexicans, breached the middle of the Mexican lines, and turned the charge into a retreat. Alexander Doniphan and his Missourians carried the day in the Battle of Sacramento Pass. The city of Chihuahua fell and Central Mexico was open for American occupation during the war.

It was a disaster for Mexico. The Mexican troops had been so confident that spectators from the town went to the pass to watch the defeat and capture the Missourians. But now the Mexican army was scattered, 304 dead and another 300 wounded. Forty Mexicans had been taken prisoner. Doniphan's casualties were two dead and seven wounded.

A Mexican priest later told Doniphan the troops from Chihuahua would have won the fight if the Missourians fought like men. Instead, said the priest, the Missourians fought like devils.

The Governor's Palace became Doniphan's headquarters and the First Missouri Volunteers savored their victory, a turning point in the Mexican War. Missourians marched into history at the Battle of Sacramento Pass on this date, the 28th of February, 1847.

****

FEBRUARY 29
JAMES CRAIG, GENERAL, LAWYER, RAILROAD BUILDER

James Craig was a military man of importance during the Civil War, but he never gained the fame of more flamboyant contemporaries. His greatest accomplishments were keeping communications lines open to the far West, and quelling guerrilla activity in Northwest Missouri. A Northwest Missouri town bears the name "Craig," not because he saved it from destruction during the war, but because he helped establish the railroad which created the town.

General James Craig, born in Pennsylvania and brought up in Ohio, was a practicing lawyer when he moved to Oregon, Missouri, in 1843 and put out his shingle. He wasted no time establishing himself and was elected a state representative from Holt County two years later. Craig raised a company of men for the Mexican War in 1847 but the group was too late to go to Mexico. They wound up chasing Indians and protecting wagon trains along the Overland Trail through Nebraska. At war's end Craig left the service and went to California. There, in the gold fields, he made several thousand dollars and came back to Missouri to practice law again, this time in St. Joseph. He became district attorney, served another term in the Missouri House, then two terms in Congress.

When the Civil War began, Craig's part of the state was a tough area. It was predominantly southern in sympathy but he became a Union Army officer. He was stationed in the Nebraska Territory to keep the mail route and telegraph lines open to the West. He had few men. The Indians stirred up trouble and the mail route shifted 100 miles farther south, further thinning his already small army. He repeatedly asked for more men to meet the Indian menace and protect communications and travelers but got little help. Craig believed the Confederacy was working with the Indians, but his force was too small to do anything about it.

In September of 1862, Major General Samuel Curtis was assigned to the newly-created Department of the Missouri. Soon after, the War Department tried to cut his force of 714 men to one-third that size. He protested loudly and won his point. Curtis later refused a request by Craig to mount an offensive against the Indians, reminding Craig that his job was to keep the overland mail routes going while the South was being subdued.

Craig wanted to be transferred to the eastern theatre, but Curtis refused to give him that transfer. Craig, tired of the Army's attitude, resigned from the service.

He did not, however, find peace at home. A year after quitting the Army, he was asked by Governor Willard Hall to become Brigadier General of the Missouri Militia. He accepted and was given command of a militia district stationed in St. Joseph. His militia had as its main duty the suppression of guerrilla activity and raids by Jayhawkers from Kansas. In an effort to soothe some of the southern sympathies in the area, Governor Gamble ordered disloyal men and returned Confederate soldiers to enroll in the militia, under bond, as a way to keep the peace. This unit became known as the Paw Paw Militia. It did fairly well at keeping out Jayhawkers but was less than enthusiastic about putting down guerrilla activity.

When Price moved into Missouri in 1864, Craig was given the tough job of controlling guerrilla bands Price sent out to distract Union forces. After the Battle of Westport the military situation quieted down. But Craig was determined to rid the state of the notorious Bloody Bill Anderson. He ordered Colonel S. P. Cox to track him down. Cox did and Anderson was killed. His guerrilla band, which included young Jesse James, was scattered. Craig then became a victim of generals operating independently of one another—sent on a mission by one, he would be ordered back to St. Joseph by another.

Finally the war ended and Craig left the service. He returned to his law practice and became a railroad builder. He was the President of the Hannibal and St. Joseph Railroad, later City Comptroller in St. Joseph. He died at the age of 71. He never sought honors, not even a military pension. Perhaps it is because he was a man who sought to serve, not to gain honor, that James Craig is not remembered as well as his more politically-oriented military contemporaries. General James Craig was born on this date, February 29th, in 1817.

Jennie
Lind
Concert
March 18,
1851

MARCH

MARCH 1
CENTRAL METHODIST

Once upon a time it was said that God would never cross the Mississippi River. But by the time Missouri came to be a state, that was obviously no longer true. God had moved west of the Mississippi and his agents had established colleges, congregations and churches. The Catholics came first. Historians tell us the Baptists and Methodists sent the first Protestant missionaries to Missouri.

Each denomination set up its own institution of higher learning, and in those days it didn't have to be too high. For a time those schools were the largest institutions in the state. The Methodists had one such institution. It was Howard High School in Fayette, which had a popularity statewide, that was perhaps greater than any other school of its time outside of St. Louis.

Its roots stretched back to the mid 1820s when Fayette Academy was opened to teach the three R's plus surveying, navigation, philosophy, chemistry, Latin and Greek with "special attention [to] the instruction of young ladies in the higher branches of female education."

In 1835, Howard College was incorporated with both male and female departments. Fire destroyed the school's building in 1838, badly damaging Fayette's hopes for being the site of the proposed state university. Classes at Howard College soon resumed, but it lasted only a few more years before its debts overwhelmed it and the property was sold in 1844.

That same year, the Reverend William T. Lucky established the Howard High School, using a part of the vacated and still incomplete college structure. His first class contained six boys. But a year later it was a coeducational institution and by 1850 room facilities in Fayette were so overloaded that students were quartered throughout the county.

Lucky started using the name "Howard High School" soon after he put the institution together. In September of 1845 the school came under the control of the Missouri Annual Conference of the Methodist Episcopal Church, South. The building was deeded to the church two years later, and it was then that the school formally became known as Howard High School. The school year of 1851-52 showed 338 students enrolled, 172 boys and 166 girls. Fayette at the time was a town of only 700 residents.

In 1852 Nathan Scarritt of Kansas City, wrote in the St. Louis *Christian Advocate:*

"Would it not be well for the two conferences, viz.: Missouri and St. Louis, to settle that they will have but one Methodist College or university, within their bounds?... Let our motto be, One Methodist College in Missouri, and Only One. This policy being settled, let a joint commission from the two conferences determine the location of said college or university at such place as they shall determine best for the interests of the whole state at large...."

A year later the Methodists decided to go ahead with a church-supported college, just one, "of the highest grade" in Missouri. Fayette, with Howard High School, entered the competition to be the location. St. Charles challenged but Fayette won.

Then, in late January of 1854, Howard High School burned. The trustees gave the site to the college's curators with the provision that the church come up with $5,000 to build a new high school at a different location. The new college building was completed in 1857. The male department was known as "Central College," and it had about a half-dozen more students than the University in Columbia. The female department was incorporated as Howard Payne College.

Like other institutions, Central had a hard time during the Civil War. Its buildings were used for hospitals, barracks and stables. it wasn't until 1871 that classes resumed.

As the school's 100th birthday neared, a change of name was discussed. "Central College" was an undistinguished name, so undistinguished that the post office had trouble remembering where it was. Mail frequently went to Central Missouri State in Warrensburg. In June of 1961 the college adopted its present name—Central Methodist College. It now operates a 60-acre campus with about 20 major study fields. It is still the only Methodist-supported college in Missouri, a status it has held since it was incorporated on this date, the first of March in 1855.

****

MARCH 2
SCHURZ

Only two years after coming to Missouri, he was elected a Senator. He was a German, an impressive newspaperman and orator. A progressive, he three times broke with his political party over corruption, overseas expansion, civil service reform, inflation and other political exploitations. He constantly took stands against those who opposed the disadvantaged, the Indians, the slaves, and supporters of the Confederacy. He was Carl Schurz, one of this nation's leading nineteenth century progressive thinkers.

Historian Floyd Shoemaker wrote, "No man on Missouri soil (although some might except Captain Nathaniel Lyon) either of native or foreign birth, so quickly changed the course of the state's political annals as did this thirty-eight-year-old German."

Carl Schurz fled his home country during the Prussian Revolution. He was twenty-three when he came to America. He spent three years in Philadelphia learning English then moved to Wisconsin. There he ran for Lieutenant Governor and lost. He was chairman of the Wisconsin delegation at the 1860 Republican convention which nominated Lincoln. He favored Lincoln's rival, Seward, but Lincoln named him American minister to Spain anyway. Schurz served only a short time before coming back to this country to become an Army General. He was one of Meade's officers at Gettysburg. He was with Howard at Chancellorsville and with Sigel at Bull Run. When the war ended, he was marching with Sherman.

Schurz was thirty-eight when he came to Missouri as editor of the *Westliche Post,* a St. Louis German newspaper. He quickly rose to become a leader in the German populace and in the Republican party. It was Schurz who organized the first challenge to the Radical Republican leadership of Charles Drake. The year was 1869, just four years after the Radical constitution had gone into effect which severely restricted the rights of those who had sympathized with the Confederacy. When Senator John Henderson's seat became vacant, the odds-on favorite to be elected was former Congressman Benjamin F. Loan of St. Joseph. He was portrayed as a willing tool of Drake, by now also a U.S. Senator. But a small group of St. Louis residents, disenchanted with Drake's antics, urged Schurz to run.

Senators were picked by the legislature in those days. Drake came back to Missouri to meet the challenge. Schurz nailed him on his position on black suffrage, saying the Drake Constitution provided an easier method for enfranchisement of former rebels than for allowing the newly-freed blacks to vote. Drake denied it. But Schurz quoted remarks his opponent had made four years earlier. When Drake denied these too, Schurz presented him with a copy of the speech, pointing to page and paragraph. Humiliated, Drake left Jefferson City before the balloting which sent Schurz to Washington.

The next year, Schurz led his battle against the extremists in the Radical movement. The time had come, he maintained, that former rebels should regain the right to vote. The national emergency was over. For three days the Radicals and the Liberals battled in their convention in Jefferson City. Finally when the Radicals inserted into the state GOP platform a plank only vaguely acknowledging the possibility that former rebels might be given a chance to vote again, the Liberals bolted the convention. They nominated Banjamin Gratz Brown as their candidate for Governor. Brown won. Democrats in the state, repressed by the Radicals, rode piggy-back with the Schurz Liberals. The Drake Radicals were crushed, never to rise again.

But the Schurz Republican wing felt only a fleeting grasp of power. The national convention of 1872 was a disaster when Brown, by now feeling betrayed by Schurz, threw his support to Horace Greeley and Greeley was badly beaten in the election.

Schurz did not seek reelection in 1874. He backed Rutherford B. Hayes for President. From 1877 to 1881 he was the Secretary of the Interior under Hayes, trying to handle Indian problems with sense and dignity. He installed a merit system in his department long before it was required by law. It was under Carl Schurz that our system of national parks began.

Always a reformer, Carl Schurz headed the National Civil Service Reform League from 1892 to 1901. He died five years later in New York at the age of 77. Carl Schurz was born on this date, the 2nd of March, 1829.

****

MARCH 3
WILKINSON: TRAITOR, SPY, AND GOVERNOR

Missouri has had some chief executives of less than glittering quality. Some have been drunkards. Some have been carousers. Some have been incompetent. But none can match the record of our first Territorial Governor, James Wilkinson, who was at various times a spy for the Spanish government, and a high ranking officer in the United States Army. Historian Duane Meyer calls Wilkinson a grafter, conniver, and traitor.

Early in his career, Wilkinson was brevetted a Brigadier General in the Continental Army and fought under General Benedict Arnold— when Arnold was still a respected officer—as well as General George Washington. But he was forced to resign when he became involved in a conspiracy against Washington. Wilkinson then became Clothier General. He lost that job when it was found his accounts weren't quite proper.

He traveled west to Kentucky. Here the settlers were uneasy because the Spanish controlled the mouth of the Mississippi, hampering their access to eastern markets by water. Wilkinson went to Estaban Miro, the Spanish Governor in New Orleans, with two ideas. He suggested Spain use its navigational control to create a Spanish-loyal faction in Kentucky, leading eventually to a revolutionary movement which would separate Kentucky from the United States. He also suggested part of Kentucky could be depopulated. Liberalized Spanish immigration policies would encourage Americans to move to Missouri. Spain thought the first proposal too dangerous. But the second one was adopted and Wilkinson was granted an annual salary of $2,000 for promoting emigration away from Kentucky. Wilkinson swore allegiance to the Spanish crown and was named an agent. He became known as Spanish secret agent 13.

Aaron Burr was Vice-President under Jefferson. He and Wilkinson had known each other in the expedition against Quebec. Burr persuaded President Jefferson to name Wilkinson as the first Territorial Governor of what later was Missouri. Wilkinson moved to St. Louis.

Wilkinson didn't go over too well with several elements of St. Louis society. He drank excessively. He aroused the fur traders' ire by trying to muscle in on their business. He even sent a message to Spanish officials in Santa Fe suggesting they arrest Lewis and Clark if they got that far south!

In 1804, Burr hatched a plan to separate the lands west of the Appalachian Mountains from the United States. He left Washington at the end of his term in March of 1805 and went to St. Louis where he involved Wilkinson. Some think his visit was to be used not only to solicit support for his plan, but also to prepare the minds of the people for another change in government.

He and Wilkinson spent about two weeks together in St. Louis. They tried to get a number of prominent citizens interested. At least one, Rufus Easton, realized what was going on and refused to participate. Wilkinson then started circulating charges of official corruption against Easton and the President refused to reappoint Easton as Judge of Louisiana. Easton went to Washington and demanded an explanation. He told Jefferson about the meetings with Burr and Wilkinson. Jefferson made Easton a U.S. Attorney, then asked him to spy on Wilkinson.

A year later the Burr plot for western revolution broke into the open. Wilkinson, attempting to shift all the blame onto Burr, sent Jefferson a letter trying to remove guilt from himself. He eventually supplied the President with a coded letter Burr had sent to him, and even gave Jefferson the key to the code. But the letter said such things as "Wilkinson will be second to Burr only" and "Wilkinson shall dictate the rank and promotion of his officers." Wilkinson was removed from office two years to the day that he took over. His successor was a direct contrast—Meriwether Lewis. Wilkinson drifted into Mexico in later years and died in 1825. James Wilkinson, traitor, spy, and the first American Territorial Governor of Missouri, was booted out of office in 1807 two years to the day after he took it on this date, March 3, 1805.

****

MARCH 4
PRESIDENT FOR A DAY?

The calendar is a tricky thing sometimes.

Since the late 1840s historians have been quibbling over whether this country went one entire day without any leadership whatsoever, or whether a Missourian filled that gap and became the shortest-termed President in American history. Four years after that controversy this same man became Vice-President, but that's generally forgotten.

David Rice Atchison always said he slept through most of his term as President of the United States. The confusing series of circumstances leads many to wonder if he really missed anything.

David Rice Atchison, a Kentuckian by birth, came to Missouri in 1830 and took up a law practice in Liberty with Alexander Doniphan. Four years later he became a member of the legislature. In 1841 he became judge of the twelfth Judicial Circuit. When Senator Lewis Linn died two years after that, Atchison was named to fill the vacancy.

Atchison's fame as a one-day President often overshadows the regard with which he was held by his colleagues in the United States Senate. He served sixteen terms as President pro tem of that body, and was elected to the post unanimously fourteen straight times.

But at the critical moment of history, the question was not whether he was the presiding officer of the Senate, but whether he was a Senator at all, let alone a President.

At noon on Sunday, March 4, 1849, the terms of President James Knox Polk and Vice-President George Dallas expired. President Zachary Taylor was to succeed Polk, but Taylor refused to be sworn in on Sunday for religious reasons.

The Presidential Succession Act said that when there is no President or Vice-President, the job goes to the presiding officer in the Senate. That was Atchison.

Or was it?

Atchison's own term as Senator from Missouri had expired on March 3. He had been reelected but he didn't take the oath for that term until the fifth. So technically he wasn't really a Senator. And if he wasn't a Senator he could hardly be President. There are those, however, who note that a man holds public office until his successor is duly elected and qualified.

For those who say Atchison was the President, he served from the end of Polk's term until 11:30 the next day—twenty-three and one half hours in office before Taylor was sworn in. On the morning of March 5, Atchison signed two minor documents as acting President. The Congressional Record lists him as President that day. But Atchison never took the oath of office as President. Many years later, according to Atchison's biographer William Parrish, the Senator would recall there had been much joking by his colleagues who wanted cabinet appointments, even for just a day. Many more are said to have chided him about the policies of his administration.

The day was uneventful for this nation. In fact, Atchison told an interviewer years later, "I went to bed. There had been two or three busy nights finishing up the work of the Senate and I slept most of that Sunday."

The controversy hides the other high office Atchison filled. He served as Vice-President of the United States from April 18, 1853, until December 4, 1854. Odd circumstances figure in that story too. President Pierce's Vice-President, William R. King, died and Atchison, who was still pro tem, officially became Vice-President. The only formal record of his term in office is a single entry in the Senate Journal which provides for his salary.

Later there was drumbeating back home for Atchison to run for President, but the effort never materialized.

Was he the President of the United States for a day? Or did the United States of America once have absolutely no national leadership for an entire day? No President? No Vice-President? Almost no Congress?

You decide about the twenty-three and one half hours David Rice Atchison might have been President, a term which started at noon on this date, March 4, 1849.

****

MARCH 5
SINEWS OF PEACE

The man from England was concerned as he rode through downtown Jefferson City in a convertible. He couldn't get his cigar lighted in the wind and feared people would be disappointed if he didn't have his well-known trademark in evidence. In Fulton, where he had sugar-cured ham for dinner, he told the hostess that the "pig had reached its highest point of evolution in this ham." After lunch he went upstairs and took a nap. For many years after, a sign would hang over the bed reading, "Winnie Slept Here." Winnie, of course, was Winston Churchill.

Still later he spoke to a special convocation. His speech carried the formal title, "The Sinews of Peace," but it would become more popularly known for a phrase he used. He was there to tell the audience that the United States and Britain should make it clear through the United Nations that Russia was not to engage in a wholesale spread of Communism. He warned of the Cold War to come. The famous phrase came two-thirds of the way through the speech:

"From Stettin in the Baltic to Trieste in the Adriatic, an *iron curtain* has descended across the continent. Behind that line lie all the capitals of the ancient states of Central and Eastern Europe. Warsaw, Berlin, Prague, Vienna, Budapest, Belgrade, Bucharest and Sofia. All these famous cities and the populations around them lie in what I must call the Soviet sphere; and all are subject in one form or another not only to Soviet influence but to a very high and, in some cases, increasing measure of control from Moscow."

Later he would say the time had come for the free world to stand strong and united against Russia:

"What is needed is a settlement, and the longer this is delayed, the more difficult it will be and the greater our dangers will become. From what I have seen of our Russian friends and allies during the war, I am convinced there is nothing they admire so much as strength and there is nothing for which they have less respect than for weakness, especially military weakness."

He recalled, perhaps in hopes people might listen better this time than they had a decade before, that he had spoken in those days but had not been heard.

"Last time I saw it all coming and cried aloud to my own fellow countrymen and to the world, but no one paid any attention. Up till the year 1933 or even 1935, Germany might have been saved from the awful fate which has overtaken her and we might all have been spared the miseries Hitler let loose upon mankind."

At the end he called for support of the then still young United Nations as the best hope for world peace.

The podium was crowded with dignitaries, including President Truman who had been the key figure in bringing Churchill to Missouri. When the president of Westminster invited Churchill, Truman had written in hand at the bottom of the letter a brief note saying if Churchill accepted, Truman would introduce him.

In the audience that day was a boy who had been excused from school in St. Louis to attend the ceremonies. He had to go back and make a report on that talk. His name was Thomas Eagleton, later a U.S. Senator.

The phrase "Iron Curtain" gained great prominence after that day, but it wasn't the first time Churchill had spoken those words. He had used them previously in a speech in the House of Commons. It took the speech in Fulton, Missouri, however, to make the phrase world famous.

Today a graceful old English church stands on the campus of Westminster College. Brought to this country from England piece by piece, the bombed-out church hulk has been restored to dazzling beauty, honoring the speech and the man who made it on this date, March 5th, 1946.

****

MARCH 6
THE MISSOURIANS OF THE ALAMO

He slipped through the fortress walls about midnight and ran into the woods where he hid in a drainage ditch, escaping the enemy forces which had encircled the area for more than a week. He carried with him a final plea for help, a final plea for some kind of action. "Let the Convention go on and make a Declaration of Independence, and we will then understand and the world will understand, what we are fighting for," it said. But there were other messages, some hastily scrawled on small pieces of paper, some only trinkets that members of the garrison wanted relatives to have. For each of the men he left behind knew he was doomed. And so John Smith, a red-haired carpenter and engineer from Hannibal, Missouri, rode into the night seeking help for the men left at the Alamo. Three days later the garrison was wiped out to the man.

A Missourian was the last member of that garrison to leave alive. He left behind other Missourians in the mission-fortress-shrine—cradle of Texas liberty. John Smith went to Texas to collect a debt. He fell in love with the land and decided to stay. When he sent word to his wife to pack up and follow him, the stories of Indians and the rough territory were too much for her. She wrote back saying she was getting a divorce and staying in Missouri.

Smith recovered from this blow and prospered. He met and married a descendant of one of the Canary Island families Phillip the fifth had sent to colonize New Spain. He became one of the three richest men in San Antonio and the first mayor of the town. When the Texans seized the city in December, three months before Santa Anna and his troops launched their siege, John Smith, a civil engineer, provided the plans of the town which enabled the 300 Texans to push the 1,700 Spanish out.

Jacob Durst, who changed his name to Darst in Texas, had loaded his wife and two children on an oxcart and creaked away from his Missouri farm in August of 1830. Six months later he found Texas to be all the promoters said it was. He settled near Gonzalez, part of the colony of another Missourian, Green DeWitt, on a grant of twenty-four acres. His land became part of a prominent oil field a century later.

Darst was at Gonzalez in 1835 when the Mexicans demanded return of a ceremonial cannon they had left there. Darst was one of eighteen Texans who hid the cannon. On October 3, 1835, the Texans recovered the cannon. Near the present town of Cost, Texas, they caught up with the Mexicans and fired a load of scrap metal-shrapnel at them. The man who touched off what is now considered to be the first shot of the Texas revolution was Jacob Darst, a Missourian.

George Washington Cottle was a member of one of Missouri's pioneering families who settled mostly in Lincoln County before 1800. In the last part of the 1820s he and several other Cottles went to Texas. He too settled in the Gonzalez area and in later years a county in Texas would be named for him.

Twenty-two-year-old Private Daniel William Cloud left Kentucky to become a successful lawyer in St. Louis. But he found too many lawyers in a town of two thousand people. He wrote his mother from St. Louis on Christmas Day, 1835, that he was disappointed. The law profession wasn't good, and Missouri farmland wasn't what he expected. So he headed for Texas. Some say he joined Davy Crockett's Tennessee Mounted Volunteers on the way. He enlisted with the Texas Volunteers at Nacogdoches, though, and was sent to San Antonio on February 23, 1836.

The men of San Antonio took refuge in an old mission when the Mexicans moved back in force. The next day Smith and another man went to Gonzalez with a message asking for help. They found thirty-two volunteers there, including Darst, Cottle, twenty-seven-year-old Private George Tumlinson, a Missouri native, and others. Smith guided them 76 miles back to San Antonio where the siege was under way.

There were others of Missouri connection inside the crumbling walls of the old mission. Captain William Charles M. Baker was one. A native Missourian, he had been in Mississippi when the call to arms appeared in the newspapers in the fall of 1835.

Twenty-three-year-old George D. Butler, a private, had gone to Texas from New Orleans. So had Private Charles H. Clark, who was probably a member of the New Orleans Grays, the military unit which provided the only surviving garrison flag at the Alamo.

Jerry Day was there. He had settled near Gonzalez too. Twenty-seven-year-old Gordon Jennings, another private in the Texas Militia, was part of the garrison.

Two cousins were there—twenty-three-year-old Private Asa Walker and thirty-three-year-old Jacob Walker. They were relatives

143

of a Jackson County, Missouri, man who became one of the great pathfinders of the West, Joseph Reddeford Walker.

These were the men John Smith left behind that midnight of March 3. Only hours after he went for help, carrying that letter from Travis signed "God and Texas, Victory or Death," the Mexicans found the drainage ditch and sealed off the last escape route. About sunrise, three days later, the attack came. It lasted about an hour.

In the final frantic minutes in the mission, Jacob Walker battled his way to the chapel for the final siege. When the Mexicans found him he was trying to give one last message to Susanna Dickinson whose husband was part of the garrison. He pleaded for his life, but he was stabbed repeatedly with bayonets and Mrs. Dickinson would recall later that the Mexicans "tossed his body on the bayonets as a farmer would toss a bundle of hay." Jacob Walker might have been among the last of the Alamo soldiers to die. (Their bodies were thrown onto massive funeral pyres and the remains buried in several places. Many of those ashes were later reinterred in a cathedral a few blocks away.)

The men of the Alamo never knew it, but even as John Smith was galloping away, the Texas Congress passed the Declaration of Independence Travis had pleaded for on their behalf.

John Smith later fought at the battle of San Jacinto and in the Mexican War. He spied behind the lines in that war. He was a Senator from Bexar County in the Texas Congress. But when he died, this last man to leave the Alamo alive was buried in an unmarked grave at Washington on the Brazos, the first Capital of Texas.

Daniel Cloud, the disappointed would-be Missouri lawyer who died in that epic battle, wrote his mother from Texas, "If we succeed, a fertile region and a grateful people will be for us our home and secure to us our reward. If we fail, death in defense of so just and so good a cause need not excite a shudder or tear."

Today the dust of Missourians is mingled with the dust of Texans, at the San Antonio de Valero Mission, just as the historical heritage of Missouri is mingled with the historical heritage of Texas and so many other states. Missourians fought and died at the Alamo, and one survived to fight again. When you visit the Alamo and read the plaque on the chapel door which says, "Be silent, friend. Here heroes died to blaze a path for other men," remember the men from

Missouri who are part of the story of the Alamo, which fell on this date, March 6, 1836.

****

MARCH 7
CHAMP

He had come to the Presidential nominating convention as the leading candidate. The consensus was that when Tammany Hall threw New York's 90 votes into his column, he'd be nominated. he finally got Tammany Hall after ten ballots and that gave him a majority. But he needed two-thirds. He started to compose his telegram of acceptance. No candidate had failed since 1844 to win the two-thirds after gaining the simple majority.

But Champ Clark was in trouble.

His real name was James Beauchamp Clark. He was known as "Champ" not because he was a champion of anything in particular, but because his family had trouble agreeing on the pronunciation of his middle name. The old English ancestors pronounced it "Beecham"—but the Americans called it "Bow-champ." So he shortened it to Champ.

Clark had come from Kentucky. He was kicked out of what was then Kentucky University in his senior year for shooting at a man. Clark graduated from a college in West Virginia, then applied for a job, as a college president. He wrote, "I have just graduated from Bethany College, with highest honors; am 23 years old, over six feet high, weigh 170 pounds, unmarried, am a Kentuckian by birth, a Campbellite in religion, a Democrat in politics and a Master Mason." He became a college president at Marshall College, the first Normal School in West Virginia. A year later he went to Cincinnati Law School, then taught school in Pike County, Missouri, until he raised enough money to go into law practice.

Clark quickly moved into politics on the county level. Then he tried for the state legislature and lost. Ten years later he won, and then tried for Congress. He won the post in 1892 and lost in 1894 as political winds changed. But in 1896 he was elected again and would not be out of Congress from that day until his death 25 years later. In 1911 he was named Speaker of the House. The next year he decided to seek the Democratic nomination for President.

Clark had supported William Jennings Bryan the three times

Bryan tried to win the Presidency. So Bryan supported Clark although Bryan was worried because the Missourian hadn't taken any positions on major issues. On the night of June 27, 1912, the Democrats started formal nominations. When Clark's name was put into the field, the floor demonstration went on for an hour and five minutes. It was after 3:00 a.m. when the New Jersey delegation nominated a college president named Woodrow Wilson.

The first ballot wasn't taken until seven o'clock the morning of June twenty-eighth. Clark had 440½ and Wilson had 324. Other candidates trailed. Through eight more ballots both men gained on the rest of the field. Then the Tammany vote went to Clark and that triggered another hour of demonstrations. But the convention wouldn't be stampeded.

Rumors began to build that Clark had promised an alliance with Wall Street to get those 90 votes. Clark denied it. On the fourteenth ballot, Bryan's home state of Nebraska passed. When the count came back, Bryan announced he would withhold his vote from Clark until the New York delegation removed itself from the Clark column. Then Bryan voted for Wilson.

The balloting went on. And on.

On the thirtieth ballot, Wilson moved into the lead. It was now July first. On the forty-second ballot, the majority went to Wilson and Clark lost Illinois. It was early on the morning of July third when the forty-sixth ballot nominated the Princeton College president. For the first time in almost seven decades a candidate with the majority couldn't hold it in the Democratic National Convention.

Clark came back to Missouri, ran for Congress, and won. He finally lost in 1920. He was then 70 years old, but he would never know what it was like to be out of office. He died March 2, 1921, just a few days before his last term was to end.

Champ Clark served twenty-six years in Congress from Missouri. He was the first Missourian to serve as Speaker of the House, a position he held for eight years. James Beauchamp "Champ" Clark was born on this date, March 7, 1850.

****

MARCH 8
ALEXANDER BUCKNER, FORGOTTEN SENATOR

The name of David Barton, Missouri's first Senator, is overshadowed by the name of Thomas Hart Benton, our second Senator. But Barton's name is a household word compared to the number of people who have heard of the third man to serve in the United States Senate from Missouri. Buckner was a Southeast Missouri resident, a prominent lodge leader and lawyer who was chosen in a compromise move that actually kept a Governor from moving up to the U.S. Senate.

Alexander Buckner succeeded David Barton after Barton had a political falling-out with Thomas Hart Benton. The people did not directly elect a Senator in Missouri. The system worked much like the Electoral College of today. The people elected their state legislators. The legislature then elected the Senators. Candidates could tell what their chances were by the party makeup of the General Assembly.

Alexander Buckner had been born in Kentucky and moved to Indiana in 1812 when it was still Indiana Territory. When slavery was excluded in Indiana, Buckner left. He was a pro-slaver all his life. He returned to Kentucky briefly and then in 1818 he came to Missouri. He brought with him his mother and five sisters. They settled in Cape Girardeau County. Buckner wasted no time becoming involved in the politics of the area. Only a few months after he arrived in Missouri, Buckner was named the Circuit Attorney for the Cape Girardeau District.

He had been the first Grand Master of the Grand Lodge of Indiana Territory, and when he came to Missouri he organized the first Masonic Lodge in this territory. It was Unity Lodge, in Jackson, near Cape Girardeau.

He was involved in the push for statehood and when the convention was called to draft Missouri's first state constitution, Alexander Buckner was one of the forty-one distinguished men elected to write that historic document.

His political power continued to build and by the mid 1820s he had worked his way up to State Senator.

In the 1830s he was named to the Missouri House and colleagues immediately started campaigning for his election to the U.S. Senate as Barton's replacement. Barton and Benton, who had gotten along well early in their political careers, were now at each other's political throats. Benton had the upper hand. Barton knew he would be out at the end of his term.

Barton, politically astute enough to recognize he would not be re-elected, started considering someone who could replace him but not yield to the Benton faction. He chose Alexander Buckner. Six names went before the General Assembly. The Jackson men wanted Governor John Miller. But Barton still had enough strength to water down Miller's support. Buckner beat Miller 35-26 in the voting.

He went on to serve an undistinguished term. He favored extending the national road from Vandalia, Illinois, to Missouri. He wanted the swamps of Southeast Missouri improved and suggested government land grants be given for construction of a canal in that area. He believed Missouri's economic condition could be strengthened only if the national bank was re-chartered and the practice of banks issuing worthless paper money stopped.

In 1833, Missouri was hit with a cholera epidemic. Alexander Buckner was one of those who caught it. He died at the age of 48. His successor was Lewis Linn.

Alexander Buckner, Missouri's forgotten third senator, was born on this date, the eighth of March, in 1785.

****

MARCH 9
BUNK

Henry Ford, the great automobile maker, once said. "History is, more or less, bunk." The great philosopher Cicero wrote, "History is the witness that testifies to the passing of time. It illumines reality, vitalizes memory, provides guidance in daily life, and brings us tidings of antiquity." It is well that there is a dedicated group of people who are more inclined to agree with Cicero than with Ford. Without them, Missouri's heritage would be virtually unknown.

In the late 1890s, the Missouri Press Association was still young. This organization of newspapermen held its fifth winter convention at the Coates House in Kansas City in January, 1898. It was during that meeting that the publisher of the Shelbina *Democrat,* W. O. L. Jewett, proposed that the president of the press group name a five-member committee to draw up plans for a state historical society.

President George Trigg, the editor of the Richmond *Conservator,* set up the committee and named Columbia publisher E. W. Stephens as its chairman. The association also decided at that meeting that the headquarters should be in Columbia.

By May, when the annual press association meeting was held, Stephens could report the University had agreed to set aside a room for the society in Academic Hall, the building now known as Jesse Hall. The committee had also drawn up a constitution and bylaws which were accepted the next day. The society was in operation, but only as an unofficial group. For some time it had no money. The expenses were defrayed by the University and society members.

Secretary Isador Loeb circulated letters to Missouri newspaper publishers seeking contributions of historic material to the society library. The result was overwhelming. In 1899 the society was incorporated and the legislature approved a bill making it a trustee of the state. That gave the society the formal substance and identification it needed. In 1901 the society hired its first full-time paid employe, Minnie K. Ogan. Sedalia lawyer Francis Asbury became the first executive secretary. He had collected books and other materials on Missouri since the immediate post-Civil War days. When he became society head, he donated his collection of 1,886 books and more than 14,000 pamphlets to the society. Thus began the society library which now contains more books and pamphlets on Missouri than any other facility in the world.

A special display was set up for the 1904 Louisiana Purchase Exposition. It contained 764 newspapers published in the state for 1903, bound into 928 volumes. Also on display were more than 1,800 books by Missouri authors. The building later burned and only quick action by Walter Williams saved the collection.

In 1903 the society published its first work, an 85-page paperbound book about its annual meeting held that year. Three years later the first edition of the *Missouri Historical Review* came off the press. It is now, as it was then, a quarterly publication. When the first issue was published, the society had 70 annual paid members and 626 editorial writers. In eight years the number of annual members grew to 538 and the society credits the magazine for it.

In the middle of the century's second decade the society was one of the leaders in a movement to build a new library on the University of Missouri campus in Columbia. The society moved into the building when it was dedicated in 1916. It is still the society's home.

The publications program continued in 1920 with the first major work published, *Journal of the Missouri Constitutional Convention of 1875.* In 1921 the society started publishing the *Messages and Proclamations of the Governors of the State of Missouri.* In 1925 executive director Floyd Shoemaker began a series of newspaper articles called "This Week in Missouri History." He later would write that "no other service has done more to stimulate popular interest in Missouri history and to encourage the inclusion of local history in the press."

In 1931 Missouri became the first midwestern state to mark completely a modern cross-state highway with historical markers. It was Highway 36. The project was funded by society president George Mahan.

For almost a half-century Floyd Shoemaker headed the society. He started in 1915 at the salary of $700 a year, with another $300 from the University. He retired in 1960 carrying the well-earned title of "Mr. Missouri." When he stepped down the society had well in excess of 300,000 books, pamphlets and bound newspapers, and more than nine million pages of microfilmed newspapers. Those items increase greatly each year. In addition to the literature the society has a valuable collection of artwork, including paintings by Benton and Bingham, editorial cartoons by Missouri's best newspaper artists, photographs, prints, maps, and manuscripts.

Shoemaker once wrote, "the society collects, publishes, restores, repairs and makes available all possible material on Missouri history!" Obviously run by people who think history anything but bunk, the State Historical Society of Missouri traces its own formal history back to the day of its incorporation, on this date, March 9, 1899.

****

MARCH 10
MISSOURI, AMERICAN TERRITORY

The flag of France had been reeled down the pole only moments earlier. Now, catching the breeze and fluttering into full view as it was run to the top was the red, white and blue of the still-young United States. A dignified, peaceful ceremony. The change of flags was not the result of conquest, but of purchase. This was the day the flag of the United States was raised over Missouri for the first time. Just seventeen years later this part of the Louisiana Territory would be a state.

Captain Amos Stoddard presided in St. Louis that day as Upper Louisiana was transferred to America from France. Stoddard had the unusual distinction of representing both sides in the ceremony while a Spanish Governor stood by, watching sadly. Just three years earlier the land had been Spanish territory. Spain had sold the land to France in 1801, a move which cast a shadow over the Jefferson administration in Washington, D.C.

Jefferson saw the expansion-minded French as a considerable threat to the western border of the United States. He also realized that French control of the port of New Orleans could be disastrous for American commerce in the west which used the Mississippi River so heavily to reach markets. He ordered Robert Livingston, minister to France, to begin negotiating for New Orleans.

Livingston himself was an interesting man. He was deaf. He spoke no French and he often quarrelled with French agents. The President had written him: "The day that France takes possession of New Orleans fixes the sentence which is to restrain her forever within her low water mark. It seals the union of two nations who in conjunction can maintain exclusive possession of the ocean. From that moment we must marry ourselves to the British fleet and nation."

Warmongers were at work in the federal government, demanding American troops be mobilized to take New Orleans. Jefferson belittled this effort at home, but emphasized it in dealings with foreign diplomats.

Bonaparte was having trouble with Santo Domingo, an island nation that had broken with the French earlier. In trying to reconquer the natives, the French spent large amounts of men and money. There could be no occupation of Louisiana until Santo Domingo was taken care of. Bonaparte soon came to see that without Santo Domingo and the Gulf ports of Florida, which Spain would not sell, Louisiana was worthless. So he turned his thoughts of empire to the East. He demanded Malta from Britain and planned moves on India and Egypt.

Napoleon decided he couldn't defend Louisiana if he moved East. He needed money to assemble his army for a campaign to take Malta, Egypt and India. He needed the friendship of the United States and that friendship could not come about as long as the

Louisiana situation continued to create friction.

Napoleon therefore offered to Livingstone and another American minister, James Monroe, the entire Louisiana area. So thunderstruck were the Americans that they found themselves at first saying all they wanted was New Orleans and Florida. Then it soaked in. Of course they would take the entire territory, even if it was beyond their instructions! The price was $15 million. That worked out to about thirteen and one half cents an acre for a territory doubling the size of the United States.

Jefferson sent Amos Stoddard and his troops to St. Louis to take command of the new land. Stoddard was told to keep administering the law as his Spanish predecessors had since the Spanish were still in command. The French had not had time to install any of their government officers. The ceremony was not without emotion. Spanish and French citizens were understandably bewildered since three flags had flown over their territory in four years. It is said the Spanish Governor, at the end of the formal ceremony, wrapped himself in his flag and left the scene, weeping.

Thus, the Louisiana Territory and what is now Missouri came under the American flag, the result of a far-away ruler turning dreams of empire in another direction. The breeze caught the American flag over Missouri on this date, March 10, in 1804.

****

MARCH 11
THE J.P.

Even today in the movies, when a boy and girl from a typical country town elope they find a friendly Justice of the Peace to perform the ceremony. But don't look for one in Missouri. The Justice of the Peace, after occupying a place of importance from the earliest days of our state, no longer exists.

The Justice of the Peace was a powerful man in our early days. Back when our government was a territorial affair located in Indiana, the Justice of the Peace did just about everything here. The system had been borrowed from the old English system of government. Five counties were provided for in what later became Missouri and a Court of Quarter Sessions of the Peace became the general county authority. The Governor, in Indiana, would appoint a necessary number of Justices of the Peace for each county. Then those J.P.s or any number of them totalling three or more would meet quarterly to function as the county's general administrative authority. Even today, many Missouri county governments retain some of the form and substance of our earliest county government. Most counties retain the now worn-out phrase, the County *Court.* The Court of Quarter Sessions, in addition to having administrative duties, also had jurisdiction in criminal cases except for capital offenses.

But the judges of these courts, and some of the later forms of the system which have led up to our present time, were not necessarily respected as judicial arbiters. One lawyer of the nineteenth century, Charles B. McAfee, recalled, "A young attorney starting out on the circuit soon learned whether he could make a lawyer of himself or not, and soon succeeded, or quit and bought a farm, *or ran for Justice of the Peace.*"

The Probate Court in those days had one judge and the ordinary duties still associated with that court. Petty civil cases were ruled on by Courts of Single Justices. Down through the years the systems were combined, redivided, redefined and refined. Missouri adopted and abandoned the Justice of the Peace system of administrative boards several times. In the early days, County Magistrates, or Justices of the Peace, sat on the County Court, often in a rotating arrangement. Finally circuit courts were developed. Justice of the Peace Courts were separate. County Courts were set aside for administration, not judicial work.

The J.P. Courts were a colorful part of our history for years, however. McAfee remembers the time an old Justice of the Peace appeared before a circuit committee for an examination to receive his formal license to become a lawyer. He and the committee wrangled over defining "law," with the applicant finally telling committee members, "You ought to know that anyone can answer such an easy question as that. If you are going to examine me, stop this trifling and ask me something hard." He never did define "law," but McAfee reports the committee recommended him for a lawyer's license which he received. As McAfee put it, "if the courts could stand it, the committee could."

In 1946 the legislature pushed a bill through which provided not only for the institution of magistrate courts, but the transition from the 140-year old system of Justices of the Peace to the new system of magistrates. Justices of the Peace were allowed to serve in that position until their terms ran out. The first Magistrates to succeed them were elected later that year.

The law brought a certain amount of professionalism to the office by requiring that Magistrates and Probate Judges be lawyers. However, the law did say a Probate Judge who was not at that time a lawyer could succeed himself. Furthermore, in another move to protect the long-serving non-attorney Justices of the Peace, the law said anyone who had served at least four years as J.P., or who was at that time holding that job, could run for the job of Magistrate and not need a law degree. But of course the system gradually faded away, even as the Magistrate court system gradually faded away. In the 1970s a constitutional change abolished Magistrate Courts and created lower-level Circuit Courts. When that happened, January 1, 1979, the Magistrate Courts disappeared.

All of this explains why today you have to go a long way to find a kindly man in a white frame house to perform the marriage ceremony while his wife plays that convenient organ in the corner. He hasn't existed in this state since Governor Donnelly signed the bill creating Magistrate Courts in Missouri on this date, March 11, 1946.

****

MARCH 12
GOVERNOR BOB, TOOTS, AND FIDDLES

He rode his horse into the Executive Mansion one day and proceeded to feed it oats from the furniture. Stories say the horse ate out of the piano or off the mantel. Tour guides at the mansion today will show you an elaborate sideboard and tell you the nicks in it are from the horse's bridle. Our fourteenth Governor was one of the most flamboyant Governors Missouri ever had. A biographer says Robert Marcellus Stewart was "a stranger to thrift but not to alcohol."

A St. Louis newspaperman once wrote about the time the French consul from St. Louis, Emile Karst, paid a visit. "For some days we were unable to find Governor Bob, who was on one of his periodical toots." Karst was an accomplished violinist and was playing that instrument when Stewart finally showed up. The Governor stated that for some time he had been courting a young lady across the street, a young lady he'd been trying to woo by playing the violin. He asked the distinguished visitor for help. The Governor took his violin, sat on the mansion porch and went through the motions of playing while Karst, hidden behind some curtains, actually performed the music. It apparently made an impact. The young lady was seen to applaud from her window. The Governor rewarded Karst by writing a pardon for a young Frenchman being held at the state prison a few blocks away.

Robert Stewart was tall with dark hair, handsome, but sometimes sloppy. He came from New York State. Stewart was 42 years old when he became Governor. He had been a state senator for 11 years, playing a key role in building the Hannibal and St. Joseph Railroad, the most successful of Missouri's early lines. As that railroad was being planned, he traveled every mile of its proposed route and raised donations for it. Eventually he raised enough to pay for a survey of the route. Stewart became the President of the railroad, a post he filled from 1849 until the year he became Governor.

As Governor, Stewart realized that railroads were not meeting their obligations to make payments on state bonds issued for their construction. He opposed the seizure of those railroads by the state, however, and none were seized until after his term. This was not as it may seem, self serving. His Hannibal and St. Joseph Railroad was the only one which did not default.

Stewart is not dealt with kindly by historians. Edwin McReynolds writes that he was "an amateur politician. He was firmly convinced that each public question had two sides and at times he seemed determined to take both of them. On the subject of secession, he straddled the fence, not timidly, but with a positive aggressive tone." In many ways, however, he was a good Governor, except when he was on one of his "toots." Stewart was elected Governor in 1857 with the backing of the anti-Benton Democrats. Other parties backed James S. Rollins, the prominent Columbia Whig. Rollins led for many days as the votes were slowly counted. But as the Ozarks totals came in, Stewart rallied and finally slipped into office on a margin of 334 votes.

Stewart could not straddle the fence on the Kansas-Missouri border war raging in those times. He finally sent Adjutant General G. A. Parsons to Western Missouri to learn the extent of the trouble and take any necessary steps to protect residents of the territory. Parsons was authorized to organize military companies, but not to cross the line into Kansas. Stewart then wrote Governor Denver of Kansas who also was concerned and Denver took similar steps. It calmed things down until John Brown began his raids in 1858.

He left office in January of 1861. In his farewell address he pleaded for moderate thinking in the tumultuous days he knew were ahead. He attacked abolition fanatics and restated his belief that slave-holders should be allowed to take their slaves, as they could take any property, into any free state and not lose possession of them. But he would not advocate secession. By her geographical position if nothing else, Stewart said, Missouri should stay in the Union. "She cannot be frightened by the past unfriendly legislation of the North nor dragooned into secession by the restrictive legislation of the extreme South. She will rather take the high position of armed neutrality....The very idea of voluntary secession is not only absurd in itself, but utterly destructive of every principle on which national faith is founded."

Stewart became a member of the Convention of ninety-nine which decided Missouri had no cause to secede. After that he commanded a Union military brigade. He was removed from command because of his excessive drinking. He went back to St. Joseph and edited a newspaper. He was 56 when he died in 1871. He never married.

Robert Marcellus Stewart, our fourteenth Governor, was born on this date, March 12, 1815.

****

MARCH 13
CARDINALS WITH HELMETS

The American Professional Football Association was formally organized in 1920, with Jim Thorpe its president. Thirteen teams paid the $100 franchise fee to become charter members. They were from all over the map: Akron, Canton, Cleveland, Columbus and Dayton in Ohio; the Buffalo, New York, All-Americans; the Rochester Jeffersons, also from New York; the Hammond (Indiana) Pros; the Detroit Heralds; the Decatur (Illinois) Staleys joined by another Illinois team from Rock Island. Chicago had two teams, the Tigers and the Cardinals.

No official standings were kept that first season, but the Chicago Cardinals finished with a 2-3-2 record. The next year they were 8-3 and in 1923, a year after the league became known as the National Football League, they finished 8-4. They dropped to 5-4-1 in 1924. In

1925 the Cardinals bounced back to 11-2-1 and were league champions.

But at the end of the season, star halfback and dropkicker Paddy Driscoll was sold to the Decatur Staleys, now renamed the Chicago Bears. Two reasons were cited: the Cardinals needed money and the Bears needed a star to offset the big name of Red Grange who was talking of organizing another league. That idea fell through, of course, and the Bears wound up with both Grange and Driscoll. Grange made his pro debut against the Cardinals on Thanksgiving Day, 1925. The game was a scoreless tie.

The Cardinals had a new owner in 1929, Dr. David Jones. He made fullback Ernie Nevers his player-coach. Nevers, a former All-American at Stanford, set an NFL record for most points scored in one game, a 40-6 Cardinal win over the Bears. The record still stood a half-century later. In 1929 the Cardinals again made history by becoming the first NFL team to have an out-of-town training camp, at Coldwater, Michigan.

Four years after Jones bought the club, he sold it to a printing firm owner and sportsman, "Blue Shirt" Charley Bidwell. Charley earned his nickname because he seldom wore any shirt that wasn't dark blue in color. The first few years were mediocre ones for Bidwell. In four years, the team was 19 and 23.

In 1946 the fortunes of the Cardinals began to look up as they posted a 6-5 record. The next year things looked even better with the former Missouri All-American "Pitchin' Paul" Christman at quarterback and a promising All-American rookie from Georgia named Charley Trippi.

But Bidwell didn't live to see his team become champions. He died in 1947. His two sons, William and Charles Jr., became the new owners. In 1948 the Cardinals won the division title but lost the league crown in a vicious snowstorm in Philadelphia. They finished 11-1. Coach Jimmy Conzleman resigned a month later. From then until the club moved to St. Louis the Chicago Cardinals were a so-so ball club. They had only two winning seasons, 6-5 in 1949 and 7-5 in 1956.

The pressures to move grew in the 50s. Television complicated things because neither Chicago team could cash in on the television revenue. No NFL game could be broadcast into an area where an NFL team was playing at home and either the Bears or the Cardinals were always at home each weekend.

St. Louis expressed an interest in the team. The Cardinals had played exhibition games there a few times. Finally the owner of the world champion Baltimore Colts, Carroll Rosenbloom, went to the Bidwell family and tried to persuade them to move the team to St. Louis. Another man entered the negotiations, Joseph Griesedieck, the President of the Falstaff Brewing Company, who bought a large minority interest.

Finally the move was negotiated. The league paid $500,000 moving costs and St. Louis gained its second Cardinal team. It wasn't a very good one. The football Cardinals had finished 2-10 their last year in Chicago. They continued to have up and down fortunes in St. Louis. Coaches came and went. So did players. There was internal dissension in the front office and finally in 1971 Bill Bidwell bought out his brother, hoping to build on a single foundation a stronger franchise and a winning team.

The Cardinals went through three straight seasons with records of 4-9-1. Finally, in 1974, the Cardinals brought a championship to the franchise and its fans. They finished 10-4, first in their conference. It was their first title in twenty-six years. They repeated as champions the next year, but both times they lost in first-round playoff games. The next year the "Cardiac Cardinals" as they were called because of their close victories, just missed the playoffs. After that, the Cardinals slid downhill quickly and were not contenders. The Cardinals started their third decade in St. Louis with a 5-11 record.

But no matter how bad things are, fans will tell you there will be glory days for the Cardinals, who moved to St. Louis on this date, March 13, 1960.

****

MARCH 14
JOHN MARMADUKE, FEARLESS AND INCORRUPTIBLE

In the dust and confusion of the Battle of Westport a young soldier from Iowa saw some blue-clad Confederate soldiers and began to pursue them. As Private James Dunlavy chased the rebels, a Confederate General ran toward him. He mistook Dunlavy for a blue-clad Confederate. It was a costly mistake. Dunlavy quickly realized what was happening and when the General was about thirty steps away, the young private leveled his rifle at him and took him prisoner. It was one of the most embarrassing moments in the General's career. A few years later, however, he would be Governor of Missouri.

John Sappington Marmaduke has been called by historian Floyd Shoemaker "probably the best trained pro-southern military man in Missouri when the Civil War erupted." He was the only son of a former Missouri Governor to also become governor. His father, Meredith Miles Marmaduke, had succeeded Thomas Reynolds when Reynolds committed suicide in 1844. John Marmaduke was a product of that politically fertile area around Arrow Rock in Central Missouri. One of his uncles was Claiborne Fox Jackson, also a Governor. John was educated at Yale, Harvard, and later West Point. As a newly commissioned lieutenant, he served with Colonel Albert Sydney Johnston in Utah.

With the outbreak of the Civil War he came back to Missouri and cast his lot with the South. Governor Jackson ordered him to make a stand at Boonville in 1861, in what became Missouri's first real Civil War battle. Marmaduke had only 600 raw recruits and was outnumbered two to one. He objected, but he was overruled. So he made a stand which lasted several hours before he had to retreat.

Marmaduke had a quick temper. He decided that as long as politicians tried to run the war, the effort would never be successful. So he resigned his commission and went to Richmond to become a regular officer in the Confederate Army. He was wounded at Shiloh and promoted to Brigadier General. He was transferred to Arkansas and the Trans-Mississippi department to command the cavalry under General Tom Hardimann.

In January, 1862, he commanded the force which moved on Springfield. He didn't capture the city but he did draw Union forces away from a chain of supply forts in the area. Other southern commands then took them and destroyed them. Marmaduke was the first commander to use cavalry as an independent strike force in this theatre of operations.

But the Confederacy was defeated disastrously at Helena, Arkansas. Out of that disappointment came a feud with another Confederate officer, General Lucien Walker. It ended in a duel and Marmaduke killed Walker. In 1864 Price made his sweep into Missouri and his troop met death and frustration at Pilot Knob, Jefferson City and finally Westport. Union forces managed to surround Price's out-

159

fit and take Marmaduke and 500 of his men captive at Westport.

Marmaduke spent the remainder of the war in a Massachusetts prison. He came back to Missouri afterwards and edited a newspaper. He won election as Governor in 1880 after failing four years earlier. He was the first former Confederate to reach that rank, a signal that old animosities were dying.

Marmaduke had served five years on the Missouri Railway Commission before his election to the state's highest office and used his understanding of railroad operations effectively during his unfortunately short term. The first railroad strike to seriously affect Missouri occurred during his administration. He took strong action which is credited with averting high property losses and personal injuries. He sponsored a bill in the legislature regulating railroads, but it failed. He immediately recalled the General Assembly into special session. And when railroad backers threatened to block action until the time limit for the session ran out, Marmaduke said that was fine with him. He'd just keep calling special sessions until the measure passed. It passed.

Although a bachelor, he became known for his Christmas parties for children in the Executive Mansion. In 1887 he died the day before the party was to be held. The weather was so bad Marmaduke was buried in Jefferson City instead of being taken home to the family burial ground at Arrow Rock. The tall spire of marble which marks his grave chronicles his military, educational and political successes, and concludes with these words: "He was fearless and incorruptible."

John Sappington Marmaduke, the only son of a Missouri Governor to serve in that same office, was born on this date, March 14, 1833.

****

MARCH 15
INITIATIVE AND REFERENDUM

Initiative and referendum are regarded now as indispensable parts of government. But it wasn't always so. As a matter of fact, the first time Missourians had a chance to accept the privilege of submitting proposed laws and amendments by petition, or overriding legislative acts at the polls, they refused.

The Socialist Labor Party endorsed the idea of direct elections in 1894. The Missouri Referendum League was formed a year later. In 1898 the People's Party, the Prohibition Party and the Missouri Single Tax League all announced their support of the idea.

The first initiative and referendum proposal in Missouri missed by only four votes of being passed in the House in 1899. The Democratic National Platform, adopted in Kansas City in 1900, called for "direct legislation whenever practicable." So in 1901 a resolution submitting the issue to Missouri voters was introduced in the legislature. This time it passed the House. But in the Senate, where the railroad lobby strongly opposed it, the resolution lost 14-13.

That put the Referendum League to work in earnest. By the next session the State Labor Federation had endorsed it. And late in the 1904 session, the legislature passed a resolution placing a constitutional amendment on the ballot. The Republican Platform of 1904 endorsed the concept, but not the specific amendment, which had come from the Democratic-controlled legislature, calling it "so cumbrous as to make its application impracticable."

Only 44 percent of those who voted for Governor that November voted on the initiative and referendum issue. It lost — 169,281 against, 115,741 in favor. It was the first time voters anywhere in the nation had refused to adopt such a plan when it was placed before them.

The Referendum League was staggered but not beaten. In 1905 resolutions were introduced to keep the matter alive in the legislature, but no real effort was made to push them to passage. In 1907 however, Governor Folk recommended the people vote again on initiative and referendum. The senate this time said yes 19-6 and the House approved the resolution 90-7.

It was not a heated campaign. It was one which relied on little speaking and much pamphleteering. A St. Louis man, who had been an activist and lobbyist throughout the entire effort, Dr. William Preston Hill, told one audience, "This system does not aim to abolish the representative form of government we now have, nor to substitute another in its place. It leaves our representative system just as it is, but guards it from abuse and from becoming misrepresentative. It will perform the same function as a safety value on an engine; silent and unnoticed when not needed, but most useful in time of danger." Four state political party platforms endorsed the proposal: The Democrats, Socialists, Prohibitionists, and the People's Party.

161

This time the Republicans rode the fence.

On November 3, 1908, the voters showed a change of heart. Forty-five percent of those who voted for Governor voted on initiative and referendum and this time it passed with 177,615 voting in favor, 147,290 against.

It took little time for the process to begin to work. In 1910 two constitutional amendments were put before the public through the initiative process. One prohibited the manufacture and sale of intoxicants in Missouri. Another would have had the State University maintained by a direct state tax levy. Both lost. Four more proposals were defeated in 1912.

In 1914 there were three proposals advanced by initiative petition. Women's suffrage was one. A road-building bond issue was another. Another one allowing taxes for special road-building was on the ballot. Referendum was first used that year when four acts of the legislature were called to the people for a vote. Everything lost. Missourians had the authority, but apparently did not yet want the responsibility.

In 1920 the second application of referendum came about. Two legislative acts were challenged: a workman's compensation act which was defeated, and a prohibition act which was approved. A constitutional amendment calling for a constitutional convention was adopted, the first time an initiative proposal was approved.

It was a long fight to gain the right, and then it was a long time before Missourians decided to use it.

Today of course, we're all familiar with the process. Nearly every time there is a state election we face a ballot with issues on it brought to us through initiative or referendum. It never could have happened if Missouri's House had not approved a Senate resolution giving Missouri voters two of their most important tools of citizenship on this date, March 15, in 1907.

****

MARCH 16
SWITZLER, JOURNALIST-HISTORIAN

He was one of Missouri's most respected newspapermen. He once wrote, "Those newspapers in the country that are conducted with enterprise, spirit and industry—that are alive (not dead) to the news and interest of the respective localities—that are just, but fearless, respectful but outspoken, promoting and conserving the best interest of the community where published—that, in short, have brains and use them vigorously, hands and employ them constantly, will become a *power* no monopoly can destroy."

But William F. Switzler was more than a newspaperman.

He was, among other things, a member of the legislature, a humanitarian and the author of one of our state's most important history books.

In the 1840s when a great humanitarian movement swept the country, Switzler was one of its most outspoken supporters. In 1846 he wrote in his newspaper in Columbia, "Let no man despise the unfortunate, poor and wretched. Earth has ills to which all are heir. Rather let us sympathize with rather than despise the unfortunate of our race." Switzler was a first-term member of the Missouri House that year. He served three terms as a Whig. In the legislature he favored the passage of acts for charters to colleges and schools, orphan homes, saving institutions, mining turnpikes, ferry services, canals and railroads, toll bridges and fire insurance companies. He secured passage of an act setting aside room in the Capitol for the first Missouri historical society. He backed construction of a bridge across the Mississippi at St. Louis.

William Switzler was born in Fayette County, Kentucky. His family moved to Fayette, Missouri, when he was seven. He was educated in Howard County and read law with the prominent judge, Abiel Leonard, and another prominent lawyer in Columbia, James S. Rollins. Switzler was twenty-two when he moved to Columbia and bought the Columbia *Patriot,* which he renamed the Columbia *Statesman* two years later. He published that paper for almost half a century. Former Missouri Attorney General North Todd Gentry would later call Switzler the "dean of Missouri journalists." He was known as a fair and just editor, but he was not afraid to criticize. Gentry said he would "write an account of a public meeting of a different political faith, and give a correct account, and he would truthfully report the speech of a political orator, then write an editorial and answer the orator's argument."

Switzler was known for a remarkable memory. Friends used to say he could give a name and number to each grain in a bushel of corn and remember it. He was a stickler for accuracy in days when stories often were written in longhand.

When Switzler went to the legislature he supported funds to buy books for prison inmates. He was one of the backers of the first wildlife game laws ever enacted in Missouri. As early as 1857 a bill was approved prohibiting the killing of prairie chickens, deer, wild turkey, and quail in Lincoln and Pike Counties at certain times of the year.

He believed in education for everybody. An attempt in 1849 to organize a Collegiate Female Institute in Columbia failed. But two years later Christian College was formed, and five years after that, Stephens College began. Switzler was on the board of Christian College, a Disciples of Christ-founded school, although he was one of Columbia's foremost Presbyterians. He also was a trustee at the University of Missouri where a building on the Columbia campus still bears his name.

He wasn't above engaging in pointed partisan fights with his newspaper. Once, when he attacked University President James Shannon for his religious zeal, Shannon barred Switzler from curators meetings and moved the school's printing to another print shop. Switzler also feuded with another rival editor named Peabody. The men got into a fistfight in the streets of Columbia.

During the Civil War, President Lincoln made Switzler military Secretary of State for Arkansas.

Switzler ran for Congress four times, but lost. In 1885 President Cleveland made him the Chief of the Bureau of Statistics. His history of statistics, published in 1888, and his history of Missouri mark him as a major Missouri author of his time; the latter book being the first comprehensive history of Missouri.

Tradition says he knew more public figures than any other person in Missouri in his time. One admirer called him "a perfect animated encyclopedia of facts pertaining to the History of Missouri." He died in 1906 at the age of 87. William Switzler, editor, legislator and one of our state's most important historians, was born on this date, March 16, 1819.

****

MARCH 17
GABE

Often in his last years he would stand at his farm near Kansas City and look to the west, his failing eyes seeing little. He was an old man. Ah, but what those eyes had seen, and what the memory could recall!

Years before, in 1822, a St. Louis newspaper carried an advertisement reading: "To enterprising young men. The subscriber wishes to engage one hundred young men to ascend the Missouri River to its source, there to be employed for one, two or three years. For particulars inquire of Major Andrew Henry, near the lead mines in the county of Washington, who will ascend with and command the party; or the subscriber near St. Louis." It was signed by William H. Ashley.

Both Ashley and Henry would make their marks on Missouri and western history. But the men who answered that ad would become even more famous, their names followed by one of the most dynamic terms of the west, *mountain man.* There was Jedediah Smith, who is called the greatest continental explorer after Lewis and Clark. There was the legendary Mike Fink. Old Hugh Glass would sign up and in months to come have his epic fight with a bear. Also signing on with that group was a young man who later would be described as the greatest mountain man of them all, an 18-year-old boy named Jim Bridger.

Bridger had been an orphan for about five years. He had worked as a flatboat operator and an apprentice blacksmith to support his sister and himself in St. Louis. But St. Louis then was at the edge of the frontier and those who ventured into it filled the streets not only with their presence but with tales that fired the young man's imagination. So Bridger signed on with the Ashley-Henry men and went West. From the beginning, his life was one grand adventure. When Glass was mauled by the bear, Bridger was one of the two men left behind by the expedition to care for him or wait until he died. The two youngsters grew scared because Indians were in the neighborhood. They left, taking all of Glass's belongings because they were certain he would die. But Glass didn't die. He crawled and limped his way 100 miles to the nearest fort. He swore vengance on those who abandoned him, but later forgave Bridger.

A year after that, Jim Bridger was exploring the Bear River and discovered the Great Salt Lake. At the time he thought it was an arm of the Pacific Ocean. In the 1830s he and another man became partners in a fur-trading company. Bridger is said to have been the second white man to have seen what is now Yellowstone National Park. John Colter is believed to have been the first, about 1808. It was Bridger, though, who brought back all the tall tales which first made the area famous. He talked about steaming springs, the sulphur pots and pools and the geysers. The folks back East couldn't believe it. But even more unbelievable were Bridger's tales of petrified forests with petrified birds singing petrified songs. Bridger even told of a time when he rode his horse right off the edge of a cliff and didn't fall because the gravity was petrified!

In 1843 he established Fort Bridger in Southwest Wyoming. It became a way station to wagon trains bound for Oregon. It was a place for wagon repairs and restocking of supplies. Rescue expeditions also went out from Fort Bridger.

His friends and competitors on the frontier knew him as "Old Gabe," and his memory of the land he had traveled proved valuable in later years. When the time came for the transcontinental railraod, organizers of the effort called on Bridger to find the best path west. Bridger and another man are given credit for finding one of the most important openings in the Rockies for the rail line—Berthoud Pass.

In 1871 Jim Bridger came back to Missouri to stay. He bought a farm near Kansas City and settled down. His sight failed and by 1875 the eyes which had beheld such marvels were totally blind. He spent the last six years of his life yearning for one more glimpse of the country he had helped open for civilization. He was 77 when he died in Kansas City in 1881.

Today as you go through the West, you find Bridger's name almost everywhere: Bridger Pass; Bridger National Forest; Bridger, Wyoming.

Seven years before he died, the place of geysers, petrified trees and petrified stories became Yellowstone National Park. He was buried in Kansas City, not far from the Missouri River which first carried him on his great journey. Jim Bridger, mountain man, was born on this date, March 17, 1804.

****

MARCH 18
A NIGHTINGALE SANG

Why would anyone want to pay $150 a ticket to hear somebody sing "Home Sweet Home," or "I Know That My Redeemer Liveth," especially when the concert was sponsored by the world's greatest huckster? It was a concert which almost didn't happen, a near miss on one of P.T. Barnum's most famous national tours and promotions.

The episode began when a steamboat nosed in at the St. Louis levee before sunup on a Friday morning. It arrived early to avoid a large crowd. The singer and her escort were quickly taken to the nearby Planter's House, the most prominent hotel in St. Louis. She was Jenny Lind and she was in St. Louis for a series of concerts.

Later that morning tickets for the first concert were auctioned off. It was customary during the tour to hold auctions for the first concert's tickets. The man who arranged the tour, Phineas T. Barnum, was the auctioneer. The first ticket brought $150, purchased by E. A. Byron. It was the highest amount paid for a ticket. The rest of the seats, about 1,000 of them, went for about $8.00 each. Five concerts were scheduled for alternate days with the last one on March 26. Outside the hall people stood hoping to hear even a few notes from the concert inside. It rained the third night but the people outside merely opened their umbrellas.

The concerts, as it turned out, almost didn't happen at all.

Soon after the party's arrival in St. Louis, Barnum was visited by Miss Lind's personal secretary who told Barnum that the St. Louis concert would have to be cancelled. He claimed the contract with Miss Lind called for 60 concerts, and the St. Louis event would be concerts 61 through 65.

But Barnum, as shrewd at composing contracts as he was at attracting performers and crowds, was well prepared for this eventuality. Barnum recalled a provision in the agreement saying if the contract was suddenly cancelled, Miss Lind would have to repay him all that he had paid her over $1,000 per concert. She had received part of the gate receipts. he figured the total amount would be $77,000.

The great promoter didn't believe Miss Lind wanted to terminate the contract. He had, on occasion, expressed his opinion about those he called her "selfish and greedy hangers on and advisers, legal and otherwise." Barnum told one of his friends he doubted the Swedish Nightingale even knew the effort was underway.

He went into another meeting with Miss Lind's secretary and told him he would agree to the cancellations. This wasn't what the secretary really wanted, of course. He quickly noted that Barnum already had lined up concerts in Louisville and Cincinnati. Barnum offered to let Miss Lind and her advisers handle them all, in exchange for reimbursement of printing costs and auditorium rental fees already paid.

Eventually the secretary asked Barnum how much he would charge to manage fifty concerts for Miss Lind. The price Barnum quoted was one million dollars. Then he told the secretary he was certain Miss Lind had not authorized him to propose the cancellation of the contract and that if she did, he wanted to see the authorization in Miss Lind's writing.

The secretary tried another tack, proposing a new contract for fifty more concerts, with Barnum being paid $1,000 per concert to promote them. Barnum flatly refused. He stated he had hired Miss Lind, she had not hired him.

The next day the secretary told Barnum it had all been a joke—the contract would continue in effect.

Jenny Lind eventually bought her contract after 93 of the 100 concerts it actually provided for. She paid the penalty fee. The other seven concerts were not as successful as those under Barnum. In time she married a piano player who was with the Barnum troupe and they went back to Europe. But a near-disaster for the tour had been averted in St. Louis when Barnum turned the table on the singer's agents.

When the concert series ended, $40,000 had been raised, of which $2,000 was given to the mayor of St. Louis for charity and immigrant relief. Advertisers capitalized on the concerts by attaching the singer's name to umbrellas, jewelry and flour.

Barnum, Lind and the rest of the group left behind in Missouri several thousand people who would never forget hearing "The Last Rose of Summer" sung by the legendary Swedish Nightingale, Jenny Lind, at a concert which almost didn't occur, on this date, March 18, 1851.

****

MARCH 19
THE HANGING JUDGE

Back when he lived in Missouri the hometown newspaper was sometimes critical of what it called his "spread-eagle oratory," and his "sky-scraping eloquence." When he became a judge he still had a tendency to make speeches from the bench. In time his courtroom became known as the "Court of the Damned" and the gate to the prison in the basement of the courthouse was known as "The Doorway to Hell." He was a Missouri Congressman who became one of the most feared judges the American West ever knew.

From the windows of his courtroom those on trial could see the gallows, gallows big enough to stretch a dozen necks at a time. But he never hanged a dozen at a time. Six was his maximum. For years, the most feared words any criminal could hear in that courtroom were, "I sentence you to be hanged by the neck until you are dead, dead, dead." It was not without reason that Isaac Parker became known as "The Hanging Judge."

From his bench as the Judge of the United States District Court for Western Arkansas, located at Fort Smith, Isaac Parker heard about 13,500 cases. He tried 344 cases punishable by death. Almost half of those convictions meant a visit with George Maledon, a hangman who took such pride in his work that he once told a friend, "They don't even twitch."

Isaac Parker was thirty-six years old when he left Missouri and became a judge. Missouri historian, folklorist and author Homer Croy says he was "an unusually handsome man, with brown hair, blue eyes and a neat, well-trimmed beard. He was a large man, six feet, and weighing almost two hundred pounds. He was genial and pleasant mannered to his friends and acquaintances. But when he passed sentence on a murderer his eyes became cold and his voice cruel. The man had committed a crime. He must be punished. The law must be carried out."

Isaac Parker was twenty-one when he went to St. Joseph, Missouri, from Ohio. He wasted no time establishing himself, winning the city attorney's job, then winning reelection without opposition.

Parker was elected prosecutor for the Ninth Circuit in 1863 and four years later was named to a six-year term as Circuit Judge. He resigned two years into that term to run for Congress. In 1870 he was successful, and was re-elected in 1872. He knew Indians, who still visited St. Joseph frequently, and in Congress he pushed for appropriations providing greater protection for the Indians.

But political times changed and in 1874 Parker knew he wouldn't be re-elected. He went to President Grant and asked for an appointment. Grant offered him Chief Justice of Utah Territory, a position Parker saw could be only temporary. He asked for something else. That's how Isaac Parker became judge of the District Court in Fort Smith, a place where the court was known to be corrupt, taking bribes and giving easy sentences. Parker's district covered more territory than any other, a territory as large as the states of Connecticut and Missouri combined, including Arkansas and what was then the Indian Territory, Oklahoma.

He opened his court on May 10, 1875. His first case was a murder charge. The jury was out of the room for half an hour before coming back with a guilty verdict. Parker handed out his first death sentence. On September 3, 1875, some 6,000 persons gathered to watch the first six men Parker had sentenced to death keep their date with the rope. The next April 21, five more men dropped to their doom and the next September 8, four more. In his career, Parker would twice hang six men at one time. He would have five men hanged at once three times. He would send four men to deaths simultaneously twice. In 21 years the gallows floor opened 35 times. Nineteen of those times were multiple hangings. They always attracted large crowds and Parker didn't mind. It was good for the public to see what happened to criminals. Later, on his death bed, aware of criticism for his stern punishments, Parker said, "I never hanged a man. The law hanged them. I was only its instrument."

He employed two hundred deputy marshalls to patrol the territory. Sixty-five of these men were killed. He kept his court open for long hours, as long as it took to transact business. He often deliberately led juries, telling them what verdict to produce.

But in 1889 Congress passed a law granting the right of appeal to the U.S. Supreme Court in all convictions where the sentence was death. Judge Parker's absolute rule came to an end. In time there was no reason to continue Parker's court and in September of 1896 the district and circuit courts for the Western District of the Indian Territory were adjourned forever. It speeded the decline of Parker's health. Just over two months later he died.

A former Missouri Congressman, Isaac Parker became the judge of the United States District Court for Western Arkansas, the "Court of the Damned," on this date, March 19, 1875.

****

MARCH 20
BINGHAM

Order Number 11 is more than just a history-making governmental edict. *Stump Speaking* is more than a political technique for addressing voters. *The County Election* is more than just a balloting contest, and *The Verdict of the People* is more than just the outcome of that balloting. They're all paintings done by a Missouri artist, soldier, State Treasurer, and college professor: George Caleb Bingham.

The picture of George Caleb Bingham which is usually circulated shows him with a full head of hair. But his hair really fell out when he was nineteen years old. Bingham had decided to walk to St. Louis but came down with a bad case of measles on the way. For a number of days he was cared for by an old woman who pushed his food through a crack in the wall of a deserted log cabin where he had taken refuge. A young doctor occasionally stopped in. Bingham finally recovered but he had no hair left.

Four years later his good friend James S. Rollins loaned him enough money to go to St. Louis and study art. Until that time, Bingham and his family had lived in Franklin, that famous trail-starting town just across the Missouri River from what is now Boonville. When Bingham's father died, George became a cabinetmaker's apprentice. For a time he thought about becoming a preacher or lawyer, but decided instead to follow his inclinations and become an artist.

Bingham finally settled at Arrow Rock in 1837. He built a small house which still stands in that historic village. He made a living painting portraits of the people in the surrounding counties. It has been said that it was as likely for a family to have a Bingham painting on the wall as it was for a family to have a Bible on the table. It was in Arrow Rock that he developed the style which would make him famous, the technique of capturing the life of rural America. It was also at Arrow Rock that Bingham became interested in politics, an interest which would be important to Missouri in the Civil War years, and an interest which has produced some of his most memorable paintings.

Bingham lived in Arrow Rock until 1845. He went to Philadelphia to the Academy of Fine Arts. But he was back in Missouri in 1844 and his interest in politics continued. Saline County sent him to the Missouri House as its representative in 1848. In 1852 he was a delegate to the national Whig convention. He had earlier won a seat in the legislature, but an opponent, E. B. Sappington, protested the three-vote Bingham victory and the results were reversed.

In the late 1850s Bingham left Missouri to go to Europe but he was back in time for the Civil War. He believed strongly in the Union.

When the pro-Union government took control of the state, Bingham became State Treasurer, serving from 1862 to '64.

Bingham was not the type of artist to cloister himself in a studio somewhere and prepare great works. At various times he also was a University of Missouri professor, the President of the Kansas City Board of Police Commissioners and in 1875 was the Adjutant General of Missouri.

But he is most noted today for his paintings, not only of peopled scenes, but of landscapes. One biographer says he painted at least 40 landscapes and never showed a cow. Bingham became famous for his political paintings as well.

When General Thomas Ewing issued Order Number 11 during the Civil War, driving western Missouri residents from their homes in an effort to clear out rebels and guerrillas, Bingham was so incensed at the resulting misery, he told the General he would do a painting that would ruin Ewing. The emotional painting, widely circulated as an etching, caused widespread anger over Ewing's order and did, as Bingham had promised, virtually ruin the man. Bingham and Ewing remained enemies for the rest of their lives. Three months after Bingham began circulating *Order Number 11,* Ewing issued Order Number 20 allowing people to go back home.

Today Bingham's paintings are valued parts of American history and our Missouri heritage. In 1978 one of his paintings was sold at auction for almost one million dollars, more money than had ever before been paid for a painting by an American. In 1976 the people of the state of Missouri contributed throusands of dollars to purchase a series of Bingham sketches from the Mercantile Library in St. Louis, keeping those works of art in Missouri. Bingham's reputation grows with the passage of time.

George Caleb Bingham died in 1879. He was 68.

Much of the flavor and style of early Missouri is still with us because it was captured in the paintings of George Caleb Bingham, who was born on March 20, 1811.

****

MARCH 21
THE SHOE BROWNS

Alanson Brown was the older of the two Brown brothers. He made five dollars picking up potatoes other workers left behind in

Rutland, Vermont, and bought a cow. He took the money from the sale of the cow, went to work in Mississippi for his uncle, and in three years he had become a partner. Two years later he sold his interest in the store for $13,000. He came to Missouri in 1871 as a delegate to a Southern Baptist Convention in St. Louis. He liked the town and returned. He tried, but couldn't get interested in, a wholesale grocery business. About this time, James Hamilton wanted to set up a shoe and boot house in the town. So the company was organized—Hamilton-Brown and Company. They sold shoes made in the East.

Back in New York, younger brother George received an offer to come West and work for Hamilton-Brown. He became a traveling shoe salesman in north Missouri and in the next four years saved about $7,000. By then George had become convinced Missourians should have shoes made in Missouri, not imported from Eastern companies. Alanson Brown and his partner were reluctant to get into the shoe manufacturing business because those who had tried in the past in St. Louis had failed. So George quit his brother's company and in November, 1878, joined with two other men to form Bryan, Brown and Company. Three years later their company was incorporated as the first wholesale shoe concern in St. Louis.

In 1893, the other partners now retired, the firm became known by the famous name it carries today, the Brown Shoe Company. Five years after that it had 1,000 employes and 50 salesmen. Alanson Brown, meanwhile, decided he and Hamilton could also make shoes. That was 1883 and within a few years their factory was the largest shoe-making plant in the world. The two men gained a reputation for paying all bills promptly in cash and requiring the same of those who owed them money.

Alanson Brown, although not the first shoemaker in St. Louis, became known as the "Father of Shoe Manufacturing in St. Louis." It is said he had two great interests, shoes and the Baptist Church. His salesmen underwent periodic two-week seminars on shoe construction, styling and marketing. Throughout the factory were signs saying, "Keep the quality up." He made employes part owners of the firm. By 1906 more than 130 employes were stockholders.

In 1904 a cartoonist named Richard Fenton Outcault was selling advertising rights to a successful cartoon character of his at the St. Louis World's Fair. John A. Busch, a sales executive for George Brown's company, bought those rights. Since then the line of children's shoes has shown in its heel the winking kid and the grinning dog named Tige. Buster Brown has become one of the world's greatest trademarks. Busch later became chairman of the Board of the Brown Shoe Company.

Alanson Brown fell ill in the second decade of the 20th century. His company's business had fallen off by about a million dollars a year and had dropped from its leadership in sales. He died in Texas of leukemia. At the time of his death, the company employed 5,000 persons and his estate totalled about seven and one half million dollars. His company had seven factories shipping a million dollars worth of shoes a month. He was also President of the Pitchfork Cattle Company which operated a 100,000 acre Texas ranch with 15,000 head of cattle on it. The company continued to decline after his death. His son took over the firm for several years, but it went out of business in the 1940s. The main office at 2031 Olive Street in St. Louis became a WPA project office.

George Warren Brown retired as president of his company in 1915 and became Chairman of the Board. By then the Brown Shoe Company was valued at $10,000,000. He died in Tucson, Arizona, in December of 1921, at the age of 68. But the Brown Shoe Company survived long afterward.

There were remarkable parallels in the lives of those two brothers named Brown. Both made their first money picking potatoes, increased their holdings by trading for livestock, studied at small eastern business schools and landed in Missouri to make their fortunes manufacturing shoes. They shared many things, including their birthdays, six years apart to the day, March 21; Alanson born in 1847 and George in 1853.

****

MARCH 22
FLAG

Our state went without an official state flag for almost a century. It didn't seem to hurt. Many flags flew over and in Missouri in that time, of course. The one we finally got, however, has been unchanged since. Missouri's Betsy Ross was the wife of a former State Senator. Her name was Elizabeth Watkins Oliver. She was from Cape Girardeau. The original state flag of Missouri, made by

Mrs. Oliver, was on display at the Capitol in Jefferson City for years.

The first flag to fly over Missouri was the banner of the French monarchy, three golden *fleur de lis* on a blue field. It was carried here by the earliest explorers and presented to the Indians as a sign of friendship. After the French and Indian War, the flag of the Spanish Kings waved over Missouri, a red banner with a diagonal cross on a white field. In 1785 Spain adopted a new flag of red and gold, the third flag Missouri had known.

France recovered the territory and ran up its tri-color. Shortly after that the Stars and Stripes of the United States flew over Missouri in 1804. Even when Missouri became a state in 1821, there was no official state flag.

The Civil War broke out and in some parts of our state the stars and bars of the Confederacy flew, and then later the Confederate battle flag. That flag was a blue, star-studded St. Andrews Cross on a red field. The Confederate government quit using the first flag because, in the smoke and dust of the battle, it was easily mistaken for the United States flag.

The Ste. Genevieve *Plain-Dealer* reported in 1861 that on the night of March third that year a flag with a state seal painted on it was flown from the St. Louis Courthouse. It was supposedly placed there by the St. Louis Minutemen, a group of young ultra-southern men. This group tried to organize a semi-military body which would be ready immediately for any hazardous action. It was thought in those days the Minutemen were planning to capture the St. Louis Arsenal with its store of arms and ammunition. The Minutemen turned out to be little more than an organization which did a lot of talking. When officials tore down the Minuteman flag, another banner made its appearance at the Minuteman offices, a blue flag with a crescent, cross and single star. The entire incident created much excitement in St. Louis but the situation eased. It wasn't until a half-century later that Missouri finally got its own flag. Surprisingly it was a combination of those two Minuteman flags.

Shortly after the turn of the century, in 1908, the Daughters of the American Revolution began to push for a state banner. The effort was led by Mrs. Robert Oliver of Cape Girardeau. The flag then became an Oliver family project. Her committee researched the design for the flag. She had her husband draft a bill to make the flag official in 1909. Her nephew, State Senator Arthur L. Oliver of Caruthersville, introduced the measure in the General Assembly. It was the second flag proposal to go before the legislature that year. The other was the so-called Holcomb Flag. It lacked anything which distinguished it as a Missouri flag, however, and the Oliver family got its bill through the House that year only to have the Senate turn it down.

In the next session, two years later, the bill was introduced again. This was the year the Capitol burned. Many things went up in smoke, including the original design of the flag painted by Miss Mary Kochitzky of Cape Girardeau. So, Mrs. Oliver went to work on another one. By the time the legislature reorganized itself after the fire, it was too late to process the flag bill. Finally in 1913 the bill went through both houses of the legislature and was signed by Governor Major.

Missouri's flag is a colorful banner with red, white and blue stripes, top to bottom. In the center is the state coat of arms. In the blue circle which encloses the coat of arms are 24 stars, signifying Missouri as the 24th state in the Union. The crescent signifies that Missouri was the second state formed in the Louisiana Purchase. The helmet signifies the enterprise and hardiness of the state and stands for sovereignty. The grizzly bears signify the courage of the people.

The original flag stayed in the Oliver family for many years. On June 14, 1961 — Flag Day — it finally went to the Capitol. Governor Hearnes accepted it on behalf of the state. Later it was framed and hung at the entrance to the rotunda.

Many flags flew over Missouri before our own. We had to wait almost a century after statehood to have a state flag. It finally came into official being the day Governor Major signed the bill designating the design as an official state symbol on this date, March 22, 1913.

****

MARCH 23
CARS

It happened in Kansas City, in May of 1901, on a clear day.

The only two cars in the entire town collided head-on.

They collided because the only two drivers in town decided to play that city's first game of "chicken."

Nobody was hurt. The cars were pulled apart and continued on their way.

One of the passengers, Dr. Eugene Carbaugh, was thrown over the curved dash of the Locomobile and hung there, his belt caught on a carbide lantern. The passenger in the other car, a horse-raiser who disliked automobiles, Ray Oliver, was thrown to the pavement and was heard to mutter as he picked himself up and dusted himself off, "I told you the damn' thing would do it."

It's one of those events no one commemorates with a plaque. But it is one of hundreds of colorful incidents in Missouri history involving the automobile.

Eight years before the Kansas City incident, Missouri's first self-propelled vehicle which could be called an automobile was built in St. Louis by a man named J.D.P. Lewis. He took an old family buggy, rigged it with batteries and a drive mechanism. He could go seven or eight miles an hour. St. Louis issued its first automobile license nine years later. Lewis received tag number one.

St. Louis's first motor car factory was built in 1898, the St. Louis Motor Carriage Company. It made the "St. Louis," producing single and later double-cylinder cars. George Dorris designed the engines. Later he would resign and found his own company in St. Louis which would produce cars bearing the Dorris name until 1926. He is credited with designing the first side-entrance car. Dorris and his sales manager, A. L. Dyke, also invented the first American-made float-feed carburetor, still used, in principle, today. Dorris produced the world's first valve-in-head engine, again a manufacturing technique which has lasted.

Dyke, meanwhile, is remembered for something else, a phrase and a business. In 1899 he established the first automobile supply house in the country. His "number one outfit" was an early-day do-it-yourself kit, which included the radiator, the steering gear, the engine, transmission, axles and wheels. He also sold appropriate attire to wear while motoring. A person fully dressed for a motor excursion in those days was said to be "all dyked out," or "all decked out" today.

The first bus in Missouri was built in St. Louis in 1898 by Ashley and Semple Scott. It was electric and carried eight passengers. The first American manufacturer of automobile axles, wheels, chassis and bodies was H. F. Borbein and Company of St. Louis in 1899.

In 1907 Joseph Moon began making the cars bearing his name. His cars had six-cylinder engines. His company also made the eight-cylinder Diana, and two luxury cars, the Windsor White Prince Phaeton and later the low-slung, front-drive Ruxton. The Moon failed during the depression. In 1919 the Gardner Motor Company started and before it too failed in the depression it made 100,000 cars. St. Louis had become a major automobile center. In fact, in 1905, a man named C. H. Laessig is believed to have built the world's first service station there.

In August, 1900, three cars raced a horse at a St. Louis picnic. The horse won. Two years later the St. Louis Police Department made officers William Stinger and James Cooney its first motor-car patrolmen in the department's first patrol car. The public called it a "skiddoo car" because when you heard it coming down the road, you were supposed to "skiddoo."

Kansas City's first car arrived in 1895 when Henry Weber optimistically called his contraption a "flyer." A White Steamer was hissing around Kansas City streets in 1899, two years before the collision we talked about earlier. By October, 1902, Kansas City had 25 cars. Six years later it had 16 times that number.

Theodore Tanner spent three years building Jefferson City's first car before its debut in 1900. Columbia's first car shattered the stillness of the night on June 4, 1905, when W. B. West arrived in his merry Oldsmobile, having motored from St. Louis in only fourteen and one half hours.

In 1902, the Kansas City Council had before it an ordinance banning cars from the streets as pests and nuisances. In those days the "snort wagons," as they were called, were often stopped for speeding by policemen on horses!

In 1905 a group of farmers tried to ban cars in Mexico, Missouri.

The state jumped into the act. By 1903 the first state law licensing automobiles had been passed and the first speed limit in the nation was set—nine miles an hour. The law also provided that before any car could pass another vehicle drawn by animals, the operator had to sound a bell or whistle to let the driver stop and get off before his animals became frightened and ran away. The first gas tax, two cents, came in 1924. The Highway Patrol was created in 1931. You didn't need a driver's license in Missouri until 1937.

Missouri continues to be a major automobile manufacturing state, years after the first speed limits were set and the first licensing of automobiles was formally begun, when the law providing those regulations was signed by the Governor on this date, March 23, 1903.

****

MARCH 24
THE ART GALLERY WHERE THE LEGISLATURE MEETS

The tall white building dominates the area around it. It sits in dignified splendor on a bluff overlooking the often lazy, sometimes angry Missouri River. There are those who say it is the eleventh structure to serve its purpose in Missouri.

It is Missouri's Capitol building.

Its story goes back to a February night in 1911 when lightning struck the 70-year-old capitol and started the fire which gutted it. Mobilization for a new building began almost immediately. When the legislature got itself settled in churches and the State Supreme Court building, it immediately passed acts calling for a statewide bond issue to finance a new building. Voters approved by 100,000 votes a three and one half million dollar bond issue that August. Ground was broken on May 6, 1913, and on June 24, 1915, the cornerstone was laid. Seven years after the construction board was formed, the building was presented to the state, ready for occupancy.

The Capitol grounds were expanded for the new building. The state bought an extra one and one half blocks south of the site of the old Capitol, then bought a tract to the west to use as the location for a power house. The Capitol campus now covers 17 acres, twice as much as the old area.

Controversy developed over the quality of stone to be used in the building. Finally the decision was made to use Burlington Limestone from the quarries at Carthage, with the exception of the interior of the third floor, where Greene County limestone was to be used.

A New York firm, Tracy and Swartwout, was hired to design the building and supervise construction. The design called for a stately dome towering 400 feet over the Missouri River. Egerton Swartwout wrote in his description of the dome, "We have too few of them. It seems to have been the idea in the last ten or fifteen years that domes are banal and mongrel roofs or parapets have usually hidden the dome which existed in the interior, and should be expressed on the exterior. A dome is one of the most beautiful forms in all architecture, and even a poor dome is effective if it is logical."

It took Missourians eight years to finish their Capitol. But the Iowa Capitol took nine years to build; 14 years were needed to put up capitols in Wisconsin, Minnesota, and Arkansas, 21 years in Illinois and 33 in New York state.

Missouri's building is anchored with 285 concrete piers extending 20 to 50 feet into solid rock. It is 437 feet long, 200 feet wide and 300 feet wide through the center. It is 247 feet tall. Nearly 5,200 tons of steel were needed to make its frame at a cost of $354,000, 240,000 feet of stone were used at a cost of $774,000. More than $125,000 was spent to purchase 4,650,000 bricks. The superstructure took almost 31,000 barrels of cement, another 12,500 barrels were used for the basement along with 9,000 cubic yards of crushed stone. The building has 134 columns. One fourth of all stone in the building is in the columns.

Aside from the dome, another important feature is the grand stairway which leads from the third, or legislative, floor to the front portico. It is 30 feet wide and at the time of its construction was said to have been the widest stairway built in modern times anywhere in the world. At the base of those stairs is a 13-by-18-foot bronze door, the largest of its time. That door and two doors next to it cost $15,000. The building is notable for its stone carvings. It has 200 carved state medallions on the rear and front porticos. Four men died working on construction of the building.

Atop the dome is a statue of Ceres, the patron goddess of agriculture. The bronze statue at the South front of the building was done by James Earl Fraser, a famous sculptor, who used a full-length portrait of Thomas Jefferson by the prominent artist Gilbert Stuart for most of the work. He used a painting of the face by Charles Wilson Peale and Jefferson's own life mask for the head. Inside are paintings by American masters of the 20th century like Oscar Berninghaus, Nathaniel Wyeth, E. L. Blumenschein and Thomas Hart Benton. Benton's paintings are the most controversial. The dynamic murals in the House Lounge so angered some legislators in the 1930s that a short-lived effort to have them painted over was started. The inside of the dome was painted by Frank Brangwyn of London and Charles A. W. Ringschede of New York. Some say the artwork inside is worth more than the building itself.

It takes more than one visit to become truly familiar with the Missouri Capitol. To visit it often is to find a new carving, a new design, a new place for the state seal, to marvel at the long hallways and legislative chambers, the artwork and the museums. It all began when Governor Herbert S. Hadley signed the acts calling for the statewide bond issue to build it on this date, March 24, 1911.

****

MARCH 25
NORMAL SCHOOL NUMBER FIVE

Like so many colleges, it started life as a single building, a so-called "Normal School." Even then, we suppose, people came up with the tiresome old question about what an "Abnormal School" would be like. Normal Schools were established primarily to provide higher education for students in several counties around them. Normal School Number Five carried its simple undistinguished name for years because it was serving the Fifth Missouri Normal School District which covered 19 counties. But Normal School Number Five had roots which extended back a quarter century before its birth. The institution that Normal School Number Five became resulted largely from the efforts of residents of a small community who wanted something better than what they had.

In 1905, the Missouri legislature decided to set up a new college. As is often done, bidding for the campus location was invited. The winning community offered eighty-six and one-eighth acres of land valued at $57,000, along with another $58,600 cash. But a key part of the proposal from that town was a building already in existence which could be used.

In the 1880s citizens of Maryville banded together to set up a school that went somewhat beyond the regular public schools of the community. Out of that effort came a seminary. The seminary was established under the management of the Maryville First Methodist Episcopal Church. The school allowed students of all faiths to attend. In July of 1887 the articles of incorporation were filed for the operating organization, the "Northwest Missouri Education and Scientific Association." The organization later became known simply as the Maryville Seminary. It was announced that the school would be opened October 1, but things still weren't ready by then. Temporary quarters were set up in store rooms.

In March of the next year a public meeting was held to organize a campus and put up a building for the Seminary. Pledges were sought, about $6,000 was collected. Propositions were entertained for donations or sales of land for the site of the school. Again, the response was strong. Eight proposals were filed and the one of

Theodore L. Robinson was chosen. His tract was ten acres and worth about $1,300.

The first building wasn't finished until 1891. Classes moved into it that year. The school's first President was O. H. Smith. The school would have only four presidents in its entire life. About a decade and a half later the state government decided to organize the Fifth Normal School District in Northwest Missouri.

The site chosen was Maryville. In September, 1905, the first board of regents was named. In 1906 the institution gained its first president, Frank Deerwester, who went to Maryville from Central Missouri State Teachers College in Warrensburg. The first session at State Normal School Number Five was in June of 1906. The student body numbered 212. By the full term, however, enrollment was 775.

Then as now the largest percentage of the students came from the immediate 19-county area. One survey, about sixty-five years after the founding, showed about 70 percent of the school's enrollment came from within a sixty-mile radius of the campus. The first session was in a high school, then later the move was made to the old seminary building. It was used until the fall of 1910 when the first new building was opened. The old seminary building is gone now, torn down in 1925. By then enrollment was past 900 and would top the 1,000 mark in some quarters, beginning with the summer quarter of 1922. Like so many colleges, the school was a college in name only in its earliest days. The majority of students were really only of high school rank for the first few years of the school's existence.

In 1919 it became Northwest Missouri State Teachers College and the state gave it the right to grant Bachelor's degrees. Thirty years later the Board of Regents, acting under state legislative authority, changed the name again, to Northwest Missouri State College. Although the word "teachers" is long gone from the school name, the primary function of the school is still to educate men and women in the field of education.

In the early 1970s, the name changed again. The legislature passed a law letting colleges which had expanded into other fields to call themselves universities. Northwest Missouri wasted no time in making the change to reflect its growth.

Northwest Missouri State University started as just plain Normal School Number Five in Maryville when the legislature approved the act creating it on this date, March 25, 1905.

****

MARCH 26
MISSOURI: THE DISTRICT OF LOUISIANA

How would you feel if the government under which you lived no longer existed? As a Missourian, how would you feel, for instance, if your state were no longer ruled by the legislative, executive and judicial branches seated in Jefferson City, but by some stranger far away? It happened to Missouri and the feeling the people had then was similar to the feeling you might experience now.

The Spanish government then in control collected no taxes and did not require military service. It allowed slavery and was tolerant of various cultural backgrounds and institutions. It had a liberal land policy. Then in 1803 the American flag was raised over this land acquired in the Louisiana Purchase. People felt apprehension, resentment, anger, and suspicion. Missouri's citizens didn't like living under a democracy at first. They had become accustomed to living under what one might call a comfortable dictatorship. They liked the idea of paying almost no taxes, owning slaves, getting sizeable grants of land from the Spanish.

The U.S. Government, however, had developed a good system for giving newly-annexed areas self-government. It involved educating people to the rights and powers they had as citizens under the United States Constitution. The process started early here. President Jefferson quickly realized the fears of the residents of the Louisiana Territory, so he looked for a man who could represent the United States in the days of transition. He needed someone who could do the job with dignity and assurance. Jefferson picked Amos Stoddard to preside over the area. Stoddard was told to reappoint Spanish officials who were still around and keep the laws virtually unchanged. Jefferson and Stoddard hoped that would have a calming effect on the citizens. Apparently it did.

In an effort to give the area more of its own identity, the federal government in 1804 divided the Louisiana Territory into two regions. To the south was the Territory of Orleans. The north was the Territory of Louisiana. If you look at an old map, you'll note our state was shaped somewhat differently in those years. For one thing, New Madrid County extended far south, to the 33rd parallel, which divided the District of Louisiana from the Territory of Orleans. At one time, New Madrid County took in almost all of what is now Arkansas.

The capital city for the District of Louisiana was in Vincennes, Indiana. General William Henry Harrison governed the territory. But Missourians weren't too happy with that arrangement. They complained that their governing body was too far away and that they really had nothing to' say about their own government. In September, 1804, a petition signed by fifteen prominent citizens was presented to Congress. It asked for a form of self-government and it asked for money for a French and English School in each county.

The next year, the area took another step toward statehood. Congress decided the District of Louisiana should become the Territory of Louisiana, with its capital at St. Louis. That separated the area from the Vincennes capital. The residents still had little voice in their government, but the government was a lot closer. In fact, they actually had no more political rights than they had under Spanish rule. It would be a few years yet before anyone would refer to the territory as Missouri and do so officially.

But it was a big step, a major step, toward statehood. The area was reduced in size to a more-or-less specific set of geographical boundaries and something more like self-government was begun when Congress divided the Louisiana Territory into two areas, one of them the District of Louisiana which later became Missouri, on this date, March 26, 1804.

****

MARCH 27
THE MILL OF WALTUS WATKINS

He didn't believe it when an expert brickmaker told him he couldn't make bricks from the dirt of his plantation. He decided to try anyway. He was an ambitious man who wanted to build a brick house, a church, a school and a mill on his plantation which he called "Bethany." In 1859 and 1860 he proved the experts wrong. Today those brick buildings still stand. They're part of Missouri's State Park System and a National Historic Landmark.

Waltus Watkins came from Kentucky where he had been born in October of 1806. He was only twenty-four when he left his friends and family to come west to Missouri. His mechanical abilities had manifested themselves several years earlier in cotton mills owned by his uncles. He had been manager of a textile mill in Frankfort,

Kentucky. Watkins set up a small cotton mill near Liberty, but ran into trouble quickly. Cotton wasn't plentiful in Northwest Missouri. He tried importing the material but that wasn't economical. The effort ended when his mill burned.

He turned to agriculture and in 1839 bought the first 80 acres of what would become a 3,600-acre plantation. The next 20 years were important ones for Waltus Watkins. The area was being rapidly settled, thanks largely to his efforts. He established his own post office and built a fine mansion to replace his log cabin. He set up a flour and grist mill and a sawmill. He became one of the founders of William Jewell College and was a member of its board of trustees for 16 years. Eight of his eleven children were born during that time.

Watkins was 55 when he decided to put up the woolen mill, the largest one west of St. Louis. But this was a time of tight money. To raise the $30,000 to put up the mill, Watkins mortgaged almost everything. The machinery was ordered from Pennsylvania and the boiler and steam engine came from a St. Louis firm. The heavy equipment was hauled up the Missouri River by steamboat, then lugged 20 miles overland to the plantation. Operations began at the mill in May of 1861.

The Liberty *Tribune* carried this notice: "In a short time I will have an assortment of woolen goods for sale which shall be as good as any made elsewhere and as low as any establishment west of Cincinnati. . . . Persons wishing to purchase anything in our line can pay in cash or produce such as wool, wheat, corn, bacon, lard, soap, and other articles too tedious to mention."

But the Civil War intervened. Raids by guerrillas from both sides forced closure of the mill. Slow delivery of some equipment, which didn't arrive until 1864, hampered the output. The Watkins family was beginning to build a reputation for its mill, however, and after the war, it began to achieve the financial prosperity Watkins had hoped for. Business picked up as money became available throughout the country. His son John joined his father in the business and the firm became known as W. L. Watkins and Son. At its peak the mill processed forty to sixty thousand pounds of woolen fleece a year.

But the hard times of the early 1870s closed in. So did competition. Costs went up. Profits went down. In 1872 Waltus Watkins signed a $10,000 mortgage against much of his land to raise needed capital. His investment in a Ray County coal mine went sour. Finally in late September of 1882 he sold all of his holdings, farm and industry, to three of his sons who formed the firm of John H. Watkins and Brothers. Waltus Watkins died in January of 1884.

Some of his landholdings were sold to pay off debts. The mill was remodeled and provisions were made for dying the woolen material it produced. But all this couldn't save Watkins Mill. In 1899 the partnership was dissolved. John Watkins kept the land on which the mill and family home were located. In time, only a few custom wool carding jobs were done and little spinning. Shortly after the turn of the century, the boiler was shut down and the machinery stopped.

In 1934 the Clay County Historical Society launched an effort to turn the plantation into a park. Progress was slow. Not until 1958 was the Watkins Mill Association, a non-profit organization, able to purchase the mill. Five years later citizens of Clay County approved a bond issue to formally take over the original plantation. The land was then deeded to the Missouri Park Board. On November 8, 1966, the United States Department of the Interior declared Watkins Mill and its surrounding area a National Historic Landmark.

Today tourists wander over the quiet grounds of the Watkins plantation, visit the machinery, and admire the home Waltus Watkins built out of bricks the experts said couldn't be made. It all began when Waltus Lockett Watkins bought the first 80 acres of what later would be his plantation, "Bethany," on this date, March 27, 1839.

****

MARCH 28
MISSOURI'S ONE-MAN CHAMBER OF COMMERCE

He wrote in his journal, "I begin my tour where other travellers have ended theirs, on the confines of the wilderness and at the last village of white inhabitants between the Mississippi River and the Pacific Ocean...." He and another man began their journey of exploration ignorant about surviving in the wilderness. They did not know how to build a fire; they knew little about hunting; knew nothing about the Indians they'd meet and really had no idea where they were going. Despite this lack of knowledge or direction, Henry

Rowe Schoolcraft set off into what he would later call a "howling wilderness."

That last village of white inhabitants he talked about was St. Louis. The "howling wilderness" is the area around Springfield and Joplin, Missouri. He and Levi Pettibone began their travels in November of 1818. The interior of Missouri was still largely unknown and Schoolcraft, a trained mineralogist with education in "chymistry" was determined to trace its rivers and learn its possibilities. In time Henry Schoolcraft would be internationally famous in various scientific and ethnological circles.

The men ran into trouble. Twice in the first four days their packhorse wandered off. Schoolcraft complains in his journal that it was hard to sleep at nights because of fears that wild animals might be lurking around. His descriptions of what they found made exciting reading in his time because they were the first detailed descriptions of what kind of land awaited potential settlers in the areas of Missouri and "Arkansaw."

Schoolcraft was a New Yorker who had studied the glass industry as a youth, and headed west after a business venture went bad. He met Moses Austin at Herculaneum and thoroughly investigated the history and work of the lead mines in the Herculaneum-Potosi area. His book, *A View of the Lead Mines of Missouri,* was published in 1819 and is still a basic source book of the early techniques of lead mining in Missouri. He compiled that book in the summer before he started his investigative tour of the southwestern part of the territory. He estimated 1,100 people were engaged in mining. Others were farmers, mechanics, manufacturers, hunters, and professional men.

"The farming class is by far the largest," he wrote, "as the fertility of the soil and the advantage of procuring lands on easy terms, and a mild climate, afford the strongest and surest prospects of gain to the emigrant. There are probably fewer mechanics than are required by the existing population. The wages of mechanics of all kinds are very high. A carpenter or bricklayer cannot be hired for less than two dollars per day, and often receives more. Other mechanics are also in demand, particularly in the new settlements; and these are increasing with such rapidity as to invite emigration of skillful and industrious artisans from all parts, with the sure prospect of success."

Later on his trip to the wilderness, Schoolcraft met hunters and isolated settlers, describing the hunters as being "a hardy, brave and independent people, rude in appearance, frank and generous who traveled without baggage, could subsist anywhere in the woods and would form the most efficient military corps in frontier warfare."

Missourians of all sorts fascinated this easterner. "Hospitality to strangers, enterprise in business, ardor in the pursuit of wealth, an elevated pride of country and perseverances under the pressure of many difficulties growing out of the infancy of the settlements are the most conspicuous traits. They are robust, frank, and daring. Taught by the hardships and dangers incident to a frontier settlement to depend for security and success upon their own individual exertions, they rely little on extraneous help and feel that true independence flows from a conviction that their own physical exertions are equal to every call, necessity and emergency of life." Writing like this prompted some to refer to Schoolcraft as "Missouri's first Chamber of Commerce."

He and Pettibone tramped through what are now the counties of Crawford, Dent and Texas, then into Wright and Douglas counties, where they followed the north fork of the White River into Arkansas. They came back into the present Taney and Stone counties, up the James River, probably near the present town of Springfield, then headed south again.

They might have reached what is now Batesville, Arkansas, then walked to where West Plains now stands. Pettibone went back to St. Louis, but Schoolcraft kept walking, wandering through the area that became Shannon, Reynolds, Iron, Madison and St. Francois counties, arriving in Potosi in February. In his journal he would mention zinc in southwest Missouri, something not really "discovered" for another 50 years.

While still in Missouri, he looked into the future and wrote that St. Louis would become the "seat of empire for that vast basin of land....Its situation in point of beauty, health and convenience is rarely equalled, and no place in the world, situated so far from the ocean, can at all compare with it for a commercial advantage."

He died in December of 1864 in New York. Henry Rowe Schoolcraft, scientist, explorer of the howling wilderness of Southwest Missouri, Missouri's one-man Chamber of Commerce, was born on this date, March 28, 1793.

****

MARCH 29
DUBOURG: CATHEDRAL BUILDER

When Missouri became a territory of the United States in 1804 a large number of the Catholic clergy in the area left and the Catholic Church suffered. The Catholic Church fell on such hard times, in fact, that the log church built in 1777 in St. Louis was not cared for. It was crumbling and falling in.

But then the right Reverend Louis William Valentine DuBourg arrived. He carried the title of Bishop of Louisiana and the Floridas. St. Louis numbered a little under 1,500 people in 1804. Ten years earlier, another priest named Dunand had written, "Having arrived in St. Louis I found the district in a pitiful state. Deprived of priests and all spiritual aid, the morals of the people were entirely corrupt and ignorance of religion was so general that the inhabitants scarcely recognized the name Catholic." Shortly after he arrived, Bishop Du-Bourg wrote, "My cathedral, which looks like a poor stable, is falling in ruins, so that a new church is absolutely necessary." Just three days after DuBourg arrived, he had plans drawn for a new cathedral.

A parish meeting was held and raised almost $4,300. At a later meeting another $1,300 came in. The biggest amount of money, however, came from the sale of the old pews in the crumbling log church for almost $6,800. Then the wealthy Chouteau family and another man loaned the church about $4,500 more. The cathedral was begun. The main part of the building was to be 134 by 40 feet. It was to be 40 feet high with five large arches on each side. A tall steeple, as tall as the building was deep, would contain several bells from France. The decorations would be surprisingly grand for a frontier church.

Twenty-one months after the plans were made the first services where held in the new church on Christmas day. But the church wasn't finished yet, and it would never become what the Bishop hoped it would be. Soon after the Christmas service in 1819 the five arches intended to separate the middle of the church from the side aisles were filled in and became outer walls. Financial times were hard. Despite the fact that the church had six paintings donated by Louis XVIII, King of France, and despite the money collected to start construction, operations suffered from lack of money. Help finally came from the Association for the Propagation of the Faith, in France, under the Archbishop of Rouen.

Bishop DuBourg gave more than just his time and effort to the building, later praised as unique in this part of the world. He furnished a number of personal items. The church organ belonged to him, received during his travels to Europe in 1815. DuBourg also succeeded in reviving the Catholic church in St. Louis. When he had first arrived, one of his contemporaries said the people weren't very interested in him. As a matter of fact, they said the Emperor of China would have been just as interesting. But so successful were the Bishop's efforts that in only thirteen years it became apparent another new church was needed.

By then Bishop DuBourg had resigned. He was succeeded by an associate, Bishop Joseph Rosati. In 1831 the cornerstone of a newer church was laid. That church is still standing as a national landmark near the Gateway Arch in St. Louis, the fourth Catholic Church on the same lot since the first one was built in 1770. Bishop DuBourg's church suffered the ignominious fate of becoming a warehouse until it was destroyed by fire in 1835.

A priest who worked closely with Bishop DuBourg, Father Felix DeAndreis, wrote, "I must confess that after God, the mention of all that has been, or will be done, is due to the rare talents, industry, experience, activity, ability, prudence, vigilance, patience, zeal—in a word, to the indefatigable perseverance of this extraordinary man, Bishop DuBourg....He preaches continually in both languages, English and French. The numerous conversions that take place should be attributed to him. He is not only at the helm, but at the sail and oars; he is everywhere; he preaches, hears confessions, baptizes, marries, assists the sick, is general, captain, sergeant, and foot-soldier."

His cathedral is gone, but the Catholic church is strong because of Bishop DuBourg. He is known as a man who brought education and faith to his people. Today when you visit the present "old cathedral" sitting in dignity on the St. Louis riverfront, remember Louis DuBourg, the Bishop who built a building and resurrected his faith among the people of Missouri. It was *his* cathedral which symbolized his efforts, a cathedral for which the cornerstone was laid on this date, March 29, 1818.

****

MARCH 30
ANOTHER THOMAS REYNOLDS, ANOTHER TRAGEDY

His body was found at the bottom of a St. Louis elevator shaft in 1887. Historians are still unsure if he jumped or fell the eighty feet to his death. His name was Thomas Reynolds. He had been Governor of Missouri. More than 40 years earlier, another Thomas Reynolds, also a Governor, ended his life with a gunshot blast. The first Thomas Reynolds was the legitimate Governor of our state. The second Thomas Reynolds was not.

Governor Claiborne Fox Jackson fled the Capital in 1861. Later that year he declared Missouri separated from the Union. By then, however, a wartime government had taken over Missouri. Hamilton Gamble was declared the new Governor. Jackson and his Confederate followers were on the outside looking in, no matter what they would claim for the next four years. When Jackson died in 1862 in Arkansas, Thomas Caute Reynolds, who had been elected Lieutenant Governor in the legitimate elections in Missouri, succeeded him as head of the Confederate government of Missouri. He gathered up what he could find of the state papers and went to Texas with them. He leased a home to use as a Governor's mansion in Marshall, Texas.

Reynolds had served with the U.S. Legation in Spain in the 1840s. Later he became a United States District Attorney in St. Louis. At one time he and a man who was also to be a Governor, B. Gratz Brown, fought a duel. Reynolds wasn't hurt, but Brown suffered a knee wound that made him limp all his life.

Reynolds was an ardent secessionist. Floyd Shoemaker described him as "a driving force behind the avowed secessionists in Missouri.... Intelligent, accomplished, he was a firm believer in the cause of the South...." So persistent was Reynolds that, had he been in a position of more power, the story of Missouri and the Confederacy might have had a different ending. Historian William Parrish said that he was "brilliant" and he "bored into the heart of every question with pitiless auger of common sense." In time Reynolds came to doubt the leadership capabilities of Governor Jackson. He insisted Sterling Price be named to head the State Militia over the objections of Jackson who wasn't seeing eye to eye with Price then.

In May, Reynolds went South to talk with Confederate leaders about secession. He asked for Confederate troops to be sent to Missouri as quickly as possible. After Jackson's death, Reynolds' role was greatly important in holding the Missouri Confederacy together. He acted quickly to gain payment for soldiers from the Confederate government. The Reynolds government established legitimate status with the Confederacy with its representatives and senators in Richmond. His vigorous efforts gave Confederate efforts legitimacy in Missouri.

In August of 1863, Reynolds became the second most powerful man in the Southwestern Confederate Department, working under Commander E. Kirby Smith to establish committees of correspondence in each county and parish, urging cooperation with Smith in the war effort. There are evidences, though, that Reynolds was a little carried away with his role sometimes. George Graham Vest once recalled Reynolds was always an even-tempered and polished gentleman, at least as much as conditions allowed. He kept a notebook of remarks made about himself by others and once called Vest on the carpet for saying something insulting. Vest, never one to sidestep things, told Reynolds, "Yes, I did say that, every word of it. I think you are going around here putting on too many airs with your little old one-horse Confederate state government, carrying your commission in your hat and the great seal of Missouri in your saddlebags. Put that in your memorandum book if you want to." Vest says Reynolds responded, "Oh, well, we'll not say any more about it." By the end of their visit, Reynolds had named Vest to a term as a Senator in Richmond, the Confederate capital city.

When the war ended, Reynolds fled to Mexico with Shelby's men. He still had the State Seal and said, "I will return it whenever Missouri has a Governor legally elected at the polls." He came back in 1869 and returned the seal to Governor McClurg, saying he hoped it would "be an augury of the speedy oblivion of past strife, and of the complete restoration of fraternal feeling."

Later he pleaded for unity, once telling a group of former Confederates, "We have played at the grand game of Civil War, and so ably as to gain the admiration of the world, and the respect of magnanimous opponents. We lost it for want of trumps, but we drew at least our fair share of honor."

In the mid 1870s President Arthur named him to a commission to investigate relations with Latin America. Reynolds spoke three languages fluently and was a logical choice. But a great tragedy occurred just before the tour. A spark from a fireplace ignited his wife's nightgown and she died later of the burns. In the late 1880s his health began to fail. He worried he would become a burden on his new wife. Shortly after that he became the second Governor Thomas Reynolds of Missouri to die tragically when his body was found at the bottom of that elevator shaft on March 30, 1887.

****

MARCH 31
THE ROOM ON THE SIXTH FLOOR

Personal memories of the fears generated among German and Japanese-American citizens during World War II have faded with the years. But the fears were very real, not only on the part of those citizens, but on the part of people who felt they had reason to fear Americans of recent German or Japanese heritage.

The stories of the impounding of Japanese-American citizens on the West Coast are familiar to us. But right here in Missouri, a sizeable counterspy operation was under way for most of the war, and for good reason. If it was natural for the federal government to be concerned about what might happen with all the Americans on the west coast who have Oriental heritage, it was also natural for people at high levels to worry about what could happen in Missouri, an area where Germans settled in large numbers.

The German people in Missouri themselves were quite conscious of their heritage. They also were aware of their neighbor's hostile feelings. Much of that same feeling had been expressed during World War I. For example, in Bollinger County, German Township was renamed Scopus Township in 1918. German Township in Madison County became Marquant Township. The old German Center School in St. Clair was renamed Valley Center School. Keyser Avenue in Columbia, although named for a family of English extraction, didn't sound right. So it was changed to Wilson Avenue. Potsdam, in Gasconade County, was renamed Pershing.

A foreign power did influence the lives of many in Missouri. Late in the war the story was revealed of a special committee established in St. Louis which had the duty to keep watch on some 7,000 Americans of German descent or of Communist leanings. In 1939 the federal government in this country decided to watch as closely as

193

possible any persons who might have Nazi tendencies. In St. Louis a special squad of detectives was organized within the police force. It worked with the FBI for the next six years. The squad, eventually numbering 14 officers, worked from an unmarked sixth floor office at the police station. What went on behind the door of that office, and who the men were who were involved, was a closely-guarded secret.

St. Louis police chief James J. Mitchell said when the squad was organized that St. Louis was a "hotbed of Un-American activity and sympathy." But he would later note, largely because of that squad and the FBI, that St. Louis did not suffer a single case of enemy-inspired sabotage, despite being one of the nation's most vital war production centers. By the spring of 1945, Mitchell was able to boast that every organized subversive society in St. Louis had been wiped out.

The squad was headed by Sergeant Harry J. Powell, a forty-year man on the force. It found loyal German-Americans and induced them to infiltrate various subversive groups. When a Congressional Committee on Un-American Activity came to St. Louis, Powell and his men were able to provide committee members with complete files on key Nazi and Communist sympathizers. About 7,000 enemy aliens and, as reports later said, "numerous fifth column groups," were investigated by that squad. In time, fifty-eight dangerous enemy aliens were jailed.

One man who had been watched closely by the squad was a German-born publicist who died before the war was over. He brought attention to himself by his frequent visits to the German Consulate in St. Louis, and his attendance at Nazi rallies which were held in St. Louis and other parts of Missouri. He finally confessed to police he was helping the Nazi Consul control Nazi sympathizers. He told Powell and his officers he had relatives in Germany the consul had threatened to harm unless he cooperated with the Germans. It was a technique which the Nazis used to influence thousands of Americans, and hundreds of Missourians.

Sometimes the squad raided places thought to be subversive group headquarters. What they found is a little astonishing to consider. But when word finally got out, spokesmen reported uncovering shortwave receivers, various kinds of weapons, cameras, and even Nazi storm trooper uniforms. It wasn't until American troops landed in Europe and were driving toward victory that word of the squad came out. With the Germans all but on their knees in

Europe, officials felt they could relax the secrecy in St. Louis surrounding that unmarked office on the sixth floor of the police station.

There were no massive jailings in Missouri. But there was a watchful eye: the secret squad—a dark secret until authorities felt they could tell the story to the public on this date, March 31, 1945.

Bonnie
& Clyde
Shootout,
April 13, 1933

APRIL

APRIL 1
THE EMPIRE BUILDER OF SOUTHEAST MISSOURI

A passenger on a train riding through the swampy woodlands of Southeast Missouri would suddenly hear the conductor cry out, "Look out, she's going to jump!" And in a minute the train *would* jump! It was because the builder of the railroad had felled two trees and laid them across a small creek south of Benton instead of building a regular bridge. The train would have to rise suddenly as the rails bent upward to get onto that bridge. It was just one of the many projects of Louis Houck, the "Empire Builder of Southeast Missouri."

When he went to Southeast Missouri and settled in Cape Girardeau, Louis Houck realized the area could be greatly developed if there was an outlet for its products. Little farming above the subsistence level was done; more could be done if there was a way to get products to market. So Houck, a good lawyer, announced in 1880 that he was retiring from practice to become a railroad builder. Eleven years earlier, the Cape Girardeau and State Line Railroad had been organized with plans to lay tracks from Cape Girardeau to the Arkansas border. But the bonds to finance it didn't sell. Louis Houck contracted with the original owners to complete the road by January of 1881. If he did, the agreement stipulated, he would own the railroad.

At 3:00 a.m. on January 1, 1881, the first locomotive arrived at Cape Girardeau. It had taken some doing because much of the work had been done in the winter cold. There had been a shortage of materials and money. To make good his promise to put a train in Cape Girardeau that day, Houck had to tear up some track already laid and put it ahead of the locomotive as it moved along!

From 1880 to 1905 Houck supervised the construction of more than 500 miles of short line railroads in Southeast Missouri and Southwest Illinois. Because of that, Southeast Missouri had more rail connections than many other parts of the state. In 1902 he incorporated all of his railroads into the St. Louis and Gulf Railroad Company. Soon afterward he sold out to the St. Louis and San Francisco Railroad Company. Some of his short line routes are still part of the Frisco system.

In the early 1870s, when Cape Girardeau was trying unsuccessfully to obtain a state normal school, Houck and another man offered to buy the necessary bonds. In the fall of 1873 Cape Girardeau was selected as a site for the school. Houck later became a member of the Board of Regents, and two years later was elected president of the Board, a position be held until his death about fifty years later in 1925.

Houck had always been a student of history and discovered that one story of early Missouri had never been told. His interest was encouraged by a large collection of old documents he found at the New Madrid County Courthouse. He planned to write a series of short sketches on the early prestatehood days, but quickly found it would take more research. So, seated on a creaking old chair and working at a walnut desk at Elmwood, he started compiling what became a 1,200-page, three-volume work still considered a standard work on early Missouri history. He employed agents to search old records in Canada, France, Spain, Cuba, and Mexico. He spent his summer vacations looking through the Library of Congress. To gain information on the Indians he had his railroad surveyors chart Indian mounds. They found, in two years, more than 2,800 of them in eastern Missouri. The books were a diversion from his railroad building. He compiled the information for them off and on for about twenty years, and took four years to dictate the manuscript. (He dictated because his handwriting was very poor. The story is told that he once gave a man a receipt for a load of hay and the man used it as a pass on Houck's railroads for years because the conductors could read nothing but the signature.) His first books came out in 1908 and a year later he published a two-volume set on the Spanish regime in Missouri.

In the foreword of the three-volume history, he wrote, "For me it has been a labor of love, absorbing for a long time all my leisure hours—diverting my mind from business cares.... Such in brief is the origin of this work, written at odd hours by one professing no literary accomplishments, but nevertheless anxious to rescue from oblivion that earlier Missouri."

He was eighty-four when he died in his beloved Southeast Missouri. Louis Houck, railroad builder, lawyer, newspaper publisher, a man who in his spare time became one of this state's greatest historians, the Empire Builder of Southeast Missouri was born on this date, the first of April, 1841.

****

198

APRIL 2
THE TAVERN AT NEW PHILADELPHIA

Long before the white man came, the Indians made good use of an outcropping of flint near the Missouri River. French hunters are thought to have been the first white men to see the territory. Lewis and Clark wrote in their journal that it would be a nice place for a town. A trading post was finally built there in 1813 and later, as traffic increased, a ferry boat landing was built and operated by an uncle of Abraham Lincoln's wife.

The town itself was born in 1829 with the pretentious name of New Philadelphia. Three governors would spring from the frontier community. It also would produce at least four first ladies, a great artist, and a world-renowned doctor.

The plan of the town was first drawn up by Meredith Miles Marmaduke, later a governor of Missouri. For a short time it was the county seat. It thrived on the river traffic that reached its peak in the 1860s but was never a large town — its biggest population was about 1,000. Stage service came. A telegraph line was installed. Slaves built the cobblestone gutters which are still there. It is said that when the first Santa Fe traders came back and slashed open their saddlebags, silver dollars rolled into those gutters.

New Philadelphia was on the downhill slide by the time the Civil War ended, and by 1873 it had shrunk to a community of 600. A major fire that year destroyed part of the town and three young men believed to have been the arsonists were lynched. The death knell was rung prematurely in 1923 when a bridge across the Missouri River was built a short distance downstream and the town's ferryboat operation closed after about 110 years of service.

But New Philadelphia would not die.

A historically minded group realized the value of the community and in the early 1920s set about to breathe new life into this slice of Missouri's past. Back in 1833, Saline County Judge Joseph Huston had bought land in New Philadelphia and put up a two and one-half story tavern. It had four rooms, an attic, and perhaps a detached brick kitchen. A two-room, two-story addition was put up in the 1840s as a grocery store, a ballroom, and a meeting hall. In the 1880s the building was enlarged again. Forty years later the Daughters of the American Revolution persuaded the state to buy the old tavern — what we could call a hotel-restaurant today. The state paid

$5,000 for it, the first historic building ever acquired by the state. It took another $20,000 to restore it.

Today visitors will note the seven original fireplaces, the portraits by George Caleb Bingham of Dr. and Mrs. John Sappington and Governor Calib Jackson. In the lobby hangs the rope connected to the old steamboat bell atop the roof, a bell rung years ago each evening to remind people to take Dr. Sappington's wonderful anti-fever pills to combat malaria.

You can eat at the tavern, visit the old seminary building, and see the town jail which supposedly had only one prisoner in its entire history. The story goes that he yelled so loudly they released him.

Water still flows down the hard-laid rock gutters.

The old lodge building is still there, as is the gunsmith's home and a doctor's office.

You can stand and look down a ravine that is Godsey's Diggin's, an improvement project which went on for seventeen years and was never finished. For seventeen years the effort was made to cut a shorter, more direct route to the river from the bluffs on which the town grew up. But the commissioners finally gave up. Steamboat traffic was waning and the river was moving away.

The courthouse still stands, an unimposing small structure which was the seat of county government in 1839 and 1840, and is said to have been the scene which formed the basis of a famous Bingham painting, "County Election."

Restoration continues. Curio shops, the artist's home, the doctor's office and the gunsmith's shop are open to the public. The mid-eighteenth century atmosphere of the town is so vivid that in the 1970s, a musical version of Mark Twain's *Tom Sawyer* was filmed there. The town was used to portray Hannibal of a century before, because it looked more like Hannibal did than Hannibal does.

The old Baptist Church has become a summer theatre, a circumstance which prompted author MacKinlay Kantor to speculate that old-time Baptists are probably rolling over in their graves.

Oh yes, one other thing. The town isn't known as New Philadelphia anymore—hasn't been since 1835. Someday, though, you owe yourself a visit to Arrow Rock, where the flavor of the 1850s lives, much of it because the state began saving it with the purchase of the old tavern on this date, the second of April, 1923.

****

APRIL 3
THE PONY

The wood-fired locomotive rushed across the Missouri prairie at record speed. Down the line a few miles a group of citizens was waiting in a telegraph office when the printer started clicking. The message read, "Something yellow, flying low, just shot through town." The message had come from Cameron at 4:49 p.m.

The train, rushing from Hannibal to St. Joseph, was carrying important cargo. It traveled so fast it set a record which would stand for a half century.

The cargo? Forty-six pieces of paper.

In a few hours those forty-six pieces of paper would constitute new pages in history.

A few minutes after that first telegraph message, another one came in from Hamilton, Missouri, saying the train had taken on more fuel. The telegraph operator said the train had been leaving enough dead pigs and cows along the right-of-way to provide a barbecue for the entire state.

A few hours later, those forty-six pieces of paper were stuffed into pockets on a saddle and by mistake were thrown onto the horse ridden by ten-year-old Billy Richardson, who had planned to accompany the real rider to the St. Joseph Ferry landing and help send him on his way. Young Billy and the other rider, Johnny Frye, dashed to the ferry boat. The mail was transferred to Frye's saddle at the riverfront. Moments later Frye was on the Kansas side of the river, a diminishing speck headed for Sacramento, California.

The Pony Express was on its way.

The advertisement attracting Richardson and others like him had appeared in February 1860. "Wanted," it read, "young skinny, wiry fellows not over eighteen. Must be expert riders willing to risk death daily. Orphans preferred. Wages...25 dollars per week."

The operation centered on Alexander Majors. He required his employees to take an oath: "While I am in the employ of A. Majors, I agree not to use profane language, not to get drunk, not to gamble, not to treat animals cruelly, and not to do anything incompatible with the conduct of a gentleman. I agree, if I violate any of the above conditions, to accept my discharge without pay for my service."

Majors expected those pledges to be signed, then he would present his employees with a Bible. They were the young men who would live and die as members of the Pony Express. On the calendar their time in the profession was short. The Pony Express existed only eighteen months. Then the telegraph and other developments put it out of business.

When the train arrived in St. Joseph that first day, its occupants were the worse for wear from the breakneck speeds on the still primitive roadbeds. The first rider, Richardson, took the letters, and stuffed them into the pockets on the saddle. There were speeches, crowds, and cheering. Richardson galloped down the river shore, boarded the steamboat, "Denver," and was on his way. Before the boat reached the other shore, Richardson and the horse jumped off, clearing the stretch of water between the bow and the land, and the first mail was on its way to California. Richardson left St. Joseph at 6:30 in the evening. Five minutes short of nine days later he reached Salt Lake.

In San Francisco a similar scene was in progress. There, James Randall, with eighty-four letters, started east.

The fastest run that would ever be made was seven days, seventeen hours, when the Pony Express carried Lincoln's first inaugural address to the West Coast. The average time was about eleven days.

Every man who rode for Majors and his two partners, William Russell and William Waddell, became hero-stuff for Americans and remain so today.

One was a former errand boy for Majors who eventually got to ride on the Pony Express although he was only fifteen at the time. He made a seventy-seven-mile run in one of the relays, but when he reached the next relay station he found the rider had been killed. He took a fresh horse and rode the next eighty-five miles. There a waiting rider took the mail on west. But the young man picked up the eastbound load and headed back. When he reached his point of origin he had covered 322 miles, virtually nonstop. It was a new record. He averaged fifteen miles per hour. At the age of fifteen Bill Cody, who later would become famous as a buffalo killer and wild west show promoter, was already a western legend.

Then there was Robert Haslam, "Pony Bob," they called him. His ride through the prairies while pursued by a band of Indians is another part of the epic story of the Pony Express—one preserved in a painting in fact. He was one of the last of the fabled riders to die, in 1912. He's buried now in Chicago and the stone on his grave was paid for by his friend, Bill Cody.

It all ended in 1861—bankrupt by a third of a million dollars. The telegraph and the railroad postal car had helped spell its end. The Pony Express died, leaving behind legends, a few scattered outposts, and some stables in St. Joseph which are now a quiet museum.

As long as America has heroes the story will be told of the Pony Express whose first rider galloped westward out of St. Joseph on this date, April 3, 1860.

****

APRIL 4
THE WIVES AND WARS OF CALIB JACKSON

He was twenty-five when he married the daughter of a famous doctor. She died only six months later. But she had a sister, so he married her. She bore him two sons and died about six years later. But she had a sister, so he asked the old doctor if he could marry the third daughter. The doctor supposedly said, "Take her, Calib. But don't come back for the old lady. She's all I got left."

Pulitzer Prize winning author MacKinlay Kantor wrote that Claiborne Fox Jackson must have been terribly hard on wives. But marrying three sisters wasn't his only achievement. Calib Jackson would die in a fight for a lost cause after reaching the state's highest office.

Jackson was a Kentuckian by birth, who went to Old Franklin when he was nineteen. Later he moved to Saline County and that's when he met the family of Dr. John Sappington.

At the age of thirty Jackson took a seat in the Missouri legislature. He was against chartering the State Bank of Missouri, but when the legislature approved it Claiborne Fox Jackson became the chief cashier of one of its branches.

He rose to become Speaker of the House.

In 1848, as a state senator and a member of the Federal Relations Committee, he returned a minority report which contained six proposals. These became the famous Jackson Resolutions which had far-reaching effects. One of those proposals challenged the power of Congress to legislate the institution of slavery. The resolutions were strongly pro states rights and instructed Missouri's congressional delegation to follow them in actions in Washington. Thomas Hart

Benton came out against them, returned to Missouri to best them, but found himself beaten after a quarter-century of representing Missouri in the U.S. Senate.

Jackson did not try for re-election to the Senate in 1852 and had a hard time winning a seat in the House. A year later he ran for Congress in a district which, it was openly charged, had been created to insure his success. But he lost. He tried again in 1856 but lost again. A year later he was named State Bank Commissioner, a job he filled until 1860. By then, party unity had been restored and the feeling grew that it was Jackson's turn to be nominated governor. Even then it took three ballots before he was finally chosen.

Although Jackson was fundamentally one of those Democrats who supported John C. Breckenridge, he favored Stephen A. Douglas nationally because of St. Louis political pressures. The national party was divided over the Douglas-Breckenridge issue, but hung together enough in Missouri to elect Jackson governor by 7,000 votes over three other candidates.

In his inaugural address he continued the expressions of the earlier Jackson Resolutions and called for Missouri to make what he called "a timely declaration of her determination to stand by her sister slave-holding states, in whose wrongs she participates and with whose institutions and people she sympathizes."

When Abraham Lincoln issued his first call for volunteers to put down a rebellion, Jackson wrote back that "not a man would the State of Missouri furnish to carry on such an unholy crusade." The governor called the legislature into session and sent to Montgomery, Alabama, for guns and mortars to be used in taking the St. Louis arsenal. The arsenal was under Union control and a prime plum for the infant Confederacy.

But a massive internal struggle was taking place within the military in St. Louis. Nathaniel Lyon was finally given command and acted to strengthen the arsenal. Jackson established a southern-leaning state militia, quartered at what was called Camp Jackson. But Lyon captured the camp.

The legislature, hearing of the bloodshed in that takeover, quickly passed Jackson's militia bills asking for 50,000 volunteers. He got many of them. But Lyon was already on the way to Jefferson City.

The Convention of 99 took over, named Hamilton Gamble interim governor, and the state stayed in the Union.

Jackson summoned a Confederate legislature that same year and it proclaimed Missouri a Confederate state, for all the good it did.

That winter, Federal forces drove Jackson and Price from Missouri. After the Battle of Pea Ridge in Arkansas, the Confederate hopes in Missouri were crushed. Jackson would not live to see the end of the war and the South repeatedly fail to regain Missouri. He died in 1862 at his Confederate headquarters in Little Rock. After the war, his body was returned to Arrow Rock for burial in the Sappington family graveyard.

Claiborne Fox Jackson, a man who reached the state's highest office but chose the wrong side and died pretending to be governor, was born on this date, the fourth of April in 1806.

****

APRIL 5
THE WEEPING JUDGE

He was a judge with an eye problem so bad he often could not read. Sometimes he wore goggles or blindfolds when he conducted court. He often had someone else read his decisions from the bench. Despite this handicap he was one of our most distinguished early jurists.

He saw many doctors in an attempt to cure the eye inflammation which prevented him from being in brightly-lighted areas at times. He once wrote his brother, "I have bathed them much in brandy and water...I have likewise applied to them as an eye water, a solution of opium...I have derived no benefit...I am satisfied that cold water is injurious.

"My eyes are not a whit better than when I returned from Philadelphia."

James Hawkins Peck never was able to get rid of the problem.

Peck came to Missouri from Tennessee, starting his law practice in 1818. He rapidly made friends with David Barton, later Missouri's first U.S. Senator.

In one of his early cases, Peck represented a Kentucky man who had a contract to deliver supplies to Council Bluffs, Iowa. A St. Louis bank had seized the firm's boats. It was an important case. By the time it was over, the man Peck represented had risen from Kentucky state representative to U.S. Senator from Kentucky.

Later, Richard M. Johnson was vice-president under Martin Van Buren.

By then Missouri was a state and Barton was a senator. The District Court of Missouri was created and Peck became its first judge. He was nominated by Barton and Johnson. He served in that post for fourteen years, until his death.

When the capital was relocated in Jefferson City, Peck commuted from St. Louis for his court's sessions.

In 1824, Congress ordered Peck's court to rule on the validity of various conflicting land claims carried over from the days of the French and Spanish governments. With no precedents to go on, Peck made his ruling in favor of the state against Antoine Soulard in the first case.

Soulard's attorney, with the unlikely name of Luke Lawless, wrote a letter published in a St. Louis newspaper criticizing the decision.

Peck charged Lawless with contempt and after two days of courtroom argument sent Lawless to jail for twenty-four hours and suspended his right to practice for eighteen months. Lawless petitioned Congress to have Peck impeached. Twice Congress refused to act but Lawless did not withdraw his petition. Finally the House impeached James Hawkins Peck in April 1830, five years after Peck had heard the Soulard case. Peck was so sure he was right he never tried to resolve the matter. The articles of impeachment charged that Peck had wrongfully and oppressively convicted and sentenced Lawless.

The trial began that December and lasted a month and a half. The prosecution's attorneys, one of whom was future President James Buchanan, charged that Peck had tried to restrict freedom of the press, had punished a man for contempt after an appeal had been filed, had imposed improper punishment in suspending a member of the bar from practice, and had shown a disposition to injure Lawless in his profession.

Peck's defense was that Lawless's letters had implied that those with land claims could not get a fair trial. Peck said it was imperative for the court to uphold its integrity.

A two-thirds majority was required to achieve conviction. The vote was twenty-two guilty, twenty-one not guilty. So Peck's career continued.

Judge Peck served for another six years with distinction although he was never able to shake off the stigma of the impeachment.

In April of 1836 he caught pneumonia riding back to St. Louis from a court session in Jefferson City and died. He was in his mid-forties.

Judge James Hawkins Peck, one of Missouri's most distinguished early jurists, the first judge of the Federal District Court of Missouri, and the key figure in one of the nation's major court cases involving the courts themselves, the weeping judge, was confirmed as a district judge on this date, April 5, in 1822.

****

APRIL 6
THE WAR TO END ALL WARS

Missouri played a distinguished role in World War I, both on the battlefield and at home. A former adjutant General of Missouri, Harvey Clark, says "Missouri was represented in practically every company, battery, corps, or contingent in the American army, and contributed its full quota to the Officers Reserve Corps, navy, regular army, aviation service, marines, the engineers, railroad troops and sanitary units." A total of 138,310 Missourians served in World War I, 11,172 of them becoming casualties. Even the Missouri mule was recognized for playing a major role.

The last Missourian had just been released from serving on the Mexican border when war was declared. The Missouri National Guard was pressed into federal service in August 1917 and was sent to Camp Doniphan, Oklahoma, and consolidated with the Kansas Guard to form the 35th Division. The soldiers (including a young captain named Harry Truman) arrived in Europe in mid-May, 1918.

The unit saw service at St. Mihel and the Argonne which General Clark described as being the "razor edge of the American advance." It fought for six days against four of the best Prussian divisions, covered eleven miles, and captured every objective. More than 4,500 Missourians were wounded and 675 were killed. Forty percent of the officers were casualties, the highest relative loss among officers of any American division in the war.

The first contingent of Missouri draftees was combined in September 1917 with men from Kansas, Nebraska, South Dakota, Colorado, Arizona, and New Mexico to become the 89th Division. They were among the last units to reach Europe but at St. Mihel they took twenty-one miles of territory and captured five towns. At the

Argonne the 89th crossed the Meuse River when the Armistice was signed. The 89th became part of the Army of Occupation in Germany. It had captured more than 5,000 prisoners, 127 artillery pieces, and 455 machine guns.

The name of Dr. William T. Fitzsimmons won't be found in many history books. A Missourian from Kansas City, when war broke out he went as a volunteer. He traveled to Belgium on the first Red Cross ship and served under the French flag and later in an American hospital. Dr. Fitzsimmons became the first American to die in France in World War I.

Eight Missourians won the Medal of Honor: Capt. Alex Skinker, Sgt. Arthur Forrest and Sgt. Michael Ellis, all of St. Louis; Pfc. Charles Barger of Mount Vernon; Pfc. Jesse Funk of New Hampton; Sgt. M. Waldo Hatler of Bolivar; Pfc. John Barkley of Blairstown, and Cpl. Harold Turner of Aurora.

There were also others of distinction: John Pershing of Lamar, the AEF Commander; Enoch Crowder of Edinburg who wrote the Selective Service Law for the war; Commander Joseph Taussig of St. Louis who commanded the first American destroyer flotilla to arrive in European waters. A St. Louis woman, Miss Julia Stinson, was in charge of all Red Cross nurses in France. A Missourian, Gregory Davison of Jefferson City, invented the depth charge used to destroy submarines. Missouri's Council of Defense, established to encourage food production, was one of the best in the nation. Almost 1,500 Missouri doctors offered their services. Kansas City supplied more doctors and nurses than any other city in the nation. A. A. Kellog of Clinton invented an instantaneous detonator for shells, allowing explosion on contact. St. Louis native Julien A. Gehrung discovered a successful treatment for nerve gas.

On January 19, 1918, merchants in Hallsville agreed not to sell candy as long as sugar was in such short supply and was needed overseas. Hallsville was the first known town in America where the merchants did that.

Former Washington University Chancellor David Houston was Secretary of Agriculture and in charge of the campaign for greater national food production.

The ambassador to Russia who exerted allied influence there was a former Missouri governor, David Francis.

When peace became a reality, the commanding general of the 35th Division, Peter Taub, gave a speech which is familiar today:

"When the boys come back, remember that brass bands and ice cream aren't the only things to a real welcome. Get busy and do something worthy....Provide each returning soldier with a job."

Missourians, never afraid of a fight, accepted their roles in the War to End All Wars, when war was declared by Congress and President Wilson on this date, April 6, 1917.

****

APRIL 7
MINE LAMOTTE

Missouri has always been one of the world's great producers of lead. For more than 200 years one particular mine in our state produced the valuable mineral, and mining of lead continues not far away today.

The French economy was beginning to sag in the late 1600s and early 1700s. So it became necessary to look for other sources of wealth in the new world. In 1715 the governor of Louisiana, Antoine de La Motte Cadillac, crossed into what later would be Missouri from Kaskaskia, a place later known as Illinois. He was looking for silver which had been reported in Missouri.

He didn't find silver but he did find a rich vein of lead ore. He stumbled onto it by following streams and Indian paths. His workers sank a small shaft and found a rich vein. Cadillac didn't stay there long, but he did leave his name. The site became known as Mine LaMotte.

Four years after the governor left, the mine was worked by another man who sank two more shafts. In 1723 French officers at Fort deChartres gave Phillipe Renault a grant of two leagues of ground at Mine LaMotte. It was the first time any government had exercised authority over the territory which would become Missouri.

Renault brought 200 workers, slaves, and mining tools from France to set up operations. He worked those mines for twenty years. The lead was shipped from Sainte Genevieve, the first permanent settlement in Missouri. The metal was shaped into horse collars and then the horses were driven to the river town, wearing as well as pulling their loads. Most of the mining was done from August through November, times of little rain, when it was easier to work in the pits.

The Kaskaskia, Chickasaw, and Osage Indians from time to time pestered the miners. Governor Cauzat once complained of the "Cheraqui" Indians raiding the mine. Only one of those raids has achieved any prominence. One spring day a strong group of Osage Indians suddenly struck. A fierce fight was waged and seven miners killed before the Indians were driven off.

Historian Duane Meyer sketched the procedure for the early mining of lead. It was simple. Miners, armed with pick and shovel, dug a hole and removed the ore. They rarely tried tunnels or mine shafts as such. Holes were rarely deeper than six feet. Smelting was also crude. The ore was placed in the ground and a big bonfire was built. The heat made the metal form pools which then solidified into lead. Only one-third of the ore actually could be processed into lead this way. It was left to Moses Austin almost a century later to devise a furnace system that would double the yield.

Mine owners came and went. Some came with high hopes and left bankrupt. Renault was one of them. He finally went back to France when he began to lose money, but the mine kept producing.

In 1861 federal officers raided the mining areas and destroyed the buildings and machinery. But it was soon put back into operation and produced 3,500 tons of lead during the conflict. By 1869, five years after the St. Joe Minerals Corporation bought the mine, it was producing about 2,200 tons a year.

The mine was closed in 1919 but reopened less than a decade later when new drilling uncovered richer deposits of lead ore.

The Great Depression caused it to close from 1931 to 1937 but it was reopened for World War II and remained open. St. Joe Minerals finally closed Mine LaMotte after almost 240 years of near continuous operations. By this time it was heralded as the oldest lead mine in the United States. In 244 years of service this mine was closed only a few times—for a depression, a shortage of ore, a war, and for an Indian fight on this date, April 7, in 1774.

****

APRIL 8
MISSOURI, THE DAIRY STATE

For years Missouri has been known as a beef producing state. In the early 1900s, however, farmers, bankers, and other businessmen began to notice the money being made by dairy farmers in other states. This produced a significant change in the kind of farming done here.

The dairy cow wasn't unknown in Missouri. Many people kept a milk cow in the back yard. Others kept a few cows and sold the milk. But it wasn't until a change in farming attitude that the state passed a law regulating the quality and purity of milk.

How much dairying did Missouri farmers do before 1900?

The author of a book written for the 1904 St. Louis World's Fair praised Missouri as an agricultural state. He devoted twenty-four pages to grain crops, but only two pages to Missouri as a dairy state.

At the time Missouri ranked first in the nation in number of farms and fifth in valuation and numbers of livestock. But dairy farmers and their stock were in the minority and were considered unimportant.

In 1905 the legislature established the office of State Dairy Commissioner. He was to inspect all creameries, public dairies, and butter and cheese factories. Four years later the Bureau of Dairying replaced the commissioner's office. This agency functioned till 1933 when the Missouri Department of Agriculture was created. These were critical years in the development of Missouri's dairy industry because of the need for increased agriculture production during World War I and probably because of farmers' increasing awareness that big money could be made milking cows, and the subsequent efforts to upgrade their herds.

At the turn of the century Missouri had about 800,000 milk cows. Half of them were virtually worthless. The milk they produced didn't offset the costs of their feed and care. But starting in 1916, about 100 state dairy clubs were formed with definite programs to replace unprofitable scrub cows and heifers with highly bred dairy cattle. More than 5,000 dairy cows were imported to become the nucleus of Missouri's rise as a dairy state.

In 1912 Missouri dairies and about fifty creameries were producing less than 12,000,000 pounds of butter. A dozen years later more than eighty creameries were making more than 60,000,000 pounds of butter. In time, Missouri would have about 3,000 small local cream-buying plants.

In 1915 Missouri was nineteenth in butter production in the nation, a decade later, eighth, and in the mid-1950s, fifth. For many years

Missouri was the nation's second biggest cheese producer. By 1946 Missouri dairy farmers produced just under four billion pounds of milk from almost 1.1 million cows. From that milk was made 13 million gallons of ice cream, 49 million pounds of cheese, and 65 million pounds of butter. Some fifty-four cheese plants were operating.

But a half century after that first dairy act we were down to forty-five cheese plants. Obviously dairy farming was changing. The cream-buying station was dying and soon would be virtually extinct. In the twenties and thirties, cream was the main part of the milk used. Small farmers sold cream to buyers and fed much of the skimmed milk to livestock.

The small farmer was rapidly dying out too. Dairying had become a major industry. New uses were found for milk which in days before would have been thrown out or made into cheese. The independent cheese maker began to disappear. By the late 1970s only about a dozen were left. Markets for nonfat dry milk had been building steadily for years. New alternatives to butter were growing in popularity.

Dairy operators found it no longer necessary to maintain huge herds of cattle. Better breeding, better feed, and better facilities were enabling the farmer to get more milk from fewer cows. As the years went by the overall production was down 25 percent. The number of cows, however, was down 70 percent. Missouri remained among the top ten states in the nation in milk production, though. The state ranked tenth in butter production and cheese-making, and fourteenth in production of ice cream.

Missouri is a modern, major dairy state and its people are consuming more wholesome products. It began with the adoption of the law creating the first State Dairy Commissioner on this date, April 8, 1905.

****

APRIL 9
THE END

Two former residents of Missouri sat across the table from each other. The dignity of the man in gray showed through even in this sad moment. Across from him, clad in blue, was a mud-splattered man. Today they would sign the document ending the war. Then Robert E. Lee climbed aboard his horse, Traveller, and went back to his vanquished troops. Ulysses Grant accepted the terms of surrender with compassion and respect for the defeated side.

The Civil War was over. Missouri had played a key role in the war, a role too often overlooked.

Those who tell Civil War stories seem to ignore the war in the West, as if nothing important happened west of Vicksburg. Cliff Edom wrote, "Wilson's Creek, Lexington, Belmont, Westport— these and other Missouri battles begrudgingly are given a spot of flyspeck proportions on national Civil War maps, the briefest mentions in history books. On a nationwide scale, historians lose sight of the hundreds of skirmishes in Missouri at out-of-the-way places such as Cross Timbers or Elliot's Mills. . . .

"But to ignore the many collisions between regular and irregular troops and to overlook the importance of guerrilla warfare in the West relegates Missouri to an erroneous and inconsequential role in the conflict. This state from beginning to the end of the war was one huge, bitter battlefield."

Missouri has been called "The Child of the Storm" from its earliest days as a state, because of the fight over slavery which resulted in the Missouri Compromise. Forty years after Missouri achieved statehood, the storm broke. The Civil War split Missouri families, political factions, social orders, military lives.

The fight at Wilson's Creek in the early going is the only battle of significance as far as those historians in the East are concerned. But there were other battles, all of them tragic, and they continued throughout the war and beyond.

Missouri had more than 1,100 battles or skirmishes within its borders. Only two other states, Virginia and Tennessee, had more. Missouri furnished more cavalrymen to the Union side than any other state except New York. No other northern state was able to put as many battalions, companies, or regiments in the field. All this was from a state ranked eleventh in the nation in slave population and eighth in national population.

Missouri, torn by its sympathies and loyalties, was exceeded only by six completely Union states in the number of men it contributed to the Union army. Missouri furnished the Union army with 109,000 men; almost 14,000 of them died. About 30,000 men fought for the Confederacy and 4,000 of them died.

Duane Meyer writes that 60 percent of the Missouri men eligible for military service in those years fought in the Civil War. No other state could match that percentage. Meyer has written an excellent summation in his book, *The Heritage of Missouri,* for years a standard school textbook:

"Of the 5,000 who formed the first and second Missouri brigades of the Confederate army after the Battle of Pea Ridge, only 800 survived the war and half of those were sick and wounded when Lee surrendered....Missourians fought and died on the battlefields of the south at Vicksburg, Shiloh, Corinth, Chickamauga. Missourians followed Sherman in his march through Georgia.

"Men of Missouri not only marched in the armies of the north and south, but led them as well. General Sterling Price and General Joseph O. Shelby distinguished themselves in the service of the Confederacy. Abraham Lincoln's two most successful generals, Ulysses S. Grant and William Tecumseh Sherman, were both residents of St. Louis at the outbreak of the war. Grant and Sherman were both onlookers in the crowd during the riot following Lyon's capture of Camp Jackson.

"The battlefields, littered with the white bones of fallen horses and foul with the stench of death and decay, remained for long months as a reminder the war is more gore than glory."

From the first skirmish—the capture of the Liberty Arsenal in April, 1861—to the last, in Carroll and Ray Counties in May 1865, more than a month after Lee surrendered, Missourians fought the Civil War. And the reconstruction period was as harsh here as anywhere in the South.

Some Missourians never surrendered. Callaway County calls itself "The Kingdom of Callaway," and claims it seceded from federal control and never came back. Price, Shelby, and others went to Mexico looking for another war rather than surrender. In many parts of Missouri the Civil War is still fought. Perhaps "argued" might be a better word. Families still express pride that their relatives fought on one side or another—or both.

But for Missourians as well as for the rest of the nation it all ended with the dignified former St. Louis resident named Lee agreeing to the terms of the mud-splattered Missourian in Blue, Grant, at Appomattox Courthouse on this date, April 9, 1865.

****

APRIL 10
PULITZER

He was broke when he came to Missouri. He'd been urged to go to St. Louis because it was just the place to become Americanized and because he would hear only English spoken. But after one of his adventures an old man told him, "You seem to be right smart and able for a furriner.... But you'll never make a successful American until yer learn to drink, chew, and smoke." Joseph Pulitzer began to have some doubts about English being spoken in St. Louis, but he did become a successful American. Today his name is nationally known.

In the middle of the nineteenth century Joseph Pulitzer was just beginning to build a reputation and it wasn't very good at times. Back then members of the legislature liked to gather at Schmidt's Hotel in Jefferson City for meetings or socializing. One of those members was Joseph Pulitzer, a skinny kid, age 22, serving illegally because he was too young. He had trouble speaking English although he had been in this country six years. Nonetheless he had led the battle against a corrupt St. Louis County government and was seeking legislation to restrict its powers. St. Louis contractor and Superintendent of Registration Edward Augustine was in Jefferson City to speak against the legislation. He had a score to settle with the young lawmaker.

When they confronted each other at Schmidt's Hotel, Augustine called Pulitzer a liar and was promptly told to watch his mouth. Pulitzer left, went to his hotel, and came back with a gun. There was an exchange of words. He pulled his pistol. Augustine jumped for him. Two shots were fired. One hit Augustine in the leg; the other went into the floor. Pulitzer was wrestled to the floor—and was later fined.

Joseph Pulitzer was widely known for his quick temper. He would carry it throughout his life as a history-changing politician and a great newspaperman. He was only seventeen when he came to this country, arriving in New York from Germany. To avoid immigration procedures he jumped off the ship and swam to shore.

Pulitzer became an American citizen in 1867. His news story about the advice the old man gave him about drinking, chewing, and smoking won him an opening on a German newspaper in St. Louis, the *Westliche Post*. Eventually he became a partner in that paper. He sold his interest, however, and bought a German-language daily paper which he ran for one day. Then he got rid of it. A few years later Pulitzer bought the bankrupt St. Louis *Post.* Three days later the backers of the much more successful St. Louis *Dispatch* decided they would rather merge with Pulitzer than try to beat him. That's how the St. Louis *Post-Dispatch* was born.

He was a crusading newspaperman fighting political corruption and vice. His vigor in that area brought on another incident, similar to the one in Jefferson City. As it happened, the heavy clothing of the day might have saved his life or at least his career. One of the targets of Pulitzer's editorial attacks met him on the street and suddenly took a swing at him. Pulitzer was carrying a gun. But by the time he had fought his way through his heavy overcoat to his hip pocket a crowd had gathered and separated the men. Whether Pulitzer could have hit his assailant had he shot at him is another thing. Without his glasses, which were knocked off in the attack, he was extremely nearsighted.

Pulitzer's employees received extraordinary treatment for that time. Each received a two-week paid vacation. Good newsboys got lavish prizes like suits of clothing and gold watches. An annual Christmas dinner was held for the staff.

In 1882 the Pulitzer family decided to go to Europe for a vacation. On the way Pulitzer stopped in New York and bought another bankrupt rag, the New York *World.* Like the *Post,* the *World* flourished under Pulitzer's hand. His battle with arch rival William Randolph Hearst for circulation is epic in journalism history.

Pulitzer's health broke while he was still relatively young, only about forty. He died in 1911, blind.

The New York *World* is gone but the *Post-Dispatch* was surviving seventy years later as a highly-respected paper with strong ties to the Pulitzer family. The Pulitzer Prizes honor his name.

Joseph Pulitzer had a superstition about the number ten. He arrived in Missouri on October 10. He cast his first important vote in the legislature on January 10. And he was born on this date, April 10, in 1847.

****

APRIL 11
THE ENGLISHMAN AND THE VULGAR MISSOURIANS

He wrote that Americans are "by nature, frank, brave, cordial, hospitable, and affectionate. Cultivation and refinement seem but to enhance their warmth of heart and ardent enthusiasm, and it is the possession of these latter qualities in a most remarkable degree, which renders an educated American one of the most endearing and generous of friends."

The writer was the great English author Charles Dickens who visited this country in 1842. He came to Missouri, and Missouri went into his books.

Dickens traveled 200 miles up the Mississippi River, a river he disliked. He called it an "enormous ditch sometimes two or three miles wide, running liquid mud." He was already homesick. So it isn't surprising he found some parts of his visit to Missouri less than sensational. By the time he reached Missouri he had become tired of the constant praise and honor heaped upon him wherever he visited. Soon after his arrival he criticized St. Louisans as rough and intolerably conceited, "tobacco spitting, slaveholding (and) vulgar."

The St. Louis Dickens found in 1842 was a city of marked contrasts and interests. Some parts of the city charmed him. The old French Quarter of the town intrigued him. "The thoroughfares are narrow and crooked, and some of the houses are very quaint and picturesque; being built of wood, with tumble-down galleries before the windows, approachable by stairs or rather ladders from the street." Near this quaint slice from the old world, he said some of the shops and tenements reminded him of Flanders, and were modern improvements as the city continued to modernize itself. "The town bids fair in a few years to improve considerably; though it is not likely ever to vie, in point of elegance or beauty, with Cincinnati," he wrote. The very location of the town was an item of great concern. He wrote, "It is very hot, lies among great rivers, and has vast tracts of undrained swampy land around it."

A trip across the river to a place known as Looking Glass Prairie was a revelation. Dickens complained of the constant, sticky mud which he said, "had no variety but in depth. Now it was only half over the wheels, now it hid the axletree, and now the coach sank down in it almost to the windows. The air resounded in all directions with the loud chirping of frogs, who, with the pigs (a coarse, ugly breed, as unwholesome-looking as though they were spontaneous growth of the country), had the whole scene to themselves."

. He marveled at the American practice of giving horses huge quantities of water when they became lathered from their labors, until the horses were swollen to about twice their natural dimensions. He spoke once of stopping a second time that day "to inflate the horses again."

Some of his relationships with his hosts did little to further goodwill. Dickens hated slavery. In his book on the travels he spent the best part of three pages listing newspaper ads showing cruelty to and mutilations of slaves. He writes of those cruelties, "Shall we whimper over legends of torture practiced on each other by the pagan Indians, and smile upon the cruelties of Christian men! Shall we, so long as these unique things last, exult above the scattered remnants of the race, and triumph in the white enjoyment of possessions?

"Rather, for me, restore the forest and the Indian village, in lieu of stars and stripes, let some poor feather flutter in the breeze."

Dickens met the spirit of the American frontier at Carondelet, where he stopped at a local tavern run by an old man who always dreamed of moving West.

"He had all his life been restless and locomotive," wrote Dickens, "with an irresistable desire for change; and was still the son of his old self; for if he had nothing to keep him at home, he said he would clean up his musket and be off to Texas tomorrow morning. He was one of the very many descendants of Cain proper to this continent, who seemed destined from the birth to serve as pioneers in the great human army, who gladly go on from year to year extending its outposts, and leaving home after home behind them, and die at last, utterly regardless of their graves being left thousands of miles behind by the wandering generation who succeeded him."

He found Missouri generally unhealthy and generally uncomfortable. He found interesting characters who would appear in his book *American Notes* and in at least one novel, *Martin Chuzzlewit.* Those books by Charles Dickens are today a valuable insight into America twenty years before the Civil War, the result of travels which brought him to Missouri on this date, April 11, in 1842.

****

APRIL 12
THE DANGDEST SCOUNDREL IN THE STATE OF MISSOURI

William Muldrow was riding across his Marion County farmland one day when he came upon a boy he didn't know. Apparently thinking he could impress the youth, Muldrow asked, "Who owns this land around here?"

The boy answered, "Old Bill Muldrow. Pap says he's the dangdest scoundrel in the State of Missouri."

Scoundrel? Perhaps. Speculator? Certainly. Not only that, but he is a figure in a Charles Dickens novel, Martin Chuzzlewit was a fictional English architect in America who ran across a man trying to recruit settlers for a town called "Eden," which was being established in the West. A big drawing of the community was nailed to the wall of the hotel room and Dickens described it as "A flourishing city too! An architectural city! There are banks, churches, cathedrals, market places, factories, hotels, stores, mansions, wharves, an exchange, a theatre, public buildings of all kinds, down to the office of the Eden *Stinger,* a daily journal; all faithfully depicted in the view before them." But Martin is dismayed because it appears from the plans there is no need for an architect.

"Well, it ain't all built," replied the agent, "not quite."

"The market place, now," said Martin. "Is that built?"

"That?" said the agent. "Let me see. No. That ain't built."

"I suppose," said Martin, "I suppose there are several architects there?"

"There ain't a single one."

So Martin and his manservant Mark Tapley go to Eden. They arrive at night. The next morning, Mark awakens and sees the settlement. It's less than twenty cabins and at least half of them are not occupied. All are rotten. "The most tottering, abject and forlorn among them was called, with great propriety, the Bank, and National Credit Office. It had some feeble props about it, but was settling deep down in the mud, past all recovery."

The inspiration for this novel, titled after its main character, *Martin Chuzzlewit,* was Marion City, a community William Muldrow forecast would be the great metropolis of the Midwest someday. He built it about ten or twelve miles north of Hannibal. When potential residents asked about the slough which ran in back of the city and overflowed at the slightest provocation, Muldrow told them it would be deepened and the river then could cut a permanent channel. That would make the city a virtual island community. He said that would be ideal.

But the floods of 1836 put the town under in more ways than one. Another of Muldrow's grand schemes died, but not before he had sold more than three-quarters of a million acres in Marion County to eastern investors, forcing the Palmyra land office to make the largest single one-year payment into the U.S. Treasury by any Missouri land office, $934,000. Muldrow and a few others he enticed planned a railroad. It became the first railroad in Missouri to be surveyed and graded. But he was fifteen years ahead of his time. The railroad went nowhere.

Then William Muldrow seized upon an idea put forth by a Presbyterian minister, David Nelson, to found Marion College, a self-supporting institution where students would work for their tuition. It became the first college chartered by the legislature. It was one of the earliest of its type. But it, too, finally failed.

Some of his ideas were ill-advised. For instance he thought of buying cattle in Southwest Missouri and driving them to Marion College farmlands, then selling them later at a profit. Unfortunately he bought the cattle in the fall, not the spring. They were not in good condition and he had no place to keep them during the severe winter; therefore he lost most of them.

Longtime Palmyra newspaper editor Jacob Sosey says Muldrow had "a malignant attack of gold fever." He went to California and stayed there for twenty years. He convinced John Sutter to buy land from the Russian Fur Company, but they couldn't get the federal government to confirm the title. He died, virtually broke, in 1872.

Some credit is given Muldrow for inventing the plow which enabled settlers to finally start breaking the prairie. The plows of the time couldn't cut the tough sod. So, supposedly, Muldrow created a giant plow that required thirteen yoke of oxen to pull it. It could turn over six-foot strips of prairie.

William Muldrow: His towns are mostly historical memories. His exploits are largely forgotten. His railroads never went anywhere. He *might* have invented a plow. "The dangdest scoundrel in the state of Missouri"? Perhaps. But it took men like him to make the American West and to bring to Missouri many of the early settlers.

William Muldrow, the man who dreamed of what became Charles

Dickens' town of Eden, was born on this date, April 12, in 1797.

****

APRIL 13
THE BEGINNING OF THE END FOR BONNIE AND CLYDE

They had come to Joplin that spring and rented a small house. They claimed to be Mr. and Mrs. W. L. Callahan. They said they were from Minnesota. She was about 4′ 10″ tall and had a narrow face. She weighed 85 pounds. She had a tatoo on the inside of her thigh. She read romance magazines, painted her toenails pink, dyed her hair red, and wrote terrible amateur poetry.

Her alleged husband was also short. He was one of eight children of an itinerant fieldhand. He had a fifth-grade education and a prison record.

They were killers.

Her real name was Bonnie Parker; his was Clyde Barrow.

They made a mistake renting that Joplin bungalow because that's where their dead-end road began. Bonnie and Clyde were part of the worst open crime wave in American history. During it, there were more homicides in Chicago in 1933 than in the entire British Isles.

Bonnie and Clyde were hoodlums who first met in Texas. Their relationship was interrupted when Clyde was jailed a month later. Bonnie helped him escape. He was caught and served two more years. A month after this release he and Bonnie tried a robbery and she wound up in jail for a short time.

A month later Clyde and some friends killed an elderly man during a Texas store holdup. Bonnie was still in prison and wasn't involved. But in 1932 she and Clyde were at a dance when Clyde and another man argued and decided to settle it outside. In the confusing events that followed, a deputy sheriff was killed. When the sheriff showed up to see what was happening, he too was gunned down.

Two months later Bonnie and Clyde shot a grocer to death in Sherman, Texas, during a robbery. Two months after that they killed a lumber dealer who tried to keep them from stealing his car. They escaped an ambush in January 1933 and killed another deputy sheriff. They fled to Joplin, Missouri, where they were joined by Clyde's brother, Buck, and his wife, Blanche.

221

Neighbors became suspicious about their behavior. There was a lot of drinking. License plates were scattered around the garage. The women didn't leave the house often, but the men would sometimes be gone for several days. Meanwhile, robberies were occurring frequently in the Springfield and Joplin areas and along Highway 66.

At dusk one evening, five policemen—three Joplin officers and two Missouri Highway Patrolmen—went to check out the bungalow. Joplin Constable J. W. Harryman got out of his car and was walking toward the garage door when he was struck by a shotgun blast from a distance of ten feet. He died instantly. Detective Harry McGinnis, close behind him, was also hit and mortally wounded.

Meanwhile, Buck Barrow was getting the car ready for escape. The women raced up and down stairs throwing things into suitcases. Barrow dashed out in the hail of lead and pushed Harryman's body to one side so the car could get past. With Clyde at the wheel, machine guns and pistols blazing, the four fled.

Later when officers were able to check the house they found important evidence. A partially finished poem called "Suicide Sal," written by Bonnie, was found along with several weapons and—most important—a roll of film. The pictures on it became famous.

There were pictures of Bonnie holding a heavy pistol and smoking a cigar, of Clyde with a brace of guns, standing in front of the car, and of Bonnie supposedly holding up Clyde with a shotgun. The photos were widely circulated and appeared in newspapers and on wanted posters. Authorities and the general public now knew for the first time who to look for.

Late July found them in Platte City, Missouri, where motel operators became suspicious because the windows were curtained with newspapers and attendants weren't allowed in the rooms. They tipped police. Sheriff Holt Coffey and his deputies called in an armored car from Kansas City. They met a withering blast of gunfire when they surrounded the motel. Three of the lawmen were wounded. The sheriff was shot three times.

One of the lawmen's bullets hit the mark though. Buck Barrow, with a terrible head wound, survived the flight to Iowa where he and his wife Blanche were captured. He died not long afterwards.

Authorities began to draw their circle tighter around the gang. Former Texas Ranger Frank Hamer was hot on their trail and for 102 days he followed it closely. He studied their personal habits, found their hideouts, and tried to learn how they thought. Some of their favorite hiding places were abandoned mines near Joplin.

In early April, 1934, Bonnie and Clyde killed three more policemen. But a month later, near Plain Dealing, Louisiana, officers were waiting for them and ended their bloody careers.

Their bullet-riddled car yielded three automatic rifles, two sawed-off shotguns, ten 20-round clips of machine gun ammunition and about 3,000 rounds of other ammunition.

It had been just over a year since they had left behind that incriminating roll of film which ended their anonymity and spelled their doom, when Bonnie and Clyde shot their way out of that Joplin bungalow on this date, April 13, 1933.

****

APRIL 14
BONNEVILLE: EXPLORER, TRAPPER, SPY?

In the spring of 1832 a privately financed expedition left Fort Osage, Missouri, bound for the Rockies. The trip was a major experiment, a test to see if wagons could really be taken over the Continental Divide and on to the West Coast. There were twenty wagons. The expedition planned to stay out for two years. The experiment succeeded. But it had other purposes—fur trapping and spying. It was led by Captain Benjamin Louis Eulalie de Bonneville.

It was through the good graces of American diplomat, author, and political firebrand Thomas Paine that Benjamin Bonneville's father was able to flee from France. The elder Bonneville was a libertarian newspaperman whose outbursts against Napoleon were not welcome.

Through Paine's influence, the younger Bonneville got into West Point. He graduated in 1815 although he was not yet twenty years old. For the first decade of his military career he was stationed at one frontier outpost after another, spending one long stretch building a road from Washington to New Orleans.

Bonneville had been to St. Louis and had heard the fur trade talk there. When he was serving at Fort Gibson in the Indian territory, the jumping-off place for the southern expeditions into the Rockies, he got the idea of working for an excursion of his own into the West. He received a two-year leave of absence from the army and gained the financial backing of Alfred Seton, one of the original Astorians—the group which helped settle the Oregon country. His official orders were to explore the area, learn all he could of the Northwest, and report back to his superior officers. All of this was officially unofficial, however. Officially, he was trapping for furs.

In May 1832 the party left Fort Osage on the Missouri River. In July Bonneville took his wagons across the Divide and set up a post on the Green River. Mountain men, most of whom never found much good about Bonneville, and many of whom united to bankrupt him, christened the outpost "Fort Nonsense," contending it could not be inhabited during the cold winters.

But it was no nonsense. The American Fur Company and the British Hudson's Bay Company had been competing strongly in the Oregon Territory for years, although a treaty had been signed with Britain allowing both sides to trade in the area. His letter back to his commanders discussed the problem of a military invasion of Oregon should one become necessary. He once wrote, "If our government ever intends taking possession of Oregon, the sooner it shall be done, the better." Clearly, Fort Nonsense was not the product of a military man playing at being a fur trader. It was a strategic outpost which could cover any expedition moving into Oregon from the United States, or block any expedition coming out of Oregon into the American hunting grounds.

Bonneville was learning what was going on, but he suffered financially. By the end of the first year he was close to bankruptcy. In 1833 he sent Old Joe Walker on a trip to California, presumably to look for furs. Some think it might have been one final, giant effort to regain financial solvency because California trading had been popular earlier. Others think it was at least partly military, testing Spanish sentiments toward the United States and probing Spanish influence in that territory. Some think that little trip also sought a southern invasion route of Oregon.

The expedition as a hunting trip was a failure. And "Bald Head" as the Indians called Bonneville, was keenly disappointed. The disappointment, reflected in the book about the Bonneville expedition by the noted author Washington Irving, overshadowed the fact that as Bernard DeVoto says, "Joe (Walker) had performed offhand one of the prodigies of Western history. Also he had increased the potential that a few years later would be called Manifest Destiny."

With Walker gone, Bonneville struck out toward Oregon, reaching

Fort Walla Walla, where the British made it clear he wasn't welcome. So he went back to Fort Nonsense. In 1834, after Walker's return, he set out for Oregon again and once more was rebuffed. William Goetzmann says it would be "somewhat difficult to account for those two treks to Oregon. But quite obviously Bonneville was probing British strength and observing their operations in the Northwest as well as trying to establish contact with the Indians in the region."

Bonneville wrapped things up in 1835 and came back to Missouri.

Upon his return, however, he learned his request for leave extension had been lost. The army had dismissed him. When the value of his journals and maps became known, though, President Jackson reinstated him. In later years he fought in the Seminole, Mexican, and Civil wars. He died in St. Louis in 1878 and is buried there.

Bonneville proved wagons could be taken West. He provided the important exploration and first map of the interior West that had its geographical features generally in order. It was an important but one of the least known American intelligence efforts of the time. And his bankrupt three and one-half years on the frontier contributed to obtaining Washington and Oregon. Captain Benjamin Bonneville, another in a long list of Missouri explorers of the West, was born on this date, April 14, 1796.

****

APRIL 15
BENTON THE ARTIST

He had been staring at the painting of a nude woman for so long some bystanders started ribbing him about it. He said the only reason he was interested in it was because he was an artist.

"Well," his tormentors suggested, "let's adjourn to the offices of the Joplin *American* and let this artist demonstrate his talents."

He did. He sketched a man in a drugstore across the street.

It was the first time Thomas Hart Benton had sketched a living person. He got a job with the paper and a start in his life career. He would be known for most of his life as a crusty duck who loved life and painted it realistically.

His granduncle was Missouri's famous U.S. Senator, Thomas Hart Benton. Although born in Neosho, the Benton who became an artist spent his youth in Joplin, a lively town he would later say had everything: "drugstores, slot machines, real estate slickers, busy preachers, and off the main street a row of houses devoted to insinuatingly decorated girls."

When Benton drew the drugstore patron for his tavern tormentors that day in Joplin, he was hired by the newspaper for fourteen dollars a week. Years later he painted a mural for the town and the city paid him $60,000.

Benton's parents were concerned about the boy's artistic ability, mainly because he had taken some charcoal and drawn a train on the wallpaper. But then, Thomas Hart Benton always would like to decorate walls. He could have been a lawyer in the family tradition but didn't want to be. He started developing as an artist. Benton attended art institutes in Chicago and Paris, but conventional art studies weren't interesting. He drew and painted independent of prevailing styles, although he did go through a period of impressionism.

He served in World War I and profited from it. His paintings began to portray things that were basic in the people and his land. He wrote his biography, *An Artist in America,* in the late 1930s and revised it in the 1950s. He travelled throughout the state sketching the common people. Those people kept appearing in his murals, which he began painting long after his career became established.

Benton had never done a mural until the New School for Social Research was built in New York. His work there drew critical fire, as would others. But there were defenders. Out of that affair, he received the chance to do a mural for the Whitney Museum, which led to a mural depicting the state of Indiana's history for the 1933 Chicago World's Fair.

On a trip back to the Midwest Benton met some old friends who suggested he do a mural for Missouri. A few weeks later the legislature passed a bill commissioning the mural Benton would call "A Social History of Missouri." But Benton didn't expect the extensive criticism which came after the mural, which covered the walls of the House Lounge at the Capitol, was finished. Some critics suggested he had tried to degrade his home state or make a joke of it. But he denied that and said he simply treated Missouri society realistically. He believed you had to see all of society, "warts and all."

In the 1930s Benton wrote of the controversy, "There are people even among the Democrats of the legislature who sponsored my job and paid me money, who seem to feel that I should have done better had I painted a sweeter picture of my home state...something a little more delicate, a little more violet-scented. This seems a bit odd because in my whole experience of Missouri Democrats, I've never run across any woodland flowers...and I don't believe I've ever seen a single Missouri Democratic politician, drunk or sober, who wouldn't bust you if he thought you mistook him for a violet."

He had little truck with those who consider themselves "society," once writing, "What is called society is, of course, like the froth on a glass of beer, of no consequence.... Below the top economic foam of Missouri, a true native life lies. Although I have painted that life as I saw it and felt it, I am not yet ready to analyze it or pass judgment upon it. Taken as a whole, I like the men and women who make the real Missouri. I get along with them."

He and Harry Truman, both fiercely individualistic men, respected one another greatly. Truman once called Benton "the best damned painter in America," and Benton called Truman "the only individual who stands out in my lifetime." Appropriately, when the Truman Library was built in Independence, Benton painted a mural for it.

In 1970 he said, "I know I've only got about five or six years left, maybe ten, but as long as I'm working, keeping busy, I don't give a damn when I go." He died in January 1975. He collapsed as he stood looking at his last mural.

Thomas Hart Benton, great artist, Missourian, was born on this date, April 15, 1889.

****

APRIL 16
STARS AND BOUNDARIES, HENRY SMITH PRITCHETT

The United States and Canada had argued and negotiated for seventy years over the boundary line between Canada and American Alaska. Sometimes the discussions became quite heated. So the commission debating the matter turned to a Missouri stargazer and asked him to draw an exact map fairly representing the claims of both countries. Henry Smith Pritchett took on a job diplomats had been unable to do for seven decades.

Look at your map. The boundary line between Alaska and Canada is the one Pritchett drew. That's not a bad accomplishment for a man whose father almost didn't let him graduate from college because of a prank.

His father was president of Howard College in Fayette and left to head up Pritchett Institute in Glasgow, Missouri.

It was at Pritchett Institute that Henry started school at the age of ten. Just eight years later he was entitled to a bachelor's degree at Howard. His father, however, a stern disciplinarian, was shocked to learn that Henry had, on the night before graduation, helped put a wagon on the roof of the college building. It took some strong arguing by Howard's president, Oran Root, to let the younger Pritchett graduate.

Henry was interested in astronomy and went on to study at the United States Naval Observatory under Professor Asaph Hall, who had discovered one of the satellites of Mars.

Interestingly, Pritchett could have become a professional sports figure. Years later he would write, "I was devoted to baseball with an intensity that I have been able to reach in few other matters." He was a catcher and the old St. Louis Browns offered him a job. But he declined on advice of his parents.

He was twenty-one when he was named assistant astronomer at the Naval Observatory. He helped build a star catalog which was, and is still, important in navigation.

Pritchett returned to Glasgow in 1880 to work with his father who then headed the Morrison Observatory, a $100,000 facility set up by a grant from a wealthy family. Just a year later he resigned to become assistant mathematics and astronomy professor at Washington University. In 1882 and 1883 he took a leave of absence to go to New Zealand to observe Venus.

Pritchett viewed railroad travel as a huge headache. There was little coordination of schedules between trains. So Pritchett made out a time schedule for railroads operating out of St. Louis. Through his study of astronomy and earth movement, he introduced a standard time schedule adopted by the Wabash Railroad. Soon all of the nation's railroads were patterning their schedules after his.

When William McKinley became president in 1897, he hired Henry Smith Pritchett to revitalize the U.S. Coast and Geodetic Survey, the nation's oldest scientific bureau. In his three years there, Pritchett made the National Bureau of Standards a separate entity and put it on its feet.

Later Pritchett became head of the Massachusetts Institute of Technology and produced marked changes in the school, especially in campus life. Some school historians point to his administration as the turning point in the history of the Institute. Pritchett brought the departments of Chemical Engineering and Applied Electricity to MIT.

By now Andrew Carnegie had established his foundation. Pritchett became the first chairman of the board of the Carnegie Foundation for the Advancement of Teaching. He held that job longer than any of his jobs, retiring in 1930 as President Emeritus. He died at the age of eighty-two in 1939.

Biographer Abraham Flexner says, "He was a reformer in every field in which he entered, and a reformer who never lost his good temper and who never displayed bitterness or disappointment....He had a consciousness of what was right which never deserted him....Opportunity never caught him unawares."

Henry Smith Pritchett, a man from a small school in a small Missouri town, who looked at the stars, formulated time, shaped the American education system and drew an important boundary line, was born on this date, April 16, 1857.

****

APRIL 17
THE FIRST GOVERNOR OF MISSOURI TERRITORY

The death of Meriwether Lewis under mysterious circumstances in 1809 left a void in frontier government. He had been governor of the District of Louisiana. A number of persons applied for the job. Why President Madison chose the man he did is still a matter of speculation. The man he picked preferred to live in Kentucky, rather than live in the area which would become known as Missouri during his term.

Despite his absences from Missouri, Benjamin Howard was regarded highly as a military leader in the nervous days of the War of 1812. He had been a congressman from Kentucky when he was first named governor of the district of Louisiana. He was about fifty years old when he took the job in 1810.

Howard was born in Lexington, Kentucky, while that area was still part of Virginia. A military man, he took part in the Indian Wars in the early 1790s and studied law after the treaties were signed. He was admitted to the bar in 1799 and became a member of the Kentucky House of Representatives a year later.

Howard was one of the applicants for the job opened by the death of Lewis. Later he would regret taking it. Some believe his military background, especially his experience in dealing with Indian troubles, was a factor in Madison naming him governor. The British had been stirring up the Indians on the frontier. Two Indian leaders, The Prophet and his brother Tecumseh, were working within the tribes trying to bring about unity in an effort to drive out the white man.

Five months after President Madison commissioned Howard as governor he arrived in St. Louis for a short stay, then went back to Kentucky. The next spring, with Indians raiding east of the Mississippi, and Missourians getting nervous about it, he returned to Missouri and took charge of local defense preparations. With help from William Clark, who was then Brigadier General of the territorial militia, he set up companies and built blockhouses in remote areas. With that work well under way, he went back to Kentucky in September.

In November 1811 General Harrison clashed with Tecumseh in an indecisive battle which came to be known as the Battle of Tippecanoe. Howard feared it might start trouble in Missouri, so he returned and took charge again. In February 1812 Indians murdered a St. Charles family. Howard acted quickly. He set up a ranger company under Nathan Boone who launched a major campaign. He met with Illinois Governor Ninian Edwards to plan joint defensive measures, and ordered stronger fortifications around St. Louis.

In June 1812 Congress declared Missouri a territory, the first time the term "Missouri" was formally affixed to the area which later would be our state. Howard called for the first territorial legislature election in November, suggesting that five counties be organized, a thirteen-member representative branch of the territorial legislature, and the area's first territorial delegate to Congress. In the spring of 1813 he ordered Fort Osage, far up the Missouri River, evacuated because it was too isolated to be effective. He decided to fortify Portage des Sioux. In April word came that Missouri had been authorized to raise ten companies of rangers to defend exposed regions.

230

The federal government sent Howard a blank commission. He could be either territorial governor or a brigadier general in the regular army. Howard already had decided not to be reappoined governor. So he became a general and offered William Clark the territorial governorship.

As commander of forces for Illinois and Missouri, Howard led an expedition up the Mississippi and across to Peoria, Illinois, which did much to check Indian aggression into Missouri.

When General Harrison ordered Howard east to Cincinnati, Missouri residents complained. So did our first congressional delegate, Edward Hempstead, and Governor Clark. The order was revoked. Clark organized an expedition to Prairie du Chein in what is now southern Wisconsin to cut off the Indians from their British allies in Canada. Howard worked to get reinforcements for the post but it fell before he could gather them.

The loss of the fort was a sad blow to Missourians. But an ever sadder one came in 1814 when news reached Missouri that General Howard had died in September. His body was returned for burial to St. Louis.

Governor Benjamin Howard. General Benjamin Howard. He preferred to live in Kentucky although he was our state's first territorial chief executive. But he answered the young territory's cries for help in a way which overshadowed any of his gubernatorial shortcomings. Benjamin Howard was appointed governor of Missouri by President Madison on this date, April 17, 1810.

****

APRIL 18
THE MARSHFIELD TORNADO

It was cloudy that day, and pretty soon it started to rain. An occasional shower at first, the showers became heavier. Soon it began to hail. Then came more rain, heavier this time. And then the sound. The sound was like that of a freight train.

This was long before storm warnings, long before radar could have picked up unsettled weather, long before radios could have blared out the news that a tornado was bearing down on Marshfield, a small town in southwest Missouri. In minutes the town was destroyed.

231

High overhead on that Sunday, the elements had been at work. Warm air and cold air had collided and begun to grow turbulent. Some of the turbulence began to move in circles growing tighter and tighter, turning faster and faster. The April showers of a Missouri spring were about to turn into a disaster for the small town about twenty-five miles northeast of Springfield.

Marshfield was only twenty-five years old. Settlement, however, dated back to the 1830s when a family named Flannagan arrived. Surveying of the town didn't come until 1856. During the Civil War it was raided several times.

In 1870 an imposing courthouse was put up with twin cupolas and an arched passageway in the center. Marshfield had become the seat of a county named for Daniel Webster. Webster had once visited Missouri as an unsuccessful candidate for the Whig nomination in 1852. He died about the time Webster County and Marshfield were being created.

The tornado had a funnel described as several hundred yards wide when it ripped into the heart of Marshfield, destroying everything for a quarter mile on either side of it. The twister came out of the south and followed the familiar tornado path in Missouri. After wiping out Marshfield, it hopscotched north, around Jefferson City, touching down at places in Miller, Morgan, Callaway, and Moniteau counties.

This wide-ranging whirlwind left several dead in the area of Jefferson City and in Moniteau and Callaway counties. But it hit Marshfield hardest. The death count reached eighty-seven; there were 150 injured. Property damage was put at $350,000. Somehow in the darkness, rescue and recovery operations began. It took several hours to get the telegraph wires back up so the rest of the world would know what had happened. As soon as the telegraph was in operation, a hurried plea for help was sent to Springfield.

When the word got out, residents of Southwest Missouri responded quickly. In Springfield, three trains carrying doctors and nurses, medical supplies and food, and a large number of women to help tend the injured went to Marshfield. The Marshfield schoolhouse was turned into a hospital and a morgue. Mattresses were laid across school desks to be used as temporary beds. The dead were taken to the courthouse yard to be identified by surviving relatives.

The second story of the courthouse was torn off. Sixteen businesses nearby had been destroyed. A block of brick buildings facing the public square was wrecked. By Wednesday, residents of

Lebanon raised $1000 in just fifteen minutes and had sent it to the stricken town. Neighboring towns also came up with donations totalling $16,700, a considerable sum in those days of small agricultural communities.

Marshfield recovered from the twister and rebuilt as most towns hit by such tragedy do. But few small towns in Missouri ever have been hit as hard by a tornado as was Marshfield that Sunday. About sixty years later a federally-financed tour guide of Missouri noted that "since then, things have gone fairly quietly, with only the rise and fall of farm prices to affect the town's tranquility."

One of the worst tornadoes in state history roared through Marshfield on this date, April 18, 1880.

****

APRIL 19
THE FATHER OF THE UNIVERSITY

Great men often fail to achieve all they could because they affiliate with the wrong political party. While they might attain prominence within their state, the possibility of national prominence is restricted not because of their talent, but because they call themselves by the wrong political name. Such is the case with the man known as "The Father of the University." He was a Whig, a party of prominence, but seldom of power. He challenged for the governorship several times but never made it. Nonetheless, James Sidney Rollins was important in shaping the history of our state.

He was a highly educated and cultured young man when he came to Missouri in the early 1830s. He had come from Kentucky, been educated in Pennsylvania, and graduated from the University of Indiana with honors.

After a year on his father's farm in Boone County he went back to Kentucky and studied law. On his return to Missouri he followed the path of many ambitious young men of the day with an eye on political achievement—he practiced law and became a newspaper publisher.

Rollins, at age twenty-four, served as a delegate to the first railroad convention west of the Mississippi River. During the rest of his public life he would serve three terms in the Missouri House, two more in the Missouri Senate and two terms in the U.S. Congress. All of this came despite his allegiance to the Whig party.

He was elected to the Missouri House when he was twenty-six. He immediately pushed for establishment of a state university with the first bill he drafted, calling for the site to be fixed for the school.

His father donated $1,500 and part of the university ended up Rollins property. The bill passed in 1839. A few years later when the university was faltering Senator Rollins asked for a commission to examine its condition and prospects. Rollins proposed state aid for the University of Missouri. The Rollins committee proposed that the legislature establish a training ground for teachers at the school. He thus became the founding father of Missouri's teachers colleges. It wasn't until the next session that the measure passed.

By now Rollins was the state's leading Whig. He was nominated for governor in 1848 at the age of thirty-six. But the Whigs were a definite minority in strongly Democratic Missouri and he lost. His popularity had grown, however, and he was nominated for the U.S. Senate. Democrats controlled the legislature too and in those days senators were elected by the General Assembly. David Rice Atchison got the nod.

In 1854 Rollins went back to the legislature and two years later when Trusten Polk resigned as governor to go to the U.S. Senate, a new election was called. Again Rollins was nominated. This time he lost to Robert Stewart by 230 votes. His political supporters complained of fraud in the late returns, but the results stood.

He was finally elected to Congress in 1861. Although a slave owner, he supported the Union. He backed a bill for a railroad and telegraph line from the Missouri River to the Pacific Ocean. Under that bill, the Union Pacific, Central Pacific, and Kansas Pacific railroads were born. He supported the Morrill Act which gave the state 330,000 acres for an agricultural college.

After two terms in the U.S. House of Representatives he stepped down, only to find his constituents more than willing to put him back in.

By then, too, the state university was in deep trouble again. It had become a camp for soldiers during the war. It would not recover from that, its decaying buildings, and its recurring debts unless it received help. Rollins proposed state aid for the university. He also drew up a bill designating the school as the University of Missouri, an institution the state would be required to maintain. He also introduced a bill establishing the agriculture and mechanical colleges at

234

the university and gave the curators the 330,000 acres he and other congressmen had approved in 1862. In 1869 he was named to the university's Board of Curators and became president of that group. He held that job until 1888, two years before his death.

A Jefferson City newspaper wrote of him at his death, "He was a progressive man and the state owes him much. Major Rollins was first to head every enterprise and the last man to become discouraged. . . . Major Rollins belonged to that hardy class of pioneers whose energy and enterprise developed Missouri into what she is today."

The father of the University of Missouri, a strong leader in education for all Missourians, was James Sidney Rollins—never a governor—but perhaps more important than many governors we have had.

James S. Rollins was born on this date, April 19, 1812.

****

APRIL 20
THE WAR COMES TO MISSOURI

In the late 1830s the United States government established an arsenal in Liberty and the citizens' minds rested easier. Before then they had lived in fear of Indian raids. Now, the militia which guarded the arsenal kept the Indians away. But then came the Civil War and the secessionists.

The lines had been quicky drawn in Missouri as the Civil War began to break out across the nation. Governor Claiborne Jackson was a secessionist. Frank Blair and General Nathaniel Lyon led the movement of those wanting to stay in the union. Blair and Lyon managed to seize the arsenal at St. Louis, short-circuiting plans by the Jackson government to take it. At the Liberty arsenal, however, there were still some 1500 stands of arms and four small cannons.

Apparently the stores there never were used to fight Indians. But every now and then the arsenal became a target. One was in late 1855 when Major Ebenezer Price and 100 volunteers seized the place and wanted to take the contents to a pro-slavery camp which would then attack the free-soilers in Kansas. This was during the time of the border war with Kansas, when skirmishes between the neighboring states were common. Major Price took three cannons, 55 rifles, 100 pistols, 20 Colt revolvers, 67 sabers and ammunition. But

Captain N. R. Beall of Fort Leavenworth told the prominent residents of the area the property would have to be returned. Almost all of it was and nobody was prosecuted or punished.

Almost six years later, Major Nathaniel Grant, the officer in charge of the arsenal, was at breakfast when a boy hurriedly entered his quarters and gave him an unsigned note from a Union man. "A company of men from across the river camped in the bottoms last night," it read. "I understand another company is at or near Liberty and that the destination of both is the arsenal."

A few minutes later, 200 armed and mounted southern sympathizers rode into the arsenal yard and demanded Grant surrender the fort and its contents. There was no thought of resistance. There couldn't be. Grant and two employees were the only ones present.

According to an 1885 history of Clay and Platte counties, "Grant contented himself by protesting vigorously against the seizure and this was allowed him with great good humor amid laughter and raillery."

Most of the stores that were taken were distributed to the Minutemen of Clay and surrounding counties. Eventually much of the material got into the hands of bushwhackers. Most of it, however, went to the troops of Jackson and Price.

The next day, Grant sent word of the event to the Chief of Ordinance in Washington and a week later he wrote, "The Union feeling has been so strong in Missouri and particularly this county, that I had no apprehension that the post would be disturbed; but it appears that the late telegraphic dispatches from other states produced much excitement among the people, and meetings have been held, and Secession flags raised in almost every town during the past week—this state of things being inaugurated by the seizure of the depot." Grant said he joined those who were "of the opinion that the state is fast drifting into the current of secession."

The raid took place on Saturday. The next Monday, secessionists held a rally at Liberty with speeches, a secessionist flag-raising, and a salute fired from a captured cannon. Conservative Unionists stayed calm and held their rally the next day. One speaker was Alexander Doniphan of Mexican War fame. He vowed neutrality saying he couldn't fight against his flag, nor could he fight against his neighbors. A resolution was passed proclaiming secession would solve nothing. But by then military companies already were being formed. Shooting would come soon after.

The arsenal buildings are long gone now. They were dismantled and hauled away in pieces just after the turn of the century. Not much remains of the site of the first aggressive act against the federal government within Missouri's borders, and the first armed action in the nation after the surrender of Fort Sumter, the capture of the Liberty Arsenal on this date, April 20, in 1861.

****

APRIL 21
THE SOUTHWEST BRANCH

The construction of railroads in Missouri was a tedious process, interrupted by weather, wars, and bankruptcy. Sixteen years after the first rail was laid in St. Louis, one railroad finally reached its destination, Springfield. Along the way were bankrupt men, a near-bankrupt state, crushed hopes, sweat and blood, and feuds.

But the railroads created new towns, gave employment to thousands, and eventually became part of one of the nation's best-known railway systems.

The railroad craze gripped the country in the early 1830s. With eastern states building railroads, the western states caught the fever, too. In 1836, the first railroad convention was held in Missouri and the legislature issued charters to a number of corporations to build rail systems. The national financial panic of 1837, however, doomed all those hopes. Not until 1851 did the legislature authorize grants of state bonds to railroad corporations.

The first railroad operations began in 1852. The first construction of tracks to the southwestern part of the state came in 1855. But the company's bonds which were to finance construction weren't sold. State loan terms were too high. Later the state came through with $4.5 million in state loans on easier terms. But it still took five years for the tracks to reach Rolla. By then the road had become the most expensive railway in Missouri. It averaged $6,580 per mile in cost.

In July 1861 the company defaulted on its loan. All but one of the railroads chartered by the state had financial problems, especially during the Civil War. By the end of the year, Missouri's railroad debt amounted to almost $3.4 million. The railroads were sold at public auction and the state lost $25 million.

There were other problems too.

Confederate raiders attacked federal troop and supply trains and tore up miles of track. During the war the federal government was asked to extend the tracks to Springfield. But the cost was considered too high. Public opinion was strong, though, and demanded the road be finished. That was when the state formally sold the railroad.

John C. Fremont, the famous pathfinder and general, bought it for about $1.3 million and extended it to Arlington where he merged it with the Atlantic and Pacific Company. The plan was for the Atlantic and Pacific Railroad to be built southwest from Springfield, across the Indian territory and on to the Pacific along the 35th parallel. The route later became the St. Louis-San Francisco Railroad, better known as the "Frisco." Ambition was greater then practicality, though. The line never did reach San Francisco.

In the summer of 1867, Supreme Court Judge James Baker called a mass meeting in the Springfield courthouse. The crowd was so large it overflowed the building. Governor Fletcher spoke for a new law allowing new financing of railroads. Baker and his group tried to drum up support from New York financiers but the past history of the railroad was against them. When the railroad had built only one-third of its line in fourteen years and couldn't even pay the operating expenses of the part it had built, not many people wanted to pour more money into it.

Finally, though, the state was able to unload the white elephant line on the South Pacific Railroad Company. The state required $300,000 in interest be paid and that the tracks be completed to the state line in Newton County by mid-June, 1872.

Slowly the tracks moved toward Springfield, with a big celebration at Lebanon. The tracks from Gasconade to Lebanon cost $16,000 a mile with one mile of work over tough terrain costing $41,000 to build. In the construction from Arlington, where Fremont had given up, to Springfield the railroad created thirteen new towns and kept 12,000 men at work.

In Springfield, though, there was dissension. Arguments had arisen over whether the railroad could come to town. Finally a group of land speculators bought land north of Springfield and induced the railroad to build through their community, promising a hotel and depot, forty acres for the railroad's shops and one-half interest in the town site. The depot was in a wooded area of North Springfield. Just before sunset early one spring day, the construction train of the

Pacific Railroad's Southwest Branch pulled alongside the depot. It was a trip that had taken more than a decade and a half. About two weeks later formal service opened on the line. Trains would leave St. Louis in the evening and reach North Springfield the next morning at 11:00 o'clock.

In time the feud between the two Springfields subsided and the towns grew together. But it would be a decade before they merged.

It had taken more than fifteen years of bankruptcy and war to get the tracks laid from St. Louis to Springfield. There would be other misfortunes and long years ahead before the system was complete. The line that became the Frisco never did reach the coast. But in Missouri the great struggle to reach its biggest goal came when the tracks of the Pacific Railroad's Southwest Branch finally reached the Springfield depot and the first train arrived on them on this date, April 21, 1870.

****

APRIL 22
THE MILK STOP THAT BECAME A PRISON

For almost a century Missouri criminals all went to one place, the Missouri State Penitentiary. Whether they were first-time check forgers or multiple offenders and killers, they were all put behind the walls on the riverfront of Jefferson City. But with the coming of the twentieth century, prison reform took hold in the country and by the 1920s it was felt in Missouri.

The push for reform of the state prison system became strong. One leader of the movement in the Missouri legislature was Representative H. O. Maxey, an attorney from Bates County. He became concerned about the Boonville State Training School after a visit there and decided the state needed an institution for older inmates.

Maxey managed to push through an appropriation in the legislature. But the money wasn't specifically earmarked for development of an intermediate reformatory. The funds were used to put up a new maximum security building at the main penitentiary.

So he tried again. In 1927 the legislature gave the go-ahead for what is now the Algoa Intermediate Reformatory. Although its techniques and facilities have improved over the years, its basic purpose remains the same—to rehabilitate young first-time offenders and offer them a solid chance in the outside world. Although the go-ahead was given in 1927, it would be three years before Governor Henry Caulfield could notify the commissioners of the Department of Penal Institutions and the necessary revenue was in the treasury to build the facility. Caulfield suggested the Penal Board, along with an advisory committee, find a suitable location for the institution.

A number of central Missouri farms were inspected. Soils were tested, and after some six weeks of inspection, it was finally unanimously agreed the farm known as the Ewing farm east of and adjacent to Prison Farm Number Three east of Jefferson City would be the place. The prison farm, known as the Algoa dairy farm informally, consisted of 319 acres, about one-half bottomland and one-half rolling red clay highland. The total package would be 776 acres. The commissioners bought the 319-acre Ewing farm for $33,000.

The first inmate stepped onto the grounds of the institution on March 1, 1932. The inmate population varies although it has stabilized in recent years. Until the Moberly Training Center was created the number of inmates sometimes reached 600. But Moberly took some of the pressure off Algoa which then had a regular population of 450 to 500 inmates.

None of the inmates at Algoa has served time in the adult prisons. Most of them are seventeen to twenty-five years old and serve sentences of up to five years.

Ninety percent of the inmates spend a half day in school. The rest work. Most receive education up to the eighth grade and some receive high school diplomas. But no prison diploma is issued. The diploma they receive carries the name of their school back home.

It began as an effort by the state to handle criminals older than those at the Boonville Training School, but still young enough they shouldn't be exposed to the harsher elements of the main penitentiary. It remains so today. The Intermediate Reformatory for Young Men, best known as the Algoa Reformatory, has been giving young men hope for a second chance since the day the legislature created it, on this date, April 22, in 1927.

****

APRIL 23
THE FIRST AMERICAN NEWSPAPER WEST OF ST. LOUIS

Man has found a number of ways to measure the advance of the frontier. Shortly after the first settlers move to an area, a saloon will be built and maybe a church. Later a school, a few miscellaneous "houses" and, not far behind, at least one newspaper will be added to make the settlement a community.

It took eleven years from the time Missouri's first newspaper was printed before the first newspaper was published in outstate Missouri. It would move, change its name, and last 120 years.

Locating a newspaper at Franklin, Missouri, might not be as far-fetched an idea as one might think. Franklin, in its brief history, was a reasonable rival of St. Louis. It was an important river town. Before the Missouri River washed it away it had 2,000 residents and its real estate values equalled those of St. Louis. It was to this growing town that Nathaniel Patten, Jr., went in 1819. He was from Massachusetts, apprenticed in the printing trade in Boston, and had failed at newspapering in Kentucky. Patten decided to try his luck in Missouri. His health was not good, a matter which would plague him throughout his career and sometimes even force him to delay the publication of his newspaper until he could recover from a particular bout of illness. He was also deaf.

The newspaper he established in Franklin was the first one west of St. Louis, and the first north of the Missouri River. It was a typical newspaper of the time, tabloid in size with four pages and five columns per page. In the prospectus for the paper, Patten promised "Truth on all occasions." He promised readers his paper would be "unshackled by the influence of any party." Patten is described by newspaper historian William Howard Taft as a sensitive and reserved individual working in a part of the country which had little patience with impartiality. Missourians demanded to know where a man stood on an issue. Therefore the proclaimed impartiality of the newspaper was unusual.

It was important in those days for a newspaper to secure a contract with the government to print the laws as they developed. It provided a stronger economic base for the paper. Patten had trouble getting that contract. But he finally received it after correspondence with Secretary of State John Quincy Adams and Senators Benton, Barton, and Scott.

Business was slow, hampered by the difficulty of getting supplies and news. Supplies cost a lot and the closest place for them was St. Louis, 160 miles away. Since the newspaper relied on other newspapers and letters to bring it news of the outside world, the sporadic mail delivery was another problem to be overcome. But the circulation grew to about 400.

Patten vigorously solicited advertising. "Notices," as they were called, appeared in the paper. Taft notes the first edition of *The Missouri Intelligencer and Boon's Lick Advertiser* contained sixteen ads. These included a notice of unclaimed mail from the post office and a woman's petition for separation from her husband.

Patten didn't like to publish letters to the editor unless the author's name was included. One of Patten's entries says, in effect, that some people hiding behind cryptic names, such as "Relief" and "Observer," wouldn't see their letters published.

"'Relief' is inadmissable," wrote Patten. "'An Observer' we do not understand, and if we did, should be unable to discern how any benefit could result from its publication. 'A Voter' is postponed until next week for want of room. It will be out of our power to publish any futher numbers of 'A Farmer' until after the election."

In 1826 Patten moved his paper to nearby Fayette and four years later shifted it to Columbia. The last edition in Franklin was printed in June of 1826. In April of 1830 he took it to Columbia. In December of 1835 came the surprise announcement that Patten was selling his paper. He cited ill health as a reason for the sale to Sinclair Kirtley and James S. Rollins. But his health apparently wasn't all that bad because within a year he had started a new paper in St. Charles.

The first American newspaper west of St. Louis lasted 120 years from the time an unhealthy man, Nathaniel Patten, went to a small, thriving but doomed town named Franklin and put out the first edition on this date, April 23, in 1819.

****

APRIL 24
THE MISSOURI COUNCIL OF DEFENSE

On April 2, 1917, Congress met in special session and heard Woodrow Wilson ask for a declaration of war against Germany. Two days later the Senate adopted the war resolution and two days after that the House approved it. Wilson signed the proclamation that same day. Three days later the Secretary of War asked the nation's governors to establish state councils of defense which would mobilize the war effort. On April 12 the movement began in Missouri.

Governor Frederick Gardner called for a war conference with representatives of Missouri cities and organizations meeting in Jefferson City. Gardner told the conference delegates, "History will repeat itself in showing that the burden of war will be placed on the shoulders of the farmers. If this war is to be won, it must be won by the work of the American farmers...." Out of that meeting came the Missouri Council of Defense.

Missouri sent thousands of troops and important leaders to fight in Europe. But almost forgotten through the passage of time is the remarkable statewide effort to support those troops. Not long after the governor made his remarks at that meeting, Mrs. Gardner took about 500 delegates to the backyard of the governor's mansion and showed them how she was cultivating a garden which would supply food for the executive family all year. Soon such gardens would become commonplace throughout the nation.

The next day the governor announced the council would be headed by F. B. Mumford, the Dean of Agriculture at the University of Missouri. Within two years the council could count 12,000 members. The council was given $100,000 on which to operate. It was the only such group given an appropriation of less than a million dollars. Surprisingly, the council did its work on only $76,000. The statistics it produced are still amazing.

Under the council's enthusiastic efforts, Missouri's crop production jumped from fourteenth in value in the nation in 1916 to fifth in 1917. Crop production, only one small part of the council's efforts, jumped. Oats production was up 87 percent. Buckwheat production was increased 61 percent. Sorghum molasses production jumped 233 percent. Production of sweet potatoes showed an 83 percent rise. Bean production: up 500 percent. Corn production was 91 percent more. In 1916 the total value of all Missouri crops was about twenty-six and one quarter million dollars. In 1917 the figure was more than five hundred forty-six million.

Farmers were asked to forget about experimentation, to grow crops with proven techniques. Bulletins and circulars were delivered by the agriculture department. Speaking campaigns were launched

243

with home demonstration agents sent out to show how to can and how to use food substitutes.

Children were urged to join the effort with Junior Garden Clubs, and by 1918 there were almost 2,500 Youth Poultry Clubs which produced thirteen and one-half million dollars in products. Pig clubs, canning clubs, sewing clubs, garden clubs and 739 bread baking clubs were formed.

In the summer of 1917 the governor asked Missouri farmers to increase their fall wheat sowing by 5 percent. The farmers increased it by 20 percent.

Missouri's council was at work elsewhere too. It tried to eliminate the use of the German language and customs which it considered injurious and a deterrent to the various government campaigns. In July 1918 it endorsed the governor's efforts to abolish the German language altogether in Missouri at all public meetings, including meetings at churches, schools, and lodges, and asked for voluntary compliance. But the council cautioned against overzealousness, saying "Loyal and zealous Americans should refrain from violence and disorders and under no circumstances and no conditions should our own people be guilty of injustice, oppression or atrocious conduct toward any class of our citizens." The number of German language newspapers in Missouri dropped from fifteen to ten and many of them started publishing partly in English.

Four-Minute Men were organized. Their main duty was to give short inspirational talks rousing the people to the necessity of sacrifice, passing along messages the government wanted circulated, or raising general patriotic fervor. A woman's committee was set up to train women to fill positions left vacant by men serving in the armed forces.

A campaign was started to use wood instead of coal as fuel in the winter of 1917 and 1918. Drives were organized to collect telescopes and binoculars for the navy. Committees also worked as part of a national campaign to enroll 2,500 student nurses and provide unskilled laborers for war industries.

The shooting stopped in November of 1918. The final commission report came out the next year.

Missouri's Council of Defense which united the state behind those in the trenches, was organized on this date, April 24, 1917.

****

APRIL 25
BULLSEYE BLEDSOE

It is 1861. The Confederate forces of Sterling Price and Calib Jackson are fleeing federal forces after the Battle of Boonville. The Union Army seeks to keep them from reaching Arkansas and an eventual linkup with a sizeable southern army. The confrontation comes at Carthage. Two six-pound cannons and one twelve-pounder, under the command of Captain Hiram Bledsoe, stop the Union advance until the southern forces can get organized. The Confederates regroup and make a camouflaged flanking movement with 2,000 unarmed men. The Union troops withdraw.

Hiram Bledsoe, known as "Bullseye" to his contemporaries, was already a veteran whose military career went back several years. When Alexander Doniphan made his famous 3,000-mile march across Mexico to conquer Santa Fe, Chihuahua, and Sacramento Pass, one of those with him was Hiram Bledsoe.

When Sterling Price organized the pro-southern Missouri Guards at the outbreak of the Civil War, Hi Bledsoe joined up. He rounded up thirteen other men in Lexington and caught a boat to Jefferson City. He got three more recruits on the boat and enough others from along the way that by the time he organized the company in Jefferson City it was sixty men strong.

Bledsoe is credited with saving Price's life once in Jefferson City, defending him from an angry group of fellow pro-southerners who thought Price had betrayed them by making an agreement with General Harney. These southerners were ready for a fight and were disappointed when Price indicated the agreement at least postponed a battle. They surrounded the general, yelling and threatening, when Bledsoe hustled his unit to the area around Price. He brought the crowd under control until Price could address them and explain the situation.

An artillery officer, Bledsoe gained respect from northerner and southerner alike. In the Battle of Carthage, Bledsoe's artillery battery kept the federal forces under Sigel at bay until southern leaders could plot the strategy which would force the men in blue to retreat. His artillery performances were remarkable when you remember that the Confederacy in Missouri often came up short of supplies. Ammunition was homemade: bolts, chains, belt buckles, iron slugs, anything. Opposing forces found that kind of fire withering. When

Price and Jackson reached Lexington they found only three old cannons in the entire town. One was a bronze nine-pounder called "Old Sacramento," a souvenir of the battle in the Mexican War. Another was an iron six-pounder made in Lexington and another was a brass six-pounder taken from the Liberty Arsenal. "Old Sacramento" was bored out to become a 12-pounder. Because of the alteration it made a peculiar sound when fired and that sound became one of encouragement to the rebels. It also was a target for northern troops who often tried to capture it but failed.

When the Confederacy collapsed in Missouri, Bledsoe stayed with the gray. He joined the regular Confederate Army in 1862. He was given four new guns and his unit was completely equipped. Years later an old Confederate artillery veteran would remark that the "history of Bledsoe's battery would be the history of the war, at least so far as the armies of Tennessee and Mississippi are concerned, to say nothing of earlier work in Missouri and Arkansas."

Bledsoe was a commander who came to life in the heat of battle. He sometimes relaxed discipline around the camp, but in the action of a fight he was a stern leader. His men became so proficient they could get off six shots a minute from each cannon. He and his cannons fought at Chickamauga, Chattanooga, Fort Hudson, and Corinth, along with other famous battles. Once he was reported killed. He wasn't, but 70 of his men were. Three weeks after the surrender at Appomattox, Bledsoe went to Hamburg, South Carolina, and gave up.

He returned to Missouri and was able to withstand the cruelty of the radicals after the war. In 1872 Governor Brown named him Presiding Judge of the Cass County Court to fill a vacancy. He was later elected to a full term on the court, then reelected. In 1878 he became the Cass County Collector and in 1892 his constituents sent him to the Missouri Senate.

The federal government came to Bullseye Bledsoe when it was trying to preserve the battlefields of the Civil War, putting him on a special commission sent to locate and mark Confederate positions at Chickamauga, Missionary Ridge, and Lookout Mountain.

Hiram Bledsoe was almost seventy-four when he died shortly before the start of a new century. He wasn't as famous as Price and Jackson or other Missouri military figures like Grant and Sherman. Nonetheless he was a distinguished figure in our state's Civil War history.

Hiram M. Bledsoe, the man his troops called "Bullseye," was born on this date, April 25, in 1825.

****

APRIL 26
THE BATTLE OF CAPE GIRARDEAU

The old fort is a public park now. During their leisure hours, soldiers stationed there used to go bowling—using 32-pound cannon balls! During the winter they dug caves in the river bluffs, finding them more comfortable than the drafty rooms at the fort. The fort was at Cape Girardeau, one of four erected to protect the city during the Civil War. It was an important city from a strategic standpoint for both sides.

The four forts which protected Cape Girardeau bore no heroic names. They were just Forts A, B, C, and D.

Federal forces who assumed control of the town in January 1861 occupied the town until August 1865. Military law was established with tight reins kept on civilians. Many Confederate sympathizers left town. By the same token, many Union supporters moved to Cape Girardeau to be protected by federal forces.

Cape Girardeau was regarded as a key jumping-off point for federal operations in that region. In addition, the Union army felt Cape Girardeau was a key to stopping any Confederate advance up the Mississippi River. District Commander Ulysses Grant kept his headquarters on a boat at Cape Girardeau for a short time before moving to Cairo, Illinois.

The Confederacy coveted the Union position and from time to time made forays into the area, coming up from Arkansas. But only once would there be what could be called "The Battle of Cape Girardeau."

General John Marmaduke, later a governor of Missouri, came north from Arkansas in 1863. He hoped to recruit southern sympathizers and disrupt federal fortifications. He had about 5,000 men with him, many poorly armed, and ten pieces of artillery. Cape Girardeau was his major target. The city had become an important supplies depot for Grant's army which was operating against Vicksburg. The South knew that capture of Cape Girardeau or the disrup-

247

tion of the supply lines to the Union forces at Vicksburg might make a difference in that beseiged Mississippi city.

Sappington divided his men and took the community of Patterson on April 20. As expected, federal forces pulled back toward Pilot Knob. Another southern force hit the northern units of General John McNeil, who had some 3,000 men at Bloomfield. Marmaduke ordered J. O. Shelby's rangers to Fredericktown in hopes McNeil would be driven from Bloomfield and flee toward Pilot Knob. If that happened, Shelby's men could sweep down and annihilate the bluecoats during their retreat. Sure enough, McNeil had to fall back. But he learned of Shelby's presence nearby and turned to Cape Girardeau. His intelligence officers had smelled the trap.

There might still have been a chance to inflict heavy damage on McNeil's men, but the messengers sent to Shelby and Marmaduke at Fredericktown were captured and it wasn't until April 25 that word reached the Confederate commanders that McNeil was in Cape Girardeau.

McNeil therefore had plenty of time to fortify himself and send for help. He ordered all women and children out of the town because he expected an artillery bombardment. He told them to take food and warm clothes. Some even sewed money into skirts and petticoats, not knowing when they'd be back.

Shelby led his men to Cape Girardeau along the Jackson road, but ran into a federal unit outside Cape Girardeau to the northwest. For a short time, the Confederates moved forward. Shelby had help from Colonel George Carter's units and drove the Union troops back to their forts.

Marmaduke gave McNeil thirty minutes to surrender. McNeil refused and counterattacked, forcing Marmaduke's men to retreat.

The firing finally ended about two o'clock in the afternoon. Marmaduke saw Union reinforcements coming upriver and ordered his men back to Jackson. With pursuit close behind, the Confederates went back to Arkansas.

Relief from Missouri for the Confederates under seige at Vicksburg was not forthcoming. Grant took the town two bloody months later.

Both sides claimed victory at Cape Girardeau. But never again did the Confederacy try to take eastern Missouri by coming up the Mississippi River. And only once more would the Confederacy launch a major thrust into Missouri from the south.

The Battle of Cape Girardeau, not major, but a strategically important fight, was fought on this date, April 26, 1863.

****

APRIL 27
THE BIG NECK AFFAIR

The man named Winn was wounded in the battle and was unable to escape with his friends. When the Indians found him, they stacked wood around him and set it afire. With flames soaring, the chief pointed to the dead Indians around him and addressed the wounded white man, "See there! You have killed all that was dear to me: my brother, my brother's wife and her child.... You are not brave, you are a dog."

With that the Indian leaped over the flames and scalped the white man, cut open his chest and cut out his heart.

The Big Neck Affair had begun.

Chief Big Neck had signed the 1824 treaty ceding the Iowa, Sac, and Fox Indian territory in the Chariton River region to the United States. It was part of the process in Missouri in which the Indians gradually gave up their lands to the oncoming white settlers. Five years after the treaty was signed a small settlement was organized about six miles west of what is now Kirksville. The white man was establishing himself quickly in that region. Under the treaty Indians couldn't settle or hunt in that territory any more. But Big Neck, described by some sources as headstrong, came back on a hunting expedition anyway.

Then he refused to return to his people's lands north of the Missouri border, apparently not understanding that he had given up all rights to the land with that five-year-old treaty. He and his band decided to go to St. Louis to complain to the Indian Commissioner, William Clark.

Big Neck and his group arrived at the white settlement on the Chariton River that June and set up camp. Tensions naturally increased. Some say the white men sold whiskey to the Indians and then stole from them when the Indians were drunk. Some say the Indians often barged into white men's homes demanding food and horses. Some of the settlers complained of missing hogs. Finally the settlers sent for help. A twenty-six-man company started from

Howard County to render aid. In July the settlers went to the Indian encampment to have it out.

When the group arrived they apparently asked the chief for an interpreter, but he didn't understand. Then somebody thought he saw an Indian point a gun at a white man.

There are reports that Big Neck had just stepped from his lodge with a peace pipe when the fight broke out. In that fight the leader of the settlers group was killed. James Winn was wounded and later killed by the Indians, and another man was hurt and left behind, later to die. Four others were wounded but escaped although one of them died later.

News of the skirmish spread and the story grew wilder as it went. When word reached Fayette three days later almost all citizens who could carry a gun got ready to leave for the campaign. About 150 persons grabbed their weapons in Randolph County and Governor Miller called out the United States troops under General Henry Leavenworth.

Federal Indian agents finally tracked down Big Neck and his men and took them to St. Louis. Authorities advised that the Indians should not be treated harshly. There was considerable doubt that the Indians really had crossed the treaty boundary line. A survey would later show they had.

In March 1830 a jury sat in judgment of Big Neck and four others. The jury members never left their seats. They handed down a verdict of *not* guilty. They ruled the investigation showed the party of white men had fired first and had been guilty of unprovoked murder.

But the affair wasn't over until Brigadier General Ignatius Owen answered some charges. Owen, from Fayette, had commanded a unit of volunteers which went to the battle site and found nothing. He was charged with disobeying the governor's orders to return home, leaving a contingent in the field to protect the frontier. He faced six charges but was acquitted of all of them.

Several years later a similar incident occurred when some people named Heatherly tried to sell whiskey to emigrating Potawatomis. The Indians refused to buy. The Heatherly family stole some Indian horses. The Indians killed two family members. The rest of the Heatherly clan spread tales of thousands of warring Indians prompting the governor to send out 200 militiamen with orders to expel all Indians from the state. A later investigation by federal authorities uncovered the truth. The report said there was no reason for the panic felt in that case either.

And so the Big Neck Affair ended, the bloodiest of the two similar incidents a dozen years apart. Both are prime examples of misunderstanding and fear on both sides. The books finally closed on the incident, though, with the acquittal of Ignatius Owen on this date, April 27, in 1830.

****

APRIL 28
A TOUR OF CURIOSITY

They had come from the East in 1846, young adventurers wanting to see the West, to sample the frontier and maybe write a book about what they saw. It wasn't uncommon in those days for easterners, especially authors, to come West and write about their experiences. Those in the East were hungry for material capturing the sweep of the West, the idiosyncracies of those who lived in it and the dangers of those who would venture out. Such was the case with the two young men, one of whom would write one of the most famous books ever penned about the American West.

"Late spring was a busy season in the city of St. Louis," he wrote. "Not only were emigrants from every part of the country preparing for the journey to Oregon and California, but an unusual number of traders were making ready their wagons and outfits for Santa Fe. The hotels were crowded and the gunsmiths and saddlers were kept constantly at work in providing arms and equipment for the different parties of travelers. Steamboats were leaving the levee and passing up the Missouri, crowded with passengers on their way to the frontier. In one of these...my friend and relative, Quincy Adams Shaw, and myself, left St. Louis...on a tour of curiosity and amusement to the Rocky Mountains."

Once the young man got on the boat he would have time to know them better. He would later write that the people on board the boat with him included Santa Fe traders, gamblers, speculators and adventurers, Oregon immigrants, mountain men, Negroes, and even a party of Kansas Indians. The boat entered the Missouri River in a drizzle and struggled upsteam for seven or eight days before reaching Westport—now Kansas City. The boat often grated on snags and spent two or three hours at a time hung up on sandbars. He was amazed at the muddy water and the mobility of the river.

Westport, he found, was filled with Indians of all tribes. There he met two men he had known in St. Louis and they encouraged him to set out across the country with them. One day he went to Independence, which he described as crowded, with a business district made up of shops catering to the emigrant trade. He said there was an incessant hammering and banging from a dozen blacksmith sheds—a profitable occupation because of the repairs needed for wagons and the shoes needed for the animals.

Later he would write that whiskey circulated more freely in Westport than could be considered safe in a place where every man carried a loaded pistol in his pocket.

When the party reached Fort Laramie, they arranged to join a band of Sioux Indians who were involved in a retaliatory war against their enemies. That war eventually fell apart. But the young man stayed with the Indians and traveled through much of what is now Wyoming. He finally returned to Fort Laramie and joined his relatives to go south. They picked up the Santa Fe Trail and returned to civilization.

It took another eight days to come back downstream to St. Louis. The levee was crowded when they returned. They found a room at the prominent hotel of the day—the Planter's House—and for the first time put on civilized eastern clothes again. A couple of days later the party left St. Louis and "after a fortnight of railroads, coaches and steamboats, (we) saw once more the familiar features of home—Boston."

The book written about his adventures is now a classic in American literature, an enduring description of a nation gathering itself for the leap West. For the next twenty-seven years he worked on an eight-volume history of France. When ill health cut down on the amount of time he could devote to writing, he became interested in raising flowers and originated several new varieties. He even wrote a book about it and became a professor on the subject at Harvard. He died in 1893 at the age of seventy.

His book was *The Oregon Trail*, complete with the vivid descriptions of frontier Missouri and a growing nation. It showed the excitement of a people pushing into a new territory.

It all began when Francis Parkman, a twenty-three-year-old

easterner, left St. Louis for a "tour of curiosity and amusement to the Rocky Mountains" on this date, April 28, in 1846.

****

APRIL 29
LAFAYETTE, HE IS HERE

The French influence in Missouri was still very strong in the decade after statehood when word got out that the famous French military hero, Lafayette, was coming to our state. The populace prepared a great reception. But then the governor of Missouri did something which left the citizens stunned and had the makings of an international insult.

General Marie Joseph Paul Roche Yves Gilbert du Motier, the Marquis de Lafayette, had been invited to America by outgoing President James Monroe and the Congress. When word reached St. Louis the citizens decided he absolutely had to visit their growing and bustling community.

Lafayette arrived in New York on August 16, 1824. A month later, on September 15, St. Louis held a big outdoor celebration to mark his arrival in the "states." Five days later a special invitation was sent to the general. The general, then in Philadelphia, accepted.

Plans were immediately made to entertain him. But they ran into a snag. St. Louis city officials doubted the legality of using the city's money to entertain the great guest. So Mayor William Carr Lane decided they should invite Governor Bates. Surely, thought Lane, if the Governor acted as host, some of the wealthier elements of St. Louis society would be more inclined to donate money for the event. Furthermore, Lane argued, if the governor took part the state might later make an appropriation to cover the expenses. But Bates flatly refused to take part. The state couldn't afford it, said Bates, and unless Lafayette could be entertained in a manner befitting his station in life, he should not be entertained at all! He added that the country had already shown Lafayette sufficient good will. Furthermore, said the governor, if Lafayette came to the Bates farm looking for him, he—Bates—would arrange not to be there.

Mayor Lane was astounded. Finally, city aldermen took a chance and used money from the city treasury to entertain the French General. Lafayette arrived in St. Louis in the spring of 1825, lucky to have made it. His steamboat had hit a snag about 120 miles from

Louisville and had sunk within ten minutes. Lafayette escaped with only part of his luggage. A carriage which had been the property of George Washington, given him by Washington's nephew, went to the bottom of the river. His party was picked up by a couple of freighters bound upstream from New Orleans.

Mayor Lane and others boarded the steamship "Natchez" to meet him. Later they went to the home of Pierre Chouteau to relax. The state, by the way, was not totally without representation. Former Governor Alexander McNair was a member of the reception committee and acted on behalf of the state.

Later they visited the home of former Territorial Governor William Clark who, twenty-two years before, had explored much of the area Lafayette's country sold to the United States. Lafayette is reported to have marveled at a set of grizzly bear claws which Clark had brought back from the Northwest.

Once during the visit, Lafayette was surprised to see an old man approaching him, dressed in the uniform of a French soldier in the American Revolution. The old man tottered up, stiffly saluted and identified himself as Alexander Bellisime, a native of Toulon, France. He had come to the colonies with Lafayette's first units during the Revolution. Years later he had settled in St. Louis and opened a tavern popular with rivermen who called him "Old Alexie." The meeting left both men deeply touched.

The rest of the day was spent driving around the city which then had a population of about 5,000. They visited the St. Louis Masonic Lodge where Lafayette and his son, George Washington Lafayette, were made honorary Masons. The climax of the visit was a dance at the City Hotel.

When it was over and Lafayette had gone, city officials totaled their expenses. Since so many people had opened their homes for entertainment or provided transportation, the city's bill for the entire day's entertainment came to only $37.

St. Louis, where some say the westernmost battle of the Revolutinary War was fought and an important victory for the future of this nation was won, had given a hero of that war a grand reception. But the day could have been a social disaster. The disaster had been avoided because Missourians would not let a governor's rudeness overcome their desire to honor the great Lafayette the day he came to Missouri, this date, April 29, 1825.

****

254

APRIL 30
MEET ME AT THE FAIR

About 200,000 people were waiting that day in St. Louis when the president, in Washington, pressed an electric key. When he did, 10,000 flags unfurled, waterfalls began to flow in Forest Park, bands began to play, and machinery began to run. For the next eight months, St. Louis would be the site of the great Louisiana Purchase Exposition, the 1904 World's Fair. It went far beyond the expectations of those who originally planned an event to celebrate the centennial of the Louisiana Purchase.

Thousands of people lined Administration Avenue — Lindell Boulevard today — for a parade. They heard John Phillip Sousa's band, a chorus singing "Hymn to the West," a speech from the Secretary of War, William Howard Taft, and another speech from Missouri's governor, David Francis, a former mayor of St. Louis.

Plans for the fair had started eight years earlier when Pierre Chouteau, a descendant of the founders of the city, proposed a memorial to be built honoring Thomas Jefferson in Forest Park. The memorial was to house documents important to the Louisiana Purchase. Two years later endorsement came from the Missouri Historical Society of St. Louis. A group was set up to plan a celebration, with Chouteau suggesting a four-block-long historic memorial on the riverfront. St. Louis businessmen were interested. Some suggested the celebration last for a week, maybe more. Federal money might be obtained.

Another group, led by publisher William Marion Reedy, started a campaign to clean up the town. They felt St. Louis couldn't invite thousands of guests until it was a model community. The city received ten million dollars in state and federal money. Street improvements were made. A smoke control ordinance was passed. The courthouse was renovated. The water supply was improved. Street lights were upgraded. New hotels were built.

Finally the fair opened.

What did people see when they walked into the fairgrounds for the Louisiana Purchase Exposition? Many hummed the hit song which came from the event, "Meet me in St. Looey, Looey; Meet me at the Fair...." Most of the forty-three states built their own exhibit buildings. Fifteen great exposition halls were laid out in a fan-shaped arrangement. One critic looked at the dozens of different buildings and examples of national architecture and called it an "astonishing pattern of elaborate and universal chaos."

At the top of Art Hill was the Palace of Art, now a part of the St. Louis Art Museum. In front of it was Festival Hall and inside that was the world's largest organ. Italian gondolas were poled throughout the grand basin and lagoons. The Missouri building, the biggest and best, was heated by steam in the cold weather and cooled by cold air in hot weather.

In the Palace of Electricity people could crowd around and hear a wireless telegraph sending messages all the way to Chicago.

In the Agriculture Building they could watch as cows were milked twice a day and see a statue of President Roosevelt carved in butter. There was also a bear made of prunes.

People marveled at a display of 100 automobiles—all in one place! And one of them had even made the trip to St. Louis all the way from New York under its own power.

There was no zoo, but the largest bird cage in the world housed birds from all around the globe.

Houses, castles, and cabins dotted the grounds. Eskimoes strolled around in their parkas. Indians lived in their tents. African pygmies wiped out swarms of sparrows with accurate bow-and-arrow shooting.

Hagenbeck's circus had elephants sliding down slides. In the Irish village a young singer delighted audiences who years later would listen to records and recall having heard John Charles Thomas at the World's Fair. In the village of old St. Louis, a young cowboy named Will Rogers spun ropes and stories simultaneously. A young pianist named Scott Joplin played the music he had made famous—ragtime.

On the Pike people could sample all kinds of new and foreign foods. It was there that the first ice cream cone was made, that people ate their first hot dog, and a delightful new drink called "iced tea" was enjoyed.

The Olympic Games were held in St. Louis that August and September. President Roosevelt visited and became the first president to make an airplane flight.

It was an exciting exposition and it ended in December. Then the buildings, only a few intended to be permanent, were torn down. Only the Art Museum, the Grand Basin, the Bird Cage, lagoons and three buildings given to Washington University are left.

Perhaps the greatest monument left from the World's Fair of 1904 is the city of St. Louis, which brought itself into the twentieth century because its citizens and leaders were too proud to have the world see it the way it was. Memories and pictures tell us it was a great exposition, Missouri's only World's Fair, which opened on this date, April 30, 1904.

Harry S.
Truman,
Born May 8,
1884

MAY

MAY 1
CALAMITY

In the 1860s, three children were out panhandling in the streets of Virginia City, Montana. The oldest was about twelve and the head of the family since her parents had died. They had come from Missouri. The death of the parents left the children to their own inclinations. The inclinations of Martha Jane, the oldest, became part of the legends of the American West. For it was Martha Jane Canary of Princeton, Missouri, who became "Calamity Jane."

One of the many people who have written about the colorful person who became known to historian and novelist alike says Calamity Jane "took the greatest pride in her ability to out-chew, out-smoke, out-swear and out-drink most of her masculine companions. Her profanity in particular, was so rich in metaphor and so varied, that it was a source of delight to discriminating audiences."

The story of Calamity Jane is a tangled mess of dime novel adventures, her own lies and drunken ramblings and a few noble moments. In all honesty, we don't know if her story as we tell it is completely true.

Her father was apparently a Mormon who did not leave Missouri in the late 1830s as others had done. Martha had just started school in Princeton when her father, Robert Canary, got a call to Kirkwood to become a lay minister. Her disrupted education never progressed further.

In the 1860s Canary decided to head for Salt Lake City. Martha Jane was twelve. Her mother died on the way west and her father died not long after reaching Virginia City. Her story is obscured in history for a few years, although she went to South Pass City, Wyoming, for a while. She fell in love with a young army officer, shared his bed, and supposedly married him. He deserted her a few weeks later.

Calamity Jane reportedly "married" about a dozen times. But her definition of marriage was different from the usually accepted one. She may have been married legally twice, and perhaps a third time—although that third time is a controversial part of her life. Harry Sinclair Drago notes that by the late 1860s she was in Virginia City working as a "dance hall girl." From time to time she worked in a brothel. Sometimes she was a camp follower for wagon trains.

She claimed to have scouted for Custer. The truth is that she might have been a teamster or mule skinner for a military unit once, but not for Custer.

She claimed to have rescued innumerable cavalry captains, ruined many stage holdups, killed hundreds of Indians. But verification of these heroic ventures does not exist.

Calamity Jane lived in the midst of men who saw her both as a comrade and an object of amusement. Her tall tales were always worth a drink or two. By the time she was in her mid-twenties she was an alcoholic.

She claimed to have met Wild Bill Hickock in Hays, Kansas, married him and had Hickock's child a few days later. While sentimentalists cling to that, historians don't regard the matter seriously.

Realistically it appears she and Hickock, another former Missourian, didn't meet until 1876 when the newly married Wild Bill was working with a wagon train in Cheyenne, Wyoming, hoping to reach the gold fields of Deadwood, South Dakota. Drago says up to then Jane had been primarily "a widely traveled, coarse, slovenly" prostitute.

Hickock was shot to death soon after. Dime novelists would make much of Jane's relationship with him, undoubtedly encouraged by Jane. But it is apparent they never lived together. He treated her with tolerance and that's about all.

Still a big name, Jane was a big attraction at the Pan American Exposition in Buffalo, New York, in 1901. She got drunk and shot up the midway. Some friends bought her a one-way ticket back west.

For a while she sold souvenir pictures of herself. By 1902 an interviewer noted she couldn't talk without being liquored up, and then she could repeat only a few stilted paragraphs of biography dotted with lies. In late July 1903 she rode into Terry, South Dakota, suffering from advanced alcoholism, pneumonia and—some say—failing eyesight resulting from a long-forgotten bout with venereal disease. She is buried in Deadwood, supposedly in accordance with her last romantic wish, next to Bill Hickock.

Calamity Jane, Martha Jane Canary, was born in Missouri on this date, the first of Mary, 1852.

****

MAY 2
THE FIRST STATE CHARTER

Statehood was just around the corner. The territory had been given permission to draft its constitution. The first thing to do was elect the delegates to the constitutional convention. After their election these men would have just thirty-two days to draw up a document which would guide Missouri in its early days of statehood. This is the distinguished group which drew up Missouri's first constitution.

All but five of the forty-one delegates were from slave states. The average age was just under thirty-eight. Only two were native Missourians. Only one delegate was opposed to slavery—Benjamin Emmons of St. Charles. Our first constitution was drafted largely by Englishmen, with two Welshmen, two Scotsmen, two Irishmen, four Scotch-Irish and one German. Only two of the forty-one were of French background despite the strong French influence on Missouri's recent past. Eight members of the group later occupied seats in one or both houses of the legislature. Sixteen had been in the Territorial General Assembly. In each of the first eleven general assemblies after statehood at least one, and sometimes as many as ten of the forty-one drafters of the state constitution served.

The oldest delegate was Col. Malcolm Henry. He was eighty-four.

Edward Bates, who would become the first federal cabinet officer from west of the Mississippi forty years later, was the youngest member of the convention. He was twenty-seven.

Three men would later serve in the United States Senate: David Barton from Missouri, Henry Dodge from Wisconsin, and Alexander Buckner also from Missouri.

Four of the men would either serve in the future, or had already served, in the lower house of the national legislature: Bates, Dodge, Samuel Hammond—a former delegate from Georgia—and John Scott, who had been Missouri's second territorial delegate and would be our first congressional delegate after statehood.

Delegate Benjamin Reeves would later be lieutenant governor. Two of the men would be or had been attorneys general—Bates for Missouri and John Rice Jones, who already had served in that job in Indiana.

Two future secretaries of state were there. Hammond would be secretary of state a decade later in South Carolina and William G.

Pettus would be Missouri's second secretary of state. Benjamin Reeves would be Missouri's second state auditor. Hiram E. Baber would be the sixth.

Two of Missouri's first three state supreme court judges were there, Jones and John Cook. Barton held the first circuit court session west of the Mississippi earlier. James Evans and Richard Thomas would be circuit judges later.

Fourteen were independently wealthy. Most of the others enjoyed large incomes from their profession, business, or holdings. Only four were in a lower economic level. Two were schoolteachers; one was a politician. The other, Baber, was a small businessman who later became a politician, state auditor, and so wealthy he supposedly lit cigars with his money.

Seven were self-educated. Others had some formal education and several had been to college. John Rice Jones probably was the best-educated. He was well versed in math and the classics, and could speak Greek, Latin, French, Spanish, Welsh, and English. He was a financier and one of the wealthiest men in the West. Unfortunately, Jones and two other delegates would not live to see the constitution go into effect. On the other hand, four lived to see the Civil War and the next constitution which came in 1865.

Three men served in the Revolutionary War as colonels. Eighteen were in the War of 1812 including two who became major generals. Four men served in the war against Chief Blackhawk. Nathan Boone was the only one to see actual service in the Mexican War.

Only ten members were lawyers. Five religions were represented: Methodist, Baptist, Presbyterian, Episcopal, and Catholic.

These then were the men who drafted our first state constitution, a solid one, brief but long-lasting. Somewhat liberal in outlook, it wasn't amended for many years. Missourians were casting ballots to elect that distinguished group of forty-one on this date, May 2, in 1820.

****

MAY 3
THE SAGE

Missouri has given the nation two of its greatest newspaper publishers in William Rockhill Nelson of the *Kansas City Star* and

Joseph Pulitzer of the *St. Louis Post-Dispatch.* One of the nation's best small town newspapermen also is claimed by Missouri. He learned his trade here, but took it to Atchison, Kansas, and became known as "The Sage of Potato Hill."

His name was E. W. Howe.

Biographer Calder Pickett describes him as "a man who came to represent country-town journalism, and country-town philosophy to much of America." For sixty years only William Allen White rivaled him as a symbol of the crusty, pithy, and quick country editor.

Howe was raised in Harrison County, Missouri. His education was sparse. His father was a circuit-riding preacher who ran off with one of his parishoners.

Howe never studied grammar. He said common fractions discouraged him. But when he was eleven or twelve his father bought a newspaper in nearby Bethany, Missouri, and young Ed became a typesetter. He was whipped by his stern father if he made too many errors. This was how he learned sentence construction. He also gained a distrust of formal education. Once Howe said the best men have not been formally educated and that college can ruin a boy.

After his father sold the paper Howe went to Gallatin to work on a paper there. Later he went to Maysville and supplemented his typesetting with some writing. It was then that he first began to realize the power of the pen. His first experience on a daily paper was in St. Joseph. Later, he left to work on newspapers in several western states, founded a paper in Golden, Colorado, and then in Falls City, Nebraska. Two years later he started the Atchison *Globe* in Kansas.

Howe gained national fame through his pointed editorial comments. The major papers began running his comments and occasionally one crops up today.

Howe was a critic of organized religion. Once he ran a poll surveying ninety-six congregational ministers. He said forty-one of them were for hell; fifty-five were against it, and that meant the anti-hell ministers had a majority of fourteen. He castigated them for accepting biblical promises of salvation but refusing to accept the threats of holy vengeance.

Howe once asked area hunters to go to Missouri to do their Sunday shooting. It wouldn't offend Missourians as much as Kansans, he wrote, because Missouri people are neither religious nor particular.

Howe lived on a high plot of ground in Atchison called Potato Hill. His comments earned him the title, "The Sage of Potato Hill." He wrote a book about small town life, *The Story of a Country Town.* In many ways it was typical of the romantic but sticky tales of the day which Howe generally disliked. It contained an air of realism, however, which most of the novels of the day never approached. It made him a national figure. The book was based in Missouri and is filled with stories of people reminiscent of those he had known in Harrison County.

Newspaper historian Frank Luther Mott says Howe's significance is that he was deeply interested in his neighbors and published a newspaper for them and of them.

E. W. Howe, the editor of the Atchison *Globe,* born in Indiana, but from the age of two until he stopped for keeps in Atchison, Kansas, was a Missourian. Missouri was always a part of his life. E. W. Howe, the Sage of Potato Hill, was born on this date, May 3, 1853.

****

MAY 4
THE SHEPHERD AND THE CALLING

The young minister had come to town while in his mid-thirties. The people in the little church were surprised by what they saw. He was about six feet two and weighed 125 pounds. He was tubercular and would fight the illness for much of his life. Church members accustomed to fire and brimstone were surprised when the preacher delivered a quiet sermon, a fireside chat type of presentation. In his spare time the young preacher made his headquarters at the office of a local lawyer. There he wrote his sermons and worked on a book about some people he had known a few years before. Often he wrote parts of it while on fishing and hunting trips with friends. It became one of the most famous novels ever written about Missouri, a book which gave its name to an entire section of our state.

For a man who started life with so little and finished life with so much, he never seemed to consider himself above the common people who filled the novels which made him rich. Once he told an interviewer, "You know, I understand my limitations. I don't write literature. I write books." Later he said, "Take your work seriously, but not yourself. My first commandment is 'Thou shalt not kid thyself.'"

His name was Harold Bell Wright.

His middle name came from friends named Bell in the area around his birthplace, Rome, New York. His first memory was of being placed on his back in a hay-filled manger under the nose of a gentle horse. He once wrote his sons, "Is it strange that with such a start I should, all my life, wish that I could be a farmer? Does it explain my love for horses? Is this why there are so many horses in my books? Is this why I do not care for automobiles and use them only because I must.... To me the difference between an automobile and a horse is the difference between Henry Ford and God."

Wright's father was an alcoholic carpenter whose life was generally marked by poverty. His mother died when he was eleven. He was passed around from relative to relative or from friend to friend. He picked up occasional schooling, supported himself by painting houses, and worked in a bookstore for a while. He was a minister for a time. Once he said, "While I served ten years as a parson, I never for a moment felt myself to be other than an amateur."

When relatives moved to the area near Springfield, Missouri, he followed, still a teen-ager; and when he first saw the Ozarks, he said they "entered his soul."

Wright was a part-time painter who supported himself with his art work. Once he went to a revival and was shocked at the ignorance of the preacher who first misread the Bible verse then preached a distorted sermon, based on the misreading. When Thanksgiving came and the preacher didn't, a citizen said to Wright, "You got edication, mister. Why cain't you preach for we-uns?" He did.

Wright married and later was divorced, a move which hurt the popularity of his books. He went to Kansas City to work and began to outline a book he wrote after moving to Lebanon, Missouri. He called it *The Shepherd of the Hills*. It stands today as his greatest work. It was released in 1907, first dramatized in 1912, filmed in 1919, 1928, and 1941. Eight of his books became movies.

Wright authored eighteen books including three more dealing with Missouri. One was a sequel to *The Shepherd of the Hills, The Calling of Dan Matthews*. Two others were *The Recreation of Brian Kent*, and *Ma Cinderella*.

The Shepherd of the Hills is the story of a city minister who goes to the Ozarks looking for meaning in life and finds himself living among the same people his artist son had known years before. He learns his son had abandoned an illegitimate son whose mother died in childbirth and left behind a bitter and lonely family. The book sold out in its first printing of 25,000 before it was actually released. Within twenty-five days the printer had gone through four more printings of 25,000 each. The first edition of the sequel, *The Calling of Dan Matthews,* was 100,000 copies.

On the day of his death in 1944, an Associated Press dispatch said, "In simple, penetrating portrayal of the lives of wholesome people... lay the strength of Wright as a fictionist. That vast mass of humanity known as the common people made up the bulk of the author's public. He wrote of what he liked to term 'life.'"

Harold Bell Wright, who wrote one of the most beloved books ever written about Missouri and through its title gave a name to a part of our state, was born on this date, May 4, 1872.

****

MAY 5
ALEXANDER McNAIR

He was a most unusual governor, perhaps one of the more practical ones. He campaigned for the office on the basis that it paid too much. His inaugural address was so short many state lawmakers who were celebrating in a nearby pub showed up a little late and missed it entirely. Then he vetoed the daily compensation and travel allowance for members of the legislature.

He was Alexander McNair, our state's first governor. His victory was a surprise to many.

Alexander McNair was from Pennsylvania where he commanded a company which helped put down the Whiskey Rebellion. McNair was one of those in the crowd when Captain Amos Stoddard ran the American flag up the pole for the first time over Missouri. From that time on he served in some kind of public capacity.

McNair was a close friend of General William Henry Harrison, the governor of the Northwest Territory. When the first Court of Common Pleas was organized—the only American government in Missouri at the time—McNair was on it.

Among other things, this court licensed ferry-boat operators at ten dollars a year and taverns at five dollars a year. The judges regarded pool tables a little more critically, charging $100 a year per table for licenses. The court allowed sheared deerskins to be used in payment of taxes—three deerskins equal to one dollar. One could pay in skins only from October to April, however. Otherwise — cash.

When St. Louis was incorporated as a city, McNair was one of the five trustees of the town. Later he became the fourth sheriff of St. Louis County. McNair rose to the rank of colonel during the War of 1812 and was adjutant and inspector general of the territorial forces. His unit of horse cavalry and rangers was a popular organization in St. Louis during that war.

McNair rose in political and financial stature during that time. He'd gone into the mercantile business in 1806 but broke it up six years later to lead his rangers. In 1811 his property assessment was $841. The richest man in St. Louis in those days was Auguste Chouteau whose assessment was $15,000. In 1811 only fourteen St. Louis residents had so-called "carriages of pleasure," and McNair was one of them.

In those days the question of land titles was important. With the shift in governments over the years, land grants became chaotic and the American government dragged its feet in settling the matter. It was McNair who joined with a dozen others to form a committee which convinced Territorial Land Registrar Frederick Bates to accept the old Spanish records as the basis for making determinations and working from there. His efforts undoubtedly stood him in good stead later when he ran for governor. In any event, it helped him become the presiding officer in the Federal Land Office in St. Louis.

That May a large public meeting was held protesting Congressional delays on the question of Missouri statehood. McNair presided.

When the time came to draw up a constitution, McNair was one of the distinguished forty-one elected to do it. He ran on a platform of unrestricted slavery and free, white male suffrage based on age, residence and tax qualification. In the deliberations he voted against high salaries other delegates favored and voted against the $2,000 annual salary for the governor.

Two days after the constitution was signed, he announced his candidacy for the governorship. McNair campaigned hard in all parts of the city. He didn't attack his opponent, explorer William Clark, but he attacked the constitutional convention for its secrecy and its failure to distribute information about the proceedings so people could see how the delegates had voted.

Clark campaigned little. He once said naming a governor was the people's job, not his.

McNair received 72 percent of the vote.

In McNair's first legislative address he proposed incorporation of a state medical society and establishment of public hospitals. He was several years ahead of his time with those ideas. Within a month he was working on his campaign pledges. He issued the first gubernatorial veto in Missouri history when he refused to endorse a bill giving lawmakers four dollars a day salary plus an extra daily dollar for legislative leaders. The measure also provided three dollars for each twenty-five miles of travel. The legislature promptly overrode those vetoes.

After his term as governor, Alexander McNair became an Osage Indian agent. On one of his visits to the Indian agency he caught a bad cold which became influenza. He was not quite fifty-one when he died.

Alexander McNair, Missouri's first state governor, was born on this date, May 5, 1775.

****

MAY 6
STEPHEN HEMPSTEAD

It is September of 1776.

The Battle of Harlem Heights has just recently been fought and the British are camped on Long Island. A small group of Americans makes a spying trip into the British camp. One of the group is captured and hanged. His name is Nathan Hale.

Others escaped to spy and fight again. One of those who got away was Stephen Hempstead. It was not his first narrow escape.

A few months before about 2,400 British soldiers had assembled below a hill north of New York and begun an orderly march up its slopes. At the top were three units of colonials. The colonials were nervous. Several already had fled back to Boston.

History tells us that they were commanded not to shoot until the men saw the whites of the British eyes. Whether or not that was said that's what happened. At fifty yards, the New Hampshire colonials tore apart the British column. One historian says the next unit melted like a wax candle against a hot plate.

The British fled.

On the left another British unit withered before the accurate colonial fire, regrouped, advanced again, and again was decimated in another fierce burst of gunfire. But they came back and the fighting was hand to hand. Finally the red tide took the crest and the colonials fled down the far slope of Breed's Hill, up and over Bunker Hill, which for some reason gave its name to the battle.

One of those who stood and fought and would now flee to fight again was Stephen Hempstead. He was a sergeant in that historic battle which cost the British 1,000 men.

A year later the British were trying to capture the key port of New York. One of the ninety Americans wounded in the battle was Stephen Hempstead.

In 1781 when the British landed at New London, Connecticut, about 160 colonials manned the defenses and fought well. They repulsed three redcoat attacks but were finally overwhelmed. The American commander, Colonel William Ledyard, offered his sword to the British commander. The Tory officer took the sword and immediately killed Ledyard. The British and Hessian troops butchered the surrendered men, leaving 85 dead immediately and 60 more hurt. Many of them died later. The town was destroyed. The man who conceived this atrocity was Benedict Arnold.

One of those to feel the steel of the bayonet at that massacre was Stephen Hempstead. The dead were dumped into the river. Only an accident kept Hempstead, still living, from being dumped into the river too.

Many years after the war ended Stephen Hempstead led a party of twenty persons to the West. Two of his sons had preceded him to the area that is now Missouri. In 1811, Hempstead, his sons, daughters, grandchildren, and other friends made their way to the settlement of St. Louis.

The Hempsteads set up a farm in what is now Bellefontaine Cemetery. When Lafayette made the famous visit to St. Louis in 1825, Hempstead was one of the three men on the welcoming committee. He was instrumental in founding the Presbyterian church in Missouri.

Stephen Hempstead would live to see Missouri achieve statehood in a land far removed from the colonies he fought to make into states. It would be fifty years after his narrow escape from death at the New London Massacre before death would claim him. He is buried in St. Louis, one of many Revolutionary War soldiers to come to Missouri to live out the dream they fought to establish.

Stephen Hempstead was born on this date, May 6, 1754.

MAY 7
THE HISTORICAL SHOEMAKER

He was called "Mr. Missouri" by some. He might have been a great musician except for a hearing defect which forced him to turn his interests elsewhere. For more than half a century he played the key role in preserving the history of Missouri. His job and his hobby became the same thing. His name was Floyd Shoemaker, and he wasn't a general or a politician. He was a historian.

In the foreword to one of his many books, Shoemaker wrote, "The history of Missouri and her people is a story dramatic and colorful, a story of enterprise and achievements. With a background that mirrors each of the various phases of American history, Missouri yet retains an individuality that lends distinctiveness to each episode in her development.

"In the early days of settlement, from the days when the rivers offered gateways to the rich fur trade of the west, through the years when Missouri's rich mines lured prospectors; when her newly opened fertile farmlands attracted homesteaders; when her publicized glories brought thousands of foreigners to her borders; when steel ribbons of railway transformed her into the stepping stone between East and West; when her infant manufacturers began to develop into great industrial cities....Missouri has been a land of promise to many.

"Her citizens, statesmen, educators, industrialists, soldiers, professional men, farmers, traders...in all fields have been people of achievement.

"To tell the story of these things...Missouri, the land of promises, and Missourians, a people of achievements...has been the aim of this work."

Floyd Shoemaker came to Missouri from Florida at the age of seven. His family moved to Bucklin, in Linn County, in 1893. He graduated from Kirksville State Teachers College where he was president of the senior class. In 1906 and 1907 he taught in the public schools of Colorado before returning to Gallatin, Missouri, to teach history and Latin.

Shoemaker went on to the University of Missouri to get his bachelor's degree and a master's. Along the way he picked up a Phi

Beta Kappa key. His master's thesis was on "The First Constitution of Missouri, 1820." He became an assistant professor of political science and public law at the university. In 1910 he was attracted to the still infant State Historical Society of Missouri which needed a librarian. Five years later he was the executive secretary of the society.

Shoemaker drew upon his intense interest in history, his skills as an organizer, and his comprehensive memory to give the new society life. By the time he retired in the spring of 1960 the State Historical Society of Missouri counted 12,000 members—the largest membership of any historical society in America.

As Missouri neared its centennial, Shoemaker began organizing his society's workers and community historians throughout the state to increase interest in the event. He even expanded his master's thesis into a book, *Missouri's Struggle for Statehood, 1804-1821*. It gave him national standing as a historical writer. His second book was *Missouri's Hall of Fame,* a collection of intimate personal sketches of distinguished Missourians. Encouraged by the reception of those books, he wrote *A History of Missouri and Missourians.* He wrote six books on Missouri history, edited or co-edited thirty others, and helped on thirty-five more.

The year before he retired he reported the society had more than 300,000 books, pamphlets and bound newspapers, and more than nine million pages of microfilmed newspapers plus many art treasures. For half a century he had been with the society—forty-five years as its leader. He died in August of 1972 at the age of 86.

The Official State Manual of 1959-60 said, "Dr. Shoemaker has dedicated his life, his prodigious talent and his energy to the building of a great historical library, to the writing of scholarly historical books and to the popularization of state history, and to bringing it within the grasp and interest of the smallest child and to the citizen."

Dr. Floyd Shoemaker was born on this date, May 7, in 1886.

****

MAY 8
HST

April 12, 1945.
A president has died.

A Missourian will succeed him. Harry Truman. Unless you count David Rice Atchison and Ulysses Grant, he is the only man from Missouri to lead this nation as its president. Fate has thrust him into that office. Three years later he will win it outright despite great odds, the rumors, the polls, a Chicago newspaper that proclaims him the loser, and a radio commentator named H. V. Kaltenborn, who found the returns hard to believe throughout the long election night.

The day after Roosevelt died and Harry Truman became president, he told some friends from the Senate, "I don't know if any of you fellows ever had a load of hay or a bull fall on you. . . . Last night the whole weight of the moon and stars fell on me. I feel a tremendous responsibility."

The people of the nation didn't know much about their new president. Vice-presidents in those days were generally forgotten men. There was some talk about connections with the Pendergast machine in Kansas City. Some remembered him as a demanding investigating committee member. Many would remember him as Captain Harry of the One Hundred Twenty-ninth Field Artillery, Thirty-fifth Division, which he helped organize during World War I.

He was a farm boy from Lamar, Missouri. His first job, at the age of eleven, was dusting bottles and washing windows in a drugstore. Later he worked for a couple of banks but ended up on the family farm near Grandview until the war broke out. Truman emerged from the war as a major in 1919 and later that year became co-owner of a men's clothing store in Kansas City. In the first year they sold $70,000 worth of clothing. The partnership ended in 1922. By then he was a judge on the Jackson County Court. He was defeated in 1924 but elected presiding judge in 1926 and was re-elected in 1930.

In 1934, with the backing of the Pendergasts, Truman beat the incumbent U.S. Senator, Roscoe Patterson of Springfield. He was re-elected in 1940. During that second term, Truman became nationally famous as the head of a committee examining the national defense program. Recommendations from that committee saved the nation an estimated $15 billion dollars.

In 1944 when Henry Wallace fell out of favor with many Democrats, Franklin Roosevelt picked Harry Truman as his running mate. When Roosevelt died, the job went to Truman.

Truman had already weathered the scandal when the Pendergast machine was broken. The machine had supported him in the race for the county court. Despite the Pendergast presence, Truman's term on the court saw expenditures of $60 million in Jackson County improvements. Bipartisan engineers who supervised the extensive road program were able to see no scandal involved in it. Truman was Pendergast's second choice for senator in 1934. Although Pendergast had not agreed with the Roosevelt policies, he saw that supporting a man who endorsed the Roosevelt proposals would be good for the syndicate. Truman was politically sharp enough to see that without the backing of the machine he couldn't win. But he was enough of his own man that he would never be the property of Tom Pendergast.

This, then, was the president, a shrewd, knowledgeable Missourian who could rise above guilt by association.

Truman had to decide on dropping the atomic bombs. He never indicated the results bothered him. The bombs helped end the war. He proposed the Fair Deal and other reforms. But what he would later call "the do-nothing 80th Congress" wouldn't cooperate. He kept this country from becoming isolationist after the war with the Truman Doctrine providing overseas aid. He installed the Marshall plan to keep Russian expansion into western Europe under control. He authorized the Berlin airlift to keep that city alive. He led this country into NATO, another effort to safeguard Europe. In 1951 he ordered American troops into Korea when the North Koreans invaded. He wouldn't order all-out war and removed General Mac-Arthur, who wanted one.

Truman too often is overlooked in the field of Civil Rights. But he spearheaded the effort to enact a national housing act which began the nation's first public housing program. He integrated the armed forces. He once said, "You can't cure a moral problem or a social problem by ignoring it. It's no service to the country to turn away from the hard problems, to ignore injustice and human suffering. It is simply not the American way of doing things. Of course there are a lot of people whose motto is 'Don't rock the boat.' They are so afraid of rocking the boat they stop rowing. We can never get ahead that way.

"If we wish to inspire the people of the world whose freedom is in jeopardy, if we wish to restore hope to those who have already lost their civil liberties, if we wish to fulfill the promise that is ours, we must correct the remaining imperfections in our practice of democracy."

Nobody gave him a chance to win against Dewey in 1948. But nobody has ever run a campaign like Harry Truman did. And, of course, he won.

He returned to private life—he called it being "promoted to private life"—in 1953 and led a quiet life in the white frame house in Independence until his death on December 26, 1972.

President Harry Truman, of Missouri, was born on this date, May 8, 1884.

****

MAY 9
WILLARD HALL

It was after the battle of Westport when a tired and battle-weary unit from Warrensburg was returning home. They heard shooting ahead and found a skirmish under way between other Union soldiers barricaded behind a stone wall and some Confederates. When the second unit showed up, the Confederates fled and the Union men went after them, leaving orders with the head of that second unit, Captain George Grover of Warrensburg, to stay behind and take the governor to Pleasant Hill.

The Governor!?!!

When the Westport veterans reached the stone wall they found an ambulance behind it, the top part of the ambulance splintered by the Confederate gunfire. Inside was Governor Willard Hall who, although shaken, was still calm enough to ask Grover if he had any whiskey. The captain did, and after a long and refreshing drink from the canteen, Hall said he was ready for the road and got back into the ambulance. He was unhurt but the Confederacy had missed another golden opportunity to change the Civil War history of Missouri by capturing the governor.

Willard Preble Hall had been governor about nine months by then, succeeding Hamilton Gamble who had died the previous January 30. Gamble, knowing his days were numbered, had suggested Hall as his lieutenant governor because he needed a smart, vigorous, dynamic man to support him and take over if necessary.

Hall was already well-known and highly respected in Missouri. He was born at Harpers Ferry, Virginia, where his father—the inventor of the first breech-loading gun—was in charge of the armory that would be famous forty years later. Hall had come to Missouri at the age of twenty. A year later he was practicing law, and four years after that he tangled with Alexander Doniphan in debate over a presidential election. Doniphan favored Henry Clay. Hall favored James Polk. The two earned each other's respect in those confrontations.

Hall was running for Congress from St. Joseph in 1846 when the chance came to join Doniphan's expedition into Mexico. He abandoned his campaign and joined up as a private. But he was still elected to Congress by 3,000 votes. By then, however, he and Doniphan were drafting a civil code for the liberated area of New Mexico. That code, known as the "Kearney Code," because it was ordered by Phil Kearney, would be the basic law in that land for forty-five years. Some think Hall did most of the work on that code.

In 1847 he finally took his seat in Washington. Hall worked for railroad legislation and government grants of swamps and wastelands which laid the groundwork for the Missouri school fund. He split with Thomas Hart Benton over repeal of the Missouri Compromise, and aligned himself with Stephen A. Douglas who believed Kansas and Nebraska should be allowed to cast their own ballots on the slavery question.

Hall believed the Union should be preserved although he favored states rights. The time came when he could no longer straddle the fence, and in 1861 Willard Hall pledged himself to the Conservative Unionist cause. He was a member of the convention in 1861 which named Gamble provisional governor after Jackson failed to take Missouri into the Confederacy with him.

Hall made it clear where he stood and was sworn in as Gamble's successor in 1864.

"I believe...that to Missouri, the Union is peace and disunion is war," he said that day. "I believe that today Missouri could be as peaceful as Illinois, if her citizens had recognized their obligations to the Constitution and laws of their country. Whatever might be said by citizens of other states, certainly Missouri has no right to complain of the general government....As a Missourian, I desire no change in the political relations that exist between this state and the government of the United States; and least of all do I desire such a change as will throw her into the arms of those who have proved unfaithful to the high trust imposed on them by a generous and confiding people."

It was apparent by then the Confederacy could not last. The radicals were beginning to stir in Missouri. In the reconstruction days to come they would exact a price from those who had sided with the South. But Hall kept his thumb on the radicals during his term. They didn't become a dominant political force until his successor, Thomas Fletcher, took over.

At the end of his term, Hall went back to St. Joseph and practiced law. He died in 1882.

Willard Preble Hall, an often overlooked Missouri governor, was born on this date, May 9, 1820.

****

MAY 10
THE BALD KNOBBERS

It is the mid 1880s. A group of Missourians has met on a treeless hill to do something about lawlessness. Their leader, a giant of a man, would later write that his group will be part of a "war between civilization and barbarism."

They called themselves the Bald Knobbers.

The group met that night on a hill called "Big Bald" or "Snapp Bald" because it had no trees at the top. You could get away with a lot of things in Taney County in those days. By the 1880s the county hadn't sent anyone to the state prison for twenty years. This bothered people like Captain Nathaniel Kinney, a former Civil War officer, Springfield saloon keeper, and an upstanding Taney County citizen.

Lucille Morris, in a book about the anti-crime movement in Southwest Missouri, says "Kinney was a big man...6 feet 7 and 275 pounds....At forty-eight years old he was a fine-appearing man and a leader around whom the citizens could rally."

He was raising finely-bred sheep, cattle, and horses near Forsyth then. He had organized the first Taney County Sunday School at Oak Grove. Sometime during the winter of 1884-85, Kinney started gathering his organization about him. In January of '85, a secret group was organized in a Forsyth warehouse. Within a few months, Kinney had organized the group which held its meeting on Bald Knob. About 100 men were there, the first of the Bald Knobbers of Missouri. The group formed a vigilante corps.

It wasn't long before the Bald Knobbers struck.

A store owner and his wife had been shot by thieves. Two of the men who did it surrendered, confident that under Taney County custom they would be released because the couple survived. But the Bald Knobbers lynched them. Word went out that hoodlums better clear out of Taney County by nightfall. Anyone finding a bundle of switches on his doorstep knew he'd better leave or face a flogging.

In March, 1886, Kinney had a run-in with a young roughneck, Andrew Cogburn, and shot him to death at Oak Grove Church. Although exonerated, Kinney found a lot of public sentiment against him. Kinney called a meeting in Forsyth attended by about 300 persons and told the crowd his only intention was to eradicate lawlessness. The group adopted a resolution promising peace, denouncing lawlessness, and protesting organization of any military company to keep the Bald Knobbers in line.

But the situation continued to deteriorate. The governor sent the Adjutant General to Taney County to investigate. General J. C. Jamison urged the Bald Knobbers to disband and on April 8, 1886, about 500 citizens met in Forsyth and publicly disbanded the organization.

But the story doesn't end there.

Not long afterward one of Kinney's friends killed a friend of Andrew Cogburn. Apparently some Bald Knobber units never quit working. In 1887 a cabin in Christian County was attacked. Two men were killed and another was wounded. A woman was injured. In time twenty-five Knobbers were arrested including the leader of the Christian County Bald Knobbers, "Bull Creek Dave" Walker and his seventeen-year-old son, William.

Trials began in August 1887.

The two Walkers and two of their companions were found guilty. The verdict: death by hanging. Four others pleaded guilty. One was fined. The other three drew long prison sentences. One day in 1889 the two Walkers and another man went to the gallows.

During this time Kinney had been trying to live peacefully. He was a witness in a lawsuit in which a man lost his business, with Kinney becoming the receiver. Later Kinney and one of the plaintiff's witnesses argued and Kinney was shot to death.

The Bald Knobbers thus passed into Missouri folklore.

Nat Kinney's farmland is mostly under water, covered by Lake Taneycomo. But Bald Knob still stands. And there are those who say that on some nights ghostly campfires appear in the woods and around them are gathered the Bald Knobbers.

It started as an anti-crime organization and became at times no better than those it fought. It all ended with the hanging of three of its leaders on this date, May 10, 1889.

****

MAY 11
ST. REGIS SEMINARY

The Indians were dressed in their finest attire. Different-colored stripes were painted on their grease-coated bodies and faces. Their hair was cut and combed into tufts. Rings were in their noses and lips. They wore headdresses, bracelets, earrings, and animal skin robes. They were the chiefs of the Osage nation. They had gone in 1820 to St. Louis to see the "Chief of the Black Robes," Louis DuBourg. They wanted a mission established.

Three years before Missouri became a state, Bishop DuBourg wrote, "Turn your eyes on hundreds of Indian tribes that seem but to wait for instruction in order to embrace the faith. How touched you would be if you could see the frequent deputations which I receive from them, the religious respect which they testify to me and the urgent prayers which they address to me, to their father, to visit them, and to give them men of God. In the midst of great sadness which the view of so many of my neglected children causes me, I am beginning to experience the consolation of seeing the seed of the word bear fruit." But it would be three years before the hopes of Bishop DuBourg and the hopes of some of the Indians were answered with a history-making institution. Unfortunately the story of that school is one of promises broken or never realized.

In 1821, Father Charles de la Croix opened a mission for the tribes and baptized many of the Indians. Later that same year he spent a dozen days on horseback to reach the villages and stayed with the Indians for ten more days. This was the time of the Monroe administration in Washington and the "era of good feeling." Foreign problems seemed taken care of. Now it was time to look at internal difficulties, especially with the Indians.

One solution was to educate them. So Congress set up a $10,000 fund for schools to be established for the instruction of young Indians. If the government approved the school, it would pay two-thirds of the cost of putting up buildings. Federal aid would be provided according to the number of pupils. The boys were to learn agricultural and mechanical arts. The girls were to be taught spinning, weaving, and sewing. About this time, DuBourg wrote to Secretary of War John Calhoun that another effective technique to help the Indians would be to send missionaries to the tribes to "harmonize them with friendly, representative Christianity."

President Monroe and Calhoun approved and promised government subsidies of $200 a year to support the missionaries. Then DuBourg suggested the formation of a seminary to train the young missionaries. Again the reaction was favorable from Washington. In addition the school would train some of the children from the Indian tribes. DuBourg was assured of an annual appropriation of $800 plus an unspecified sum to finance a suitable building if the school were started. The school was built at a cost of about $200, and was named St. Francis Regis Academy.

In January of the next year the newly established Bureau of Indian Affairs told DuBourg it wouldn't pay $800. It would pay only $100 per student, or $500 for the five enrolled. DuBourg accused the federal government of welching on its earlier deal. By the time the school closed, the federal government had come across with $3,100. Total maintenance costs had been more than $10,000. No money ever came for the building.

The school was not a success. It was hard to teach Indians to eat with table utensils, say English prayers, and work in the fields. The tribes were not farmers and the boys did not like being farmers.

The federal government complained that further aid would not be forthcoming for a school that wasn't any closer to the tribes than St. Regis. So in 1830 Father Felix Van Quickenborne wrote that he was no longer admitting pupils and was preparing to set up operations closer to the tribes themselves. The last student left the school June 30, 1831. In its short history the school received only thirty boys. Only ten were full-blooded Indians. They represented five tribes.

When the seminary closed, its relations with the government ended. But the relations with the Indians continued for years. Some of the students later became major supporters of Jesuit efforts in the Indian villages. The Jesuits continued for years to be active and popular among the Indians.

St. Regis Seminary in Florissant was the first of its kind in America, the first to be subsidized by the federal government. It opened its doors when the first students arrived on this date, May 11, 1824.

****

MAY 12
THE POLITICAL TOOLE

The role of Missourians in the settlement of the West would fill volumes. They were first to cross an important pass, blaze a major trail, settle an area which would later become a state. Missourians also have helped others organize their governments and gain statehood. One of them is Joseph Kemp Toole who, as Governor of Montana, faced a unique situation when that territory became a state.

Joseph Kemp Toole was nineteen when he went to Montana to practice law. He was born in Savannah, Missouri, and attended public school in St. Joseph. After graduating from Western Military Academy in Newcastle, Kentucky, he read law for a while in St. Joseph. Then he went west to join his brother.

Just a year after Toole was admitted to the Montana Bar he became a district attorney in the Territory. At the age of twenty-eight he was a delegate in the Territorial House of Representatives. When he was thirty he became the president of the Territorial Council. Joseph Kemp Toole had rapidly become an important leader among Montana Democrats. He was one of the most vigorous leaders in the push for statehood. By 1884 his efforts and those of others had brought about a constitutional convention which drafted a proposed state charter he later presented to Congress.

But that constitution ran afoul of a political hassle which involved a number of other potential states. Democrats and Republicans both claimed control of Montana politics. The Democrats in Congress that year made the admission of Montana contingent on the advancement of New Mexico to statehood. The Democrats hoped to win control of New Mexico politics. The Republicans, meanwhile, sought to strengthen their hand in Washington and demanded the splitting of the Dakota Territory into two states since Republicans in those areas would be strongly on their side. As a result the Montana matter died.

Toole was elected a Territorial delegate for the next two Congresses and kept up the statehood pressure. He supported free coinage of silver, an important mineral in Montana. He backed legislation for building railroads, bridges, and public facilities. He favored the founding of Indian reservations. He sought legislation protecting sheep ranchers. In 1889, he was one of those who backed the omnibus bill admitting Montana, Washington, and the two Dakotas into the Union. The new constitutional convention began work that July. Toole was one of seven persons there who had served in the convention five years earlier. He was one of twenty-two lawyers in that seventy-five-man delegation.

When debate for organizing the legislature came up, Toole made proposals far ahead of his time. Some wanted sixteen Senators, one from each county. But Toole argued the upper chamber, at least, should be apportioned according to population—one man, one vote. He said it was against democratic principles to give 300 voters in Dawson County as much lawmaking power as 10,000 citizens in Silver Bow County. But his ideas failed. He also wanted to make each stockholder in a corporation responsible for his share of the debts incurred by that corporation and make each director responsible for money embezzled or misapplied by other officers during their terms. Opposition to that came up immediately. Critics said it would ruin half the corporations in the state.

Toole was elected Montana's first governor, though, at the age of thirty-eight. He faced chaos when he called the first legislature into session. There had been some bitterly contested elections which didn't help. Democrats and Republicans were not on speaking terms. But worse, there were no provisions in the state constitution providing for a meeting place for the Montana General Assembly. So the two parties met in two separate locations for the House. The Senate went twenty-four days before the Democrats finally joined the Republicans to make a quorum.

Toole served four years as governor then went back to his law practice. But in November of 1900 he was elected to another term. He was reelected in 1904. Ill health forced his retirement from the governorship in April of 1908. He lived another twenty-one years. After leaving the governorship Toole divided his time between his home in Montana's capital city of Helena and San Francisco. He died in 1929 at the age of seventy-eight.

Joseph Kemp Toole made little or no contribution to Missouri. But he was a Missourian who made a sizable contribution to the settling of a nation. Joseph Kemp Toole, leader of Montana, three-term governor of that state, was born in Savannah, Missouri, on this date, May 12, 1851.

****

MAY 13
3000

The Chicago Cubs and the St. Louis Cardinals were playing a game in Chicago that meant nothing in the standings. It was too early to know this game would mean nothing in the pennant race, though. It was still spring, when baseball fortunes are yet to be made. The home team lost. But the story wasn't the score or how the game was played. The story is who played it—one man named Stan Musial.

Twenty years earlier he had broken into baseball with the Williamson minor league club. He was a pitcher but not a very good one. In the first three and one-third innings he was rapped for six hits. He escaped without taking the loss. His hitting was more distinguished that day than his pitching. He hit a double. Three years later Musial was 18-5 for another minor league club. But the next time he pitched was in 1952, against Frankie Baumholtz of the Chicago Cubs in the last game of the season.

Musial finally made it to the major leagues after about three and one-half years in the minors. He started the second game of the doubleheader against the Boston Braves. He hit a single and a double that day. The Cardinals won 3-2.

He had hoped to get hit 3,000 before the home folks, but the home stand had ended with him one hit away. He was on the bench in Chicago, put there in hopes he wouldn't be needed until the team got back to St. Louis.

But Musial was needed in Chicago.

The Cardinals trailed 3-1 with one out in the sixth inning and a man on. Cub reliever Moe Drabowsky was on the mound. Musial had not been hitting Drabowsky well. In 1957 he was only 4 for 16 against him. He had failed to hit in his only two chances against Drabowsky in 1958.

Musial dug in at the plate, feet close together, the body coiled at the waist, the bat held straight up.

The first pitch was a curve, low and outside.

The next one was good, but Stan swung and fouled it back to the screen.

The next one was good too, and Stan swung and fouled it out of play.

Two strikes and a ball now.

The next pitch, low, ball two.

Another good one, a swing....

A fly ball into left field, twisting, twisting...foul.

And then it came.

On Drabowsky's sixth pitch, Musial hit a shot into left field, driving in the run. Stan wound up at second base. The game was stopped. The Cub fans gave him a standing ovation. Umpire Frank Dascoli retrieved the ball and gave it to Musial who threw it to coach Terry Moore in the dugout.

Stan Musial, a seven-time national league batting champion, had become the first major leaguer to reach 3,000 hits since Paul Waner in 1942.

Musial closed out his career September 29, 1963, going 2 for 3 with a run batted in. He left the game in the sixth inning when Curt Flood came in as a pinch runner. The Cardinals won that game as they had won the first in which he appeared for them 22 years earlier, 3-2.

When Stan Musial stepped down only seven other men had achieved 3,000 hits and only one had more hits than he had. It took eighteen years before his record of having more hits than any other National Leaguer fell—to Pete Rose, who was playing second base for Cincinnati the day Musial finally retired.

His records went on and on: most games played by a national leaguer, most at bats, most total bases in a career, most seasons of 100 or more games played, most years leading in doubles and triples, most seasons leading in runs scored, most seasons hitting over .300.

In 1954 he hit 5 home runs in a double header, finishing the day 6 for 8 at the plate with 6 runs scored and 9 runs driven in. In July of 1962 he hit 3 home runs in a row against the Mets. Four times in 1948 he had 5 hits in one game. He won the Most Valuable Player Award three times. Musial was Player of the Decade in the 1950s. And he had enough left that in his next-to-last season, when he was almost forty-two years old, he still hit .330.

Today a stylized statue of him stands in front of Busch Stadium.

Stan Musial still considers hit number 3,000 one of his greatest thrills—the double he hit against the Chicago Cubs on this date, May 13, 1958.

****

MAY 14
THE CORPS AND ITS DISCOVERIES

The journal read:

"All the preparations being completed, we left our encampment. This spot is at the mouth of Wood River, a small stream which empties itself into the Mississippi, opposite to the entrance of the Missouri. Not being able to set sail before 4:00 o'clock p.m., we did not make more than four miles and encamped on the first island opposite a small creek called Cold Water."

The Corps of Discovery, led by William Clark and Meriwether Lewis, had started its historic journey into the unknown.

The two met in the mid 1790s when both were under the command of General Mad Anthony Wayne in the Whiskey Rebellion. Lewis was an infantry captain. Clark, a lieutenant, would resign his rank about 1795. Lewis kept his rank until he became the personal secretary of Thomas Jefferson.

The United States more or less fell into the purchase of the vast Louisiana Territory, originally seeking only to buy New Orleans. Suddenly Jefferson had on his hands land of unknown value. He had to investigate it. He wrote to his personal secretary, Lewis. "The object of your mission," read the letter, "is to explore the Missouri River and such principal streams of it, as, by its course and communication with the waters of the Pacific Ocean, whether the Columbia, Oregon, Colorado, or any other river, may offer the most direct and practicable water communication across the continent, for the purpose of commerce."

The Corps was to study the area geologically and geographically, make peace with the Indians, note the wildlife and catalog the trees and other plants. The expedition was to study the economy of the natives, their dress, their diseases, and morals. Jefferson wanted reports on the minerals of the territory, volcanic activity, and climate.

Lewis offered Clark equal rank in the expedition. But the War Department overruled him and made Clark a lieutenant. However, the

284

two men referred to each other as equals. Lewis always spoke of "Captain Clark," and Clark always referred to himself the same way. Bernard DeVoto says, however, that Lewis was the actual commander by the natural set of his personality and Clark was the perfect executive officer.

Jefferson suggested a dozen men would be a good number for the trip. But by the time the group had been assembled, it numbered about twenty-five. One member of the expedition not normally listed was Scammon, a big Newfoundland dog belonging to Lewis. Clark brought along his slave, York, who would become an object of wonder to the Indians they would meet later. Many had never seen a black man before.

The men studied at length the reports of the early explorers of the river. They were not the first men to go upstream on the Missouri. Others had made limited trips as much as 1,500 miles upstream on early trading and hunting trips. But there was little known about what lay beyond the headwaters of the muddy river. They loaded their three crafts with twenty-one bales of presents for the Indians and at least twenty barrels of flour, seven of salt, fifty kegs of pork, another fifty bushels of meal, tools, and medicine. One of the men took along a violin which would break the monotony with music for square dances and astonish the Indians.

Eight days after the start they camped at what is now the village of Chesterfield in St. Louis County and made their first trade with the Kickapoo Indians. For much of May and June they traveled across Missouri learning about the Missouri River at a good time, honing the navigational skills they would need upstream where the waters would be rougher.

It was the first of June when they reached the Osage River and two days later they camped near what would be Jefferson City. They reached what is now Kansas City on June 26.

Lewis and Clark lost two expedition members. One, a Frenchman named Liberte, deserted. The other, Sergeant Charles Floyd, died of a "biliose Chorlick," perhaps a ruptured appendix, near the present town of Sioux City, Iowa. Today a 100-foot tall monument marks the resting place of the only member of the expedition to die during the trip.

In November of 1805 the expedition reached the Pacific. Many people had given them up for lost by the time they returned to St. Louis in September of 1806. They were far from lost. In fact the things they found are still marvels today. Descriptions in the journals are valuable parts of our history. Their voyage gave America a vital foothold in the Northwest. Historians still exclaim over the significance of the trip and the two men who led it.

The twenty-five members of the Corps of Discovery started their history-making voyage on this date, May 14, 1804.

****

MAY 15
JESUIT'S BARK AND THE FRONTIER DOCTOR

Once he read a pamphlet telling about some Jesuit priests who were working in Peru. They used water from a particular pond and stayed healthy. Others, who used different pond water, became sick. Those who stayed well did so, it seems, because the water of their pond was impregnated with the properties of the bark of certain nearby trees. The doctor believed the story about the so-called "Jesuit's Bark," or "Peruvian Bark," and it made him a famous man, one of Missouri's most distinguished citizens.

It is said Dr. John Sappington kept a coffin under his bed stocked with apples and nuts for visiting grandchildren until the time came for him to use it. He was the father-in-law of Governor Meredith Miles Marmaduke, the grandfather-in-law of Governor John S. Marmaduke and the father-in-law three times of Governor Claiborne Fox Jackson. His great-great-great-granddaughter became the prominent actress, Ginger Rogers. One biographer noted that by blood, marriage, or in a business way, John Sappington was connected with almost every prominent family in central Missouri.

Dr. John Sappington was born about two months before the signing of the Declaration of Independence. His father was a Nashville doctor. Sappington studied with him and received a degree from a medical school in Philadelphia. He came to Missouri in 1817 and two years later settled in Saline County on a farm west of Arrow Rock.

Sappington read the account of the Peruvian missionaries and the marvelous tree bark. Although the qualities of the drug extracted from the bark had been known for about 250 years, it had never caught on well in America. In fact, Sappington said that it took him some time to get rid of the prejudices which had been hammered into him at medical school where teachers spoke out against the material. They taught that taking the drug—quinine—was harmful.

On the frontier in those days, malaria and other fevers were killers. Communities were ravaged by them in the late summers. In 1832, Sappington, having tested the drug extensively, began to manufacture "Doctor John Sappington's Anti-Fever Pills." He didn't say what was in them until twelve years later when they had been circulated nationwide and gained acceptance. Then he published his *Theory and Treatment of Fevers,* a small book regarded as one of the most important medical volumes of his time. Sappington explained the treatment of illnesses and revealed the formula for his anti-fever pills: one grain of quinine, three-quarters grain of licorice, one-quarter grain of myrrh and oil of sassafras. Patients were to take them every two hours until the fever broke.

Sappington once rode horseback to Philadelphia to attend medical lectures and present his views on quinine. In those days quinine was so scarce in the United States that when his first order was filled by a Philadelphia firm, he was able to put their entire stock in his saddle-bags with room left.

Sappington eventually had twenty-five salesmen on the road peddling his pills. He insisted they themselves take three pills a day to prevent catching malaria. The salesmen traveled through malaria-stricken areas and never came down with the disease. Once someone suggested ringing the bell on the roof of the Arrow Rock tavern to remind area residents to take their pills. It became custom each evening at dusk for the bell to ring and for residents of Arrow Rock to take their anti-fever medicine.

In the first decade of manufacture, one million boxes of pills were sold. After that Sappington published his little book and gave away his secret.

Dr. Sappington also dabbled in other areas such as the Santa Fe trade, politics, and real estate. He accumulated a considerable fortune, some of which still exists in the form of a trust fund for indigent children of Saline County.

He died in 1856 at the age of eighty. One will never be able to measure the lives saved or the agony avoided because a Missouri physician was unafraid to test and develop quinine. Dr. John Sappington of Arrow Rock, was born on this date, May 15, 1776.

****

MAY 16
GET ME ABIEL LEONARD

When the Mormons appealed for help from Governor Dunklin, he suggested they seek their own relief through the courts and hire their own attorney. The Mormons wanted only one man. When former Governor Miller was involved in a lawsuit, he wanted only one man. When Thomas Hart Benton was once sued, one of the men he specifically hired to defend him was Abiel Leonard.

When citizens of Boonville and Hannibal saw their towns threatened by lawsuits over land grants, they hired Abiel Leonard to represent them. And when a similar lawsuit challenged the very location of the capital city of Missouri, the legislature appropriated $1,000 to hire Abiel Leonard. A man once rode all the way from Springfield to Fayette in the dead of winter to hire him. The man was stopped only by the icy Missouri River. A man accused of a Columbia stabbing once asked him *not* to assist in the prosecution.

Abiel Leonard might have been a minister of renown if he had followed his early training. But economics decided otherwise. He said later he injured his eyes "studying Greek at nights" and left Dartmouth after two years. He started reading law in New York. But poverty drove him west. Leonard became ill in St. Charles, Missouri Territory, and it was some time before he resumed his journey. In St. Charles he met a young lawyer named Peyton Hayden, one of the first attorneys in outstate Missouri.

Leonard walked to Franklin with his belongings tied to a stick and carried over his shoulder. He is believed to have taught school for a while in Franklin while waiting for his credentials to be approved. But his practice was centered in Fayette and Boonville. For a while Leonard took almost any case to get himself established. One of his clients once won a judgment of $2.37½. But in three years Leonard was a success.

Abiel Leonard was hardly a matinee idol. He was only five feet four. He never weighed more than 100 pounds. He was distressingly ugly. W.V.N. Bay, who wrote of lawyers he had known in the nineteenth century, once said Leonard's face was "a compound of wrinkles, yellow jaundice, and jurisprudence." Judge John Phillips of Kansas City said Leonard was "so ugly as to attract attention." His swearing was worthy of note. Leonard's handwriting was so bad that a friend wrote to him, "Drop me a line on this subject that I will be able to read."

288

Leonard had a powerful voice, a quick and independent mind, and burning black eyes. He had a will to succeed. He was aggressive. His desire to win gained the respect of many. He never lacked courage. Once a horse thief was jailed in Fayette. A lynch mob arrived, led by a man who said he would shoot anyone who got in the way. Leonard blocked his path and told the man to "shoot and be damned." While they were arguing the thief committed suicide in his cell.

In 1824, as circuit attorney, Leonard prosecuted a man and lost. The man challenged him to a duel. Leonard accepted and killed the man. But the incident marked him. Never again was he a prosecutor. Another incident, however, increased his fame. This was the defense of Judge David Todd who was impeached in 1828. Todd was acquitted.

Leonard went to the legislature in 1834 and played a major role in the last revision of the criminal code in Missouri until the late 1970s. In 1854 he moved to the Missouri Supreme Court. He wasn't above setting precedent if he felt the law on the books not proper to the case. But his health wasn't good and after one term he went back to his home, "Oakwood," in Fayette.

Leonard was an important Whig party leader, a political realist who built his political strength so quietly many of his friends never realized the depth of his involvement. But retirement would be a tragedy for him. His family fortunes had turned downward. Some of his land deals hadn't worked out. He was heavily in debt and the depression hurt more. The last three years of his life were poverty-stricken. His wife once secretly wrote to their son who was studying in Berlin at the time, "It is imperative for you to go to work as soon as possible. . . . I do not see how we can live. Your father's property is not worth anything and he is not able to do anything." It was a sad end to a distinguished life. He died in March of 1863, not quite 66 years old, deeply in debt—owing $28,000 to one man alone.

His home still stands on a hill near Fayette.

Abiel Leonard was one of Missouri's foremost early lawyers and Supreme Court judges. Few lawyers were as respected in Missouri history as Abiel Leonard, born on this date, May 16, 1797.

****

MAY 17
BLIND BOONE

Blind Boone as he was known, never saw a piano. He never saw a piece of music. But he was blessed with a beautiful talent and an amazing memory that overcame his handicap.

Born in a Warrensburg army camp during the Civil War, John William Boone came down with brain fever at the age of six months. His life was saved only because his mother allowed a camp doctor to remove his eyes.

He was five years old when his mother gave him a tin whistle, his first musical instrument. A few years later he had a harmonica. John Boone was only nine years old when he was sent to the St. Louis School for the Blind, to learn a trade and receive some education. He found a piano, though, and started skipping his lessons to play it. School authorities closed up the piano and gave him a broom. The boy ran away.

A twelve-year-old blind black boy in St. Louis had little future. For some time he wandered around, performing on the harmonica or any other instrument he could find. One day an orchestra conductor named A. J. Kerry found him in the streets and paid his way home.

Boone formed a "penny whistle band" in Warrensburg with other youngsters playing tambourine, triangle, and harmonica. They played in the Warrensburg area for some time. Eventually he came under the management of Mark Cromwell, or rather, the exploitation of Mark Cromwell. Cromwell and Boone trouped around Central Missouri with the manager taking most of the money. Often they had to walk from town to town. Once Cromwell disguised him as a girl to escape creditors and once he even lost Boone in a card game and then kidnapped him back.

Boone was sixteen when he arrived in Columbia. One day he walked into Kirkley's Book and Music Store and asked to play the piano. He met John Lange, Jr., a young black teamster who did some hauling for a clerk in the store. The clerk suggested Lange become Boone's agent. The partnership created that day lasted forty years.

Boone later married Lange's sister Eugenia.

Their concerts were not successful at first. Then a music teacher at Iowa State University convinced Boone he should learn some of the classics and for an entire summer she played classical music which Boone listened to and memorized on the first hearing.

He combined the classics with many of the traditional Negro music of the time and did much in the next four decades to bring black music to the concert stages of America, Canada, and Europe.

In his peak years he made two or three appearances a day, six days a week. Once he was paid $17,000 for a single appearance.

Boone was hard on pianos. It is believed he owned seventeen of them in his long career. He could ruin an ordinary piano playing a dramatic composition. The Chickering Piano Company began to build special instruments for him, the last being a nine-foot concert grand with a solid oak case strung in England in 1891. It is believed to be the largest of its kind.

After Lange's death, Boone fell onto hard times under a number of poor managers. He died in poverty in October 1927 at the age of sixty-three. Boone carried an elaborate watch with him throughout his career, a watch he said cost $1,000. It could tell the time of day, the day, the month, the phase of the moon, and strike the quarter hour. It was set with diamonds. After his death his wife hocked the watch in Columbia for $50 to pay her way out of town. She never returned for the watch.

Boone's last great piano gathered dust for years before being used for a Blind Boone Memorial Foundation concert in 1961 in Columbia. The concert was a failure and the piano went to pay for the services of the man who played it. Boone's house became a funeral home. Most of his music was lost.

In Missouri's sesquicentennial year, 1971, interest in Boone was rekindled. The piano was purchased and returned to Columbia. But it had a cracked sounding board and was little more than a museum piece. A massive, successful, effort was launched to find and mark Boone's grave.

He was a man who needed no eyes to express his remarkable talents, John William "Blind" Boone, born on this date, May 17, 1864.

****

MAY 18
VICKSBURG

The seige had gone on for weeks. The garrison was so badly weakened, hungry, and sick there were fears it could not turn back another attack if one came. So the commander decided to surrender. He and the opposing general worked out terms of the capitulation under a tree on the battlefield. Later the losing general, John Pemberton, would say, "If I had 10,000 more Missourians I would have won and carried the war." Maybe one reason he lost was because the other side had more Missourians than he did, including a couple of Missouri generals who would make the difference in the next two years.

This was Vicksburg.

It was the battle at Vicksburg that made a Missouri general named U.S. Grant into a national figure and silenced his long-time detractors. He worked for months to take Vicksburg. He tried from the north with another Missourian, William Sherman, and through central Mississippi but failed both times. Then he tried five times in the winter of 1862 and the spring of '63 to move in from the south and east, but failed. Finally he moved through the Louisiana swamps and marshes to the west bank of the Mississippi, thirty miles below Vicksburg. From then on it was a matter of tightening the noose.

Frank Blair gained the respect of General Sherman at Vicksburg. Up to now Sherman had discounted Blair as an "erratic and unstable" man, a Missouri politician. But Blair led an advance in a withering Confederate crossfire and held his ground although taking casualties of almost 500 before he fell back.

The Battle of Champions Hill came on May 14. Missourians led by General Peter Osterhouse and General Grant met a brigade under the command of Colonel Francis Cockrell and Brigadier General Martin Green, both Missourians. Cockrell, later a Missouri governor, was wounded five times and taken prisoner three times. Later he would be the only Missouri senator other than Benton to serve thirty years in Congress. When Cockrell and Green finally collapsed, the way was clear to Vicksburg.

For forty-seven days and nights, Missourians faced each other 50 to 600 yards apart. Pemberton and 32,600 men faced the Union army and navy with 75,000 men. There were 42 Missouri companies at Vicksburg, 27 of them on the Union side. Only Missouri and Kentucky had units on both sides of this fight, and only Missouri had units facing each other.

In the heavy fighting of the first assault, the 6th Confederate Missouri took the battle flag of the 8th Missouri Federal Infantry.

Blair's troops led the way for the 15th Corps assaults that day and three days later. In the second attack, Blair's troops attacked three times but were repulsed by the First Missouri Confederate Brigade. Fifty Missourians of Blair's unit managed to put a flag at the outer edge of the Confederate parapet before taking refuge in a trench where a bomb exploded, killing twenty-one of them.

Brigadier General Joseph Mower and his 11th Missouri Infantry also planted their colors on the Confederate lines. But Mower, who earlier looked over the battlefield and said, "Good God! No man can return alive," was killed in the first fire.

Federals breached the lines once, but Greene and his Missourians pushed them back in the last assault of the Vicksburg engagement.

Missourians counted their casualties on both sides: 101 Federal dead, 517 wounded, six missing; 113 Confederates killed, 446 wounded. More than one-third of the men in their respective brigades were casualties.

On May 25 a truce was called allowing both sides to bury their dead. Missourians met friends and one account tells of a Confederate soldier meeting his brother who was fighting for the Union. The two sat on a log talking until the armistice was over.

General John Bowen of St. Louis was finally designated to carry the white flag to Grant and ask for a surrender meeting. Vicksburg fell on Independence Day, 1863. Twelve days later Bowen died from illness in a Union camp. Jefferson Davis sent a telegram thanking the Missourians for their fighting and General Sherman said that if any troops could have carried and held the trenches and battlements in the fights in May, the Missourians under Blair would have.

Today there are fifty markers designating where Missourians fought at Vicksburg. In no other battle of the Civil War did so many men from the same state fight each other from opposing sides.

The glory goes to the generals, seldom to the men who fight and die. Only one general died at Vicksburg—a Missourian. The rest of the blood was spilled by the average soldiers, many of them Missourians, at the seige of Vicksburg, which began on this date, May 18, 1863.

****

MAY 19
VAN HORN AND THE EFFORT TO REMOVE KANSAS CITY

Kansas City was being challenged by St. Joseph, Missouri, and Leavenworth, Kansas, to determine which would become *the* great commercial metropolis of the far west. Kansas City civic leaders needed to take decisive action to make their community the great commercial hub they dreamed of. One of the strongest steps was taken by a newspaper publisher who tried to split Kansas City away from Missouri entirely and put it into Kansas.

He almost succeeded.

Robert Thomas Van Horn was a newspaperman and lawyer by trade. When he was fifteen he had become an apprentice printer for a Pennsylvania newspaper. At nineteen he struck out to seek his fortune. He was a journeyman printer, a boatman on the Erie Canal and then on the Mississippi River. Finally he studied law in Ohio, was admitted to the bar at the age of twenty-six, and set up a practice. Five years later he decided to go farther west and arrived in Kansas City, then a town of about 500 people.

The Kansas City *Enterprise,* a one-year-old newspaper, was ready to sell. Van Horn bought it for $250 cash with the rest to come later. He immediately changed the name to the *Western Journal of Commerce.* Three years later he changed its name again to the Kansas City *Journal.* For forty years the newspaper played an important role in shaping the commercial outlook of the city.

He used the newspaper constantly to push for expansion, civic development, and continued enterprise by the residents of Kansas City. But he believed the state of Kansas was the logical trade area. So in the late 1850s, Van Horn and Mobillon W. McGee started an effort to get Kansas City included in the Territory of Kansas. McGee was a member of the Kansas territorial legislature although there was some question about the legality of his service there.

These were the days of the border war. McGee wanted Kansas City on the Kansas side because it would be a solid proslavery influence. Van Horn was less interested in slavery than he was in the commercial growth of his town. These two men with differing philosophies worked to deprive Missouri of what is now its second largest metropolitan area.

They proposed a slight boundary change which would put sixty square miles of Missouri into Kansas. That sixty-square-mile area would include Kansas City and Westport.

Both legislatures were in favor of the effort. A third man, whose name was never revealed by the other two for reasons soon to become apparent, went to Washington to present the case to Congress.

No word was heard from him for weeks.

Finally Van Horn learned the man had met a young woman shortly after arriving in Washington, had fallen hopelessly in love, married, and had gone to Europe instead of taking the Kansas City issue to Congress which would have had to approve the boundary change. By then the attitude of the state lawmakers in Missouri had changed and approval no longer seemed possible. Kansas came into the Union a free state and the Civil War further killed the Kansas City issue.

In 1873 Van Horn's annexation idea was resurrected with a new twist. Kansas offered to buy Kansas City. Missouri's legislature refused. Three years later a bill was introduced in Congress to change Missouri's western border to put Kansas City into Kansas. The measure died in committee. In 1879 another attempt was made, but Missouri's legislature again turned it down. As it worked out, the best chance Kansas had to take Kansas City away from Missouri vanished in a Washington romance and honeymoon in the 1850s.

Van Horn was the mayor of Kansas City when the Civil War broke out. He enlisted in the army and was elected to the state Senate while he was away. He backed railroad legislation and was instrumental in having bills passed putting a railroad bridge across the Missouri River at Kansas City, a key to making the city a great commercial hub.

He served in Congress from 1864 to 1880, was one of the early boosters of Oklahoma statehood. He served a thirteen-month interim term in Congress in 1896 and '97.

Van Horn was district collector of internal revenue under Grant and was one of 306 delegates who stood for a third term for Grant.

He died in 1916 at his home, "Honeywood," at the age of ninety-two. Robert Thomas Van Horn, editor, soldier, congressman, politician, lawyer, a constant supporter of an effort to do better and be better, a driving force in the shaping of the success of Kansas City regardless of the state it was in, was born on this date, May 19, 1824.

****

MAY 20
SLIM THE LONE EAGLE

It was raining that early morning in New York, and the ground was soft. The airplane at the end of the runway seemed small. The young pilot sloshed through the water and mud, checked the craft and climbed aboard. He was tired, perhaps not as sharp as he might be had he been able to rest during the night. But he hadn't.

The motor was started at about 7:40 a.m. It had been warmed up for about twelve minutes while the pilot and ground crew checked things out. The little plane was heavily loaded, slow to gain speed on the mushy runway. A tractor blocked the end of the runway, along with telephone lines, a hill, and some trees. But the plane lifted off, cleared the tractor by fifteen feet, the lines by twenty and made it over the hill and trees.

A Missouri National Guardsman named Lindbergh was on his way into the rising sun and into the history books, flying a plane financed by Missourians and named for a Missouri city.

Charles Lindbergh had taken his first airplane flight only seven years before. Since then he had barnstormed all over the Midwest. Several times he crashed. Once he jumped from his plane and his parachute almost failed to open. Once he tried a take-off from a city street, but hit a hole in the roadway and ended up with his airplane stuck halfway into a drugstore.

In 1924, Charles Lindbergh, son of a congressman, decided to take in the International Air Races at St. Louis. The bomber races were under way when he got there. So he landed his plane, a Curtiss Jenny, on a nearby hill. That evening he flew it to the airfield. He sold the airplane and bought another. He headed south with a stop in Perryville, where he made a little money taking passengers up. Then he went farther south and that March reported to Brooks Field for pilot instruction in the army.

Lindbergh received his pilot's wings and returned to St. Louis to do more barnstorming. This was about the same time the post office department decided to get into the air mail business. He wound up staying in St. Louis waiting for the bids to be announced because he had an offer to fly the mail. In St. Louis he gave more flight lessons, an employee of the Robertson Aircraft Corporation. In November 1925 he enlisted in the 110th Observation Squadron of the Missouri National Guard, stationed at Lambert Field. Sometimes members of the squadron had to supplement the meager appropriations with their own paychecks, but young men who wanted to fly as badly as Lindberg didn't mind. The next April the mail service started.

That September Lindbergh ran out of fuel on a run from St. Louis to Chicago and bailed out in the fog. The plane crashed not far away, just missing a farmhouse. Lindbergh himself came down in a cornfield and had a hard time convincing the farmer he had jumped out of an airplane. Only a few weeks later it happened again and he bailed out only to land on top of a barbed wire fence. The fence broke his fall and the barbs didn't cut through his flying suit.

Even after those experiences the thought of flying from New York to Paris began to grow. His friends were skeptical. Here was a guy who had trouble flying from St. Louis to Chicago, and he wanted to fly across the entire Atlantic Ocean!

In December 1926 with financial backing from a number of St. Louis businessmen, Lindbergh started planning the type of plane he needed. He decided on a single-engine plane because it produced less air resistence and gave greater cruising range.

It wasn't until the last day of February 1927 that he ordered the airplane from Ryan Aircraft of San Diego, California. It was simply constructed. After a few test flights Lindbergh decided to fly the plane to the city for which it would be named. Two days later the Spirit of St. Louis landed in its namesake city. The next morning he flew to New York. The trip took nine hours.

He had hoped to take off on the nineteenth but the weather was bad. Lindbergh planned a number of social activities for the next few days until the weather cleared, but that night word came that the weather would break the next day. So the night of the nineteenth he went back to his hotel to rest for a couple of hours. But he got involved in final preparations and didn't get any sleep.

The next morning he lifted off from the muddy runway in that little silver plane. Thirty-three hours later he and the plane were in Paris. The first solo flight across the Atlantic Ocean was completed. Charles Lindbergh had made history at the age of twenty-five. The Spirit of St. Louis would become one of the best-known airplanes in the world.

Charles Lindbergh, the "Lone Eagle," was doing more than flying to Paris that day when he took off from Roosevelt Field. Charles Lindbergh and the Spirit of St. Louis started a flight into history on this date, May 20, 1927.

****

MAY 21
FORT CARONDELET

Spanish settlers in early Missouri had been bothered by the Osage Indians for some time when the Territorial governor-general decided he had enough of what he called "mildness." He abolished all trade with the tribes, hoping to cut off their supply of guns and ammunition.

One suggestion the governor-general, Baron Francisco de-Carondelet, offered was to incite other tribes to go to war against the Osages. He reasoned that would occupy them elsewhere so they wouldn't bother the settlers! But the threat of an invasion from the north loomed. There was fear of a possible alliance of the tribes with the French. It was time for a major policy adjustment—a way to pacify the Osages but still maintain control over them.

About this time a prominent St. Louis leader, Auguste Chouteau, expressed interest in expanding his business to include dealings with the Osages. Chouteau had received government permission to trade with the Indians as early as 1777 and had come to know them well. In Chouteau both the Spanish and the Indians had a valued and influential friend.

Chouteau went to New Orleans and met with Carondelet. He offered to establish a fort near the main Osage village. Auguste's brother, Pierre, would be the commandant. The plans submitted in 1794 called for the fort to be built of logs, brick, and stone. A barracks building would be constructed and fortified with tiles of slate or brick and defended with four cannons or swivel guns. It was to form a thirty-two-foot square structure with the first floor ten feet high, the second floor nine feet high and the garret about six to eight feet high.

The main door was to be wide and high, six and one-half feet by five feet. It was to be anchored with iron hinges, a lock and bolts. The second floor of the fort building would be surrounded by a stockade six inches thick and sixteen feet high. The Spanish government agreed to pay for twenty militiamen to defend the post at salaries of 100 pesos a year.

Chouteau was given authority to conduct trading with the Indians for six years. At the end of that time the fort and its functions would be turned over to the Spanish if the government wanted it.

In December of 1795, Carondelet was able to write to his superiors that the fort had been completed, "The savages have let our settlements alone during the year—so much that they have not committed one murder, and on the other hand have restored various army horses which their war parties had stolen, although the full number of these were not returned. The inhabitants have succeeded in cultivating the fields and in working some lead mines that are very rich, but which their fear of the Osages had compelled them to abandon."

The fort was named for the governor general in New Orleans. It was probably the nucleus for a small French settlement in Vernon County, the first white settlement in that area. It was the westernmost fort erected in Missouri during the Spanish occupation of Upper Louisiana.

The Chouteau contract expired in 1800 and was not renewed.

The fort went to pieces rather quickly. The Indians apparently took some of the armaments. In 1806, when General James Wilkinson and Zebulon Pike set out on a trip to the southwest, they stopped at the Osage villages and were saluted by a discharge from four swivel guns! Pike could find no trace of the fort.

No great fights occurred at Fort Carondelet. No great treaties were drafted there. There were no great sieges. But Fort Carondelet, the westernmost fort in Spanish Louisiana, had helped with an important struggle, the struggle to settle Missouri and forge a path to settlement of the entire American West. It succeeded where harsher measures had failed against the Indians. It gave the area peace so settlers could move in. It increased the Chouteau fortune, but it also increased the security of the frontier settler. That was its most important function.

Fort Carondelet was created when Auguste Chouteau and the Spanish government agreed on its plans and location on this date, May 21, 1794.

****

MAY 22
THE JOPLIN GHOST

The first round leaders in the golf tournament that March were Emmett French, Jimmy Hines, and a guy from Joplin, Missouri. They shot 70s in the first round. But in the second round the Missourian went ahead by one stroke with a 72. He shot an even par 70 on the third round to hold the lead. On the fourth round, Craig Wood took the early clubhouse lead with a 285 total. But he had to wait to see if the pressure would get to the twenty-five-year-old Missourian who had already become a startling figure on the pro golf tour.

He started shakily that day, but got a birdie on the tenth hole and knocked in another one on the seventeenth. All he needed on the last hole was a par. He had a good drive, pitched to within twenty-five feet of the pin. The first putt rolled short. But the next one went in for a 284 total. Horton Smith of Joplin had just won the first Masters Golf Tournament ever held. It was March, 1934.

Let's go back to February of 1930 in Savannah, Georgia, to the Savannah Open. A classic duel took place. In the first round the great Bobby Jones broke the course record with a 67. In the second round the twenty-one-year-old pro from Joplin smashed that mark with a 66. The next day Jones stormed back with another record, a 65. On the final day, Horton Smith came back and although he didn't set another course record, he did beat Bobby Jones for the championship by one stroke. It was the last time Jones ever lost in formal competition.

Horton Smith took up golf at the age of twelve. He seldom missed a chance to watch other golfers. At the age of seventeen he played in three mid-summer open tournaments in Missouri, matching himself against recognized experts. He worked for a year as a pro's assistant in Springfield, learning all he could about making clubs. By March 1927 he was convinced he had to play a lot of golf to become a professional. So he became the pro at Sedalia and later that year at Jefferson City, working three days a week each place.

Smith was tall, six and one-half feet and driver-thin at 163 pounds. His height and stature gave his clubhead great momentum despite a short swing. He turned pro when he was eighteen, becoming one of the first golf professionals, along with Walter Hagen, Australian Joe Kirkwood, Leo Diegel, and Wild Bill Melhorn. In 1929 when Smith won the LaGorce Open, he mailed the $1,000 check back to his father in Joplin to show him golf could be a profitable business.

Smith and Hagen got together for a grinding series of exhibition matches around the country, playing five or six times a week. Once they played eleven days in a row just before the National Open. Another time they played thirty-three days in a row. "The Haig" liked to gamble and insisted on a bet of a dollar a stroke. By the time the two men played 100 exhibitions, Smith owed Hagen $22. It was this kind of barnstorming, however, that created pro golf and opened the sport to the people.

In May of 1929 Smith won his first major golf title, the French Open, the first of thirty-three major titles he'd win in his career. He not only won the first Masters Tournament in 1934 but the third one, in 1936, holing a fifty-foot chip shot on the fourteenth hole of the last round and canning a couple of long puts on fifteen and seventeen. He competed in every Masters until his death although it became more difficult as the years went by and Hodgkins disease took its toll. He was president of the Professional Golfers Association in 1952 through 1954.

In the fall of 1963 Smith collapsed at Atlanta while watching the Ryder Cup golfers start their final round. He recovered and watched the finish. But he died a few days later in Detroit at the age of fifty-five.

Horton Smith was the twentieth golfer named to Pro Golf's Hall of Fame. He is in the Helms Foundation Hall of Fame which recognizes great athletes from all sports, and he is in the Missouri Sports Hall of Fame. Horton Smith, "The Joplin Ghost," winner of the first Masters and a founding father of professional golf, was born on May 22, 1908.

****

MAY 23
ZACK WHEAT

Wallace Clement was a veteran left fielder for the Brooklyn Dodgers in 1909 when a young rookie with unimpressive minor league credentials was brought up. When the rookie was assigned to left field, Clement told him, "It's always nice to see you young fellows come up and give us regulars a rest." The rookie gave him a rest, all right! Clement's career with the Dodgers effectively ended when Zachariah Davis Wheat began what would become a great major league career.

Charlie Ebbets owned the Dodgers and the field manager was Wilbert Robinson. The Dodgers sometimes were called "Superbas" although they weren't very superb. Somebody occasionally referred to them as the "Robins" because of the influence of Robinson. When one of the great baseball scouts of the day, Larry Sutton, showed up in Brooklyn late that season of 1909 with Zack Wheat in tow, Robinson asked, "What did he hit at Mobile?"

"Oh, about .245," said Sutton.

".245! What do you expect me to do with him?"

"Just put him in the outfield; that's where he plays. I don't care what he hit," Sutton shot back.

Wheat was a Missouri farm boy, born in a rural area between Hamilton and Kingston. He got into semi-pro baseball in 1905 with a club in Enterprise, Kansas. He sent his pay back to his recently widowed mother. He spent a year with Shreveport in the Texas League, hitting only .268. He was hitting .246 at Mobile the next year when Sutton took him to Brooklyn. He played twenty-six games that year in the majors and hit .304. Wheat played the outfield for eighteen years. Half a century after he started he still led the Dodgers in games played, at bats, singles, doubles, triples, and total bases.

He hit from the left side but threw right-handed.

Three years after going to the Dodgers, Wheat succeeded in getting an old Kansas City friend called up, a fella named Casey Stengel.

Although Zack Wheat played in two World Series he never played with a world champion. In 1916 he led the Dodgers to the National League championship with a .312 batting average and set a Dodger record by hitting in twenty-nine straight games. After that season he and teammate Hi Meyers decided to hold out for more money. Meyers got his money by craftily borrowing livestock so that when Ebbets visited him it would appear Meyers was running a prosperous livestock operation in Ohio and really couldn't afford to play ball for what Ebbets offered. Meyers, in reality, owned one cow, one horse, and some chickens.

Wheat was back on his farm near Polo, Missouri, and didn't need any tricks. He just demanded more money. He and Ebbets argued and Ebbets went back to Brooklyn in a huff. Finally a sportswriter, Abe Yager, sent a fake telegram to Wheat signed C. H. Ebbets, ordering Wheat to report to spring training at once. Wheat, thinking Ebbets had finally decided to meet his demands, showed up immediately. Ebbets denounced the telegram as a fake and the two started arguing again before the sportswriters stepped in and suggested they go off in a corner somewhere and settle it sensibly. An hour later Wheat had signed his contract. It was months before Yager had nerve enough to tell Ebbets he had sent the telegram.

Wheat, like a number of other Dodgers, suffered from injuries that year. The Dodgers had a terrible season, although Wheat hit .312. The next season he and Eddie Roush of Cincinnati fought for the batting championship before Wheat won it by two percentage points. He hit .335. He had back-to-back seasons of .375 in 1923 and '24.

Ebbets died in the spring of the next year and Robinson was named the new team president, moving up to the front office. Wheat was made acting manager. But Wheat couldn't cut it as a manager and Robinson returned to the dugout to pep things up. It confused some folks who asked who was running the show. Robinson said Wheat was and went back to the grandstand. But a few games later, Robinson went back to managing full time and Wheat went back to left field to have what might have been his best major league season. He hit .359 with 14 homers, the same number of triples, 42 doubles and a total of 221 hits that year.

The next year, though, he hit .290 and was given his unconditional release. He was thirty-eight. The Philadelphia Athletics picked him up and he hit .324 for them in 88 games. That was it for the major league career.

Wheat went to Kansas City after his retirement and ran a bowling alley. He joined the Kansas City police force for a time but retired after an automobile accident hospitalized him for about five months with multiple injuries. Then he bought and operated a fishing and hunting resort at Sunrise Beach on the Lake of the Ozarks. He died in March of 1972 in Sedalia. He was 83.

In 1959 he was voted into baseball's Hall of Fame, just two years after his Dodgers had left Brooklyn and the field where he played. Many today will tell you the best outfielder the Dodgers ever had was a Missouri farm boy named Zack Wheat, born on this date, May 23, 1888.

****

MAY 24
BATTLE OF THE SINKHOLE

Great Britain badly underestimated the people of the American frontier in the war of 1812. The British had forged an alliance with the Indians in hopes of terrorizing Americans in the West. But the Americans weren't going to be driven from their land. They defeated the British and Indians, turning a minor battle into a significant frontier campaign.

It was known as the Battle of the Sinkhole.

Britain had convinced the midwestern and northern Indian tribes they should unite and drive the white man from the West. If that happened, and the British could gain control of the American East, the Indians would be allowed to live in peace on the western half of the continent. That, generally stated, and perhaps over-simplified, is what prompted Indian raids throughout Missouri during that period.

Forts were built for the safety of settlers. One of them, Fort Howard, was constructed in what is now Lincoln County, at the mouth of the Cuivre River. Missourians were concerned about the information they'd been receiving on British plans to bring about a great confederation of the Indians. They asked federal officials in Washington for help. But little help and little encouragement came. Missourians were pretty much on their own in defending themselves during the war.

Daniel Boone's son, Nathan, organized five regiments of Missouri Rangers. The rangers were widely known as excellent marksmen. They supplied their own weapons and ammunition and had fast horses.

One morning, five of Boone's rangers left Fort Howard, heading downriver by canoe for a house about a quarter-mile away. Indians were waiting and ambushed them. Three of the men were killed. another would die of his wounds. One man escaped. A group of twenty rangers nearby heard the gunshots and rode into the fight. The Indians took off. Some of them escaped through a nearby wooded area. But most of them took refuge in a nearby sinkhole. The hole had rocky ledges and the area was brushy. The battle went on for about three hours that afternoon. The Rangers could get no closer than forty-five or fifty feet before they had to expose themselves to fire from the entrenched Indians.

One of the rangers, Lieutenant Edward Spears, devised a plan for breaching the Indian defenses. He tried but was killed. Finally some of the group decided to build a mobile rock battery which would protect them as they worked their way to the hole. But night fell and the effort to storm the Indian position behind the portable rock wall had to be abandoned.

The fight went on all night. By the next morning, the rangers counted six people dead. At least seven Indians were killed. More might have been but were carried off by their friends in the dark. Several Indians were wounded with fourteen white men. The fighting at the sinkhole broke off when more Indians attacked Fort Howard and the rangers were forced to leave and help the fort.

This wasn't a major battle, just a skirmish in a much larger war with major engagements elsewhere. But it began a longer effort. The rangers now started an offensive against the Indians and the British and pushed them back to the Great Lakes. The Missourians outmaneuvered the British and the Indians in that push north. Once the rangers swam with their horses across the Mississippi River at night near Fort Mason, Iowa, attacking the British before dawn.

Dreams of British conquest of the American West ended with the Treaty of Ghent in 1815. The Missouri Rangers did much to make the British conception of the bumbling frontiersman crumble.

One of the places this became abundantly clear was in the Battle of the Sinkhole, fought in Lincoln County, Missouri, on this date, May 24, 1815.

****

MAY 25
THE IRON MOUNTAIN LINE

Many railroad men carried pets with them in days past. One was an engineer named Jerry Phalen of the St. Louis, Iron Mountain, and Southern Railroad, who had a small mongrel dog in the cab with him one day. The dog, named Dick, latched on to Phalen's pants leg and began tugging at him. The engineer thought something might be wrong with the dog's bed. Phelan stepped across the cab to check.

He had no sooner stepped across the cab than the side drive rod snapped. The rod whirled around and stripped the engineer's side of the cab right off the locomotive.

It took quite a while before Phalen could reach over and shut down the damaged locomotive. He climbed down out of the remnants of the cab, removed what was left of the rod, then took the train on to Fredericktown.

You can mark it down to another experience of an intuitive animal saving a man's life. You can also mark it down as part of the colorful history of the Iron Mountain Railroad.

When the legislature decided to help finance railroad construction in Missouri, it set out five routes. One was from St. Louis south to the Iron Mountain and Pilot Knob area. There were provisions that the railroad could go on farther south, eventually. The company was incorporated in 1851. But by the time the first five years had gone by, only twelve miles of track were down. When all eighty-six miles had been laid, it was estimated the cost for the entire route was about $47,600 a mile. The state finally had to pump several million dollars into the project as it did with other railroads. The St. Louis County Court put up money for the work too, but later released the railroad from further payment on interest on those funds in appreciation for the facilities.

There were good years for the railroad at a time when many railroads were having financial troubles. From 1860 to 1863 the railroad showed it was making money. But expenses were going up and more were expected. Sure enough they came, and the financial position of the line was weakened. Backers of the railroad started missing payments or delayed making them. The St. Louis and Iron Mountain Railroad was one of those that went back under state ownership because of poor finances.

In 1866 the state finally sold the railroad along with the Cairo and Fulton Railroad for only $900,000—a massive financial loss for the state on its railroad investment. The new owners extended the Iron Mountain line, completing that work in 1869. Except for having to use a ferry, the railroad had a continuous connection between St. Louis and cities on the Gulf of Mexico. In the 1870s the road was consolidated with others to form the St. Louis, Iron Mountain and Southern Railroad Company.

When the infamous eastern speculator Jay Gould decided to try his hand at railroading, the Iron Mountain route was one of those he used in his battles against the Union Pacific and the Chicago, Burlington and Quincy. Historians note that Gould, who also controlled the Missouri Pacific at one time, cared little about the condition of the railroads. He was a speculator, a manipulator, a man not above buying a judge or congressman or a legislature or two if he had to. He was more interested in the money the manipulation of railroad stock would bring him than the railroad itself. The Missouri Pacific turned out to be Gould's strongest railroad property. MOPAC bought the Iron Mountain Railroad in the 1880s.

The story of the dog rescuing the engineer isn't the only colorful story concerning this railroad either. In January of 1874 the James gang captured the tiny village of Gads Hill, flagged down an Iron Mountain train, and robbed it. The take was about $2,000—some say—but Jesse gave the engineer his own handwritten press release complete with headline reading, "The Most Daring Train Robbery on Record!"

One day in 1858, about 400 people climbed aboard one of the Iron Mountain trains and headed south from St. Louis. At stations along the way, crowds gathered to greet the nine-car train. Cannon fire welcomed it when it reached Pilot Knob. It was probably the most distinguished day in the railroad's history. It certainly was one of the few such days in the thirty-year-life of the line, the day the first passengers rode the Iron Mountain Railroad, May 25, 1858.

****

MAY 26
THE BATTLE OF ST. LOUIS: WHAT IF?

Bunker Hill, Valley Forge, Charleston, Lexington, Philadelphia, Yorktown. These are places one normally associates with the American Revolution. But the war was fought far to the west of those places too. We even had a significant Revolutionary War battle fought in Missouri. Had it not turned out as it did, America as we know it might not exist today.

Britain wanted to regain the Northwest Territory. In February, 1780, a force of 950 Indians and French and English traders was mobilized on the Fox and Wisconsin rivers. The group began to move south.

The security system was so poor that Patrick Henry had time to find out about it, send a letter to St. Louis and warn Commandant Fernando DeLeyba of the pending attack. Furthermore, DeLeyba had almost two months to finish fortifying his town!

The Spanish had remained technically neutral before formally declaring war on Britain in July 1779. Spain had designs far beyond those on this continent. It wanted to regain Gibraltar, regain Florida, and stop some illicit trade.

307

When DeLeyba heard his country had declared war, he immediately prepared for military operations. He didn't want to fortify the city using public funds, so he passed the hat. The public came up with the money and DeLeyba sweetened the pot with a donation from his own pocket. St. Louis then was a city of 800 people, mostly French settlers from Illinois. The city was sixteen years old and had about 100 homes. It was a firmly established river trading post.

Nearby was an old fort which had fallen into disrepair, Fort Don Carlos. DeLeyba had five cannons removed from the fort and placed at strategic points along the fortifications around the town. DeLeyba called up other soldiers from Spanish outposts in the area, St. Charles and Carondelet. About 280 militiamen showed up along with twenty-nine regular Spanish soldiers. Women and children took refuge at DeLeyba's house, guarded by twenty men in case the Indians breached the defenses. So everything was ready when the attack came at 1:00 o'clock that spring afternoon.

The attackers numbered less than 950. When they attacked they were surprised by fire from the five cannons. The cannon fire didn't kill very many but it did frighten the Menominee and Winnebago Indians who made up the attacking forces. Many of them fled.

DeLeyba has been criticized because he supposedly ordered the gates to the city closed which left several farmers and their families stranded outside the walls. Some people say he was drunk during the entire battle. Nonetheless, the attackers couldn't break through the fortifications. The battle raged on for about two hours before the British and Indians withdrew to the northeast and attacked the farmers. Official British reports say the Indians took thirty-three scalps and twenty-four prisoners. DeLeyba claimed fifteen whites and seven slaves were killed, six whites and one slave wounded, and fifty-seven whites and thirteen slaves were captured.

The British and Indians withdrew quickly. But they left behind angry St. Louis citizens who had contributed much money and time to fortify the city only to see the gates closed too soon. To add to the situation, when the Indians returned some of their white captives, DeLeyba refused to give the Indians any presents. The citizens wrote a letter to New Orleans demanding DeLeyba's replacement. But DeLeyba would die, still in office, a few weeks later.

You don't read about the fight in many textbooks on the Revolution. Most authors are too concerned with the Continental Army and George Washington. But one might wonder if the Revolution would have succeeded if the British had gained control of the Mississippi and the West and been able to move against the colonials from the West, a fortified North, and from the sea.

And if the Spanish had not beaten the British at St. Louis, Spain could not have sold this land to the French who, in turn, could not have sold this land to the United States.

Would we be British subjects today if the people of Spanish St. Louis had not turned back the British forces on this date, May 26, 1780?

****

MAY 27
THE TRAGIC PROPHECY OF IRL HICKS

Missouri averages about one tornado each year per 10,000 square miles of area. Occassionally, despite what might sound like long odds against it, one of those twisters hits a densely populated area. In the summer of 1895, a St. Louis minister named Irl Hicks predicted a major tornado for the St. Louis area, basing his predictions on the position of the moon and planets. That prediction failed to come true and people didn't take his second one too seriously.

They should have.

Hicks forecast another tornado for May 17, 1896. He missed by only ten days.

St. Louis City hospital was caring for 400 patients that day. In addition to various ailments, infirmities and injuries, the patients had to put up with the hot and humid weather of an early St. Louis spring. The heat was finally broken by a strong, cooling wind out of the northwest. Then it clouded up in the west. And out of those clouds, a funnel-shaped tail dropped to the earth.

It was nearly 6:00 p.m.

The tornado hit the southwestern section first, rushing over Lafayette Park and heading northeast. For the next seven miles, the tornado laid waste the city of St. Louis.

The Reverend Hicks had been watching developments all day. He saw the barometer falling all afternoon and knew what it meant. As the clouds gathered, Hicks ordered his porters to close all storm doors of his observatory and took his friends to the northwest corner of the building which he thought would be the safest place in case a tornado hit.

One of the twister's first targets was the city hospital. The high winds crushed the walls. Surprisingly only one person was killed, but scores were injured. The city jail was hit. The prisoners were panic-stricken. They had absolutely no way to flee to safety. They were trapped in their barred cells. Part of the jail collapsed and guards were able to maintain order only by keeping the inmates at pistol point. At one of the police substations the jailer set the prisoners free when the storm tore off the top floor of the building.

Horse races were under way at the fairgrounds and the crowd had been too busy to notice the approach of the storm until it was upon them. The curtain and sunshades around the clubhouse and grandstand were destroyed. People panicked. Some fled to the basement. Some ran to the track in the driving rain where they were ordered to lie down. The roof was lifted off the grandstand and hurled to the ground. Only a few people were hurt.

The levees were next, where several steamers were tied up. Some of them broke free and were driven across the Mississippi River and grounded on the Illinois side. The superstructure of the Eads Bridge was torn off. A passenger train which only minutes before had crossed the bridge was overturned.

The tornado struck just as many workers were going home. Power and gas were knocked out in many parts of the city and shut off in others to avoid fires from downed power lines. Firemen had trouble getting their wagons through the debris in the streets to reach the blazes that broke out. Fortunately, a drenching rain helped control the fires.

All night in the rain and the darkness rescuers searched for survivors. Often they were guided only by moans or cries for help.

It wasn't until dawn that St. Louisians learned the true tragedy of the storm. The area of destruction was seven miles long, ranging from one block to one mile wide. Along Sixth Street, the old business section, debris was piled ten feet high. Twelve thousand buildings were damaged. Most of them were uninsured. Property damage was estimated at $10 million. Across the river, half of East St. Louis was flat. Hundreds of people had been hurt, at least 140 people killed. Thirteen bodies were recovered from the ruins of a boarding house whose walls had collapsed.

Curious onlookers flocked to the stricken city where they interfered with salvage and rescue efforts. Sightseers and looters came from as far away as Chicago! The military and all available policemen were called out. It was estimated 140,000 people arrived by train in one day to see the damage.

Volunteer groups quickly formed to help the storm-ravaged residents. St. Louis began the slow move toward recovery. Food lines were set up. Living quarters were found for those without homes. One meeting collected more than $15,000 in a few moments and relief funds eventually totalled about $140,000 to help 8,000 families.

St. Louis survived the worst tornado in American history up to that time. The prediction of the Reverend Irl Hicks came true on this date, May 27, 1896.

****

MAY 28
THE MANSION IS HIS MONUMENT

The year was 1856 when two men faced each other on a sandbar in the Mississippi River, ready to fight a duel. Not only did they disagree over the so-called Know-Nothing movement in St. Louis, but they also disagreed on the conduct of the duel. Having reached this point—challenge, acceptance, arrival—they could not decide how they'd try to kill one another. Benjamin Brown wanted to fight the duel using rifles at eighty yards. Thomas C. Reynolds, who would later be Governor of Missouri's Confederate Government in Exile, had poor eyesight and said he couldn't see beyond thirty yards.

So they decided on pistols at twelve paces.

Reynolds wasn't hurt, but he shot Brown in the leg and Brown limped for the rest of his life.

Brown arrived in Missouri at the age of twenty-three and became a law associate of Frank Blair. In the 1850s he allied with Thomas Hart Benton and others who wanted to stop the spread of slavery. The stand was popular with many of the Germans in the St. Louis area and gained Brown a seat in the Missouri House in 1852. Late in his second, and last, term he said slavery in Missouri would end for economic reasons. Historian Floyd Shoemaker says Brown's speech is regarded by some as the beginning of the free-soil movement in Missouri. Brown ran for governor on the Free-Soil ticket that year but lost by 500 votes. His repeated attacks on slavery in his newspaper in the 1850s was one of the reasons he and Reynolds fought their duel.

Brown was one of the organizers of the Republican party in Missouri. He was a delegate to the Chicago convention of 1860 which nominated Abraham Lincoln.

In December of 1863 Brown was elected to the United States Senate despite criticism of him from the *Missouri Statesmen,* which said he was "a radical of the worst sort." Brown served until the spring of 1867. By then the true Radicals had taken over the state government with a stern attitude toward reconstruction. But Brown, along with Carl Schurz, Joseph Pulitzer and some others, led a liberal Republican faction to oppose the radicals. Schurz was elected to the Senate and Brown swept into the governor's mansion by 40,000 votes.

He returned to Jefferson City, a town he knew well as a legislator, the town where he had met his wife. Mary Gunn was the daughter of the state printer when he first saw her, swinging on the front gate of the family home just across the street from the present governor's mansion. Three months later they were married. He was thirty-two. She was half his age.

One of the first items of legislative business under his administration was doing something about the governor's mansion. The house occupied by his immediate predecessor was dilapidated. The Browns spent their time at their home in St. Louis as much as possible. The bill for the new mansion was passed three months later and construction started later that year. The new mansion was finished before the end of the year. The columns at the front door of the mansion were donated by Brown, quarried at his mines in Iron County.

As governor, Brown angered many of his liberal colleagues with his patronage appointments. Once he wrote that he wanted to upgrade the state's civil service based on "the fitness of the applicants, rather than to the political opinions they may have previously entertained." He once called out the militia to put down the Ku Klux Klan in southeast Missouri.

He didn't like the idea of throwing people into prison for minor offenses. He favored what today is called rehabilitation and tried repeatedly to get the legislature to approve reformatories for juveniles. Brown opposed capital punishment. He stayed all executions during his term.

He was interested in trying for a national office in 1872. As one of the leaders of the break with Grantism two years earlier he had attracted nationwide attention. But when Schurz betrayed him at the 1872 national convention, Brown turned things around, gained the presidential nomination for New York newspaperman Horace Greeley and put himself on the ticket as vice-president. Greeley was by then virtually insane and they lost badly. Their loss spelled the end of the Liberal Republican Party nationally as well as in Missouri. At the end of his term as governor, Brown went back to St. Louis and practiced law.

In 1885 he was a referee in a major railroad case being heard in St. Louis Federal Court when he became ill. He died a short time later at the age of fifty-nine.

B. Gratz Brown, a governor, U.S. Senator, political leader, limping duelist, was born on this date, May 28, 1826.

****

MAY 29
A LONG CEREMONY FOR A SHORT TERM

A new governor was going to be sworn in. The House chamber was filled with state officials. Spectators had jammed the gallery. Each man was in his place and the ceremony was due to start. But it didn't. There was a flurry at the activity at the front of the chamber and then everybody just sat. It would turn out to be the longest ceremony on record to inaugurate a governor. As it turned out, this governor would serve the shortest term on record in Missouri.

Trusten Polk was to be sworn in that day. But just as the ceremony was to begin somebody realized there was no Bible to be used for taking the oath. While spectators sat a search was going on. But there didn't seem to be a single Bible in the entire capital!

Finally, after a long wait, somebody rushed in with a Bible. They'd found one about five blocks down the street—at the state prison.

With that Trusten Polk began his short term.

Only eight days later, Polk was elected by a joint session of the legislature to the United States Senate. He resigned as governor after fifty-three days in office.

Polk was born in Delaware. He wanted to be a minister but heeded his father's wishes and became a lawyer. After graduating from Yale in 1831 he studied law for two years with long-time Delaware Attorney General James Rogers. Later Polk spent two years studying law at Yale.

He came to Missouri in 1835 and began practicing law in St. Louis. In 1843 he was elected city counselor. A year later, at the age of thirty-three, his health deteriorated. He went south to regain his vitality. After a year he travelled in the northern states and Canada, all the while observing the educational systems. While he was gone he was elected to the Constitutional Convention of 1845, where he headed the committee on education.

He aligned with David Rice Atchison, Claiborne Jackson, William C. Price, and others in an effort to unseat Thomas Hart Benton. They succeeded although Atchison would later say it cost him his public career.

In 1856 Benton tried to reestablish himself as an office-holder. He ran against Polk and Robert Ewing for governor but finished in third place. Thomas C. Reynolds, later a Confederate governor, wrote that the "election of 1856 completely demolished the Benton party in Missouri."

Polk was inaugurated on January 5, 1857. In his inaugural speech he called for increased railroad development and advocated the establishment of nine new state banks. His closing remarks would be his creed:

"I may often go wrong, even while doing the best I can. When right, I shall often be thought wrong by those whose positions will not command a view of the whole ground. Prone to error and exposed to misconstruction, I feel myself impelled to appeal for guidance and support to that Divine Wisdom and Power whose interposition...I know I shall constantly need."

But history cut short his term as governor and put him in the United States Senate. Like his fellow Missouri Senator, James Green, Trusten Polk was pro-southern. In March of 1858 he called for the admission to the Union of Kansas with a constitution allowing slavery if the citizens wanted it. His pro-southern attitudes soon put him in jeopardy in the chamber as the north-south friction grew.

In January of 1861, a few days after the secession of Mississippi, Florida, and Alabama, Polk proposed a series of irrepealable amendments to the constitution. Those amendments, among other things, would recognize the right of property in slaves and the right of an owner to take them into free territories and maintain possession of them. Polk further maintained the federal government could not coerce a seceding state back into the Union. He left Congress soon after. A few months later he was expelled for making secessionist speeches, for being in open rebellion against the government, and for helping finance secession newspapers in southern Missouri.

Polk became a Confederate Colonel. Later he was a prisoner of war, was exchanged, and for a time was the judge of the Confederate Military Courts of the Department of the Mississippi.

After the war he went to Mexico with Shelby but returned a few years later, regained his law library and other confiscated belongings and became a lawyer again.

He died in 1876 at the age of 64.

Trusten Polk, a man with a stormy political career, was born on this date, May 29, 1811.

****

MAY 30
THE SON

His father was an alcoholic who failed repeatedly. He couldn't keep a job, partly because of his own inability, sometimes because of misfortune. He tried farming but failed there, too. But he never gave up. Neither did his son, Frederick Dent Grant. The father, of course, was later a famous general and president of the United States, a man scorned by historians and contemporaries. But when Ulysses Grant was dying, his son gave up all he had to be with him.

Ulysses Grant's roommate in his days at West Point was Frederick Dent of St. Louis. When Grant was stationed at Jefferson Barricks soon after graduation, he became a familiar figure at the Dent home. He and Julia Dent were engaged in 1844 but didn't get married until 1848. In between times, Grant was fighting in the Mexican War and once saved his former roommate and future brother-in-law's life at the Battle of Molina Del Ray.

Two years after the Grants were married, their son was born. They named him after the husband's former roommate Frederick. It wasn't an easy world for Fred Grant to grow up in. By now his father was no longer in the army. He decided to become a farmer and built a log cabin in the country. He called the place "Hardscrabble." The boy grew up in unfortunate and poverty-stricken surroundings. Fred was only eight when he caught a bad case of typhoid which left him deaf for a short time.

Ulysses Grant finally gave up on St. Louis and moved to Galena, Illinois.

Fred was only eleven when the Civil War came. His father had gone back to the military, apparently the only place where he could make a go of it.

He followed in his father's footsteps by going to West Point. When he graduated, his father—by then the president—offered to put up as much as $8,000 to put Fred into farming, then subsidize him with $2,500 a year for another three or four years. The president suggested Fred grow olives, figs, almonds, and fruit. But Fred stayed in the military.

He surveyed in the west and became General Sherman's aide during a tour of the Mediterranean.

By 1874 he had become a White House aide. That fall he married the daughter of the founder of the famed Palmer House Hotel in Chicago. Fred, by now a lieutenant colonel, drove to the wedding in an open wagon pulled by a brace of immaculately groomed army mules.

In later years, after his father's term as president was over, he and his father invested heavily with some speculators and went broke. Fred had to rent his home and move in with his parents. In 1884 the elder Grant learned he had throat cancer. The family was bankrupt but publishers put up almost one-half million dollars for Grant's memoirs. That December, Fred resigned from the army to help his father write those books. It took seven months.

In 1888, President Benjamin Harrison named Frederick Grant as envoy to Vienna. When President Cleveland took office, Grant came home although Cleveland wanted him to stay. He worked with Theodore Roosevelt on the New York Board of Police Commissioners and was a Brigadier General in the Spanish-American War. Fred Grant died in 1912, a few years after he had served under President McKinley as the military governor of Puerto Rico.

Frederick Dent Grant, diplomat, general, military governor, a son, was born on this date, May 30, 1850.

****

MAY 31
THE WOMAN BEHIND THE SUCCESSFUL MAN

The young newlyweds stood before the bride's father, a senator known for quick flashes of anger and bull-headedness. The two were there to tell him they had eloped. The bride was seventeen. The groom was twenty-eight, a lieutenant in the army with little money and little opportunity for promotion in those times. Her parents had not approved of their courtship. Once they forbade the young officer from seeing her and once arranged for him to be stationed far away for a year in hopes of breaking things up. But it didn't work. So now the two stood waiting for the bride's father to explode.

She was Jessie Benton Fremont. She and John C. Fremont were married in October. They broke the news to Senator Thomas Hart Benton, the bride's father, in November. As expected, he was enraged and ordered the lieutenant out of the house. But Jessie defiantly grabbed her husband's hand and silenced her father with the words of Ruth: "Whither thou goest, I will go, and where thou lodgest, I will lodge; thy people shall be my people, and thy God my God."

The senator knew his daughter was stubborn—after all, she was his daughter. Jessie stayed at home, all right, but John moved in.

The two were separated again almost immediately. John had been authorized to take an expedition into the country between the Missouri River and the Rocky Mountains, examining South Pass as a good crossing to Oregon. When he returned he had to write his report quickly, for a second expedition was in the wind. In the winter of 1842 and '43, he and Jessie compiled a report notable as much for its literary style as its scientific information.

John couldn't write well, so he dictated his account to Jessie, who scribbled madly for four hours every day. Their book made John a national figure.

Jessie stayed behind on the next expedition, too, and it's a good thing she did because she headed off a letter to John from the War Department asking why he took a cannon with him. She was afraid John would be recalled, and that her father's hope of this expedition helping America take control of the Pacific slope of the Rockies would be crushed.

In 1846 John was named major in a battalion of California Mounted Volunteers. Then he was ordered to become acting governor of California. He argued with his superior officers, however, and was court-martialled for mutiny. Jessie fought hard for John's acquittal, twice taking Kit Carson to see the president asking for dismissal of the charges. They weren't dismissed and John was drummed out of the army.

317

Fremont made his fourth expedition to California in 1848. It ended in disaster. Jessie, meanwhile, had a miserable trip across the Isthmus of Panama and boat trip up the west coast.

The Fremonts bought a large California estate on which gold was found. John was elected a U.S. Senator. Later their home burned and one of their children died. Jessie's strength carried both of them through. John wrote, "It was she who remained dry-eyed to comfort me, for I was so unmanned over the cruelty of this bereavement. Her calm stoicism, so superior to mere resignation, soon shamed me into control."

John ran for president in 1856 but lost. He was the first Republican presidential candidate.

They were not wealthy. When Horace Greeley visited the Fremonts in California he marveled at how well Jessie dressed, not knowing she had—with two days warning—cut up two old cashmere dresses to make one new one. She had made some of John's white undershirts into new frocks for their daughters, and had cut down a linen dress shirt for their son to wear.

During the Civil War, John was given command of the Western Department. They were stationed in St. Louis. But he couldn't handle the job and was removed. Jessie was violently angry and twice appealed to President Lincoln without results. After leaving the army, John tried various business deals without success. Jessie helped him write the first volume of his memoirs. It was a sales failure. There was no second volume.

In 1890 John died, shortly after being restored to the army as a retired major general which gave the Fremonts their first adequate income in fifteen years. When he died, their son Charles wrote to his sister Elizabeth, "Of what effect this is going to be on mother, I don't dare think. And when I do think, I doubt whether the cruelest result would not be the kindest. They lived in each other so that I don't think there is any life left for the one left."

Jessie died two days after Christmas in 1902. She was seventy-eight.

Jessie Benton Fremont was born on this day, May 31, 1824.

Casey Stengel's
"Bird" Hat Tip, June 6, 1918

JUNE

JUNE 1
DEADLY DISSENT

The loyalty oath required of all professional people was instituted in Missouri just after the Civil War. The oath had its critics, of course— one of them Missouri's most outstanding statesman, a confidant of Lincoln. He immediately launched a speech-making tour throughout the state opposing the oath.

Frank Blair, a long-time Republican and staunch backer of Abraham Lincoln, dropped out of the Republican party when his fears of radical control of the party materialized after the war. He lost friends and gained enemies for attacking the proposals he saw as revenge against the South and those Missourians who, in good conscience, had cast their lot with the losing side. One of his major speeches was set for Warrensburg.

Blair's enemies knew about it and had threatened his life if he spoke. On the day of the speech, friends visited him at a Warrensburg hotel and warned him again that if he spoke, somebody might try to kill him. As a matter of fact, they said, it appeared fairly definite an attempt would be made.

It was two o'clock in the afternoon when Frank Blair walked to the speaker's platform in Warrensburg. The crowd was sizable, a benefit for a potential assassin. A potential killer, however, would have to escape through that crowd, which, it turned out, was distinctly pro-Blair.

After only a few minutes of the speech a man identified as "Old Bill" Stevens shouted that Blair was a liar. The interruption was brief as officers and Blair's friends hustled Stevens out of the area.

But he came back and again called Blair a liar.

Stevens had several other men scattered throughout the crowd, and on that signal they rushed the speaker's platform.

The crowd fought to stop them. There were shouts, cursing. A knife flashed. A man died.

When the crowd finally stopped the attack, Stevens and his men were forced away from the area. Two men were on the ground—one dead, another badly wounded.

Frank Blair waited calmly for the incident to end and then, with little indication he had even seen what was going on, continued his speech, lacing the Radical Republicans.

On the ground near the speaker's stand lay the body of Jim

Stevens, the son of the man who started the incident by calling Blair a liar.

Blair's speech continued until about 6:00 o'clock that evening. It was a four-hour tirade against the injustices of the Radical Republican administration in the state of Missouri.

At the November St. Louis municipal election in 1865, Frank Blair presented himself to vote with his own oath saying he was loyal to the United States government. He said there was no reason to take the state oath because he never had been disloyal to the state. He was not allowed to cast a ballot. He filed suit and lost it at the Circuit Court level. He then appealed to the Missouri Supreme Court, but the state court unanimously ruled the state could make any rule it wanted on who could vote, based on whatever conditions it deemed best. He appealed to the U.S. Supreme Court.

In January 1870 the U.S. Supreme Court voted to sustain the Missouri court ruling. By then, of course, public sentiment was changing. A constitutional amendment was passed allowing blacks to vote, and Missourians were beginning to think if that could happen maybe disenfranchised whites should be able to vote again too.

Eventually Frank Blair would win, not through the courts but because times changed. He would live to see it happen because he escaped death that day at Warrensburg, June 1, 1866.

****

JUNE 2
THE IRON BRIGADE

It was a long time after the Civil War ended before some devout Southerners surrendered. Among them was a group of soldiers under General Joseph O. Shelby—remnants of a proud group of Missourians who called themselves "The Iron Brigade."

The nucleus of the Iron Brigade was formed not long after Fort Sumter. Shelby organized and equipped, at his own expense, a company of horsemen who joined the State Guards and served as cavalry scouts during the campaign of 1861.

Later, after battles at Carthage, Wilson's Creek, and Lexington, and military operations in Mississippi, Shelby took the men on forced marches into northwestern Arkansas. There, at Frog Bayou, he and General Vard Cockrell joined forces and returned to Missouri to recruit. Shelby, by now a member of the regular Confederate army, gathered about 1,000 raw recruits at Waverly in four days.

Cockrell, meanwhile, raided Jackson County and was pursued by Federals back to Arkansas. Shelby and his men left two days after Cockrell started his retreat and in an exhausting march of eight days, finally reached Coon Creek, Arkansas. There General Thomas Carmichael organized Shelby's units and two other regiments into a 2,000 men brigade with Shelby as its commander. It was September 9, 1862. The Iron Brigade had become a formal military unit.

That winter the unit was placed under the command of Missouri General John Sappington Marmaduke, the last major general appointed in the Confederate army, a future governor of Missouri. For some time they were bivouacked in Arkansas and were often forced to go foraging for food because of supply delays.

Once Shelby reportedly saw one of his men carrying a sack, dripping blood, across his saddle. When asked about the contents Private Dick Gentry said he had been having his clothes washed. Shelby reportedly said, "You'd better get back to camp before your clothes bleed to death." Private Gentry was sent to the guardhouse but was later released when a quarter of fresh pork was sent to Shelby's headquarters. The general said there was no need to imprison a man for doing his laundry.

The brilliance of the Iron Brigade is shown in an 1863 foray, when the unit captured Neosho and emptied the federal depot of 400 Sharps carbines and 460 new Colt revolvers. In July of that year the unit made a raid hoping to keep federal reinforcements from going into Arkansas.

In October when the federals finally found Shelby, the Iron Brigade escaped in a frigid rain and snow storm. His cavalry was the most effective unit in this theatre of the war. They traveled light, with few supplies, struck rapidly, never stayed around for a pitched battle and when cornered, knew enough to run.

In the spring of 1865 the war ended, but not for Shelby.

He told his men he would never surrender. "This Missouri division surrender? My God! Soldiers, it is more terrible than death! You, the young and the brave of poor Missouri.... It is too horrible to contemplate."

One day he lined up his thousand men at Corsicanna, Texas, and told them the war was over. But a war was brewing in Mexico and Shelby was sure the Mexican government would welcome men who wanted to fight. Five hundred of them rode south. The rest started the long trip home.

As the 500 crossed the Rio Grande they lowered the now-tattered regimental banner into the waters, a symbol that the Iron Brigade would never quit. It was July 4, 1865, almost three months after Appomattox.

The Mexican experience was a disappointment to Shelby and his men. In 1867 they came back to Missouri.

For many years, survivors of the Iron Brigade looked back with great pride on their service with Shelby and the day the great cavalry unit gathered for the last time and Shelby announced the Iron Brigade's duties were over, on this date, June 2, 1865.

****

JUNE 3
MISSOURI'S FIRST CONGRESSIONAL DELEGATE

He walked to Missouri from Vincennes, Indiana, his entire wardrobe carried on his back in a small bundle. He settled in St. Charles where he stayed a year to learn French, then moved to St. Louis. In his mid-thirties, Edward Hempstead began a career which would earn him respect as one of our state's most able lawyers. That respect would also put him in Washington as the first congressional delegate Missouri ever had.

Although not well-educated, Edward Hempstead had what is called "native intelligence." He was a forceful presence in the courtroom. It was said that he "possessed strong sense and fine talent for special pleading. He had a sharp, fierce, and barking manner of speaking, which had great effect upon jurors and generally awed them into acquiescence with his own views. His style became very popular and was widely imitated by young attorneys."

He was born in Connecticut in 1770 and spent a year in Vincennes before coming to Missouri. Just two years after crossing the Mississippi he was named Deputy Attorney General for the Districts of St. Louis and St. Charles. Three years after that he was appointed attorney general by Governor Lewis. He allied himself with two other young lawyers of the day, Rufus Easton and William Carr, to oppose many of the policies of Lewis's predecessor, Governor James Wilkinson.

Wilkinson's group was mostly the old French and those who wanted to protect their extensive Spanish land holdings. Hempstead, Carr, and Easton were leaders of the new American faction which was ambitious politically and in land speculation. The whole thing led to a big upheaval in territorial government.

So quickly did Hempstead achieve prominence that he was one of the eight original trustees of the city when St. Louis was incorporated four years after he arrived. It was Hempstead, conscious of the city's French heritage and aware that five of the eight board members were French, who recommended that all ordinances be written in French as well as English.

Hempstead's biggest battle in Congress was for a change in American policy concerning the Spanish land grants in his home territory. It was a confused situation because of the rapid change from Spanish to French to American ownership. Many of the old grants from Spain were not recognized by the United States. But Hempstead contended the title of lands in the Louisiana Territory should be based on the Spanish records. He argued France had never taken actual possession of the land, leaving Spanish officials to command the territory during the short period of French ownership. He charged that any acts of Congress reducing or overturning the Spanish land titles violated international treaty standards.

Hempstead contended that recognition of the Spanish grants would calm the fears of the old-timers and ease the uncertainty many felt about being Americans. "Liberality," he wrote, "will secure the affections of those you have made part of your family; it will root old attachments while a more rigid plan will occasion distrust and dissatisfaction." Congress passed his bill.

Hempstead persuaded Congress to enact a provision that all land not owned by individuals or held in commons be reserved for the support of schools. He also introduced a law allowing the right of preemption by settlers. Many had moved onto public lands, in violation of law, and set up homesteads. The act was passed, allowing those persons to buy for two dollars an acre, on credit if necessary, the land they had occupied. It was the first recognition of any rights of a settler to homestead government land west of the Mississippi.

His term over, Hempstead returned to his St. Louis law practice. He brought his family to St. Louis and worked with his father, Stephen, to organize the Presbyterian church in St. Louis, the first church of that denomination west of the Mississippi.

In August of 1817 he was thrown from a horse and suffered a head injury. Six days later, while arguing a case, he collapsed and died. He was only 47. The first sermon preached in that new St. Louis Presbyterian Church was at his funeral.

Edward Hempstead, Missouri's first congressional delegate, a man who laid the basis for homesteading in the west half a century before the actual passage of the Homestead Act, was born on this date, June 3, 1770.

****

JUNE 4
MISSOURI (I) (A)

It wasn't until 1812 that this area acquired the formal name "Missouri." Or is it "Missoura?" And just what does the word of varying pronunciations really mean?

The situation didn't get unwieldy until the state of Louisiana was admitted to the Union. That caused confusion because Louisiana had been known as the Territory of Orleans, and the term "Louisiana" had been applied to an area to the north—what is now Missouri.

When Louisiana became a state in April 1812, Congress created the Territory of Missouri and made it a second class territory. It included all of the Louisiana Purchase except the state of Louisiana. Seven years later the Territory of Arkansas was laid out and Missouri assumed, generally, its well-known boundaries of today. In 1836 the Platte Purchase completed the northwest corner of Missouri, the area that is now Atchison, Nodaway, Holt, Andrew, Platte, and Buchanan counties.

How to pronounce the name of our state always has been a problem. The famous writer, Eugene Field, a Missourian, once wrote, "He lives in Mizzoura, where the people are so set in ante-bellum notions that they vote for Jackson yet." In the early 1930s Dr. Allen W. Read published a scholarly study of how to pronounce Missouri. He found that the majority of residents of the state pronounce it "Mizzourah." Those same people, however, were generally careless in other pronunciations, saying such things as "I have went," and "I seen your friend." Another source notes that the two s's in Missouri are not pronounced as they are in Mississippi, and that the last two letters, "ri," must certainly be pronounced "re." One wonders why the state name isn't pronounced "Missoury" instead of "Mizzourah." One person

325

suggested it become Missouro, so that using the abbreviation "Mo" can be justified. An 1897 study of 200 prominent residents of the state found 80 percent of them liked "Missoury," a compromise of sorts.

What does Missouri mean?

Floyd Shoemaker says it often has been thought to mean "muddy water." Back in 1673, he notes, Marquette and Joliet reached the mouth of the Missouri River. They called it the "Pe-kit-a-noui," an Indian name meaning "River of the Muddy Water." At the river mouth was an Indian village whose inhabitants used large log canoes. Marquette called the village, "Ou-Missouri," meaning "town of the large canoes," although some translate it as "people of the wooden canoes."

Explorers later referred to the river as being the river of the "Missouris,"referring to the Indians who lived near it. The Missouris at one time were a tribe of Sioux Indians.

Robert Ramsey, who made a career of studying the way Missouri places were named, says the Indian tribe was called the Missouris by their bitterest enemies, the Algonquins, who eventually annihilated them. In the Fox Indian language (the Foxes were part of the Algonquins) it probably means "People with Big Canoes." The Missouris called themselves the Niutachi, meaning "People Who Dwell at the Mouth of the River." They called the river the "Nishodse," which in the Sioux language means "Muddy Water." Ramsey notes, therefore, the familiar nickname for the river, "The Big Muddy," might not be too far from wrong.

The entire problem might never have reached these proportions if Louisiana had been admitted to the Union as the State of Orleans and we were left with the name "Louisiana." Little did Congress realize what long-lasting arguments it started when it organized the Territory of Missoury (or is it Mizzourah) on this date, June 4, 1812.

****

JUNE 5
HAWKEN, FIREARMS AND FIREMEN

To the frontiersman, the rifle was his life. It brought him his food. It protected him from danger. He could lose everything but as long as he had a rifle he could get it all back—his clothes, shelter, money from the sale of skins. When the frontier began to open west of the Mississippi, those who went into it quickly learned they needed a gun hefty enough to do the job. The result was a rifle made in Missouri by two brothers.

One of the most desired parts of any gun collection is the graceful Kentucky long rifle. These weapons, the kind we visualize carried by Boone and Crockett, made names for themselves in the Revolutionary War and the years afterward. But as the frontier went west, something more practical was needed. The frontiersman didn't need a weapon that was six feet long. He needed something which would fire a ball heavy enough to bring down big game, not just the squirrels, rabbits, and deer the Kentucky backwoodsman shot.

Samuel Hawken had served in the War of 1812, then joined his brother Jacob in St. Louis. Jake's gun shop already had become famous in St. Louis. Gun historian Charles Hanson says "their uniform quality, accuracy, and dependability made Hawken rifles the universal standard on the frontier."

The Hawkens began by modifying Kentucky rifles; then they began making their own weapons. Their rifles had short barrels which were needed for handling ease while chasing a target on horseback. They were not graceful or decorative; Hawken rifles were tough and functional. If you fell off a horse and landed on the weapon, it would not break, as the fragile Kentucky rifle might. The barrels, of soft metal, were lightly rifled for greater accuracy and minimum recoil. Author Francis Parkman was astonished when a hunter armed with a Hawken repeatedly killed buffalo at distances beyond 300 yards. The Hawkens also made a few pistols, now extremely rare.

Jacob Hawken died of cholera in 1849 and Sam kept the company going. So respected were the brothers that in 1847 another young gunsmith wrote a letter to Sam asking if he should set up his operations in St. Louis too. His name was Samuel Colt.

Sam Hawken is remembered for other things in St. Louis. Once, after a neighborhood fire, Hawken was kidded by a friendly fireman about the need for a fire department in that area. So Hawken started the effort which resulted in the founding of the Northern Fire Company. So popular was Hawken that in 1845, when the new reel-wagon was purchased from the famous Agnew firefighting company of Philadelphia, the firemen named it the "Sam Hawken."

Sam Hawken was almost seventy when he decided it was time to follow his rifles west, time to see Pikes Peak. The gold rush was on and Sam decided to seek another fortune. His account of the trip, published in a St. Louis newspaper in the fall of 1859, tells of his becoming bogged down many times in the mud. He tells of meeting and criticizing those persons who had hardly wet a pan in the mountain streams before giving up and coming home.

Sam ran a gun shop in Denver for a short time but came back to Missouri after a year in the west. He later sold the gun company to one of his top associates, J. P. Gemmer, who kept it going until 1915.

Sam retired to his farm about eleven miles west of St. Louis. He occasionally visited the old shop and the last Hawken rifle he built is now on display at the Jefferson Memorial building in St. Louis.

He died at the age of ninety-one in 1884, having outlived most of the men to whom a Hawken rifle was a necessity, not a keepsake. Samuel T. Hawken, who helped give the world one of its greatest firearms, came to St. Louis to begin making those guns on this date, June 5, 1822.

****

JUNE 6
THE BIRD

He was a sports hero at Central High School in Kansas City, a football and basketball player, a pitcher and infielder on the school baseball team. They called him "Dutch" and many would remember him as a kid who got into fights during basketball games. He wanted to be a dentist for a while, but one day—the story goes—he hoisted a patient seated in a dental chair clear to the ceiling while daydreaming about baseball. He emerged years later as the biggest winner and the biggest loser in baseball history—Casey Stengel.

The first professional team Stengel signed with folded before he ever played a game for them. For the rest of his life he complained they owed him two weeks salary. When Stengel was still in the minor leagues, he liked to practice sliding. Between innings, on the way to the dugout or back to the field, he'd throw his glove ahead of him and slide toward it.

In 1912, at the age of twenty-three, Casey finally reached the Brooklyn Dodgers. The first thing he saw when he entered the clubhouse was a crap game. The first thing he did as a member of the Dodgers was lose twenty dollars rolling the dice.

The greatest single day of his career came in the first game of the

328

1923 World Series against a team he would later manage—the Yankees. The game was tied and the count was three and two on Stengel. The Yankees had Bullet Joe Busch on the mound. The great Damon Runyon watched and wrote:

"This is the way Old Casey Stengel ran running his home run home when two were out in the ninth and the score was tied and the ball still bounding inside the Yankee Yard.

"His warped old legs bending beneath him at every stride.

"His arms flying back and forth like those of a man swimming with a crawl stroke.

"His flanks heaving, his breath whistling, his head far back. Yankee infielders, passed by Old Casey Stengel as he was running his home run home, said Casey was muttering to himself, adjuring himself to greater speed as a jockey mutters to his horse in a race, saying 'Go on, Casey, go on!'

"The warped old legs, twisted and bent by many a year of baseball campaigning, just barely held out under Old Casey Stengel until he reached the plate, running his home run home.

"Then he collapsed."

The "Old Casey" Runyon described was thirty-four then. He ran oddly because he had a bruised heel and lost the rubber padding in his shoe as he rounded second base. He thought he'd lost the whole shoe.

In game three he homered into the right field stands, over the head of Babe Ruth. The Giants lost the series, but Stengel outplayed the Great Babe.

The next year he was traded to Boston and ended his major league career there. Stengel hacked around as a minor league manager for years and even was part owner of one club.

He finally became a major league manager with the Boston Braves, a team so poor it changed its name briefly to the Boston Bees. They did no better under Stengel. Back to the minors after five years in Boston, he managed the old American Association team in Kansas City for a year.

Then the New York Yankees hired him. Dave Egan of the Boston *Record* wrote in 1949 that with the hiring of Casey Stengel, the Yankees automatically eliminated themselves from the pennant race.

But Egan had to eat those words. The Yankees won in 1949. Until Stengel was fired in 1960 the Yankees won ten pennants and seven world championships in twelve years. Stengel moved to the Mets in

1962 as that team's first manager. The Mets lost their first nine games and for the next seven years were the worst team in baseball history. Casey retired in 1965 after he broke his hip. He said he couldn't strut out to the mound like he used to.

There's another Stengel story people like to tell.

Back when he was with the Dodgers, the Pittsburgh fans were giving him a hard time one day. He couldn't take it lying down. He found a sparrow which had stunned itself by flying into the outfield wall and put it under his cap. When the Pittsburgh fans got on him during his next trip to the plate, Casey turned, executed a courtly bow, tipped his hat and the bird flew out.

Yes, they'll always be telling Casey Stengel stories, stories about a man some think is Missouri's greatest gift to the game. Maybe somebody will even try to tell one the way Casey talked, a peculiar brand of English the sportswriters dubbed "Stengalese." And maybe they'll get around to telling about the time Casey Stengel tipped his hat in Pittsburgh and a bird flew out from under it on this date, June 6, 1918.

****

JUNE 7
LIVING FOR THE CHILDREN

Sometimes when the governor is sitting at his large desk in his office at the Capitol, he looks up to see a series of large paintings of famous Missouri historical figures. One of those large paintings is of a woman, a schoolteacher. She is dressed in the long dress of the nineteenth century. One small girl, obviously a little unsure of herself at school, clings to her dress. Another small girl clutches a doll and stares out at the viewer of the picture. Written on the blackboard behind the woman and her two pupils in the painting are the words, "Let us live for the children." For most of her almost seventy-three years, she did.

The woman is Susan Elizabeth Blow. She created the kindergarten.

Susan Blow discovered the European philosophy of education while still a young woman. She was especially interested in the works of German educators and became a follower of the philosophy of education advanced by the German thinker, Friedrich Froebel. But she turned that philosophy into practicality.

Susan Blow grew up in a time when educated women were rare. If a family had money to send someone to school—this was before the days of free public schools—it was usually the boys. Although Susan came from a well-to-do and enlightened family, she had this same problem.

Her father was Henry Taylor Blow, state senator, briefly the American Minister to Venezuela, a congressman and later a minister to Brazil. The family lived in Carondelet, moving there when Susan was six. She was sent to a small French school for a short time when she was five. But it would be five years later before she received more formal schooling, about eight months of private tutoring. From the time she was twelve until she was fourteen she attended no schools. She did have a governess help her polish her French. She could read, however, and read the Bible and pored through the books in her father's library.

When she was fourteen her father set up a school in Carondelet which she attended for a couple of years. Then she went to New York for two years to attend a private school.

Susan was in her late twenties when her father became the ambassador to Brazil. In the fifteen months they were there, she learned Portuguese. Afterwards on a tour of Europe with her family, she became exposed to the Froebel educational ideas. On her return to St. Louis in 1872 she brought with her a dream for a practical kindergarten. Her father wanted to finance it, but Susan wanted it to be part of the public school movement. She found an ally in the forward-thinking Superintendent of Schools, William Torrey Harris.

In 1873 the first kindergarten was opened in the Des Peres School at Carondelet. It was an instant success.

The school was so overwhelmingly popular that Harris wrote forty pages about it in his annual report two years later. Susan had twenty students that first day and the number quickly grew to more than forty. At the end of the second year there were sixty-eight.

The children were taught to be clean, polite, and to exercise daily. They were taught to recognize forms, shapes, and numbers. They were encouraged to draw, to fold paper, and to model clay.

Educational leaders from across the nation examined her kindergarten and looked at her techniques for instructing teachers. Susan's innovations in the educational field became the basis for the true beginnings of the kindergarten movement in America. All of this was done by the time she was thirty-three.

Her health was uncertain and she moved from St. Louis to Boston, then to New York. She wrote her first book in the mid 1890s and followed it with three others, plus translations and interpretations from Froebel's books on the education of children.

She started lecturing in 1895 and quit in 1916 just a month before she died.

Millions of children enroll each year in the educational system she helped found. Only a few parents realize the debt they owe this remarkable Missouri woman, Susan Elizabeth Blow, who spent her life living for the children, born on this date, June 7, 1843.

****

JUNE 8
THE AGENCY OF EQUALITY

For too many years Missouri, like most other states in the nation, had standards—written or unwritten—which would not allow people of differing races to use the same hospitals, barber and beauty shops, hotels or motels, water fountains, cemeteries or bathrooms. But in 1954 came the U.S. Supreme Court ruling on desegregation of the schools. Three years later the Missouri General Assembly passed a bill creating the Missouri Commission on Human Rights. It was originally intended as an educational agency. It could investigate instances of discrimination, but only hope to resolve the problems through persuasion and education, hoping to foster mutual respect between the parties involved. Governor James Blair spoke of the commission as "a dream I have had for years."

It was only a temporary commission at first, to serve three years. Its budget was $9,000. But by the time the commission celebrated its tenth anniversary, it had grown to thirty-one full-time employees and had become a permanent arm of state government with a budget of more than $350,000.

The commission wasted little time going to work. Its study of the status of Human Rights in Missouri was soon adopted as a model to be sent to all states by President Eisenhower's Commission on Civil Rights. Within its first eighteen months the Commission documented more than forty complaints of discrimination in districts where legislators claimed there were no violations of civil rights. Such actions led the governor to ask the legislature to make the commission permanent. On the second anniversary of the creation of the temporary body, Governor Blair signed the bill making it permanent.

In 1961 more responsibilities were added to it. Now it could administer the State Fair Employment Practices Act which made it illegal to discriminate because of race, religion, creed, color, national origin, ancestry or sex in advertising for jobs, hiring, promoting, firing or admission to labor organizations or apprenticeship training programs.

In 1965, the commission was given the responsibility of enforcing the State Public Accommodations Act which made it illegal for any business offering any goods, services, privileges, facilities, advantages, and accommodations, to discriminate. The only businesses not covered were barber and beauty shops, but later legislation included them.

In January 1959 Governor Blair said, "When I...administered the oath to the Human Rights Commission I told them that their utmost responsibility was to uphold the rights of every woman and man. No circumstance has come to change my views. I still believe what I said to them, and on what I said I intend to stand firmly.

"I still require of them acknowledgment and protection of those rights. They have, I think, been faithful. In the struggle for man's rights, none of us can be a neutralist. We cannot stand above or aside from this battle. We must always remain combatants....We must gather together on this earth the freedoms that belong to all of us—and who shall tell us that we have not the right to share them."

The road hasn't always been smooth. The commission has had to face charges of ineptitude, mismanagement, racial prejudices within the agency itself, picking leaders and commission members who do not have the time or the expertise to grapple with the issue.

In 1976 Governor Bond asked all members of the commission to resign so new ones could be appointed who would have more expertise in the field.

Remarkable strides were made in the first quarter-century of the life of the commission. But it is obvious from the mere existence of the agency and the necessity of keeping it alive and expanding its responsibilities that there is still much to be done. The Missouri Commission on Human Rights was created when Governor James Blair signed the bill on this date, June 8, 1957.

****

JUNE 9
DOC, MR. SPEAKER, COLONEL, MAYOR

He was a practicing dentist in Festus in 1932 when a banker walked in one day and said, "Doctor, I was just out at Hillsboro and I filed you for Representative."

This was a complete surprise to the doctor who wasn't at all excited about getting into politics. But he ran, was elected, and eventually carved a historic place in the annals of the Missouri legislature. He didn't like Missouri's capital city when he arrived to serve his first term, and the townspeople didn't look too kindly on members of the legislature either. Ironically, he would later be mayor of that town for twelve years.

Had not his father died when young John was a youth he might have been a farmer near Cincinnati, Ohio. He thought about being a lawyer, but his brother was a professor at the Kansas City Dental College so John Christy moved to Kansas City and studied dentistry.

He decided to practice in a small town because his health was bad. He headed toward Vandalia, Illinois, where his wife's parents lived. But while in St. Louis between trains he picked up a newspaper and saw an ad for a dental office for sale in Festus, south of St. Louis. That short-circuited his plans for going to Illinois and altered the future of Missouri.

In 1932 Christy was elected to the House of Representatives. The only time he'd been to Jefferson City before was to take his state dental examinations. He couldn't even find his way around the Capitol. That first term in the House he was chairman of the Military Affairs Committee. In his second term he was named Speaker of the House — one of the most powerful posts in state government. He was picked as Speaker in his next term, and in his fourth and final term in the House he was Speaker again. For the first time a man had served three consecutive terms as Speaker of the House of Representatives. Christy once said it was fun the first time, not so much fun the second time, and hell the third time.

Christy had caught the eye of Tom Pendergast in Kansas City. Pendergast told Christy he'd get the Pendergast support for Lieutenant Governor four years later. But four years later Boss Tom had run afoul of the law and nephew Jim was in charge. Jim told Christy to file but his formal endorsement never came. Lieutenant Governor Frank Harris filed for a third term.

Christy had been in the National Guard for years and during World War II was named to a high position in the Selective Service System.

A few years later Christy was asked to run again for Lieutenant Governor. But he couldn't because of his military career. He suggested the mayor of Jefferson City try for the job. That man did, and won. Eight years later, former mayor James T. Blair became governor.

Christy more or less switched places with Blair. In the 1960s he ran for mayor of Jefferson City and won. He would serve three terms, deciding not to seek a fourth because of his advancing age. He left office in 1975, at the age of seventy-seven.

Three decades earlier when he went to Jefferson City as a freshman legislator he asked why the city didn't have any large industries. He was told the city didn't want industry, that it was a white-collar town. Under John Christy the city's industrial base boomed. For years he led the fight before the legislature for a local-option sales tax. For some time he was almost the only voice being heard pushing for that legislation. It finally came and Missouri cities today are better for it.

He died early in 1978. John Christy, whose life and the history of our state were altered by a St. Louis newspaper ad offering a dentist's office for sale, was born on this date, June 9, 1897.

****

JUNE 10
GUY B. PARK, SURPRISE GOVERNOR

He was practically unknown to the majority of Missourians, and not known at all nationwide. He didn't become a candidate until a month before the election. But he piled up one of the biggest winning margins of any governor in Missouri history. He was backed by Tom Pendergast and was such a party man that the Capitol came to be called "Uncle Tom's Cabin." He was Guy B. Park, a governor who inherited first a nomination then a state during a depression.

Park called for a reduction of government expenses at all levels as soon as he was inaugurated. He expressed his allegiance to the Roosevelt New Deal in his inaugural remarks saying, "It is the function of government to aid and protect, to relieve distress, and to promote happiness and prosperity." He told his audience on inauguration day that these aims could be met without what he called "oppressive taxation."

Park wasted no time cutting state expenses by reducing the costs of state department operations. It wasn't a popular move with many state employees, but the biggest part of the cost of operating a government or business is salaries. Many state employees were laid off. Some state departments were rearranged to take up activities of those agencies which were reduced. But Park also strongly backed education and believed firmly the time had come to upgrade the prisons and other state institutions. Despite the depression he convinced the voters they should approve a $10 million bond issue for education and corrections. That would be supplemented with about $7 million in federal money. To further increase the state's income, Missouri's first statewide sales tax was approved during the depression administration of Guy B. Park.

Park instituted other financially efficient policies. He established a department of the budget to supervise state expenditures and present a budget all in one lump. He brought centralized purchasing to state government, a process allowing a savings on purchases. It was during the Park administration that Missouri provided its first old age pensions.

Guy Park had lived in the Platte City area most of his life. He was a lawyer. In 1922 he became a member of the convention chosen to draft a new state constitution. The convention's efforts were unsuccessful. Missouri wouldn't have a new constitution until twenty-three years later. Park became a Circuit Judge in 1923 and served in that position until October of 1932 when he ran for governor. He was an associate of Francis Wilson, who had been selected as the Democratic nominee for governor in the August primary. But less than a month before the November election, Francis Wilson died. The Pendergasts went into a huddle and picked the relatively unknown Guy B. Park. So powerful was the Democratic Party in 1932 that Park won the governorship by the biggest margin of any winner up to that time.

In November of 1933 Park's daughter Henrietta was married in the governor's mansion to J. Marvin Krause of St. Louis. It was the first wedding in the mansion of a daughter whose father was still in office. It was an event that wouldn't be repeated until three and one-half decades later during the Hearnes administration.

Governor Park's wife, Eleanora, wrote a book about the wives of Missouri's governors, assembling for the first time a concise and comprehensive history of the women who have served as first ladies of Missouri.

After his term as governor was over, Park went back to Platte City. He set up a law practice in Kansas City and lived the rest of his life as a lawyer, although he never returned to a judgeship. He died in 1946 at the age of seventy-four.

In a time when pump priming was an important feature in putting an economy back on its feet, Guy Park had to walk the thin line between cutting back and going ahead. He knew he had to reduce costs of government in Missouri but still increase the flow of money so Missourians could live, purchase, and work even during a depression. He walked that tightrope successfully to the surprise of many. Guy B. Park, who made the most of a gubernatorial nomination dropped in his lap, was born on this date, June 10, in 1872.

****

JUNE 11
RED ROVER

When David Sans was brought on board for treatment, he had the hospital facilities all to himself for a while. It wasn't long before four other patients joined him. Sans probably couldn't have cared less that he was the first patient to use the new quarters. David Sans, a seaman aboard the gunboat *Benton,* had cholera. It was 1862 and he was the first patient taken aboard the first hospital ship in American history. It was built in Missouri.

The ship was two years old when the Confederacy bought it in New Orleans and made it into a floating barracks for men of the Confederate Floating Battery "New Orleans." Originally it had been a commercial sidewheeler built in Cape Girardeau, Missouri in 1859. It was called "Red Rover."

Red Rover didn't stay in Confederate hands long. In the winter of 1861 the ship went up the Mississippi as far as Island Number 10, near New Madrid, to help blockade the federal's western gunboat flotilla. In March, 1862, the Union mortar fleet and gunboat flotilla started bombarding that island and the Confederate fleet. The Red Rover was hit by a piece of shell which penetrated all of its decks and pierced its bottom. The confederates abandoned the ship and a Union gunboat, the "Mound City," captured it. From that day the Red Rover was a Union vessel.

The Red Rover displaced 786 tons but took only eight feet of water with its wide, shallow hull. It could make nine knots, maximum, upstream. It cruised at five. Repairs were made on the bottom of the boat before it was sent upstream to St. Louis. There it was outfitted to become a floating summer hospital for the western flotilla. A Boston doctor was the senior medical officer, a position he kept for the rest of the war.

In June of 1862 the Red Rover became part of the flotilla. It reported to Cairo, Illinois, with stores aboard for her crew for three months, and medical supplies for 200 men for an equal amount of time. She also carried 200 tons of ice. A couple of days after arriving at the Cairo Naval Depot, the ship was described by army quartermaster George Wise as being the most complete of her kind that ever floated. "She has bathrooms, laundry, elevators for the sick from the lower to upper decks, amputating rooms, nine different water closets, gauze blinds to the windows to keep the cinders and smoke from annoying the sick, two separate kitchens for the sick and the well, a regular corps of nurses, and two water closets on every deck." The nurses at that time were men. In the first three days the ship carried fifty-six patients. Within a week the ship was in the thick of the Mississippi River war.

On one trip with wounded to army hospitals in Illinois, the Mother Superior of the Sisters of the Holy Cross at Memphis, Sister Angela, volunteered herself and some of the other members of her order to accompany the ship and its wounded on a temporary basis. They became the first women floating nurses in American military history. Many nuns worked on the boat at various times during the war.

In the first twenty days, the ship had 109 patients. From July to September of 1862, the ship had 211 patients.

In 1862 Congress transferred the Western Gunboat Fleet from the War Department to the Navy Department. On October 1, 1862, when the transfer became effective, the United States Navy got its first hospital ship—the Red Rover. On Christmas eve, 1862, several nuns were transferred to the Red Rover from the Army Hospital at Mound City to be on permanent assignment aboard the ship. They were the forerunners of the Navy Nurse Corps and became the first women nurses to formally serve a permanent station aboard a navy hospital ship.

In the spring of 1863 the ship was at Vicksburg to handle the wounded from that seige. After Vicksburg fell, the ship worked the length of the river delivering supplies and caring for the sick and wounded. In April, 1864, the Red Rover was at Memphis when Confederate General Nathaniel Bedford Forrest captured part of the town. On the riverfront the Union Ironclad Essex was caught with its steam down, unable to escape if the Confederates took the city. The Essex was lashed to the Red Rover which was prepared to get the ironclad out into the current and try to thrash its way upstream out of the battle area. This didn't have to be done. Forrest finally was driven off.

The Red Rover's last supply voyage was late in 1864. It was a berthed hospital ship for the rest of its career, until November of 1865 when the last eleven patients were transferred to another ship. At the end of the year the ship was sold to civilians.

The Red Rover handled almost 2,500 patients. Only 157 died, a tribute to the skill of the staff and the facilities aboard this first hospital ship. Dr. Bixby, who headed the medical team on the Red Rover, went back to Boston after the war and became a prominent physician in the East.

The Red Rover, after being sold to a private owner for $45,000, drifted into obscurity and decay, its significance overlooked and forgotten for years. Nobody was there to preserve the navy's first hospital ship, built in Missouri, which accepted David Sans as its first patient on this date, June 11, 1862.

****

JUNE 12
A FINAL TRY FOR PEACE

While some parts of the nation were eager to fight at the beginning of the Civil War, Missouri was still trying to remain neutral. This effort was headed for failure. Missourians tried for peace in word and deed, but when the step was taken across the line, war came quickly. This isn't to say people hadn't chosen sides. The governor wanted secession. Those siding with the Union position had other ideas. The two sides clashed across a conference table in St. Louis and Missouri went to war.

The meeting in St. Louis that day was scheduled between the forces of Frank Blair and Nathaniel Lyon, who wanted Missouri to stay with the Union, and with Governor Claiborne Fox Jackson and General Sterling Price, who believed Missouri should cast its lot with the South. Both sides hoped to avoid conflict. But their views were so different there was no room for compromise. Blair and Lyon talked of complete neutrality. Jackson and Price wanted Missouri to be, at the least, a staging area for prosouthern forces. When the negotiations reached a final impasse it was Lyon who said, "This means war."

The story of Missouri's entry into the war actually goes back several years, the years in which the nation plummeted toward the great internal struggle. A key figure in the early stages was General William S. Harney, commander of the Department of the West. Harney was incapable of dealing with the growing storm. He had strong connections with the South. With the advent of the war he was torn in his sympathies. Many asked whether he was fit to command the Union forces or take strong action which would be necessary to keep federal forces in control of Missouri. Harney hoped to play a neutral role. On May 21, 1861, he and General Price worked out an agreement which was unacceptable to Unionist leader Frank Blair. Harney agreed to take no action against General Price as long as Price made no aggressive move. Price was thus allowed to use the state militia to keep the peace in Missouri. This, of course, played right into the hands of Price and Jackson. Blair realized this and started working on President Lincoln, persuading him to replace Harney with the fiery pro-Union officer, Nathaniel Lyon.

The critical meeting in St. Louis became known as the Planter's House Conference, taking its name from the famous St. Louis hotel in which it was held. When Lyon told Price "This means war," Jackson realized he could not hope to keep Missouri a southern-leaning neutral state. He returned to Jefferson City, burning bridges behind him. By the flickering lantern light on the train that night, the governor drafted a declaration of war.

Jackson accused the United States government of inflicting unparalleled and unprovoked outrages on the state. Referring to the Convention of 99 which had taken over legislative powers of the state, he said, "The enactments of your legislature have been nullified; your volunteer soldiers have been taken prisoners." He was referring to the capture of Camp Jackson by Lyon's forces a few days before. There had been shooting at Camp Jackson and a few other places, prompting Jackson to say, "Unoffending and defenseless men, women, and children have been ruthlessly shot down and murdered; and other indignities have been heaped upon your state." Because his attempts to keep Missouri out of the war had failed, Jackson called for 50,000 men to form a state militia to repel the invasion of Missouri by those forces acting on behalf of the United States government.

340

As soon as the train arrived in Jefferson City the governor's secretary hurried out to distribute the document. By daybreak it had gone all over the state. Price already had decided the first stand would be made at Boonville if necessary.

A frantic assemblage of state papers and materials began in Jefferson City as Jackson prepared to take state government with him. Word soon arrived that Lyon was preparing to come upstream with troops to take the city. Just forty-eight hours later Lyon was in the capital city with three steamboats and 2,000 men.

Jackson by then was in Boonville. He would never return to Jefferson City, dying long before the end of the war. Lyon was in Jefferson City long enough to secure the town, then headed upstream for the first battlefield confrontation with Jackson and Price.

Missouri was fully at war.

Four years of destruction, desolation, death, and division lay ahead for Missouri. Price and Jackson were pushed out of the state within a few weeks and Price never could regain Missouri for the South. Nathaniel Lyon's bold and forceful military strokes kept Missouri in federal hands, even though he himself would be killed in the first two months of the conflict.

Our state formally entered the Civil War when Governor Claiborne Fox Jackson issued his proclamation calling for help to repel invaders from the United States government on this date, June 12, 1861.

****

JUNE 13
WEBSTER AND MISSOURI

A poet once wrote:

> The boundless prairies learned his name,
> His words the mountain echoes knew,
> The Northern breezes swept his fame
> From icy lakes to warm bayou.

Perhaps that is why Daniel Webster was so well-known in Missouri, and why he was so warmly greeted on his only known trip to our state. We have towns, counties, and schools named for him, another indication of the respect Missourians felt for the senator from Massachusetts.

Daniel Webster needed the trip he took West in the last third of the 1830s. He had grown tired of fighting against strong odds in fourteen years as a senator. He was disappointed that his battle against the policies of Andrew Jackson had lost. A new session of Congress was coming and Webster saw little chance to push through meaningful legislation. He was also heavily in debt. His biographer, Claude Fuess, writes that Webster felt if he could get away from the turmoil of the Senate for a year or two, he might yet have a chance to become president. Two years before the trip, Webster started telling friends he planned to withdraw from the Senate as soon as possible. He was just plain tired.

Everywhere he was greeted like a king, for Daniel Webster, along with Henry Clay and John Calhoun, were considerably better known than most members of Congress and probably as well known as many presidents. He had little rest, making many addresses, many of them lengthy. Welcoming committees wined and dined the celebrity almost to the point of exhaustion.

His family and his godson, William Pitt Fessenden, were with him on the trip. If the pace was tiring for a seasoned politician it was even more so for the family members. Fessenden wrote that when the group reached St. Louis, Mrs. Webster and their daughter, Julia, "are sick and tired with glory. Their fatigue must be excessive, and, as to the show, Mrs. Webster, though proud of her husband, has little taste for it, and poor Julia has none at all."

The city of St. Louis had a welcoming committee who chartered a boat, met the Websters downriver from Jefferson Barracks and took them on a tour past the St. Louis wharf so they could see the city. Then they returned to the Market Street landing and officially entered the town.

Webster's speech, says Fuess, had an informality and humor about it which fitted the occasion of the huge barbecue held in his honor. Webster declared to the 5,000 or so people at the barbecue that he owed, as he put it, "the self-same responsibility to Missouri as to Massachusetts," his home state.

Reaction to the speech was mixed. Historian Elihu Shepard said the speech kept the audience's "rapturous attention for eighty minutes." Another St. Louis historian, J. T. Scharf, said the crowd's admiration was "one of the grandest demonstrations that ever took place in this country in honor of any public man." But the Jacksonian newspaper, the *Missouri Argus,* was less complimentary. The *Argus* called the speech a miserable and complete failure and said Webster, as an orator, was "almost below mediocrity."

Webster spent several days in St. Louis before going upriver to Alton, then to Springfield and Chicago. He wouldn't get back to his eastern home for another month. Apparently the visit refreshed him enough to continue as a senator. Later he served as Secretary of State under three presidents.

Today Missouri remembers the senator with towns like Webster Groves and Marshfield, named for Webster's home, and Webster County. There is a Webster College and several other "Webster" schools.

Daniel Webster came West in search of himself and his public. He found both when he stopped in St. Louis on this date, June 13, 1837.

****

JUNE 14
THE HOLLOW MOTTO

The emphasis at the 1916 Democratic National Convention was to be Americanism. Woodrow Wilson, a cinch for renomination, knew that unity should be the theme—unity in the face of increasing complications and military threats in Europe. The convention in St. Louis beginning on Flag Day opened with the singing of "America," then the "Star Spangled Banner." Out of that convention would come one of the most misunderstood phrases in American political history.

The delegates attending the Democratic Convention in St. Louis weren't as interested in Americanism as Wilson and his backers had hoped. Things got out of hand when former New York Governor Martin Glynn rose to give the keynote speech. What happened in the minutes that followed turned the entire convention upside down. Glynn, an experienced orator, began by justifying President Wilson's foreign policy of neutrality as "truly American as the American flag." He said every great American president from Washington to Cleveland had followed that policy. The crowd began to respond when he discussed Grant's difficulties with Spain; Harrison's problems with Chile; Lincoln's difficulties with France and England. In each case, Glynn said, America might have gone to war if the president had not settled the problem peaceably. Glynn had more examples but he didn't want to bore his listeners. He had caught their interest, however, and when he tried to go on to another topic, he was urged to continue with the one under discussion. And so he went on, surprised, but enjoying the feel an orator has when a crowd is his.

As the enthusiasm built, some people grew alarmed. But Glynn kept going, saying the policy he was describing did not satisfy "those who revel in destruction and find pleasure in despair, the fire eater or the swashbuckler," but it did satisfy "those who worship at the altar of the God of Peace. It does satisfy the mothers of the land at whose hearth and fireside no jingoist has placed an empty chair. It does satisfy the daughters of this land, for whom brag and bluster have sent no husband, no sweetheart and no brother to the mouldering dissolution of the grave. It does satisfy the fathers of this land, and the sons of this land, who will fight for our flag, and die for our flag, when Reason primes the rifle, when Honor draws the sword, when Justice breathes a blessing on the standards they uphold."

The audience rose to its feet, cheers drowning out Glynn. William Jennings Bryan wept in the press box.

Shortly after noon the next day speeches resumed. The emotion continued to build, especially when convention chairman Ollie James proclaimed that Wilson, without orphaning a single child, widowing a single mother, firing a single gun or shedding a single drop of blood had "wrung from the most militant spirit that ever brooded above a battlefield an acknowledgement of American rights and an agreement to American demands." The crowd made him repeat the statement verbatim. This triggered a 21-minute demonstration which so drained the delegates they adjourned soon after.

That night, Wilson was nominated by a vote of 1,092 to one.

The platform still had to be approved. It was written mostly by Wilson but someone had inserted into it a plank which noted he had "preserved the vital interests of our government and its citizens and *kept us out of war.*"

Wilson and his advisors knew the delegates were mistaken by thinking he could keep the country out of war just because he'd been able to do so up to then. Wilson hoped not to fight, but he believed America was slowly being sucked into the European conflict.

Wilson called for a strong prepared army. He called for a unification of nations to stop or prevent wars. Later he complained about the delegates, "They talk of me as though I were a God. But any little German lieutenant can put us into war at any time by some calculated outrage."

The phrase, "He kept us out of war," became the rallying cry of the convention and the hopes of the American peace movement in those times. The convention in St. Louis ended with the party unified to re-elect Woodrow Wilson, but unified behind a phrase Wilson knew was false: "He kept us out of war."

Woodrow Wilson won with that phrase, beating the former Supreme Court Judge Charles Evans Hughes by almost 600,000 votes. A year later, not long after his second inaugural, he could keep us out of war no longer.

Woodrow Wilson ran and won on an issue he did not want and one the public didn't understand, a phrase born at the Democratic National Convention which opened in St. Louis on this date, June 14, 1916.

****

JUNE 15
THE OCCUPIED CAPITAL CITY

The smoke-belching sidewheeler which had been working its way upstream for the last two days nosed into the landing on the riverfront. It was Saturday and although the community appeared quiet on the surface, it was in confusion and turmoil. About three days earlier the city had been thrown into chaos when the governor and a general rushed back from St. Louis, then fled.

Uncertainty prevailed.

It was mid-afternoon. Men began to file off the boat. They were wearing uniforms of federal soldiers. The capital city of Missouri was about to become an occupied town. Union forces seized the city without a shot being fired. They occupied the city for four years, all the while knowing the governor, the lieutenant governor, and hundreds of Confederate soldiers wanted to regain it. But the city lost in the first few hours of the Civil War in Missouri was never regained.

Just a few days before, negotiations which many had hoped would keep the war out of Missouri and Missouri out of the war broke off in St. Louis. General Nathaniel Lyon told Governor Jackson and General Price, "Rather than concede to the State of Missouri the right to demand that my government shall not enlist troops within her limits or bring troops into the state whenever it pleases, or move its troops at its own will into, and out of or through the state; rather than concede to the State of Missouri for one single instant the right to dictate to my government in any manner, however unimportant, I would see every man, woman and child in the state dead and buried."

345

Lyon immediately saw that federal forces must control the Missouri River. The day after the Planter's House Conference, he started loading men on boats to go upstream. Lyon and his troops unloaded about two or three o'clock Saturday afternoon just below the state penitentiary. The troops immediately seized the high land near the prison then marched through town to the Capitol where they ran up the American flag.

A newspaper correspondent for the *Missouri Democrat* in St. Louis wrote, "Hot is a word which but faintly conveys the idea of the unpleasant sensation experienced by your correspondent while marching through the streets of the capital of the state." He wrote his column that day while seated in the cupola of the Capitol. "After such a sensation, it is decidedly pleasant to sit here, in the shade of the cupola, where cool breezes fan the heated brow, with the glorious emblem of our nationality again before the eyes of the citizens here, who have been strangers to its presence so long. Enthusiastic cheers greeted the appearance of the flag, the city band meanwhile playing a tune which delighted all hearts having still left a spark of loyalty within them."

The tune was "The Star Spangled Banner."

A check was made of the penitentiary. Eight cannon cartridges and parts of some gun carriages were found within the walls and were confiscated.

Most of the troops stayed on the boats. After Colonel Henry Boernstein's regiment arrived that evening, many of the first units ashore went back to the boats. The next day the steamers left at midafternoon bound for Boonville and the first Civil War battle in the state. Word had come that Southerners had 1,000 men and a few cannons fortifying the city.

Boernstein's troops stayed behind when Lyon and his men went upstream. Life became quiet in Jefferson City. New York *Times* correspondent Albert D. Richardson wrote he found troops "standing in the shade of [the Capitol's] portico and rotunda, lying on beds of hay in its passages and upon carpets in the legislative halls."

As for the disarray in the Capitol and the Executive Mansion, Richardson wrote the governor had obviously left town quickly because the mansion was a mess. "Sofas were overturned, carpets torn up and littered with letters and public documents. Tables, chairs, damask curtains, cigar boxes, champagne bottles, ink stands, books, private letters, and family knick-knacks were scattered everywhere in chaotic confusion."

346

The Confederates tried to retake Jefferson City in the fall of 1864 with a campaign which ended with the Battle of Westport. Jefferson City stayed in federal hands throughout the war as did the Missouri River.

The Capital City of Missouri, inhabited by an army of occupation for the Civil War, was taken without a shot being fired, on this date, June 15, 1861.

****

JUNE 16
FRANKLIN

The town is gone now. But once it was one of the most flourishing towns in the entire state, once one of the important trade centers of the West. It was the beginning point of one of America's most important trails west and an important way station on another important commercial thoroughfare, the Missouri River. But it was the river that eventually brought about the downfall and ultimate disappearance of the community of Franklin.

Within the first decade of the nineteenth century, Nathan and Daniel Morgan Boone, sons of Daniel Boone, discovered large stores of salt in central Missouri. The area became known as "Boon's Lick Country." Settlers came into the area midway through the second decade and eventually laid out a town. They named it for Benjamin Franklin.

The public square contained two acres. The main streets were eighty-seven feet wide. The town grew rapidly and became a flourishing commercial and cultural center. Many Kentuckians came to the area and brought with them an important part of their background—a race track which went into operation in 1819. A library was set up, then a newspaper—the first newspaper west of St. Louis—the *Missouri Intelligencer and Boon's Lick Advertiser.*

An expedition commanded by Major Stephen Long, which provided the first person to climb Pike's Peak (Pike saw it but never got to it), stopped at Franklin in 1819. An expedition report says the town was quite large for being on the edge of the frontier with about 120 single-story log cabins, several two-story frame buildings and two more made of bricks, thirteen shops, four taverns, a couple of billiard rooms, a two-story prison, a post office, and a courthouse.

That same year the Baptists organized a congregation in the town and the Methodists formed a congregation a year later. No actual house of worship was ever constructed in Franklin, however. In 1820, four stage coaches began operating.

In 1821 William Becknell and Benjamin Cooper left Franklin bound for Santa Fe. The Mexican people had successfully overthrown Spain and traders were quick to see a profit in trading with the new government. Cooper was stopped by Indians and came back, but Becknell made it safely to Santa Fe. He returned in January of 1822. His stories of the phenomenal profits to be made dealing with the Mexicans triggered the rise of the Santa Fe Trail as a major trade route to the west.

Wagon trains began to form on the main street. They moved out and across the Missouri River by ferryboat at Arrow Rock, traveled to Fort Osage and then west and south into Kansas and on to Santa Fe.

The county seat was moved from Franklin to Fayette in 1823. By then Howard County had been divided into three counties: Howard, Boone, and Cooper. Fayette was the geographical center of what was left of Howard. During those days the population of Franklin ranged in the neighborhood of 1,500 to 1,700 persons.

In the late 1820s the Missouri River started to shift its course. High waters had hurt the town's riverfront in the few years before and in 1828 a large part of the town went into the river. The residents began to move back from the river's edge and established a new settlement. Four years later city officials decided if anything of the town was to be saved, it must be moved.

A large effort began to relocate the community. Many of the houses of the old town were moved about two miles back and the settlement became known as New Franklin. Some of the old settlers built a village just west of New Franklin and carried with them the original town name.

At one time, only St. Louis was a bigger city than Franklin.

One lasting contribution of Franklin was a 16-year-old boy who ran away from the saddler's shop where he worked to go West in 1826. Kit Carson would find his destiny elsewhere, not in what we now call "Old" Franklin, the community which opened a new door to American expansion in the south and west, a community which was able to trace its short but influential life back to the day its site was chosen, on this date, June 16, 1816.

****

JUNE 17
UNION STATION MASSACRE

It was about 7:00 o'clock in the morning when the Missouri Pacific passenger train pulled into the station in Kansas City. In the crowd of passengers were four men who met four other men. They began to walk quickly to the parking lot where cars awaited them. But as they got into the cars, three other men appeared, armed with submachine guns and automatic pistols. In a few minutes the Kansas City Union Station Massacre was over. Five men were dead; two others were critically wounded.

The events leading to the shooting stretched back several months and covered many miles. On October 9, 1930, the deputy warden at the federal prison in Leavenworth, Kansas, noticed his complete set of Shakespeare's works was missing. Also missing was a trustee assigned to his home, a midwestern hoodlum named Frank "Jelly" Nash.

Nash went to Chicago. There he made connections with a small-time hood, Verne Miller. In July 1932 FBI officers arrested four gangsters in Kansas City. They were friends of Nash who was now living in Kansas City with his mistress. Nash heard about the arrest and went into hiding, taking Verne Miller with him to Wisconsin.

On Memorial Day, 1933, eleven more Leavenworth inmates escaped, using guns supposedly smuggled to them by Nash. Two of them joined Nash for a midwestern crime spree. Federal authorities finally tracked Nash to Hot Springs, Arkansas, and arrested him.

Somebody saw the agents take Nash into custody and thought a man was being kidnapped. Police were called and twice before getting out of Arkansas the FBI agents were stopped by local authorities. It made the agents jumpy. They started thinking the entire thing was a plot to slow them down so the underworld could plan an ambush farther up the road. So they switched to a train and telegraphed Kansas City asking for reinforcements to meet them at Union Station.

In the meantime, Polk County, Missouri, sheriff Jack Killingsworth had stopped at a garage in Bolivar. A car was being worked on there which belonged to Charles Arthur "Pretty Boy" Floyd and his cohort, Adam Richetti. The two men kidnapped the sheriff and fled to Kansas City.

Nash's mistress had received word of the capture of her lover. She told Verne Miller who contacted the head of the Kansas City mob, Johnny Lazia, and asked for help.

Lazia said he had heard of a couple of guys who just blew into town in a hurry—Floyd and Richetti. Since Lazia wanted to stay clear of any trouble, he suggested outsiders like those two might be the men to do the job. Miller, Floyd, and Richetti drank some beer and plotted the ambush at Union Station.

The next morning Nash and FBI agents started to get in their car at the railroad station when Floyd, Richetti, and Miller toting machine guns and pistols appeared. City policeman W. J. Grooms pulled his pistol. Floyd and his men immediately opened fire. The car was filled with holes. Above the roar of the guns was heard the voice of Nash, screaming "Don't shoot me...!" But he could not avoid the bullets. In seconds five men were dead including Nash. One, somehow, was unhurt. Identification of the assailants was impossible, although a woman in charge of Traveler's Aid insisted one was Pretty Boy Floyd.

J. Edgar Hoover ordered the FBI to launch an intensive search for Floyd and the others. Some people urged Congress to declare martial law because of the murders.

The massacre became a turning point in the FBI story. Hoover had his men trained by the military in the use of specialized weapons. He ordered his men to take criminals alive if possible, dead if necessary. Congress passed a crime law package, enacting strict penalties for robbery, kidnapping, assault, or murder of a federal officer, and transportation of stolen property across state lines. The massacre triggered efforts which ultimately brought the crime wave of the '30s under control.

Meanwhile officers raided Miller's Kansas City home and found it empty, except for some beer bottles checked for fingerprints a few days later. One of the fingerprints belonged to Adam Richetti.

Verne Miller by now had fled to Detroit. He was later found dead.

In the summer of 1934 Johnny Lazia was shot to death with one of the guns used at Union Station. The local connection was made and a squealer confirmed to police who the three men were at Union Station. Floyd and Richetti had gone back East. They wrecked their car in Ohio and Richetti was captured. Floyd got away but was finally caught.

Richetti was returned to Missouri, tried, and convicted for his part of the massacre. On October 7, 1938, the tiny cyanide pills dropped into the bucket of acid beneath Adam Richetti's chair in the gas chamber of the Missouri State Penitentiary. Moments later the last of the trio was dead.

It had been more than five years since five men had died in a hail of machine gun and automatic pistol bullets in the Kansas City Union Station Massacre, on this date, June 17, 1933.

****

JUNE 18
THE WHIG CONVENTION AT ROCHEPORT

In 1840, Martin Van Buren was seeking the presidency against William Henry Harrison. Van Buren was a Democrat. Harrison belonged to the now-vanished party, the Whigs. It was a hotly contested race nationwide and a state like Missouri, where politics had been slow to catch on after statehood, found itself wrapped up in the race.

In 1840 the Whigs held a state convention at the bustling river town of Rocheport, in Boone County. There has not been a state convention like it since. It was to be the famous "log cabin, coonskin cap, and hard cider" campaign. It started with an article in a Baltimore newspaper which commented: "Upon condition of his receiving a pension of $2,000 and a barrel of cider, General Harrison would no doubt consent to withdraw his pretensions and spend his days in a log cabin on the banks of the Ohio."

The Whigs hooked onto that idea. They adroitly made the "log cabin and hard cider" the symbol of a man of the people. The Whigs also did some things we consider modern today. They brought the campaign slogan into use. "Tippecanoe and Tyler too" referred to a battle Harrison had fought, Tippecanoe, and to vice-presidential candidate John Tyler. The Whigs used rallies, emblems, floats, campaign hats, and portable log cabins to push their ticket. Another popular campaign slogan was, "Matty's policy, 50 cts a day and soup; Our policy, $2 a day and roast beef."

A dense grove of trees stood on a hill just outside Rocheport, and there three speakers stands were put up. Missouri Whigs flocked to Rocheport in astounding numbers. As near as anybody could figure, 6,000 to 10,000 people attended that convention. Considering the state had only about 400,000 people in those days, it was a remarkable turnout. Later, when the election was held, the total number of Whig

351

votes totalled only 23,000, making the convention turnout even more impressive. Imagine today how many people would be on hand if 43 percent of the members of one of today's major political parties in Missouri were to show up in one place!

For three days the Whigs came and listened to the speakers and vowed to see their candidates elected. One historian says the scene at Rocheport, with all of its tents and covered wagons, resembled a military encampment with only uniformed figures and firearms missing.

Locating the convention at a river town in the central part of the state was not an accident. The river provided easy access to metropolitan Whigs. Three steamboats carrying St. Louis delegates arrived. With those delegates came banners, flags, and bands. One source says the lead steamer in that fleet of three displayed a large portrait of General Harrison, "the sight of which, when the boat touched the shore at Rocheport, moved the assembled thousands with uncontrollable enthusiasm that found expressions in shouts of rapture."

The speakers were notable. Among them was Daniel Webster's son Fletcher, General Alexander Doniphan, James S. Rollins, and George Caleb Bingham. The speakers were allowed to talk only ninety minutes at a time.

The results of all this enthusiasm are mixed. The Whigs could gain no state offices of importance. A Democrat, Thomas Reynolds, was picked for governor. John Clark, the Whig, lost. John Miller and John Edwards, both Democrats, were picked over Whig candidates E. M. Samuel and George C. Sibley for other important posts.

Nationally, however, Harrison won—the first time in forty years an organized political party was beaten for the presidency. But the Whigs would never be powerful enough to wrestle political domination away from the Democrats in Missouri. It wasn't for lack of efforts such as the most remarkable political rally in state history, when 10,000 people attended the Whig Convention at Rocheport on this date, June 18, 1840.

****

JUNE 19
HANDICAP

The term "handicap" is a familiar one in sports. It is a way of penalizing the more talented performer to make him more competitive with less gifted competitors. For example, a fast horse in a field of slower ones carries extra weight. It's a system of golf strokes that makes a poor golfer a little more competitive.

But to one golfer the word "handicap" had a special meaning.

The U.S. Open Golf Tournament is one of the greatest of American sporting events. It is what its title claims, a United States Open. Anyone can enter. Through a series of qualifying matches on local or area courses, golfers earn the right to play in the Open itself—a final 72-hole competition.

The scene that year was the Baltusrol Country Club in Springfield, New Jersey. The leaders were tightly bunched after completion of the first two rounds. It was the last day. Under the rules then used by the Professional Golfers Association, the last two rounds were played on the same day, 18 holes in the morning and the other 18 in the afternoon. Any golfer who could stand up to the gruelling finish deserved to be the champion.

In later years many would remember a valiant Ken Venturi battling heat and fatigue in another dramatic open tournament. When the last putt rolled in, the only thing he had energy enough to say was, "My God, I've won the Open."

The heat wasn't quite that blistering at Baltusrol that day when twenty-nine-year-old Dick Mayer, and thirty-seven-year-old Ed Furgol, and an up-and-coming pro Gene Littler started the final 36 holes. Littler, who had been on the pro tour for only six months after winning the National Amateur Tournament the year before, got into early trouble. Coming up the fairway to the last hole he needed a birdie to tie for the lead. (A birdie is one shot under par for a hole.) His first shot was a beauty. But the second shot on the 545-yard par 5 hole went into the trap on the left. Still he was able to recover and pitched to within 8 feet of the pin. Littler lined up his fourth shot, a putt of 8 feet, and rolled it 2 feet past the cup. He tapped in from there but had to be content with a par, one shot out of first place.

Dick Mayer came up to that last hole needing only a par. But just as he drove the ball, a spectator yelled. The shot sliced off to the right into the trees. Shaken, he took a provisional drive but hit it into the right rough. He played that one and stroked his next shot onto the fairway. An approach to the green from 70 feet left him with a tough 12-foot putt. When he finally rolled the ball in, he had 7, a double bogey, two strokes over par for that final hole. He had shot himself out of the tournament title on the seventy-second, and last, hole.

Word got back to the course's fifteenth hole, the sixty-ninth of the tournament. There Ed Furgol was playing a consistent round of golf. But now there was more pressure because he knew precisely what he had to do. Furgol had shot a 71 in the morning round and had a one-stroke lead on Mayer. He parred the first 6 holes in the afternoon round but had three-putted each of the next 2. The putt on the eighth hole was less than 3 feet. But he regained his composure after that and ran off a string of ten straight pars. Par was needed on the last hole for Furgol to win. His first shot went into the trees on the left and he had to play his second shot onto the adjoining fairway. But a marvelous chip shot put the ball at the edge of the green. A putt from there put the ball within 6 feet.

And then he rolled it in.

Ed Furgol had won—the first St. Louisan to win the Open. Furgol was the pro at the Westwood Country Club in St. Louis then.

These were the days before golfers became rich almost overnight if they won a major tournament. Furgol's winning check was $6,000. That night he was introduced on Ed Sullivan's television show.

The handicap? Most pro golfers don't use handicaps. But he had no choice.

When Ed Furgol was twelve years old he was playing on some parallel bars near his home of Utica, New York. He fell and landed on his left elbow. Surgeons operated on the arm three times but their success was limited. Ed Furgol's arm was left permanently cocked at the elbow. He had to stand closer to the ball than most golfers and chop viciously at it with his right arm. Despite this unorthodox style, however, he won the U.S. Open.

Ed Furgol, the golf pro from Missouri, whose left arm was ten inches shorter than his right arm, won the U.S. Open on this date, June 19, 1954.

****

JUNE 20
MASTEN GREGORY:
TWENTY-FOUR HOURS TO VICTORY

Four o'clock in the afternoon. The French countryside has become quiet, except for a public address announcer counting down the seconds.

Fifty-one men are standing on one side of a narrow roadway.

Across that road are fifty-one low and powerful racing cars.

At four o'clock the signal is given. The men dash to their cars, start them and begin what many feel is an insane dash into the first turn. It's the "LeMans Start" and this is the place where the phrase was born, LeMans, France. Today a Missourian will win the world's most famous automobile endurance race.

LeMans is a long way from the streets of Kansas City where a nineteen-year-old kid got his thrills in an old Ford, drag racing through stoplights. Masten Gregory is remembered by some in his hometown as "that wild Gregory boy" who took his motor racing seriously from the beginning. He even used to make his girl friend get out of his car before a drag race, not because he was concerned about her safety, but because she was extra weight!

Masten Gregory came from a wealthy family. He was born on February 29, 1932. Cars were more interesting to him than books. He never graduated from high school. His brother-in-law owned an Allard, one of the first cars of that type in Kansas City, in the early 1950s. Allards were brawny machines and Masten Gregory had to have one. When he came into his share of the family fortune, he bought his own Allard. He ran his first race a month before he was 21. His car lasted five laps. Two months later he entered the car in the 12-Hour Grand Prix of Endurance at Sebring, Florida. He was running third when mechanical trouble put him out.

Gregory bought a Jaguar and drove it in 1953, in San Francisco to his first victory. The next year he was invited to run in his first international event—the 1,000 kilometers of Argentina. He didn't win but he bought the Ferrari that did and went to Europe with it, finishing fourth in the twelve-hour endurance race at Reims, France. He was third in a sports car race at Lisbon, Portugal, then posted victories at Aintree, England, and at Nassau in the famed Speed Week. The Ferrari factory offered to keep his cars in good repair although he wasn't made a member of the factory racing team.

In 1957 Gregory finished fifth in the standings for the World Grand Prix Driving Championship. He was one of the first Americans to do well on the European formula one circuits. But it was sports car racing he preferred. He won the tough 1,000 kilometer race at Nurburgring, Germany, co-driving a Maserati, in 1961.

Masten Gregory became known as a man who stepped out of crashing automobiles while they were still crashing. Once in England he was forced off the track at 135 miles per hour. He later said he tried several things to bring the car back under control but nothing worked. He saw he was going to smash into an embankment so, he said, "I stood up on the seat and stepped over the side."

In the early 1960s, the Ford Motor Company launched an assault on winning the world's most prestigious endurance race—the 24 Hours of LeMans. Gregory and Richie Ginther, another American, went out in 1964 with a broken transmission. Ford felt Gregory drove its cars too hard and did not invite him back to the LeMans team the next year. So he looked up an old friend with a Ferrari. The car had an engine half the size of the Fords. When the flag dropped, Masten Gregory, a man known for breaking and crashing cars, began the steadiest drive of his life. He and co-driver Jochen Rindt, who would later become a Grand Prix champion but not live to receive the crown, circulated the twisting eight-mile course smoothly and regularly. After 21 hours they took the lead and held it the rest of the way. They won by five laps and came within one lap of the race record. Only 14 of the 51 starters finished.

In 1969, Gregory wrote, "I think now I probably won't be killed in an accident. I find that a strange thought." A few years later the Ferrari he drove to victory at LeMans was put on display at the Indianapolis Motor Speedway Museum. Gregory had driven at Indianapolis a few times, but with little success. He retired from active racing and took up residence in Europe.

Masten Gregory, the first Missouri driver to make it big on the great tracks of Europe, won the LeMans 24 Hour Grand Prix of Endurance on this date, June 20, in 1965.

****

JUNE 21
LOUISIANA ACADEMY

In 1811, Henry Marie Brackenridge wrote in his journal that a limestone building was being constructed at Ste. Genevieve, but those who were setting up the building weren't receiving the support they needed. Brackenridge is generally regarded as Missouri's first career author. He was writing in his journal about the building of the Ste. Genevieve Academy. Three years earlier, the territorial legislature had incorporated the academy and established a board of trustees which numbered twenty-one people. The incorporation law had some forward-looking provisions. No religious discrimination was to be exhibited in the hiring of a teacher. Indian and poor children would be admitted tuition-free. Although the school was for men, the trustees were ordered to set up an academy for women as soon as the money became available. These were certainly unique standards. For a state to recognize educational possibilities for Indians and women in those days was rare. It was still many years before the education of women became widely accepted. As Brackenridge noted, the money was slow coming in.

The first classes were set for the spring of 1810. Daniel Barry was the first instructor. He proposed teaching English, French, Latin, Greek, math, surveying, logic, metaphysics, geography, and natural and moral philosophy. We don't know if he actually got started on those ambitious goals. We do know that less than a year later another candidate applied for the job—Edward Mann Butler, a pioneer Kentucky historian.

By the summer of 1814, however, the academy had gone under. The trustees sold it to merchant William Shannon. Four years later he provided the bond for the establishment of a new academy, or to turn over the property for the use of an academy to be established later. The state granted the academy a new charter in 1824. Other charters were granted in 1849 and 1853, as the school continued having trouble.

In 1847 a fund-raising campaign was launched to refurbish the school for the poor of the area. Eighty citizens pledged money or materials. The effort was a success and the school had its finest hours in the next dozen years.

Firmin Rozier took charge in 1849 and supervised about forty pupils. He expanded the building and by 1861 was listed as the principal with four instructors working for him. The next year the school was closed. Not enough people could be found to teach.

In time the Ste. Genevieve School District purchased and reconditioned the old building. For several years it was used as a school for retarded children, but in the early 1970s it became vacant again and fell into disrepair.

In the late 1970s a private foundation that oversees and encourages historic preservation and renovation in Ste. Genevieve turned its attention to the old Academy. The foundation got a 99-year lease on the building which they used for foundation offices and local arts and crafts displays.

On the face of it, the academy was a failure almost from the word "go." But it is important because it started the academy movement in Missouri. For many years academies provided most of the higher education of the times, as well as a good part of the elementary education. By the end of the Civil War, Missouri had 110 academies. Some of them exist today as colleges.

The legislation to establish Ste. Genevieve Academy was the first legislation on schools in what is now the state of Missouri. It came about just five years after this area became American property. The school was the first institution of its kind incorporated in this territory, when the Louisiana Territorial Legislature incorporated Ste. Genevieve Academy on this date, June 21, 1808.

****

JUNE 22
THE JOURNAL OF PIERRE ANTOINE TABEAU

Lewis and Clark were not the first explorers to go up the Missouri River. On their way upstream, they met a party led by Regis Loisel. He had taken with him a middle-aged man as secretary. This man's account of life along the Missouri River is one of the finest we have available.

Pierre Antoine Tabeau traced his ancestry back to one of the early families of Ste. Genevieve. His mother was the great-granddaughter of Jean Valle, whose brother, Louis-Charles, was a direct ancestor of the Valle family of Missouri's first permanent settlement.

Tabeau became a trader after completing his formal education in Quebec. He traveled to Illinois about the time of the American Revolution and became an American citizen in 1785. He was a member of the second expedition up the Missouri River sponsored by the Missouri Company.

Tabeau was a trader, but his interest in his trip went far beyond trading. His journal offers a fine description of travel up the Missouri and the dangers of the trip in the early 1800s.

He described the swirls and eddies, the floating logs and sandbars which gave the rivermen fits. He also included descriptions of plants, geography, animals, and birds.

Tabeau told about the Indians and the trading the expedition did with them.

Lewis and Clark ran into trouble with the Indians early in their voyage. A band of Sioux Indians almost ended the expedition, but some gunboat diplomacy and forceful action by the expedition's leaders kept an uneasy situation from becoming an ugly incident that might have wiped out most of the party. With that experience still in mind, the party might have been wary about its forthcoming encounter with the Ree Indians some days later.

Loisel had left Tabeau with the Rees. As a matter of fact, Tabeau was living in the lodge of the chief. He and his assistant, Joseph Gravelines, provided the liaison between the Indians and Lewis and Clark.

He reported the Rees didn't want liquor unless someone paid them to drink it. They believed that friends would not give another man a drink which makes him a fool. Therefore, the Rees felt that if someone wanted to laugh at their expense, he should pay the Indians for his pleasure. This attitude astonished Lewis and Clark.

Tabeau also found the morality of the Missouri River Indians puzzling. A husband might offer his wife to another man for night or more, but the wife faced severe punishment if she did the offering herself. The feeling was that the men owned the women in the villages and it was simply good hospitality to share one's possessions. There is some record, not specifically described in Lewis and Clark's journals, that members of the expedition accepted that hospitality. Tabeau's journal describes the fertility rites of the Mandans so graphically that when the books were first published, the editor retreated to the obscurity of printing in Latin some of the more intriguing descriptions.

Later that winter, Tabeau and Gravelines were able to warn Lewis and Clark to watch out for other Sioux tribes upriver.

Tabeau returned to St. Louis in 1805 and later went to Canada where he died in 1820. His journal would be valuable for years to come as a study of the Upper Missouri River Indians and the way they lived. His contribution to the Lewis and Clark expedition, although generally unknown, is significant.

Pierre Antoine Tabeau made his first entry in his history-making journal on this date, June 22, in 1804.

****

JUNE 23
COACH

Their father raised his four boys strictly. One said later, "He didn't give us any money to spend so that we couldn't get into trouble. He didn't spare the rod...and he worked the tar out of us." The father promised his sons he'd give each a gold watch if they reached twenty-one without smoking or drinking. All four claimed their watches.

More than a quarter century later the most famous of the four boys would write, "Since the coach should be an example to the many aspiring young athletes in the community, he should not drink, smoke, or swear in public. ...He must be above reproach in all financial, moral and social dealings."

The man's name is Don Faurot.

For a man who achieved the notoriety Don Faurot did on the gridiron, he took a surprising attitude toward football and collegiate sports in general. In 1950 Faurot wrote, "The department of athletics is only one part of the show, not the main event." A coach should live with and associate with respectable people, join church and civic clubs. "In the face of all problems," he wrote, "a coach should maintain his ideals and never lose sight of his ultimate objectives. he should strive to be a square shooter if he expects to stay long in the profession."

In 1941 Don Faurot came up with his innovation. Some call it "the Missouri T," or the "sliding T." But it is best known as the "split T" formation. The standard T-formation has the three backs lining up side-by-side behind the quarterback. By the late 30s and early 40s, it had been highly refined. The single-wing attack had been at its peak for years. Don Faurot decided there had to be something new.

Faurot had been the coach at Missouri for six years and had taken a badly damaged football program back to national prominence. When he lost his great all-purpose tailback Paul Christmas, Faurot developed a style which stressed flexibility and the multiple option. His 1941 team was 8-1 and was called by some his greatest squad. It led the nation in rushing, averaging 307 yards a game. It outscored opponents 226-37.

Missouri went to the Sugar Bowl in 1941 where it ran into a rain-soaked field and a Fordham team which played a tough defensive game. Fordham, on a freak play in the mud, scored a safety and won the game 2-0. Faurot never would win a bowl game, but in the first eight years the split-T was used, Missouri won more than 70 percent of its games, finishing in the top ten nationally in rushing and total offense for many of the next several years.

It was an offense which led Missouri to run a national record of 105 plays in one game in 1949. Best of all, that record came against arch rival Kansas. Missouri gained 667 yards that day.

Faurot liked the system. It was more explosive, required less talent, pressured the defense and made the lineman's job simpler.

The man who invented this system was one of four brothers from Mountain Grove who lettered in football at the University of Missouri, so the Faurot heritage was strong before he ever became coach there. No other family equals the record of four brothers lettering in football at the university. Don got his degree in agriculture. He not only lettered in football, but he played the outfield in baseball and was captain of the basketball team.

After leaving Missouri as a student, Don Faurot became head football coach at Northeast Missouri State Teachers College in Kirksville. In nine years there his teams won the conference title seven times. His team was riding a 27-game streak when Missouri hired him.

He replaced Frank Carideo who had won three games in three years. Twenty of Faurot's most promising players were flunking out. He admitted the job of getting the team back in shape would be tough. His first year at Missouri the team was 3-3-3. But by 1939 Missouri had its first post-season bowl invitation.

The coach went into the navy in World War II, coaching teams at training bases. He had two assistants who would learn the Faurot system all too well—Bud Wilkinson and Jim Tatum. Wilkinson would later win almost everything at Oklahoma (including too many games against Missouri), while Tatum would build a powerhouse at Maryland.

Faurot turned down many invitations to move. He retired after the 1956 Missouri football season. His record with the Tigers was 101-79-10. His career mark was 164-92-13.

Faurot stayed on as athletic director until reaching mandatory retirement at seventy. When that happened, the playing field at Memorial Stadium was named Faurot Field. Back in 1925 when Don Faurot was a student, he helped lay the sod on that field. For twenty years his teams performed there. When he retired, the football stadium capacity had been doubled. A new track, dressing rooms, practice field and an 18-hole golf course had been added to the athletic facilities. The original debt on the stadium and the basketball fieldhouse had been paid, largely from gate receipts during the Faurot years.

A football coach who admitted athletics "is only one part of the show, not the main event," one of the great coaches in the nation, Don Faurot, was born on this date, June 23, in 1902.

****

JUNE 24
THE SHORT UNHAPPY PUBLIC LIFE OF JOHN EDWARDS

He once wrote: "The governorship is a despicable office for any man to be condemned to hold. Two of my predecessors have resigned before their terms were out and a third committed suicide. I have been compelled to go armed to protect myself." One might assume an aging statesman overwhelmed by the office would have written those words. But surely, one might think, the youngest governor in Missouri history at the height of his political career would find the office exciting.

John Cummins Edwards didn't.

Governor Edwards was a Kentuckian who called himself a Tennessean. He spent his public life in Missouri and the majority of his life in California. His job as governor of Missouri was almost the last time he was in public life.

Edwards was born in Kentucky. His family moved to Tennessee soon afterwards. He was twenty-two when he came to Missouri and settled in Jefferson City. When he was only twenty-four he was appointed Missouri's Secretary of State. Five years later he became a member of the legislature representing Cole County. Edwards was thirty-one in 1837 when Governor Boggs suggested him for a seat on the Missouri Supreme Court. For political reasons his nomination never reached the state Senate for confirmation. He served a term in Congress when he was thirty-six, then came back to Missouri to run for the governorship and win.

Edwards was thirty-eight when he took office, the youngest governor in Missouri history up to that time. He was a bachelor until later in life. When he was governor his sister served as hostess for official functions.

Edwards believed in limited government. He thought the answer to recovery from the depression of 1837 and its lingering after-effects lay in the labor of the people. He felt the legislature should pass no laws to force equality or inequality upon anyone, and should make internal improvements only if the money was available.

He was a forward-looking governor, though, who urged a railroad be built from Hannibal to St. Joseph fifteen years before one was started. He settled the famous Honey War, a disagreement with Iowa over part of Missouri's northern border. During his term the legislature urged the federal government to improve the Osage River and passed stronger laws for the recovery of fugitive slaves. The legislature also approved laws for the instruction of the deaf, dumb, and blind, and for a state insane asylum.

The General Assembly also passed a so-called "woman's bill" which didn't impress Edwards. It was meant to exempt a woman's property owned before marriage from any liabilities assumed after marriage. Edwards didn't think it offered much protection. He wrote, "A separate property would change the character of the wife. In the management of her estate she would lose the woman, and become in character a man. All that was soft and tender and enduring would vanish and she would grow sturdy, obstinate and masculine, as in the case where effeminate husbands surrender the reigns of government to their wives."

He was governor during the Mexican War, and it was his orders which sent Doniphan on his epic expedition into Mexico.

During the second year of his term he called for a constitutional convention. The legislature had adopted nineteen new counties which diluted the legislative representation from the bigger counties. The 1820 Constitution limited the number of members of the General Assembly. The convention met for fifty-eight days and cost $15,000. Voters turned down the proposed charter. Historians say the effort to put the judiciary on an elective basis was one reason for the refusal. The effort was an outgrowth of Edwards' own experience in trying to gain a Supreme Court position.

He began to push for development of Missouri resources halfway through his term, saying it would help improve Missouri trade relations with the East. In his last message to the legislature, he suggested an incorporation law be passed as a step toward developing manufacturing and diversifying the state's economy.

Edwards left office in 1848 at age forty-two. He'd been bitten by the gold bug and went west almost immediately. He settled in

Stockton, California, was a businessman for a short time there, and bought a ranch where he raised stock and grain. He made his last appearance in public office when he served as mayor of Stockton in 1851.

In 1854, at forty-eight, Edwards married a nineteen-year-old French woman. They had eleven children. After twenty years of ranching he went back to Stockton where he died at the age of eighty-two. His wife outlived him by thirty-seven years. She died at the age of ninety-one in 1925.

John Cummins Edwards was the youngest governor in Missouri history in his day. He was a young man whose political star rose quickly; but he seemed to burn himself out by the time he was in his early forties. John Cummins Edwards was born on this date, June 24, 1806.

****

JUNE 25
ROSE AND THE KEWPIE

Publishers back East sometimes received illustrations for their books and magazines wrapped around sticks. The drawings had come from the Missouri Ozarks and had been carried on horseback many miles to reach the railroad so they could be shipped East. Once the young artist sold the family cow and rode a horse forty miles to Springfield to catch a train for the East where a new novel of hers was being considered for publication. The author and artist was a sensitive young woman who left the world mysterious poetry, beautiful drawings, a whimsical character known worldwide and two intriguing true-life love stories. She was a woman who was at ease with the intellectual and society circles in the East and with the people of the Ozarks. Some say she is the Rose in the song, "Rose of Washington Square."

Her name was Rose O'Neil.

One day Rose O'Neill dreamed a dream which made her famous. She dreamed a group of little, jolly, cupid-like fellows with fat stomachs and tiny feet were scurrying around. She described them as benevolent elf creatures who did good deeds in a funny way. She began to draw them and called them Kewpies.

Rose O'Neill was an accomplished artist, already well-known nationally when she dreamed up the idea of the Kewpie. She used them for illustrating magazine articles. The editor of the *Ladies Home Journal,* Edward Bok, suggested she use them to illustrate her own stories which she wrote in verse.

The Kewpie got its first national exposure in that magazine. Bok then encouraged Rose to start making figurine dolls of them. Children had begun to write asking for a Kewpie they could hold. It became a national craze, not only with dolls, but with kewpie cloth for children's clothes, kewpie soap, cutout books, printed dolls to stuff, rattles, toy pianos, and kewpie dishes among other things. An original kewpie doll today is a valuable collector's item.

Rose O'Neill came to Missouri by way of Nebraska, following her father to Southwest Missouri when she was nineteen, in 1893. The Ozarks captured her heart and held her for the rest of her life. She found the people were like "characters in delightful ballads and legends. They were horseback people and we always saw them swaying to the riders' rhythm," she wrote. "I did not know what was growing in the fields...but I liked the green of it...I forgot my fears and shouted with joy. I called it the tangle and my extravagant heart was tangled in it for good."

Three years later, Gay Latham, a young man she had known in Omaha, went to the Ozarks and they were married. They moved to New York where she became an illustrator for *Puck* magazine. But Rose and this man who had followed her halfway across the country disagreed on spending her income. They separated and she went back to the Ozarks. By then she had fallen in love with young magazine editor Harry Leon Wilson. In June, 1902, he gave up his magazine work in New York, went to her home called Bonnie Brook, and married Rose. That summer and winter she wrote her first novel. He wrote two, including a best-seller, *The Spender.* Wilson was later described as America's most refreshing author. He is best remembered today for one story, *Ruggles of Red Gap.* But their marriage was doomed.

By then, however, the Kewpies were being made in thirty factories in Germany, and Rose was famous around the world. In 1922 she published her first volume of poetry and illustrated it with nine drawings. The book was called *The Master Mistress.* It is a collection of compelling poems about life and death. Even in a poem about creation of life, she interwove the mystery of death:

"The maker said, 'Thy work is done.
Stand up, my clay, my sullen son.
Stand up til seventy years have passed,
And you are crumbled clay at last.'"

But she also could write of the softness of love and its mysteries:

"You thought I loved you,
  Because I smiled.
You did not know the dread of stars that drove me,
You could not know the mirth of moons that move me,
Nor all the winds that weep me wild.
  You thought I loved you
    Because I smiled."

There was passion in her writings too:

"There is too much meaning
Where the trees are leaning!
And the rocks conferring
Make a fearful stirring;
The wind along the leaves has made me mad!"

She kept writing poetry and drawing until she died in April 1944, not quite seventy years old, in Springfield. Rose was buried at Bonnie Brook. Three years later fire destroyed the house which had become a landmark during her lifetime.

She was a woman who couldn't explain her creativity and her abilities: "I never know how anything comes to me. There doesn't seem to be any intelligence in it." She was a woman of mystery, love, gentleness, and mischievousness, as seen in her drawings, her writings and her life, which began for Rose O'Neill on this date, June 25, 1874.

****

JUNE 26
THOMAS HENNINGS, FREEDOM FIGHTER

Seldom have the individual freedoms which built and sustain America come under such strong attack as in the hottest years of the cold war, the years from the end of World War II through much of the 1950s. These were years which saw constant efforts to undermine the fundamental rights to speak and think as one wished.

For ten crucial years a senator from Missouri fought the erosion of those basic rights with the Bill of Rights as his battle flag. One of the greatest fighters for individual Americans in those terrifying years was Thomas Hennings.

Soon after Thomas Hennings defeated incumbent U.S. Senator Forrest Donnell in 1950, he was asked about his campaign which had concentrated on attacks against the activities of Wisconsin Senator Joseph McCarthy. Hennings answered, "It is automatic with me to be in sympathy with the rights of the individual."

Hennings was the son of a prominent St. Louis jurist, a record-setting track star and athletic hero at Soldan High School. While a student at Cornell University he decided on a legal career. He got his law degree at Washington University while working as a track coach and English teacher. Upon graduation Hennings became an Assistant Circuit Attorney. He ran up the enviable record of 2,340 convictions out of 2,548 felony cases he handled.

In 1934 he campaigned as a Roosevelt new dealer and was elected to Congress. He was reelected in 1936 and '38. He had supported civil rights legislation and had many blacks on his staff. In 1937 he had supported FDR's effort to pack the Supreme Court, a point of importance to remember in considering his later career. Hennings also became known during this time as a two-fisted drinker.

In June of 1940 his concern for individual freedoms was evident in a speech urging moderation in the enactment of subversive control acts. He said the nation must resist the natural inclination to refuse freedom of expression to those who criticize or condemn our form of government.

Hennings served a term as Circuit Attorney in St. Louis. He was married, divorced, remarried. He was a naval aide to Puerto Rico Governor Rexford Tugwell. He didn't get along well with Tugwell and returned to private law practice.

Hennings won a slim victory in the 1950 Democratic senatorial primary, although President Truman and the state party leaders favored his opponent. On the first day of his general election campaign Hennings told a Moberly audience there is an obligation to preserve fundamental liberties along with maintaining internal security. He blasted McCarthyism as primarily a political, naked desire for advantage. McCarthy came to Missouri to talk against him. He waved around a list of alleged Communists who had infiltrated government. But Hennings won by 93,000 votes.

He immediately confronted McCarthy in the Senate as a member of a committee investigating McCarthy's campaign practices. Hennings attacked the abuses of the congressional committee investigative powers, nowhere better exemplified than in McCarthy's own committee activities. In the next session Hennings and Senator Estes Kefauver of Tennessee finished a long and thorough investigation of McCarthy and brought out a well-documented expose of the senator.

When a censure resolution was finally drafted, only one of the forty-six charges against McCarthy stood. It was made by Hennings. Hennings biographer Donald Kemper warns against giving Hennings all the credit for the McCarthy downfall, but says the Missouri senator had the greatest impact with his relentless pressure and investigation.

Hennings later found himself fighting the Eisenhower administration's loyalty-security measures, viewing them as harmful to liberty and justice, finding in their arbitrary judgments a violation of the fundamental and constitutional rights of due process.

He once said the Supreme Court was not above criticism, but that any congressional restrictions on the independence of the high court would disrupt the delicate system of checks and balances which kept the nation alive. He believed if the court were limited in any way, the first casualty after that would be individual human rights.

Early in 1960, Hennings learned he was suffering from terminal cancer. He continued, though, to fight for civil liberties and fought the abused authority of the executive branch to withhold information of national and international importance from Congress and from the American citizen. He fought against wiretapping. He was concerned in his last months with legal help for indigents, the rights of the mentally ill, and post office censorship powers. He believed that without free thought and communication there can be no democracy.

The day of his death, his office released a letter he had written back to Missouri. In it he said he hoped Democrats would not prejudge a candidate for president because of his religion. He urged Missourians to remain faithful to the constitutional guarantees of religious liberty. He died on September 13, 1960. Thomas Hennings was fifty-seven. Less than two months later, John Kennedy was elected our first Catholic president.

Kemper says Hennings "firmly maintained that a democratic nation was not worth saving from communism if in the process it lost the principles which made it democratic....He believed that democratic principles constituted the means rather than the price of victory."

In a world which sometimes begins to believe security is best based on the forfeiture of freedom, it is good to remember Senator Thomas Hennings of Missouri, who was born on this date, June 25, 1903.

****

JUNE 27
THE FIRST MAJOR NOMINATING CONVENTION WEST OF THE MISSISSIPPI

Democrats that year crowded into St. Louis. They had won their first congressional majority in eighteen years just two years earlier. Things looked great for 1876. Only three southern states were still in post-Civil War radical hands. The party was regaining its strength. The 1873 depression had hurt the Republicans, as had the scandals of the Grant administration. Those delegates in St. Louis would nominate the only man in American history to win and lose the same presidential election.

While delegates were meeting at the first national party presidential nominating convention west of the Mississippi, the governor of New York sat quietly in Albany, 1,500 miles to the east. He held interviews at his home at 138 Eagle Street. He met with consultants and worked on a lawsuit to which he was a party. Samuel Jones Tilden, the overwhelming favorite for the nomination, had gained fame by attacking the corrupt political machine of William Marcy Tweed—Tammany Hall. As governor he had pushed through a tax cut, governmental reorganization, and other moves against corruption in high places. And he had attracted the attention of party reformers. Tilden was sixty-two, a millionaire railroad lawyer and a fiscal conservative. His strongest challenger for the Democratic nomination was former Indiana senator and governor Thomas Hendricks who had the backing of Tammany Hall and those favoring a paper money economy.

St. Louis in 1876 was the nation's fourth largest city. Five to eight thousand people crammed into the Merchants Exchange for the convention although only 983 of them were certified to vote and some of those 983 had only half a vote.

It was hot the first day. Few delegates were able to keep their coats on very long. Temporary chairman Henry Watterson, a Louisville newspaper publisher, enlivened the meeting by telling the crowd, "Partisan misrule and sectional misdirection" had been responsible for the ills of the nation. "It is the issue, not the man, that should engage us," he said, to drive the corrupt from the party and from government.

Later that afternoon the platform, written by Manton Marble, a newspaperman from the New York *World,* was read to the convention. It was based on Tilden's thoughts. Reform was needed, it said. It supported the principles of majority rule, civil control of the military, separation of church and state, popular education and equality before the law. Each of the nine planks began with the words, "Reform is necessary." Reform was necessary to eliminate corruption, establish a strong currency, national credit, stop waste in public lands, eliminate sectional rivalries, and improve civil service.

The next day seven names were placed in nomination. The opposition couldn't muster the votes to master their hopes and Tilden finished with 441½ votes on the first ballot. He needed 492. Hendricks was far back with 140½. On the second ballot the votes began to change. Colorado gave Tilden six, Georgia ten, Illinois four. Arkansas and Iowa each switched two, then Iowa added four more. Illinois added another pair. Tilden needed only nineteen more for nomination. The Missouri delegation threw twenty-one votes into the Tilden column and that put him over the top.

Back in Albany, Tilden went for a carriage ride as the balloting started. A friend thought he should stay by the telegraph at the Capitol. But Tilden said no, the tally wouldn't be known until about 9:30 p.m. Tilden knew the workings of the convention well. Nine thirty was precisely the time the convention adjourned in St. Louis and the telegram arrived in Albany telling Tilden he had been nominated as the Democratic candidate for president of the United States.

He read it calmly. Turning to friends he said, "The nomination was not made by leaders of the party. It was the people who made it. They want reform. They have wanted it for a long while, and in looking about they became convinced," and here he pointed to himself, "that it is to be found here." At Sedalia, Missouri, that night, 100 guns were fired in celebration.

The next day Hendricks was nominated as vice-president, eating the words many a presidential candidate utters—that he would not accept the second position on the ballot.

There were critics of the ticket, but generally this first nominating convention west of the Mississippi left delegates pleased. They had, after all, picked a winner. Samuel Tilden was elected America's nineteenth president by the popular margin of 264,000 votes.

Well, almost.

There were three crucial disputed states and his opponent was judged to have carried them. When the Electoral College tallied its totals, Tilden had 184. Rutherford B. Hayes, beaten by more than a quarter-million popular votes, had 185. Rutherford B. Hayes would serve as the nineteenth president of the United States.

America can never forget the man on whom the worst political joke in the country's history was played, Samuel Tilden, a man chosen at the first major party nominating convention west of the Mississippi River which began in St. Louis on this date, June 27, 1876.

****

JUNE 28
THE LEGACY OF ANNIE BAXTER

The fourteenth Democratic candidate on the ballot in Jasper County that day was the most controversial figure in the election. The issue was whether the candidate could legally hold the office of County Clerk, despite the assertion by an opposing newspaper that the candidate was "the best man on the Democratic ticket." The problem was that the candidate was not a man at all, but a woman. The year was 1890, thirty years before women could vote. But Jasper Countians on that day made Anna White Baxter the first woman elected to public office by popular vote in Missouri.

She was twenty-six years old, prim and professional-looking in comtemporary illustrations, the daughter of a Carthage furniture factory owner. Shortly after her high school graduation in 1882 she went to work in the office of county clerk George Blakeney. In November 1885 she was appointed a deputy to County Clerk John Wilson, then continued working for John Rhoads who succeeded him.

371

In 1890 she was nominated by the Democrats to be Rhoads' successor. The Carthage *Evening Press,* a Republican newspaper, noted that state laws spoke in terms of "he," clearly meaning women could not hold that job: "It has often been decided that the right of citizenship does not carry with it political rights."

The Carthage *Democrat,* edited by future Secretary of State Cornelius Roach, defended her, noting a law saying "words importing the masculine gender only may be extended to females also." But the *Evening Press* responded, "If the sentences convey the political right of women to hold elective office, they convey also the political right of women to vote, and this is something the *Democrat,* or the party it seeks to represent in this state, do not want and will not advocate.

"Women and children are citizens for certain purposes...but unfortunately for women, the laws of Democratic Missouri, which read 'he' in telling who may vote or hold office, cannot be construed to read 'she' and for a paper to claim to the contrary is to make itself the laughing stock of the community."

Annie Baxter's opponent was Julius Fischer, a Joplin bank clerk. She won, carrying nineteen of the county's thirty precincts, 4,040 to 3,572. The Carthage *Press* afterward mused, "If it shall be decided that a woman who cannot vote is eligible to hold certain offices there will be plenty of women candidates before the convention two years hence. There are several positions on the state ticket that women could aspire to and fill with good grace."

On November 26, twenty-three days after the election, Fischer filed an election challenge. Addressing Mrs. Baxter in his suit, he charged, "you were ineligable (sic) to be nominated or elected...for the reason that you were a female, and married." And he charged the Democratic party with nominating her in an obvious effort to defraud him of the office.

Annie's response in her gracefully decorative, but businesslike handwriting was brief and pointed, charging Fischer was "ineligible to be elected...in this, you are not, and was not then a citizen of the United States...being at said time an unnaturalized foreigner and being an alien."

The case was moved to Springfield and on January 27, 1892, the court ruled Fischer was not entitled to the office and that Annie Baxter, having won the plurality of votes cast, and having assumed the office, could keep it.

"She has won the spurs and is entitled to wear them," commented the *Kansas City Times.* The *Kansas City Star* said she would "Henceforth be a historical character in Missouri."

The issue of whether a woman could be elected county clerk, by the way, was finally decided in a court case from St. Clair County in 1897. The Missouri Supreme Court ruled there was no reason a woman couldn't take that job.

She caused some other problems too. She made her husband, a former store clerk she had married in 1885, her deputy at a salary of $125 a month. That didn't set well with the opposition press.

But at the county Democratic convention in 1894 she was renominated, and the cry of convention leader William Carter of Carthage, "God Bless Annie Baxter!" became the party's rallying cry. 1894 was the year of the Republican sweep in Missouri though and Annie Baxter lost by almost 1,100 votes. There is no record that she ever sought public office again. When Cornelius Roach became Secretary of State, however, she became state lands registrar and later, an honorary colonel on the staff of Governor Gardner—the first woman ever given that ceremonial title.

Anna W. Baxter died in 1944 in Jefferson City, twenty-four years after women were allowed to vote in Missouri; twenty-two years after Mellcene Smith of University City and Sara Turner of Jackson County were elected Missouri's first women state representatives. Eight years after she died, Leonor Sullivan of St. Louis became Missouri's first woman member of Congress. In 1972, Mary Gant of Kansas City became Missouri's first woman state senator.

They, and those who will come after them in these and higher offices, live the legacy of Annie Baxter who thirty years before women could vote proved, in the words of contemporary accounts, "that the wearing of trousers is not one of the duties of the county clerk," and "that women can fill a place of trust and honor as well as his majesty, man." Anna White Baxter of Carthage, Missouri, died on this date, June 28, 1944.

****

JUNE 29
ROBERT STUART, FORGOTTEN PIONEER OF THE OREGON TRAIL.

Wilson Price Hunt laid the groundwork for what would later become the Oregon Trail as he went west from St. Louis to Astoria, Oregon, in 1811, but it remained for another man to make the most important contribution to that famous trail. He did it traveling East. So successful was his trip that a St. Louis newspaper, in publishing an interview with him, said there should be no reason wagons couldn't make the trip west to Oregon because there was no obstruction to block the way. But it would be years before Robert Stuart's advice was followed.

Stuart came from Scotland. He entered the fur trading enterprise of John Jacob Astor in the Northwest. In 1810 and 1811, Stuart took a ship around the Horn to get to the Oregon coast while Wilson Hunt was leading an overland expedition. They set up the trading post of Astoria. Stuart was able to establish good relations with many of the Oregon and Washington Indian tribes. Once a friendly subchief warned him of a plot to surprise the post with an attack.

When his party was attacked in March of 1812, Stuart took command and negotiated for the withdrawal of the Indians. He and his men were able to finish their trip across country with no further trouble. He was only twenty-seven at the time but contemporaries called him "brave and prudent," and "self-possessed and fearless."

It became necessary later in 1812 to send messages back to New York. The only way to do that was to send a party back across the uncivilized country between Astoria and St. Louis. Stuart took six men with him and started out, but one of the men was unable to take the strain of the trip. He went insane and was sent back to Astoria. The early part of their trip followed the path Hunt had taken on the way west. They used canoes and went up the Columbia River, then on through Oregon and Idaho.

Crow Indians had plagued the white men in the area before. Hoping to avoid them, the Stuart party made a fairly useless detour to the north. They struggled to cross the Tetons and finally reached Jackson Hole. Their supplies ran short, and they almost starved to death before they killed a buffalo. It was during this time that one member of the group suggested the party should determine by chance which of their number would be killed and eaten so the rest would survive. Stuart refused to allow that.

The way they got out of Jackson Hole was important. Instead of going north, back to the trail Hunt had followed west, they picked up an old Indian trail that led them to what later became known as South Pass. On Friday, October 23, 1812, they found it at the south end of the Wind River range of the Rocky Mountains. Stuart's was the first white expedition to travel through the passage going east, and it appears he was the first to publicly state that such a pass existed as a logical route to Oregon. His party wintered on the Sweetwater River and in December camped on the Platte in what is now Nebraska. They followed the Platte to its junction with the Missouri, then traveled the Missouri to St. Louis.

On April 13, 1813, Stuart and his party met an Indian who told them the Americans and British were at war again. The two countries had been fighting for ten months. War had been declared before the party left Oregon, but the communications were slow and nobody there knew about it until after Stuart had gone.

They finally arrived in St. Louis on April 30, 1813, where historian William Goetzmann says they were treated as if they were "the second coming of the Great Lewis and Clark."

Stuart stayed in the employ of Astor's company until a realignment with a new owner excluded him in 1834. He moved to Detroit where he built the city's first brick house. He was the state treasurer of Michigan later and for a time the Superintendent of Indian Affairs. He died in 1844 at the age of fifty-nine.

In spite of Stuart's discovery and the publicity it received, it would be another decade before the first white trappers would go through South Pass westbound. Bernard DeVoto says it wasn't until the mid-1830s that the route could logically be called "The Oregon Trail."

Settlers moving west, striking out from Independence and St. Joseph for the promised land of the West owed much to Robert Stuart, who left Astoria, Oregon, bound for Missouri on this date, June 19, 1812.

****

JUNE 30
WHAT STATE SONG?

In 1900 the Jefferson City *Missouri State Tribune* noted that fame and fortune awaited the author of a state song. It even printed its own suggestion—a work by D. E. Grayson with music by B. J. Wrightsman. It was called "Missouri."

But it didn't catch on.

Nothing did for about half a century, despite contests in which the state put up prize money. What we finally ended up with is a song which has little to do with Missouri and is sometimes known by a title which has absolutely nothing to do with Missouri.

The terminology of the state song is reminiscent of Stephen Foster. The only place the Show Me State is mentioned is a reference to a song the singer supposedly learned while a child in Missouri.

> Hush-a-bye my baby, slumber time is comin' soon;
> Rest yo' head upon my breast while Mommie hums a tune;
> The sandman is callin' where shadows are fallin'
> While the soft breezes sigh as in days long gone by.
> *Way down in Missouri,* where I heard this melody
> When I was a little child on my mommie's knee....

The origins of this masterpiece of a state song are vague. It's a mellow song about Dixie, old folks at home, and the like which seemed to become our state song when others failed primarily because a president from Missouri liked it.

Actually, he hated it.

The quest for a state song became a serious venture in 1908 when the DAR announced a contest. The group had twenty-six entries and picked three finalists, but couldn't decide on a winner.

Governor Hadley backed a contest in 1909 in which he promised $500 for the best lyrics and another $500 for the best music. More than 1,000 entries were filed. Most of them concentrated on characteristic Missouri symbols: the mule, the schools, the Show Me motto, the hogs, the apples, and so forth. Some were sentimental songs. In 1911 the judges, all musicians, picked the lyrics of Mrs. Lizzie Chambers Hull of St. Louis.

> Missouri fair, we bring to thee
> Hearts full of love and loyalty;
> Thou central star, thou brightest gem

Of all the brightest diadem...
Missouri.

But they never found appropriate music to match.

At six legislative sessions after that a proposed state song was introduced, using the words of Mrs. Hull. Nothing happened. Twice in the years before World War I, a song by Mrs. Anna Brosius Korn of Trenton was performed in the chambers of the Missouri House of Representatives. The House never passed a bill recognizing it as a state song. In the 1930s, nationally known composer Percy Weinrich of Joplin—who penned such hits as "Put on Your Old Gray Bonnet," "When You Wore a Tulip," "Sail Along Silvery Moon," "Moonlight Bay"—wrote what he called "32 bars of the get up and go spirit of Missourians." It might have gotten up but it went nowhere.

When Harry Truman became president, interest was revived in an old song which supposedly was his favorite, "Hush-a-Bye My Baby," known to many as the Missouri Waltz. In 1949 the Missouri Waltz became our state song, succeeding where other songs more appropriate to the state had failed.

Where did it come from?

Most agree it was first published and arranged by Frederick Knight Logan, a noted musician from Oskaloosa, Iowa. He supposedly picked it up from John Valentine Eppel, an orchestra leader from Fort Dodge, Iowa. Eppel's band, incidentally, couldn't read a note of music. Eppel could read music. The band just played along. Eppel is said to have heard the song from an old Missouri black man who had learned it from his mother.

In Moberly, some residents give credit for the song to Dab Hannah, a black piano player. But in Oskaloosa, they say a black dancing teacher, Henry Clay Cooper, gave the melody to Logan.

Another story is that Edgar Lee Settle of New Franklin, a pianist and performer in traveling shows, got it from a musical team on the show circuit. They supposedly got it from an old black man down South.

J. Boulton Settle, the editor of the New Franklin *News,* claimed Edgar Settle composed it, and called it originally the "Graveyard Waltz." And New York columnist Bill Corum claimed Edgar was playing the tune in Moberly one night when John Eppel—remember him—heard it.

Anyway it was first published about 1916 as "Hush-a-Bye-My

Baby." It swept the country and for many years was the second largest selling sheet music selection in America.

In 1924, Ernest C. Krohn wrote in a monograph that "it seems improbable that any one song will ever become a state song." But a quarter century later, an improbable song did.

When Harry Truman took office the Missouri Waltz regained national prominence. How this song, apparently written in Iowa, first performed in Iowa, ever got the word "Missouri" attached to it is a puzzle. Even today, many wonder if it is really an adequate symbol of our state.

Many years after Truman left office, he was asked if it really was his favorite song. "You ought to read the words and then you'd see why it's kind of obnoxious as a state song," he answered.

It wasn't until a Missourian went to the White House that the Missouri legislature gave us a state song, meaningless though it might be to Missouri, and the governor signed the law making it the state song, on this date, June 30, in 1949.

****

To order *Across Our Wide Missouri,* volume 2 (July through December) contact:
Herald House/Independence Press
P.O. Box HH
Independence, MO 64055
816/252-5010